Reinventing Anthropology

REINVENTING
ANTHROPOLOGY

Edited by
Dell Hymes

Pantheon Books
A Division of Random House, New York

Library of Congress Cataloging in Publication Data

Hymes, Dell H.   Reinventing Anthropology.

(Pantheon antitextbooks)
Includes bibliographies.
1. Anthropology—Study and teaching—United States—
Addresses, essays, lectures. 2. Ethnology—Addresses,
essays, lectures. I. Title.
GN43.A2H9   301.2   72-3400   ISBN 0-394-46827-9

Manufactured in the United States of America by
The Haddon Craftsmen, Inc., Scranton, Pa.

9 8 7 6 5 4 3 2

FIRST EDITION

Contents

I · Introduction

The Use of Anthropology: Critical, Political, Personal

Dell Hymes

Anthropology will survive in a changing world by allowing itself to perish in order to be born again under a new guise.
—*Claude Lévi-Strauss* (1966, p. 126)

Thou met'st with things dying, I with things newborn.
—*Shakespeare,* The Winter's Tale, *III, iii*

I

IF ANTHROPOLOGY did not exist, would it have to be invented? If it were reinvented, would it be the anthropology we have now?

To both questions, the answer, I think, is no. What, after all, is this anthropology, that its absence would be noticed or that cannot be done severally by its parts or by other disciplines? If it is unique in its unifying perspective, where are its holistic, integrating works? Does anyone write about "Anthropology" as a whole except in the smorgasbord of textbooks or as a committee? If it has a natural unity, why does its makeup differ so much from one country and national tradition to another, even from one department to another? Who can read the program of the annual meetings of the Association and find in it the profile of a science? Would an objective enthnographer, observing organized anthropology today, not conclude that its structure reflects adaptation to a past, not present, environment, that it is essentially a survival? That from the viewpoint of the next, last, generation of the twentieth century, it will be found one of

> the remains of crude old culture which have passed into harmful superstition [of which] It is a harsher, and at times even painful, office of ethnography to expose . . . and to mark . . . out for destruction. (Tylor, [1871] 1958, Vol. 2, p. 539)

But, some will say, if anthropology did not exist, who would do what anthropologists do? Without a tradition of doing it, of course, some of it might be found not worth doing; the rest could be distributed readily within a general science of man. To be sure, if one had the present architecture of the study of man with only anthropology missing, something like academic anthropology might begin, as it did begin, with the "unappropriated odds and ends of other sciences" (Kroeber, 1923, p. 2), with "work that we are doing now because no one else cares for it" (Boas, 1904, p. 523). But that is unlikely. The situation in which anthropology found a niche as an academic profession in the United States around the turn of this century is gone. The implicit division of labor—anthropology on Indian reservations and in uncivilized places abroad, sociology at home and in Europe—has quite broken down. The American quietly interviewing and observing in a foreign community today is likely to be a sociologist, a political scientist, a social psychologist, or even an economist. The person tape-recording African oral traditions may turn out to be a historian. Conversely, the student wanting to study urban problems or political power in the United States, or setting out for a field site in Luxembourg, outside Paris, or near the Mediterranean, is likely to be in anthropology.

The fact of the matter is th..t if the study of man were being invented now, there would be no apparent need for an entity corresponding to anthropology as we have it in the United States today. Its organization is essentially arbitrary, in relation to the realities it studies, in terms of the needs of both science and society. And whatever the internal alignments of a freshly designed study of man, no portion would be able to take or keep for itself a name such as "anthropology," appropriate only to the whole. While no one can wipe the slate suddenly clean and reinvent the study of man from scratch, there are indications that a reconstruction is, in fact, coming about rather steadily.

The prospects are unfavorable for the "anthropology" we now have either to grow to fulfill its self-conception and aspirations, or to maintain its present form. Although conceiving of itself as the science of man, it has never fully become such, in scope of either subject matter or participation. It is not a universal discipline; nor is it likely to become one. Under its present name it cannot perhaps escape its history as an expression of a certain period in the discovery, then domination, of the rest of the world by European and North American societies.[1] Most of the world has done without something called anthropology, seems willing enough to forego it now, and can even be positively hostile to it. The very existence of an autonomous discipline that specializes in the study of others has always been somewhat problematic. People everywhere today, especially (and rightly) third world peoples, increasingly resist being subjects of inquiry, especially for purposes not their own; and anthropologists increasingly find the business of inquiring and knowing about others a source of dilemmas—so much so that some abandon the classical identity of the anthropologist, preferring to say that one should study only one's own kind.

When anthropology in the United States was implicitly united around the study of the American Indian, most leading specialists in Indians were found within that circle, and it led in pioneering necessary methods of study. Everyone at least knew the names of the same ethnic units and culture areas. That implicit source of cohesiveness is gone. A hundred topical and regional orientations bloom beyond any would-be gardener's control. A single goal to which all lines of work can be said to contribute can hardly be articulated, and the various lines are commonly dependent, each in its way, upon facilities, training, and cooperation from outside official anthropology. Already it is clear that only small departments, or departments artificially narrow in control, can pretend to common purpose. Often enough, departmental meetings must be confined to procedural details; an appearance of harmony requires avoidance of matters of intellectual substance.

We tend to take departmental organization for granted, and the response of some in these troubling times is to cling more tightly to it, in the name of "general anthropology," "standards," or some other code word for maintaining the comfort of a status quo. Yet to do so is to reify something that is rather recent, something that is largely a product of the expansion of universities and of the role of the United States in the world following World War II. True, in the United States today, anthropology is predominantly an academic profession, organized in departments; but it was an academic profession in many places before it had departments of its own; it was a profession in museums and government before it was academic; and it was a scientific tradition before it became professionalized at all. The hegemony of departmental anthropology is relatively recent, and, it begins to appear, a transitory stage.

One factor is that the number of anthropologists outside departments grows steadily, and an influence proportionate to their numbers, when it comes, will markedly change the consciousness of the field. More generally, the needs, both scientific and social, to which anthropological research can genuinely speak transcend departmental and even academic limits. It is in the nature of anthropology that it can fulfill itself only as a universal possession of mankind. The crux is whether or not adherents of the partial anthropology we now have can look beyond present structure to a greater tradition and find new forms to realize it.

The future of anthropology in the United States is thus a question of whether its present institutional context, essentially the graduate department, will prove to have been chrysalis or coffin. If anthropology remains confined there, it may wax as an instrument of domination, wane into irrelevance, or—more likely—combine both fates. It is unlikely to contribute much to the liberation of mankind.

The issue can be stated with a further pair of fundamental questions. How much of what goes on in departments is for the sake of mankind's self-knowledge (let alone liberation), and how much for the sake of perpetuating, extending, and propagating departments? How much of anthropology is as it is today because of a genuine need for anthropology, how much because of the requirements of institutions in which anthropology finds itself?

Too many questions, too many objections, many will say. Forget the difficulty of defining anthropology or even of identifying it. We have a certain tradition, a certain ethos. Let anthropology be what anthropologists do. Sol Tax was wise indeed when he defined anthropology (1955) as simply an association of people who have agreed to continue in communication with each other. Why ask if our anthropology could be invented now? It's enough that it has been invented. It has grown and prospered, and continues to grow a little even in these hard times. We deal in actual worlds, not speculative ones, and this actual world is good enough; we manage.

This book is for people for whom "the way things are" is not reason enough for the way things are, who find fundamental questions pertinent and in need of personal answer, those for whom security, prosperity, and self-interest are not sufficient reasons for choices they make; who think that if an official "study of man" does not answer to the needs of men, it ought to be changed; who ask of anthropology what they ask of themselves—responsiveness, critical awareness, ethical concern, human relevance, a clear connection between what is to be done and the interests of mankind.

Prosperity, after all, is not necessarily a sign of a profession's intellectual health. The present appearances of anthropology may be deceptive. Though a small discipline, it does have, relative to its own past, many departments, many students. But spread of departments may be merely spread of a cultural pattern within the academy, a momentum of imitation, not fresh response. Current attractiveness to students may be due to a superficial, quickly sated, interest in the exotic or to a serious interest that meets with disappointment.

There *is* a certain tradition, a certain ethos, yes, and it informs our concern, or we would not speak of reinventing anthropology rather than of abandoning it. But much has to change, to be rethought from the foundation, if what has invigorated anthropology at its best is to survive. In one sense, anthropology is indeed a continuing association, is what those who associate do. But everything depends on the boundaries set to association and on the directions given, as Tax himself said (1955, p. 326). If the mold of departmental anthropology remains unchallenged and unchanged, then not only will anthropology not be reinvented, it will disappear. Not the name, not professionals calling themselves "anthropologists," but a reason for being, a relationship between the "mythical charter" of the field as a "science of man," for man, and actual practice. "Anthropology" will indeed be "what anthropologists do," and what they do will be a hodgepodge of vested interests, in which those who care about the true interests of mankind will find little place.

No one in this book seeks to impose answers in these regards; rather we seek to help build a community in which answers, not necessarily the same for all, can freely be found. We think that such a community is, in fact, being built today, partly publicly, often enough privately and quietly. There is genuine indication that anthropology in the United States *is* being reinvented and that the next generation will see its transformation. The surge of reconsideration, of which this book is but one instance,[2] indicates in itself that one period is coming to an end, another emerging. The present form of anthropology answers, I think, to the prediction made to another purpose by Robinson Jeffers ([1939] 1965, p. 63):

> There is a change felt in the rhythm of events, as when an
>   exhausted horse
> Falters and recovers, then the rhythm of the running hoof-
>   beats is changed; he will run miles yet,
> But he must fall.

Here is the sense in which this book may deserve the description "radical." It attempts to go to the root of anthropology itself, as an institutional fact, and considers the possibility of its disappearance. Some anthropologists, radical in other respects, are not so in this, in that they take for granted the maintenance of a separate anthropology, even assigning it a special eminence (e.g. Moore, 1971). If many of the theoretical issues debated in Marxist, socialist, and radical circles (these being overlapping) do not find expression here, the book is radical in a sense that Marx would approve, indeed demand. It does not hesitate to question the appearances of its own world, seeking to comprehend historically and to transform the structure underlying them.[3]

II

There are many traditions in anthropology. A museum or department of any age has one that partly defines a distinctive culture, and it would be the strength of a serious history of anthropology to touch on the individual contexts in which anthropology has grown, and to capture something of their "structures of feeling"—the lived cultures of the particular times and places, and the selective traditions that join one to another (cf. Williams, 1965, pp. 64–66).

I shall sketch here what I believe to be the "great tradition" in which anthropology participates and within which it should seek its future in serving mankind. One might call the tradition itself "anthropology," but only if one bears in mind that the tradition transcends organized disciplines and named boundaries. Official anthropology may be its servant but never its sole custodian, can be a center of it but never the circumference. Not all "anthropologists" serve it, and many who do bear other labels. This being the case, in fact, whoever adopts and furthers the tradition has precedent for claiming a part in it and for invoking the name. Indeed, the logic inherent in the tradition is to become universal, not only as to what is known of man, but also as to participation in the community of knowers.

The tradition is complex and has a checkered history, as will be seen, but it can be stated simply: "The *general* problem of the evolution of mankind." It was stated in those words, with that emphasis, by Franz Boas (1904, p. 523) in an essay to which I shall want to return several times. Boas is perhaps remembered now mostly as a name, except by those whose work continues to build on his (as is the case for students of several American Indian languages and cultures) and by historians. In his professional life, and for a while after his death in 1942, his figure dominated American anthropology. The 1904 essay was written within a few years of the launching of the *American Anthropologist* on its present career (1898) and of the founding of the American Anthropological Association (1902), in a period when men who were to shape academic anthropology in the United States were getting degrees with Boas in the department he had founded at Columbia.

Boas has been much discussed for his ideas and scholarly methods, but very little for his work as an organizer of anthropology. (The important exception is in the work of Stocking [1960, 1968].) Yet his intellectual impact depends in part on the fact that he worked at the center of a crucial period, when the base of anthropology shifted from government museums and private sources to the university, a period of the institutionalization, and one might say, domestication, of anthropology as an academic discipline in this country. Boas saw the beginning of a process of which we begin to see the end. Such a figure, viewing something at the point of formation, against a larger history, may see more clearly and more wholly than those who later take the new formation for granted. This seems to me true of Boas in this essay. Now that the formation once again cannot be taken for granted, the essay seems pertinent in ways it could not have been during the intervening years.[4]

Commenting on the students attracted to anthropology in the years before he wrote, Boas said (1904, p. 522):

> The best among them were gradually permeated by the fundamental spirit of anthropological research, which consists in the appreciation of the necessity of studying all forms of human culture, because the variety of its forms can alone throw light upon the history of its development, past and future.

On the origins of anthropology, he remarked that early observations of other peoples by themselves remained curiosities (1904, p. 514):

> It was only when their relation to our own civilization became the subject of inquiry that the foundations of anthropology were laid.

There are then two primary moments in the constitution of a general anthropology: interest in other peoples and their ways of life, and concern to explain them within a frame of reference that includes ourselves. Following Boas, who here follows the Enlightenment and its nineteenth-century successors, one adds: concern for explanation within a developmental perspective, a developmental perspective that comprehends the many diverse lines of human history in terms of the growth of rational command of the realities and resources of human life, toward ultimate fulfillment of human potentiality.

Let me expand on the character of these three aspects of anthropology, as background to an account of what their history suggests for our present prospects.

First, interest of the sort that matters here is not the

automatic result of contact with others—many journeys show only pursuit of trade, conquest, pleasure, escape. The interest requires some mode of description, one that may be generalized and used at home as well as abroad. Concern to explain must go beyond stereotypes and pigeonholes ("savages," "Stone Age tribes"). It requires some mode of comparison, in a frame of reference that can comprise all cases. Anthropology may begin in curiosity and savor the specific, but it leads ideally into universality—ideally, a concrete universality that mediates between the particular and the general, whether in the phonology of languages or the history of peoples. Boas was himself always clear as to the two orientations, indeed motivations, within anthropology, as within other sciences—the one seeking the unity of general laws, the other attracted to the unity of complex phenomena (1904, p. 16). The ultimate concern of the anthropological tradition, then, is with both "common humanity and diverse cultures," to use the title of an excellent essay on the theme (Kluckhohn, 1959), to explain both the similarities and the differences in the condition of mankind, to get at what is common *through* the differences that have arisen through the interaction of men with external nature and each other in different settings.

To be more concrete, this general anthropology seeks to illuminate both what is cultural and what is Navajo about Navajo culture, what is true of Navajo because it is a language, what true because it is the language of the Navajo, what is recurrent, what specific to the Navajo as a population and as a people in history.

Concern with only what is common, with similarities, universals, may constitute a philosophical anthropology, a psychology or biology, characterizing man as an abstract being. Concern with only the general contour of development, general laws, or a single lever of explanation, may constitute a sociology or history of a certain kind. Concern with only what is different may yield precise ethnography and ethnology. Neither kind of concern alone can constitute the anthropology of the tradition intended here. And at their worst, the one-sidedness of the one may lead to the imposition of *a priori* notions, distortion, and the rationalization of injustice; that of the other may never rise above exoticism or may devolve into sterile empiricism.

Second, in its concern with "the fundamental thought of the development of the culture of mankind as a whole" (Boas, 1904, p. 514), the tradition intended here implicates the "philosophy of history," in one sense of that term. It is a sense not in much repute and one cultivated by even the greatest of anthropologists only apologetically.[5] Yet what we know as anthropology grew out of the emergence of the "general problem of the evolution of mankind" in the Enlightenment, and has informed what we trace as anthropology throughout its subsequent history. As Boas' essay shows, to solve the problem of the philosophy of history empirically, rather than speculatively, was the great motivation for him, as it had been for Tylor and Morgan. Those who do not acknowledge assumptions about the course of history make assumptions about it nevertheless, assumptions perhaps made pernicious by being suppressed.

It is obviously in the nature of the dimension of human life central to anthropology—the cultural—to implicate historical process. No attempt at explanation in anthropology can escape historical assumptions (Kluckhohn, 1946); sociocultural phenomena can neither be reduced entirely to external conditions nor extricated from the matrix of change. Thus far, of course, one might have only particular lines of evolutionary history. The *general* problem involves some view of the whole. Diamond (1963, 1964a, b) has trenchantly shown that major anthropologists, seeking some general context and meaning for their work, have always broached some view of the course of human history. Boas, Lowie, Kroeber, Sapir, Whorf, Redfield, White, Steward, have all done so. Individual views differ in their weighting of two emphases that Diamond calls "prospective" and "retrospective"—the one a focus on the possibilities of a rational future, freed from past superstition, prejudice, war, and want, the other a focus on a renewed sense of the possibilities of human nature and culture through knowledge of cultural worlds already formed. The tone may be varyingly optimistic or pessimistic. Yet life is impossible without something for which one can hope. Recognizing ourselves as members of an emerging world community, we cannot avoid hope (or despair) for it. When we study local communities, we cannot escape assumptions, open or hidden, as to that for which they hope and as to what can be hoped for them.

The *general* problem, then, is not simply empirical—what has occurred; nor only methodological and theoretical—how to study what has occurred, how best explain it. It is also a moral problem, a problem of one's commitments in, and to, the world. Anthropologists have indeed commonly thought of themselves as belonging to the "party of humanity" (cf. Gay, 1971, pp. 262–90), and the world view Gay ascribes to the Enlightenment, a *passionate rationalism*[6] and a *tragic humanism*, is not alien to anthropologists. It is, I would urge, the view best suited to them.

Let me try to avoid possible misunderstandings. To speak of the "general" problem of human evolution does not mean to indulge in purely abstract or *a priori* schema, with regard to either past or future. Boas himself (1908, p. 7) stressed explanation of differences and the interest of actual histories, as well as general laws. And to speak of the evolution of mankind, although it implies a concern with the outcome, does not imply a belief in inevitable progress. "Progress" can, in fact, be used to rationalize environmental destruction and social waste, open or covert oppression. It would be hard not to agree with the conclusion of a leading scholar (Manuel, 1965, pp. 161–62):

> In the midst of universal dread of nuclear annihilation, worldwide social revolution, internecine racial wars, the spectacle of fat-land inhabitants committing suicide by overfeeding and of barren lands incapable of preventing the mass starvation of their hungry, the assurances of the prophets

of the new spirituality [he includes four seemingly diverse groups—theologians, neo-evolutionists, neo-Marxists, and modern cyclical theorists] often seem Utopian, even a hollow joke. The victims of the twentieth-century slaughterhouse refuse to believe it.

Yet the tradition intended here requires a conception of the future, indeed a "Utopian" conception (taking "Utopian" in the positive sense of a projected ideal, not the negative sense of an unrealizable dream) and a theory of progress as well.[7] That requirement withstands the widespread repudiation of what have been known as philosophies of history, not only by scholars of historical thought (such as Manuel), but also by analysts of historical methodology. Interest in such analysis has grown rapidly, and anthropologists have much to learn from the results. Yet I do not think the tradition intended here has been shown to be untenable; rather, I think it can be shown to be inescapable. Let me consider a representative book, the best I know.

ON THE PHILOSOPHY
OF HISTORY

Danto ([1965] 1968, p. 11) quite rejects substantive philosophies of history:

> Using just the same sense of significance as historians do, which presupposes that the events are set in a story, philosophers of history seek for the significance of events before the later events, in connection with which the former *acquire* significance, have happened. The pattern they project into the future is a narrative structure.[8]

Such critiques appear to be directed at certain famous nineteenth-century instances, especially Marxism (the one specified by Danto). That the anthropological tradition is implicated appears to escape notice. The criticism is not always fair to men in the tradition being rejected. (Scots Enlightenment figures such as Adam Ferguson and Adam

Smith, Victorian evolutionists such as Tylor and Morgan, and the pivotal figures, Hegel and Marx, anticipated, but did not prescribe, the narrative of the historical future.) The true force of a Marxian approach is not simply deterministic, but rooted in a conception of man as creative and emerging into freedom through the labor process (cf. Marx [1857] 1964, pp. 84–5; *Das Kapital*, Vol. I, Part 3, Ch. 8, section 1; and Stern, 1949, pp. 342–43); not directed essentially to an apparent pattern of history as a whole, but to the underlying structure of relations and causes as manifested in concrete situations, a point brought out by Lévi-Strauss (1953, p. 61).[9]

The critiques further seem to share an assumption that we are best without any substantive philosophy of history at all. In this they reflect, one suspects, a climate of opinion that welcomes the "end of ideology," for which philosophies of history, "Utopian visions," threaten despotism and sacred wars conducted in their name. In this view, celebrated in the 1950s (cf. Smith, [1964] 1971), one should accept present American life as the best of possible worlds, and there could be no responsible disagreement over ends. Today many view alternative conceptions of what society can be as essential. The threat of totalitarian control in the name of a conception of the future is to be answered by open participation in formulation and criticism of what goals constitute genuine progress, what conditions for the realization of goals are acceptable costs. To scorn conceptions of this sort (especially among scholars and movements for change) is to play into the hands of those who are already busy shaping our future by their power to implement their own. Every government, every political force, has some avowed philosophy of the history it seeks to realize. Are those intelligent enough to analyze philosophically to withdraw from civic life or become mindless or cynical servants of powers that be?

Danto himself remarks (p. 14) that "scientists make unexceptionable claims on the future, as do all of us in practical life." He further holds that the explanatory part of a philosophy of history (such as Marxism or evolutionary anthropology), when not connected with a descriptive part (i.e., a narrative projection), is not a philosophy of history in the sense he rejects, but a contribution to social science.[10] But if, as scientists and citizens, we make claims on the future, grounded in theory, but without a script written in advance, do we not, in fact, act in terms of a substantive philosophy of history? Is not the important distinction among substantive philosophies of history between those that are open-ended and those that are closed?

Indeed, the fallacy would seem to be in critiques of substantive philosophy of history which, while purporting only to explicate the normal practice of historians, have the effect of severing connection between history and the future, so as to make not only a philosophy of history, but also meaning and rationality in ordinary life, logically impossible. True, the significance of events, their meaningfulness, may depend upon their relation to later events (as argued by Danto); it may be only in terms of such a relation that significance appears. But it is not the case (as assumed by Danto) that the relation must be that of *certain knowledge* of a later state of affairs. The significance of past or present events may appear in relation to a conceptual vantage point, whose temporal location is immaterial. Where the later states of affairs are in the future, the relation may be one, not of foreknowledge, but of anticipation; not of augury, but of feedback. If such a relation is granted in science and practical life, then it has a place in comprehension of the present in relation to the future as part of "the general problem of the evolution of mankind." Its place is a matter of the place of scientific and practical rationality in shaping human history. The difference between science, practical affairs, and our efforts to comprehend and make our own history is a difference of degree, not of kind.

If, indeed, we cannot certainly know the next chapter, yet must anticipate it; cannot promise the overcoming of destruction and degradation, yet must work toward it; cannot guarantee a future state of affairs, yet can affect the odds by knowledge of such patterns and causal relations as history affords; if both in anthropological work and personal lives, we cannot avoid assumptions as to how the future will unfold from present change; if the very choice between scholarship and social action implies an assumption as to the time remaining to a way of life; then there seems no alternative but to integrate into anthropological work an explicit concern with the philosophy of history. Only so can the assumptions of our work be integral with the assumptions of our lives. For what can I hope? What is its relation to what is known of the course and bases of human history? These are questions we cannot escape.

We are told often enough that some epistemological, ontological, ethical theory is inevitably implicit in human life, and urged to come to an explicit understanding of our own premises in these regards, since we cannot avoid premises. We should be told the same with regard to the philosophy of history. Explicit understanding can indeed give foundations and direction to what may otherwise appear an infinite regress of relativity, when epistemological, ontological, and ethical questions are raised (cf. Scholte's essay in this volume).[11] The stereotype of past philosophies of history can be jettisoned by insisting on substituting realistic terms in any characterization: for "narrative," one can substitute "plan"; for "timeless Utopia," "agenda"; for prophesy," "rational hope"; for "the meaning of history," "meaningfulness in history" and the chance of constructing it.

In sum, a vital philosophical connection between human history and the human future seems clear and necessary. A special contribution of anthropology is to represent the claims of the "retrospective" view in any synthesis (cf. Diamond's paper in this volume, and the conclusion of Diamond, 1963); to serve, in the spirit of Boas (1904, p. 524),

as a check to an exaggerated valuation of the standpoint of our own period, which we are only too liable to consider the ultimate goal of human evolution, thus depriving our-selves of the benefits to be gained from the teachings of other cultures and hindering an objective criticism of our own work.[12]

I have dwelt on the justification of a philosophy of history, because I think that the justification of anthropology re-quires it. It is not only that the two share a common origin and development; it is a question of any possible future for anthropology. Eric Wolf is, I think, right when, in con-cluding a fine book, he states (1964, p. 96):

> The anthropological point of vantage is that of a world culture struggling to be born. As a scientist, the anthro-pologist both represents its embryonic possibilities and works to create it. If that culture fails, so will anthropology. . . .[13]

The foundation of that point of vantage and effort lies in a philosophy of history.

AS TO THE HISTORY OF THE TRADITION

Let me now highlight the development of the tradition in which anthropology participates, as it leads to a view of anthropology's future.

Boas himself singled out Herder as honored precursor, as did Kroeber, Lowie, and Sapir at other times, and Herder is indeed the seminal Enlightenment figure in the German tradition, a man who developed a sympathetic understand-ing of the validity of diverse cultures that echoes in Boas and among ourselves. Boas' citation of

> Herder's *Ideen zur [Philosophie der] Geschichte der Mensch-heit* [1784–1791],[14] in which perhaps for the first time the fundamental thought of the development of the culture of mankind as a whole is clearly expressed

is verbally interesting in two respects: "Fundamental" (or "foundation") seems to recur whenever Boas mentions the conception he (and I) take as the basis of anthropology, and

"Philosophie" is omitted from Herder's title. Indeed, although Boas found (1904, p. 514) "the fundamental concept of anthropology well formulated by the rationalists who preceded the French Revolution," he excused himself from discussing such work (1904, p. 513):

> The speculative anthropology of the eighteenth and of the early part of the nineteenth century is distinct in its scope and method from the science which is called anthropology at the present time and is not included in our discussion.

The road, in fact, goes further on. We have no adequate history of anthropolgy and no account of anthropologists' consciousness of their history, but individual anthropologists have many diverse reasons for tracing individual strands to one or another early point in time. Relevant observations, significant data collection, may begin in the mid-nineteenth century in some parts of Oceania and the New World, but reach back to any century since the fifteenth in others (with some of the best work in the sixteenth); and, for some regions, to medieval times or to classical antiquity. The history of a problem may go back in a similar way—that of the origin of the American Indian and the peopling of the Americas has a significant history since the sixteenth century (cf. Rowe, 1964; Huddleston, 1967).

Affinities of method, theory, or spirit may bring an earlier writer into one's personal pantheon—Montaigne's relativism, for example (though he has claims, too, as a collector and ethnological commentator), St. Thomas Aquinas' resolution of the relation between the local and universal in the realm of law, Lucretius' naturalism in explaining the origin of culture. Still, a decade or so ago, active consciousness of a general anthropology did not usually go back beyond Boas and other academic founders, save for a few major figures, notably Powell, Morgan, and Tylor, of the latter part of the nineteenth century.

Awareness of the formation of anthropological and ethnological societies in the first part of the century has since grown (Tax, 1955; Stocking, 1971b), together with a sense of the "ethnological" question that so concerned the period (cf. Gruber, 1967, 1970; Stocking, 1972). At the same time, general scholarship and a number of anthropologists have rediscovered the central relevance of the eighteenth-century Enlightenment, revaluing the seminal role of Rousseau, for example, and recognizing once again the common origin of the modern social sciences, among them anthropology, there. (Cf. LeClerc, 1972, appendix; Diamond, 1964a, b; Gay, 1969; Voget, 1968, 1969–70.) A few efforts have begun to trace the general story through the whole history of European exploration back to the Renaissance (Hodgen, 1964; Rowe, 1964, 1965; Slotkin, 1965). And some have recognized the place of classical antiquity (Kluckhohn, 1961).

The full story, I believe, does begin in the Greek Enlightenment of the fifth century B.C.—not from a search for the earliest possible ancestor, a classical training (I have none), or a plain liking for Herodotus (I do have that), but because, if one takes seriously various conditions for the emergence of anthropology that have been proposed, various indications of the presence of anthropological interest that have been suggested, then classical antiquity, beginning with the Greeks, is indeed the first case. The spatial horizon was not the whole world, but it was a sufficiently diverse world. Exploration, trade, and migration had flourished in the seventh and sixth centuries B.C., as the Greeks ranged the Mediterranean and Black Seas, and the experience was reflected in a development of geography and in literary references (as when Prometheus' peak, in Aeschylus' play, overlooks a vast arc of the peoples of the world, just as the fall of Milton's Satan was to do). The temporal horizon was greater for Plato than for most Europeans before well into the nineteenth century, for Plato speculated in terms of evolutionary developments over nine thousand years. There was also—and this would seem indispensable—some sense of distance from received tradition, in consequence of internal social and intellectual change. Alongside ethnographic curiosity and information, there had developed an independent intellectual life and serious reflection on fundamental questions; attitudes toward received beliefs ranged from rationalization and skepticism to replacement.

In this context arose universal conceptions of physical and of human nature, and a sense of human diversity and history as being subject to inquiry. There were instances of explanation in terms of invariant relations between human natures and environment; reconstruction of earlier stages of cultural history through the comparative method; ethnological inference on the basis of linguistic affinity; naturalistic explanation of the evolution of man and culture (Democritus' lost *Life of Hellas*, if Lucretius' *On the Nature of Things* does derive from it); and the beginnings of scholarly continuity (around Aristotle and his successor). Institutionalization of anthropological inquiry failed to occur (except marginally, in respect to the useful arts of medicine and geography, and as an aspect of national history), but for a time the possibility of a Herodotus and of occasional successors did exist. Compiling rather systematic ethnology and integrating it into a world history—the story of the confrontation of East (Persia) and West (Greece)—Herodotus set a precedent which first expressed "the fundamental thought of the development of the culture of mankind as a whole."

I suggest that this was the first moment of greatness in the tradition intended here, the assumption being that "greatness" does not mean beyond criticism, but has to do with what was done with what there was to work with, has to do with the opportunity that was seized. Herodotus did not, of course, escape his times or his personal outlook, but he accomplished something decisively greater in human scope and rationality than anything before. Each subsequent period that we can think of as marked with greatness will resemble his, in that an opportunity was seized to find order in newly perceived diversity, to try to explain a new horizon of knowledge in regard to human nature and culture, against a background of a sense of the inadequacy of received perspectives, and of a hope for the future.

After a new and wider wave of exploration, after a struggle against received tradition, European leaders of the Enlightenment arrived at new formulations of "the fundamental thought of the development of the culture of mankind as a whole," conceived in terms of the "history of manners" and "natural history." Various theories of society's evolutionary stages (commonly four) were advanced and debated (Herder among others cited execptions to unilinear evolution), and a consistent "cultural materialist" explanation was given by men such as William Robertson and John Millar. They had indeed not only a descriptive concept of culture ("manners and customs"), but also a theoretical one (phrased in terms of "education" by Buffon and others, and with the term "culture" itself by Hobbes and Pufendorf in the late seventeenth century, as by Kant, Herder, and others in the late eighteenth). The principal figures were conscious of a debt to classical antiquity, but also of a distinct advantage—knowledge from the new horizon of the New World, and remoter Africa and Asia, requiring to be integrated into a general view.

The first part of the nineteenth century saw continuing exploration and ethnography, the formation of anthropological societies, the rise of a Romantic re-evaluation of national traditions, folk cultures, and the Middle Ages. Attention was focused on the origins of particular peoples and on the question of the original unity of mankind. A "typological" evolutionary perspective (civilized vs. savage, with grades between sometimes of "semicivilized," "barbarian") continued to be assumed, notably in America (see Pearce, 1953, Chs. 3–5). The next great period, the Victorian, was coincident with the last surge of European division and domination of the world. Writers were conscious already of a loss of pristine ethnography.[15] The felt inadequacy of received perspectives is suggested by focus on institutions of law, inheritance, marriage, and is clear in the approach of Morgan to property, of Tylor to religion (cf. Burrows, 1966; Diamond, 1964a; Stocking, 1971b). The principal figures were conscious of eighteenth-century precedent, variously citing Montesquieu, Lord Kames, Millar, and so on. They were conscious also of a distinct advantage—knowledge of the great age of mankind, extending to a prehistoric condition more primitive than that of any contemporary people. In regard to this new horizon, which stimulated both him and Morgan in their major books, Tylor wrote ([1871] 1958, p. 54):

> Criticizing an eighteenth-century ethnologist is like criticizing an eighteenth-century geologist. The old writer may have been far abler than his modern critic, but he had not the same materials. Especially he wanted the guidance of Prehistoric Archaeology, a department of research only established on a scientific footing within the last few years.

The first part of the twentieth century saw an anthropology that, as it became institutionalized, had grown continuously in works and workers. Conscious criticism of received tradition was, of course, present. Underlying the diversity of the period are two common elements of special importance to us here, for it was, I think, also a period of greatness in the study of the "general problem of the evolution of mankind." First, evolution was not so much studied as assumed (on this, more below). Second, it was a period like its predecessors, associated with knowledge of a new horizon, requiring to be integrated into a general view. The horizon was not in space, as with the Enlightenment, nor in time, as with the Victorians, but in ethnography itself.

The principal figures were, naturally, conscious of nineteenth-century precedent in the ordering of ethnographic data, but also of a distinct advantage—a new *quality* of knowledge through their own practice. What marks the period most of all is that its principal figures were themselves field workers, unlike most Victorians or Enlightenment writers generally. More precisely, over the course of the generations encompassing the work and training given by Boas and his students, and Malinowski and Radcliffe-Brown and their students, the academically respectable terms of discussion of other ways of life changed. One can see it through the years in journals. Problems of personal bias and *a priori* description would remain; but a combination of personal practice and public critique changed standards of description and comparison irreversibly. The accomplishment can be called *methodological relativism*. (It is linked with what Willis in his paper in this volume calls *scientific antiracism,* and Benedict's *Patterns of Culture* [1934] is its main public expression in the United States.)

The shift in accepted practice should be seen as the fundamental contribution of the period, for the tradition intended here, although it was made often unremarked in the midst of overt controversy over the "superorganic" conception of culture, "functionalism," historical method, and the like. Boas, Sapir, and Kroeber established new standards for describing and discussing languages in terms of their "own genius"; Malinowski established new standards for field work to describe cultures in terms of their own internal relationships. All were part of a common accomplishment in dealing with units, patterns, and relationships in concrete, yet universally relevant, detail. That accomplishment should not be sold short today for failings in the self-conscious theoretical efforts of those who brought it about, for it (serious ethnography) is the main asset cultural and social anthropology bring today to a unified social science.[16]

The period since World War II has seen great growth in anthropology in personnel and geographic range.[17] In the study of human evolution as a whole one may find a final expansion of horizon, as it were, in time, through intensified comparative studies of primates, as well as through genetically oriented research that deepens the explanation of human nature. In prehistory one may sense a new precision in scope, integrating new data with new modes of interpretation in a domain unchallenged by others. In cultural and social anthropology there is often enough spurt and spirit, but due, at its best, to stimulation from without (linguistics, mathematics, psychology, ethology), and, at its worst, to a mistaken impression of novelty due to isolation from other fields and ignorance of prior developments in their own. Most of the best work has been a development of "methodological relativism" in both American and British varieties, aiming at improved description of cultures in their own terms and through their own eyes (or minds, as it were), and at fuller understanding of the principles of organization in communities of which kinship is the major matrix and metaphor. (Lévi-Strauss has described his work in this regard as a continuation of that of Engels! [1963, pp. 339–40])

Evolutionary conceptions have indeed returned to prominence, just as such conceptions came into prominence in the latter part of the eighteenth and nineteenth centuries. But this time the prominence is not associated with a new horizon, consciousness of advantage, or any mark of greatness that comes from wrestling with new data and problems in tension with a cultural need. For, despite theoretical controversy, the conception returned without much struggle simply because it had never been lost (cf. Bock, 1956). The heralded repudiation of cultural evolution by Boas and his students was a repudiation, not of general evolution, but of particular accounts of it and of a particular mode of explanation on which they were based (cf. the necessity of modern Marxist thinking to repudiate particular simplified accounts and models of explanation developed within official Marxism [Hobsbawm, 1964, pp. 19–20, 64–65]). Demonstration of exceptions to postulated sequences of universal development became a "paradigm" in the generation Boas shaped, as his Eskimo evidence that abstract primitive art need not develop out of naturalistic art was followed by examples from rules of descent, social groupings, religion, and so on. Inconsistency between classifications on the basis of race, languages, and cultural traits had exposed simplistic thinking about named peoples as eternal evolutionary units (Boas, 1904, p. 518) and encouraged closer-grained study of historical relations in geographically controlled settings, a kind of study for which Boas' work on the 1890s folk tales on the North Pacific Coast established the paradigm in American anthropology (cf. Spier, 1931; Chaney, 1972, pp. 2–3). (Historical-geographical perspectives indeed flourished in many disciplines and countries in the decades just before and after the turn of the twentieth century). Attention was focused on specific processes of change (which might lead to general laws of change) and indigenous patterns in terms of which historically acquired traits were reinterpreted and ordered (the Boasian form of methodological relativism in the sphere of culture [cf. Hymes, 1970]).

But Boas and the Boasians remained evolutionists in the typological sense. The Boas who wrote *The Mind of Primitive Man* to demonstrate the potential equality of all mankind still retained a clear conception of "primitive" vs. "civilized." His chapter headings said as much. The great Boasians who shared his views were not embarrassed to write books with such titles as *Primitive Society* (Lowie, 1921), *Primitive Religion* (Lowie, 1924), *Primitive Man as Philosopher* (Radin, 1927), or to give courses and scientific lectures on "primitive languages" (Sapir; Whorf). When Leslie White and others pointed out the obvious and inescapable after World War II, there was a collapse within a few years of what had seemed an impregnable, hard-won position of science (cf. Bock, 1952). Now almost everyone could be a cultural evolutionist again.

How much has changed, however, beyond the change in status of the term "evolution" itself, from taboo to popularity? Not enough, I think. Anthropological evolutionary work has corrected fundamental flaws of the preceding period in certain respects, but the future of the discipline as a whole is bound up with an as yet partial and ambiguous response to others.

In developing universally adequate descriptive concepts, many participants in methodological relativism tend also to level or reduce them. No difficulty appeared in the sphere of language, when phonological and grammatical categories and processes were recast, so that Kwakiutl and

Takelma, Greek and Latin, could be seen as cases within a common framework. In the sociocultural sphere categories such as "law," "politics," "religion," also were given definitions such that all applied equally to all communities. It became difficult to speak of differences in complexity or adequacy of institutions, and particularly difficult to recognize the emergence of levels of organization such as the tribe and the state. The movement was in part against the ethnocentric side of evolutionary thought, an impulse to defend in "primitive" communities the existence of valued categories that European bias had often denied them ("no laws, no religion, no state, no X"). But the paradigm tendency sometimes overreached itself, as when the putative discovery of private property in hunting and gathering bands was later shown to have reflected, not aboriginal conditions, but incorporation in the fur trade. (See Leacock's important monograph, 1954.)

The revival of the evolutionary perspective has provided a framework for correcting these flaws. Ecological and economic determinants gained new prominence; levels of sociocultural integration and development were restored to legitimacy and significance; and much worthwhile work has been done. In regard to the *"general* problem of the evolution of mankind," however, great limitations appear.

It is from the vantage point of political science, economics, sociology perhaps, that the period since World War II has appeared as a new horizon, providing knowledge from the expanded sphere of American interests and personal research. Anthropologists have been part of this expansion of American social science, however much they have wished to dissociate themselves from it, playing little effective critical role.

Some may recall when it was standard fare in introductory anthropology courses for the instructor to set up and shoot down in turn series of stock fallacies, having to do with a unilinear set of evolutionary stages or with some single center of cultural diffusion, and to attack ethnocentric biases associated with such fallacies as false and demeaning to the creativity of most of the world's peoples. Just such modes of thought became the stock in trade of much of what passes for social science in public life in the generation of anthropology's great expansion since World War II. Yet anthropologists who bridled at explaining aboriginal cultures in such terms had little to say when political scientists, sociologists, economists, administrators (and perhaps some anthropologists), explained contemporary third-world societies in such terms. Put aside here the triune evolutionary model that has helped shape Reisman's *The Lonely Crowd*, McLuhan's *Understanding Media*, and Margaret Mead's *Culture and Commitment*. The common coin has been "developed" vs. "underdeveloped," or "modern" vs. "traditional." I submit that these are equivalents to the "civilized" and "primitive" of a preceding era, still a polar evolutionary model, combined often enough with the notion of a center of diffusion to less fortunate peoples. (For the early ethnologist Elliot Rivers, the center was Egypt; for us, it is ourselves.) Why is it that anthropologists, so well equipped to expose the error of such thinking in Englishmen and Marxists, have been so little heard from as such thinking proliferated all about them?

What it suggests is a trained incapacity to rise above one's professional subject and into the modern world and a view of anthropology as equivalent only to ethnology. One perhaps thinks seriously about the relationship before European discovery between aboriginal Oceania and Southeast Asia, but not in the same terms about the relationship today between the United States and either. The Boas who denounced World War I and the covert use of anthropologists as spies, and whose last words expressed his lifelong fight against racism, as part of what he saw as the general mission of anthropology, would much more likely have been consistent. Another possibility, not in conflict with that preceding one, is that most anthropologists view the modern world, and the place of their society in it, in terms not much different from the typological, polar evolutionary thinking that has persisted throughout American history, as American society has had, with troubled conscience, to come to terms with the peoples and ways of life it has dominated and often enough destroyed. (Again, see Pearce's penetrating account of the settler's view of the savage and Indian as admirable and doomed [1953]. Have not many anthropologists made analogous assumptions about cultures and peoples today so that phenomena of the sort reported by Clemmer in this volume can surprise them?)

Anthropologists have only partly broached a new horizon peculiarly proper to themselves. The new horizon has to do with Wolf's thesis that "the anthropological point of vantage is that of a world culture struggling to be born." It has to do with a challenge to realize the implications of anthropology's own regulative idea, that of culture. Throughout most of the career of anthropology, the cultures of the world's peoples have been thought of in terms of a model of differentiation (not to exclude a common underlying basis). Boas phrased it thus (1908, p. 7):

> Anthropological research leads us to two fundamental questions: Why are the tribes and nations of the world different, and how have the present differences developed?

The interest might be in tracing an original unity as well as explaining the differentiation. The diversity might be thought of as a laboratory, a field of independent cases, or as an irreplaceable mirror to ourselves (Lévi-Strauss, 1966, p. 27). The model retains some value, but it has given much of anthropology what Mintz (1970, p. 14) has called its own "preoccupation with purity," by which people influenced by "civilization," especially "Western civilization," are less interesting, and people superficially like ourselves least interesting of all.

> Houses constructed of old Coca-Cola signs, a cuisine littered with canned corned beef and imported Spanish olives, ritual shot through with the cross and the palm leaf, languages

seemingly pasted together with "ungrammatical" Indo-European usages [Mintz has Caribbean Creoles in mind], all observed within the reach of radio and television—these are not the things anthropologists' dreams are made of.

Yet, Mintz points out (1970, p. 14):

we have begun to learn that it is the carriers of *these* cultures, both as victims and aggressors, who are asking today's questions, and providing irresistible answers. It becomes no longer a matter of what we shall do for them, but of what they must know, and have, in order to do for themselves. The search for an anthropology concerned with the widest issues of modern life has hence paralleled the search of the Westernized for a voice in the modern world.

There are Indian communities in the United States where no one (until just recently) has ever gone to study the way of life as it was at the time he or she was there; where the amalgam and direction of actual life are invisible (cf. Fontana, 1968). The problem is a long-standing one. There was strong resistance to publishing studies of acculturation in the official journal in the 1930s, on the ground that they were "not anthropology." Some anthropologists stopped studying Indians in the 1930s, because they had become just like any other minority group. There are today more and more exceptions to the picture Mintz paints, yet the image of anthropologists as exclusively students of "distinctive others" remains deeply ingrained.

Much of my own work is in the "distinctive other" tradition, and will continue to be, but I think that anthropologists who insist on it do anthropology a disservice. On the one hand, to take the study of a distinctive cultural tradition seriously entails, as Boasians insisted, a considerable commitment, including the kind of command of language one expects of a classical or Oriental scholar. There is a perennial place for the thorough scholarly commitment to any cultural tradition, but not for the "hit and run" tactics of many field workers.[18] On the other hand, justifications for this image of anthropological research, other than long-term humanistic commitment, hardly hold water.

The most common claim is the necessity of "culture shock" and objectivity in the study of a culture very different from one's own. Objectivity and culture shock, first of all, are somewhat in conflict.[19] The more objectivity, the less likely the culture shock. Culture shock itself can be most powerful when one discovers how different and distant one's own colleagues, neighbors, or fellow citizens are in their view of the world. (Hortense Powdermaker reported that she first understood the power of taboo, not in Polynesia, but later in a southern American town.) The relativistic objectivity sought from field work has been gained by many historians and philosophers through the centuries without field work (cf. Collingwood, 1939, p. 180). It is true that an outsider may notice what an insider takes for granted, but ethnographic research increasingly depends not on impressions, but on systematic inquiry of a sort that gives great advantage to members of the culture themselves (cf. Hale's paper in this volume). It can be argued that contributions penetrating enough to be theoretically significant are most likely to come from study of the cultural circumstances of which one has the most and most rapidly available background knowledge, namely, one's own.

In short, it is not a sufficient reason to study another culture simply because it is "other." Ethically and politically, too, there must be good reasons to inflict yet one more American inquirer on another part of the world.

Instead of taking for granted that a doctoral candidate in anthropology *will* do (exotic) field work, let us require candidates to demonstrate that they should be *allowed* to.

Most of all, the model of so much of the anthropological tradition—diversification—is anachronistic. It bespeaks the period of the peopling of the world, by God or migration: Who are they? Where did they come from? What were they put there to tell us? The relationship of cultures and communities in the world today is dominantly one of *reintegra-*

tion within complex units. Cultural anthropologists are perhaps better off in this respect than linguists, whose rich development of comparative-historical method for a century and a half is entirely adapted to studying the results and processes of diversification, at a time when genetic diversification of language may almost never happen again. Linguists have hardly any means (though sociolinguistics is beginning to provide some) for understanding, even seeing, the major processes of change among languages today, as they become specialized into niches relative to one another, in multilingual communities, educational systems, new nations, and so on. Nevertheless, relative failure to see the ways of life of American Indian reservations as *their cultures now,* novel unities shaped by historical experience of a century or more (cf. Walker, 1972); the inability to see the reality of Afro-American culture (see Szwed's paper) or foundations of resistance and rebellion (see papers by Clemmer and Caulfield)—such things point to an inadequate sense of the nature of culture itself. In origin, the metaphor of *culture* (as in Hobbes and Pufendorf) did indeed imply cultivation, as did the related use in German of *Bildung*; it was a processual term. Too often today we implicitly think of culture as what is completed, as works, not the working, to recall W. von Humboldt's discussion of language as *ergon* (product), not *energia* (activity).

The answer to this problem, at once theoretical and practical, was given, I think, by Sapir, when he separated the notion of culture from the notion of shared heritage and referred it to the processes of interaction in which identity and personal meaning emerge ([1934], 1949, [1938], 1949; cf. Aberle, 1960; Hymes, 1964, p. 29, n. 8; 1970, pp. 265–68; 1972b).[20] In effect, Sapir showed that the degree to which a cultural feature is shared, although important, is not part of its status as a cultural feature. That status depends not upon the fact, but upon its capacity for being shared. A poem written down and kept in one's drawer is cultural, whether or not it is ever known to others. It was perhaps the achievement of Tylor to help establish the notion of culture in terms of mankind as a whole (cf. Boas 1904, pp. 516–17), and of Boas to help establish the study, in their own terms, of human cultures (cf. Stocking, 1968, pp. 69–90). Our task may be to establish the study of the *cultural* as a universal and personal dimension of human efforts toward the future.

It is, after all, only in terms of such a conception of the culture as emergent, as potentially sharable as well as shared tradition, that we can understand our own situation. We are all in the situation of those in "traditional" societies, whose "modernization" we often consider. The homes in which we were born are frequently houses now torn down; the church in which we married is now a parking lot; the streets in which we played, the bits of water by which we mused, are mutilated or gone; where we live now probably is not where we will die. If the need of much of the world is to transform itself economically in order to achieve some parity of power and well-being, we, too, must often share in the need to forge new self-identities, to cope with new relations among cultural features, in order to salvage some kind of meaningfulness and symbolic self-preservation for a lifetime. We are all challenged and undermined by technological changes instituted by forces outside our control, forces which may take no note of our traditions or aspirations.

We have, then, everywhere the interplay between the cultural as traditional and the cultural as emergent. This is to touch upon an old theme, known by various names— *Gemeinschaft* vs. *Gesellschaft,* "genuine" vs. "spurious" culture (Sapir), in part Diamond's "retrospective" and "prospective" views. In the study of language it has taken on new importance in terms of socially organized ways of speaking that cut across the dimensions of "languages," as shown by Bernstein's much misunderstood notions of "restricted" and "elaborated" codes (see the treatment in Hymes, 1972a, b) and Habermas' analysis of the conflict in modern society between the spheres of symbolic interaction

and the sphere of technologically or bureaucratically motivated instrumental communication, the latter increasingly invading the former (Habermas, 1971; Schroyer,
1971). The degree to which modes of communication are
explicit and self-correcting as to presuppositions, the degree
to which they permit the expression or assumption of personal meanings, the conditions under which persons can
gain access to the acquisition of kinds of communicative
competence or opportunity to display them in performance,
for which responsibility is freely taken—such questions go
to the heart of the contribution that a linguistics reconstituted in the spirit of the anthropological tradition would
address. (Despite their personal political radicalism or liberalism, many linguists pursue a formalized, impersonal
linguistics that is itself cut off from the possibility of any
such contribution [cf. Hymes, 1972b].) Such questions also
raise the general issue of the relation between conscious and
unconscious knowledge. Sapir early spoke for the claims of
taken-for-granted, tacit knowledge and understanding
([1927] 1949, p. 559):

> Complete analysis and the conscious control that comes with
> a complete analysis are at best but the medicine of society,
> not its food.

Harris, reviewing Sapir's writings a decade after his death,
gave perhaps the best gloss (1951, p. 330):

> Which means: Don't take it as food; but also: Do take it as
> medicine.[21]

The opportunity, then, is this: to employ our ethnographic
tradition of work, and such ethnological insight as informs
it, in the study of the emergence of cultural form in concrete
settings and in relation to a world society. It is an opportunity comparable to those recognized and taken in the
periods passed in review, whose greatness consisted in
comprehending a new horizon as part of the whole, and of
advancing self-understanding through analysis of the bases

of the whole of human culture, thus enlarged. The horizon for us is not essentially remote in space or in time, nor in deepening of our practice (although all these may be involved), but in learning to see the shape of the cultural, and the forms taken by cultural identity, as they emerge and constitute our future.

This opportunity challenges the isolation of anthropology within its departmental traditions of recent generations. It gives new meaning to Boas' comment on "the *general* problem or the evolution of mankind" (1904, p. 523):

> We may still recognize in it the ultimate aim of anthropology in the wider sense of the term, but we must understand that it will be reached by cooperation between all the mental (i.e., social and cultural) sciences and the efforts of the anthropologist.

To the organizational challenge, on which the outcome of the scientific and social challenge depends, let me now turn.

III

The future of anthropology, it was said above, depends upon whether its present institutional context proves chrysalis or coffin. Let us quickly review the present situation in terms of its fundamental factor—what anthropologists are trained to do and what, we hope, they are able to do.

In the first decade of this century, Boas could both contrast anthropology's ultimate aim "in the wider sense of the term" to its more restricted actual scope and be precise about the latter (1904, p. 523; cf. 1908, p. 9):

> The historical development of the work of anthropologists seems to single out clearly a domain of knowledge that heretofore has not been treated by any other science. It is the biological history of mankind in all its varieties; linguistics applied to people without written languages; the ethnology of people without historic records; and prehistoric archaeology.

Boas could also be frank about the unprincipled basis of anthropology's domain (1908, p. 9):

> It will be recognized that this limitation of the field of work of the anthropologist is more or less accidental, and originated because other sciences occupied part of the ground before the development of modern anthropology.

And he could be frank about the dependence of anthropologists on other fields in their actual practice (1904, p. 523):

> It is true that these limits are constantly being overstepped, but the unbiased observer will recognize that in all other fields special knowledge is required which cannot be supplied by general anthropology.

Hardly anyone would recognize the substance of those characterizations of three generations ago as anthropology's "assigned special task," as its "clearly singled out" domain of knowledge. (The contents of the *American Anthropologist* and of the meetings of the American Anthropological Association show as much.) One finds in many anthropology departments today a commitment to the *form* of that characterization, the fourfold gospel—biological, linguistic, ethnological, and archaeological. Yet *within* each of the four fields "special knowledge is required which cannot be supplied by general anthropology."

Competence in two of the four fields have long required external support for facilities and training (biological and linguistic anthropology). Indeed, Boas foretold their separation as parts of biology and linguistics, because of their specialized methods (1904, p. 523):

> Problems may be set by the general anthropologist. They will be solved by the biologist. . . . I think the time is not far distant . . . when linguistics and biology will continue and develop the work that we are doing now because no one else cares for it.

The archaeology-prehistory quarter has also become increasingly interdependent with geology and other natural sciences, for dating, identifications, and control of interpretations, and with various sectors of humanistic disciplines, for work in classical, medieval, colonial, and industrial archaeology. Such interdependence also holds for genuine competence in the various aspects of cultural or social anthropology, even if cultural and social anthropologists are not always willing to grant it. Whether research is oriented topically ("economic anthropology," "psychological anthropology," "anthropology of religion," and so on) or regionally (West Africa, Latin America, etc.), essential parts of the training are not available within anthropology departments.

The plain fact is that there are such things as "political anthropology," "economic anthropology," "anthropology of religion" only because there is such a thing as "anthropology." They exist because of the organization of academic life, not the organization of reality. Guiana does not have one politics for anthropologists, another for political scientists; Latin America does not have one economics for anthropologists, another for economists; there is no theory of religion that is anthropological, as opposed to sociological, or to the understanding of religion developed by students of the history of religions. If religion is a single subject, it is the same subject for all. Too often our publications and careers have been built on the ploy of a putative contribution to the "anthropology of X" or "X anthropology." These are sometimes legitimations of new topics, no doubt, but legitimations required by a border-guard mentality. It is, in general, as ludicrous to speak of "theory in anthropology" (in contrast to theory in all of social science) as it would be to speak of "linguistic theory (Bantu)" in contrast to "linguistic theory (French)," as if the provenience of the language called for a different general theory of language. Such things belie the very conception of anthropology as a discipline universal in its concerns and in the openness of its founding.[22]

Such provincialism was not designed to frustrate and

fragment the contribution of a science of man to mankind, but has that effect. The consequence of professionalism and focus on disciplinary identity and growth is to divert much of the energy of students of man to rivalry with each other and away from human problems. The problem is obviously general to the social sciences. One sociologist (Birnbaum, 1971, p. 131) writes in terms valid for anthropology as well; it, too, shares in

> the general crisis of the social sciences. Originally intended to apprehend human history so as to fulfill the history of mankind, the social sciences . . . have broken down in two ways. The intention of apprehending history has been renounced in favor of a total capitulation to the scientific division of labor; abstractly recognized, the historicity of mankind is denied in scientific practice. This last contents itself with a fragmented description of a fragmented reality. In the second place, social science has become another instrument of domination, rather than a mode of liberation. Not the least contribution of those who sense themselves to be in the [anthropological] tradition is the insistence that the original humanist intent . . . be incorporated in contemporary practice; not the least of ironies is the fact that [anthropologists] are often as incapable as any others of realizing that intent.[23]

What, then, can be done? A small step is to commit oneself never to trade again on such titles as "anthropology of X" and to accept that either one has something to say about X or one does not. Beyond that, three general strategies seem possible: to retrench, to let go, to relax.

To retrench. One might return to Boas' anticipation that soon (1904, p. 523):

> anthropology pure and simple will deal with the customs and beliefs of the less civilized people only.

Taking the prehistoric record of custom and belief into account, "anthropology" would then be archaeology and ethnology. Its subject matter, like its sometime claim to be a general science, would be a stage of human history, not the whole. There would be honesty and dignity in that role, fulfilling the impulse to anthropology as the third wave of the humanities, after classical and Oriental studies, as the philology of peoples without philologies of their own (cf. Radin, 1933). The role of interpreter of a stage and type of human culture is indeed well established. (In Lévi-Strauss' phrase, when an object comes to Paris whose code is known, it goes to the Louvre; when the code is not known, it goes to the Musée de l'Homme.) One could return to the accurate titles of the turn of the century, when a museum or monograph series could be explicitly concerned with "Archaeology and Ethnology."

This would be the choice of becoming a branch of history, though still as a social science (Worsley, 1970, p. 128). It would still involve its own lines of interdependence with other disciplines (as in the third alternative). Many wish to retain this aspect of anthropology, but I know of no one who wishes to reduce anthropology to it.[24]

To let go. What, then, if the anthropological holding company is dissolved? Most of the component interests would find equally appropriate lodging elsewhere. A strong case could be made for departments of prehistory and/or archaeology, to which pertinent aspects of biology, linguistics, and ethnology could be attached (paleontology, linguistic prehistory, the historical ethnology of peoples investigated archaeologically as well). Indeed, while I do not wish to idealize prehistoric science, which can fall short of its own standards, and whose social basis sometimes opens it to hazards, it is probably the healthiest component of anthropology today. Cooperation is developed with other sciences, a divison of labor within the subject is recognized, so that there are places for each of the required talents: field work, interpretation, teaching; the intrinsic value of the materials studied is recognized and their preservation provided for. The scientific ideal of cumulative, collaborative research is perhaps better realized there than anywhere else in anthropology.[25]

Human biology cannot exist without the facilities of programs in biology and medicine, and anthropologically minded students of human biology could flourish as well or better there as among cultural and social anthropologists. Students of language owe a great debt to anthropology for its role in developing modern linguistics, but whereas departments of anthropology used to employ a linguist or two, a better case might be made today that departments of linguistics should employ an anthropologist or two. It really no longer makes much sense to pretend to train anthropologists in "practical linguistics"; it would make considerable sense to train linguists in "practical ethnography."

What, then, of the cultural and social anthropologists? These are, of course, the largest group, some of whom are the most threatened by centrifugal tendencies, which would deprive them of the illusion of a domain of the study of man of which they are intellectual overlords. No general rule can apply.

Clearly, a social or cultural anthropology competent to deal with contemporary societies must integrate itself with the main line of social theory that has attempted to deal with the shaping of the modern world—the line from Marx, Weber, Durkheim, and others through to contemporary sociology (on which cf. Lazarsfeld *et al.*, 1967; Colfax and Roach, 1971), political science, economics, and aspects of history and law. Conceptual integration with sociology is indeed well under way. A good many social anthropologists accept that the theoretical basis of anthropology and sociology must be the same (cf. Worsley, 1970, p. 129), as do many sociologists (cf. Smelser, 1967, p. 20). A corollary of this is that the attempt to distinguish "cultural" from "social" anthropology must be abandoned.

As to individuals, some would prefer integrated social science programs; others would prosper in settings that facilitated research with one or another topical or regional focus; still others would be at loss, unable any longer to teach "introductory anthropology," "anthropology of X," and the like, and having instead to confront those great symbols so often invoked, "man," "culture," "society," nakedly in a free market. The wisest would argue that cultural and social anthropology have certain distinctive strengths, born of their special concerns, but of general value—especially, a critical perspective, due to a long-standing concern with the full range of human experience, and the cultivation of a practice of personal research.

In the practice there is a traditional place for openness to phenomena in ways not predefined by theory or design—attentiveness to complex phenomena, to phenomena of interest, perhaps aesthetic, for their own sake, to the sensory, as well as intellectual, aspects of the subject (cf. Kroeber, 1959). These comparative and practical perspectives, though not unique to formal anthropology, are specially husbanded there, and might well be impaired, if the study of man were to be united under the guidance of others who lose touch with experience in concern for methodology, who forget the ends of social knowledge in elaborating its means, or who are unwittingly or unconcernedly culture-bound.

Such an argument would renew Boas' early view of departmental anthropology (1904, p. 523):

> Conscious of the invigorating influence of our point of view and of the grandeur of a single all-compassing science of man, enthusiastic anthropologists may proclaim the mastery of anthropology over older sciences that have achieved where we are still struggling with methods, that have built up noble structures where chaos reigns with us; the trend of development points in another direction, in the continuance of each science by itself, assisted where may be by anthropological methods.

And again (1908, p. 10):

> With the increase of our knowledge of the peoples of the world, specialization must increase, and anthropology will become more and more *a method* [Boas' emphasis] that may be applied by a great number of sciences, rather than a science by itself.

If, then, the justification for the maintenance, within the general study of man, of the branch called "anthropology" is that it husbands certain valuable methodological perspectives (ethnological, ethnographic),[26] the justification must be also that these perspectives are freely available to the general study of man; that "anthropologists" enter freely into competition in method and theory in such a general study of man, forsaking provincial claims; that the role of "anthropology" as a named node within the structure of a general study of man be accepted as one of mediating, not of isolating, the "anthropological" part with respect to the rest.

This strategy is the most reasonable, inasmuch as "letting go" of departmental structure, however much wished for, will come but slowly. Throughout the country and across the disciplines, the wish to break the "lockstep of the departments" is felt, but strongly resisted by those entrenched within them. The strategy with regard to departmental boundary maintenance, then, is:

To relax. The strategy has two aspects, one specific to the official four components of anthropology, the other more general. First, as to the relations of the components among themselves, American anthropology and its departments today are a social club, not a science or common discipline, as Lloyd Fallers pointed out once to a distressed audience of anthropologists. Social and cultural anthropology tends to consider itself central and to dominate the other three. At best, however, sociocultural anthropology stands in relation to the other three rather as philosophy once did to physics, psychology, and so on. It is an arena in which some general ideas are maintained, some problems defined, but not where the work gets done, because it is not where the way in which to do the work is known. Early in this century, some philosophers felt free to discuss the logical necessity of a concept of "ether" in physics, and some sociocultural anthropologists feel free today to define matters for specialists in the other three fields, even though the methods and training of the latter have run through at least one revolution since the sociocultural anthropologist's remembered graduate days. A first move must be to get this particular monkey off the back of the other three.[27]

A second step is to abandon the pretense that students are to master all four fields as an intellectually relevant matter. Perhaps an honest admission that it is for social reasons—one will be associating with such people within future departments—would be all right. And, of course, any student with a reason for mastering relations among two or more of the fields should be given every encouragement. But no one should be forced to dissemble about it. Boas (1904, pp. 523–24) could maintain that the field anthropologist should know the principles and results of linguistics, biological anthropology, and ethnologic-archaeological work (he joined the two in this context), but the context of problems in which he made the statement (essentially the history of peoples) no longer holds for more than a few students. The principles and methods which students may need to know are immensely various from one to another. Yet, to a considerable extent, obeisance to tradition, to the youthful *rites de passage* of their professors, and the political claims of each component, is exacted. This must stop.

All thus far is, of course, with regard to departments continuing the fourfold schema. There is no compelling reason for departments to do so—any one or more of the components might be let go, depending on strengths outside a department and the direction within it; and new departments can legitimately single out special patterns and directions of their own (as some have indeed done).

The nub of the matter is that the pretense of official coherence within anthropology acts as a barrier to the coherence that minds free to inquire into problems might actually find. Productive scholars know that problems lead where they will and that relevance commonly leads across disciplinary boundaries. Yet many an insecure academic compensates for his own lack or loss of intellectual virility by making it difficult or impossible for students and junior colleagues to benefit from theirs.[28]

There are sure tests for this, tests for what may be considered ideological and institutional, as against intellectual, criteria of relevance. Intellectual criteria involve questions such as: "Can you prove it?" "What does it show?" "If you want to do that, you'll have to learn X (a genuine prerequisite)." "Where does it lead?" Ideological and institutional criteria involve statements such as: "That's not anthropology." "That's all very well, but first you should study X" (an unrelated subject, a tradition in the field, favored by the person in question, or both). "You're not an anthropologist if you haven't done/studied X." (To this dichotomy should be added an intermediate category of personally responsible answers, such as "I don't know about that, you should ask X" (who, in fact, does know) and "That's an interesting idea, but this department will never let you do it."

In the early formation of departmental anthropology, the watchword, "That's not anthropology" may have been useful, somewhat like the union label; even though it violated the openness and expansiveness one associates with the early period, the academy had become the source of employment, departments the form of the academy, and one had to protect one's niche. Today one should react to the utterance of "That's not anthropology" as one would to an omen of intellectual death. For that is what it is.

Many of the best young people attracted to anthropology today leave it, and the causes are not hard to find. They are attracted by a vision of anthropology as a genuinely general study of man and find it a patchwork of feudal baronies. Recently I have met undergraduate students whose passion for anthropology restores faith that such a thing can exist. One colleague, initially suspicious of the students (the context was one of internal rebellion) was affected in the same way. Moved, he reflected that he had experienced that same feeling of inspiration in anthropology once thirty years before, in a summer spent in the field with Clyde Kluckhohn; he had not encountered it since. The occasion for the meeting was an internal crisis in a department devoted to general anthropology!—general anthropology defined as four separate, equal subdisciplines, each equally important, the requirements of each and of the set being mechanically interpreted and imposed. (Younger faculty were criticized for spending time with students on subjects of special student concern, such as problems of ethics in field work; that was "unprofessional" behavior.) Students entering anthropology with a dedication to it as a general field were being driven out of it. Entering with excitement about anthropology as a context in which meaningful problems could be pursued where they led, they encountered anthropology defined as a table of organization.

This analysis might be mistaken as a call for specialization in narrow components. It should be clear that nothing could be further from the truth. What is true is that even departments claiming to train in "general anthropology" hire in specialties, often enough specialists with degrees outside anthropology (linguistics, folklore, geology, genetics). Nevertheless, the point here is to call for a general anthropology that is an "organization of diversity," as opposed to a "replication of uniformity" (to employ terms introduced by A. F. C. Wallace). The purpose is to denounce a *bureaucratic* conception of general anthropology, while advocating a *personal* conception in the most vigorous terms. Given the arbitrariness of institutionalized boundaries in relation to human reality, the *personal* approach is the more adaptive— if one's goal is truly knowledge.[29]

The philosopher Collingwood once sought to describe the defining characteristic of philosophy in these words (1933, p. 184):

> It follows from the peculiar nature of philosophy that each philosopher, if he genuinely does make his own contribution to knowledge, cannot be merely adding another item to an inventory; he must be shaping afresh in his own mind the

idea of philosophy as a whole. And conversely, it is only by attempting this task, formidable as it is, that he can make any contribution, however modest, to the general advancement of philosophy; for until he has confronted this problem, the work which he is doing, whatever else it may be, is not genuinely philosophical work, since it lacks one of the distinctive marks of philosophical thinking.

These words apply to anthropology today, and have applied to the best anthropologists throughout history. One person's general anthropology need not be another's. There is no single packaged anthropology to be served to one and all. If the person attracted to anthropology has nothing of anthropological curiosity and reflectiveness, no training can produce more than a walking textbook or loyal servant. If the individual does have the spark of genuine inquiry, then the purpose of training is to nourish that spark, to enable the individual talent to come to fruition, mastering the particular skills and subjects required, and, it may be hoped, ultimately reshaping some part of the tradition in the light of the outcome. Though it may seem so to a bureaucratic mind, individuation of training is not fragmentation, but a way of enabling each to master his or her best vantage point on the whole. One of the high costs of the bureaucratic approach is the teaching of the irrelevant by, and to, the unwilling. In the approach intended here, regarding linguistics, for example, one student would be directed to historical linguistics and language classification, another to grammatical theory and psycholinguistics, another to dialectology, another to forget about the subject altogether.

The true coherence of anthropology, then, is personal. It is not official or bureaucratic. The issue is not between general anthropology and fragmentation, but between a bureaucratic general anthropology, whose latent function is the protection of academic comfort and privilege, and a personal general anthropology, whose function is the advancement of knowledge and the welfare of mankind.

Herein lies a fundamental part of "reinventing" anthropology. Each anthropologist must reinvent it, as a general field, for him or herself, following personal interest and talent where best they lead. The legitimate purpose of anthropological training is to facilitate this process. It has no other.

Such a conception may be thought to erase the boundary between anthropology and philosophy, not only with regard to history, but quite generally. I think that the boundary is indeed erased, if not by Collingwood's criterion, then by the exigencies of the situation in which anthropologists find themselves. The intellectual, political, and moral dilemmas facing anthropology call for reflection, analysis, and commitment that transcend the role of ordinary scientist or journeyman scholar. Unreflecting perpetuation of present practice will guarantee subservience to corrupt ends, sterile obsolescence, or both. Sartre once addressed the question, "For whom does one write?" Each anthropologist must address an analogous question. By virtue of its subject matter, anthropology is unavoidably a political and ethical discipline, not merely an empirical specialty. It is founded in a personal commitment that has inescapably a reflective, philosophical dimension. Indeed, the present surge of interest in philosophical questions among anthropologists reflects the widespread sense of political and ethical concern.

IV

The fundamental fact that shapes the future of anthropology is that it deals in knowledge of others. Such knowledge has always implied ethical and political responsibilities, and today the "others" whom anthropologists have studied make those responsibilities explicit and unavoidable. One must consider the consequences for those among whom one works of simply being there, of learning about them, and of what becomes of what is learned.

These responsibilities are widely discussed among anthropologists, and it would be frivolous to pretend to settle the serious disagreements that remain. I can only point to certain dimensions of the problem that seem to me essential, yet not always kept in mind.

We have to deal first with what Galtung (1967) has aptly termed "scientific colonialism." His point is this: if by "colonialism" we mean a situation whereby the center of gravity of a nation is no longer in that nation itself, but in some other nation, then the term has a scientific application. Political colonialism is well known, and economic colonialism, whereby, despite political independence, crucial economic transactions are centered elsewhere, is becoming well known. *Scientific colonialism* is a process whereby the center of gravity for acquisition of knowledge about a people is located elsewhere.

> There are many ways in which this can happen. One is to claim the right of unlimited access to data from other countries. Another is to export data about the country to one's own home country for processing into "manufactured goods," such as books and articles. . . . This is essentially similar to what happens when raw materials are exported at a low price and reimported as manufactured goods at a very high cost. The most important, most creative, most entrepreneurial, most rewarding, and most difficult phases of the process take place abroad (p. 296).

Many anthropologists have recognized the inequity of the practices that constitute scientific colonialism and have initiated efforts to overcome them, seeking to publish in the language of the country from which the data come, to provide reports of their work, to help train local researchers. So much is only courtesy, though some have yet to learn that much. The lesson of Project Camelot has been fairly widely learned, and earlier perhaps by anthropologists, who are more likely to be sensitive to such a situation, than by social scientists generally.[30] Yet the more recent crisis concerning anthropological research in Thailand[31] shows that the threat of the subversion of anthropology to the aims of counterinsurgency is permanent in a country devoted to a posture in the world of which Vietnam shows us only the extreme of a continuum. Indeed, in the context of a thoroughgoing analysis of the relation of the United States to the rest of the world as essentially colonial or imperial, one would have to conclude that the Thailand controversy is but the tip of an iceberg. The difference between counterinsurgency and much ordinary research is not fundamental; it is not that one is clandestine and the other not (the liberal issue), but that one (Moore, 1971, p. 40):

> is addressed to the counterrevolutionary aspects of imperialism while the latter is addressed to techniques of economic penetration.

In short, *cui bono?* Who is the public for one's research? Who receives it and utilizes it, intended public or not? It is perhaps true that the Czarist regime could not have benefited from reading Lenin's *State and Revolution,* no matter how many copies it obtained, but there are many instances in which specific information about communities, and simply general understanding of structures and processes, redounds to the advantage of those at the top. It has become generally recognized that information directly injurious should not be provided, but there is a less obvious, more profound obligation as well. It is to work toward ways in which the knowledge one obtains can be helpful to those from whom it comes. Not to do so is to be "neutral" on the side of the existing structure of domination.

The basis of this view was well stated in the first paragraph of resolutions proposed by the Radical Caucus at the 1969 Annual Meeting of the American Anthropological Association:

> Anthropology since its inception has contained a dual but contradictory heritage. On the one hand it derives from a humanistic tradition of concern with people. On the other hand, anthropology is a discipline developed alongside and within the growth of the colonial and imperial powers. By

what they have studied (and what they have not studied) anthropologists have assisted in, or at least acquiesced to, the goals of imperialist policy. It is becoming increasingly apparent to many that these two traditions are in contradiction.

Such statements, and the actions that follow from them, are often considered "political." They are. The difficulty is that many anthropologists have a double standard in this regard. The usual practice of anthropology is regarded as apolitical. It is not. At the meetings just cited a resolution condemning renewed expressions of scientific racism was passed and hailed with resounding applause. What expressed the taken-for-granted, "scientific" (i.e. apolitical) views of the Association was noted with some disdain next day in the *New Orleans Times-Picayune,* as the political stand that it indeed was, for it expressed, I believe properly, a union of knowledge and social values.

The instance is representative. On some matters there is a broad consensus that might be labeled one of "liberal humanism." Issues that speak to the general rights of man or the plight of an underdog command broad support. Though political in the world at large, within anthropology they appear expressions of felt truth. An issue that departs from present ethos or that reveals an unresolved split appears as politicization, particularly when concern for the oppressed begins to lead to confrontation with the oppressor.

There has been a surge of effort, generally applauded, to protect peoples and their cultures from "progress" that brings cultural destruction (ethnocide) and destruction of identity, if not also of body.[32] There is also a surge of effort, a controversial one, to study those who administer and direct affairs.[33] Unless this effort succeeds, anthropology, though it may define its subject in other terms, will remain mainly a defensive source of knowledge about the exploited of the world for those who exploit them. The peoples whom anthropologists define as scientific problems are commonly regarded by administrations and governments as social ones. But who is a problem to whom? An essential part of a critical, truly general anthropology is not to leave such definitions of the situation unexamined.

Who is the problem to whom? Whom does one's knowledge help? What responsibility must one take for the outcome of one's work? The questions are inescapable, yet the answers are not invariant. I would hope to see the consensual ethos of anthropology move from a liberal humanism, defending the powerless, to a socialist humanism, confronting the powerful and seeking to transform the structure of power. Yet one can have no illusion of unanimity on all issues. In World War I, as Norman Thomas once put it, socialists were killing each other as cheerfully as Christians. The present divisions in the professedly socialist world are notorious. More generally, anthropologists tend to understand and sympathize with the particular peoples they study. When the peoples are in conflict, so may be the sympathies of anthropologists, whatever their general convictions. Biafra was such a case, the Middle East is another. Nor is it adequate to think entirely in terms of responsibility to the community one studies (as Jorgensen [1971] does), if ethical principles are joined to a radical purpose. What of studies of bureaucracies and corporations? We tend to be hypnotized by the situation in Southeast Asia or with Indians, where the bully and the victim are clear to us. But most politically oriented anthropologists know at least one government in the world whose interest they would defend against some constituent community, even though their preference would be to mediate a dual responsibility. In a given country three conscientious anthropologists might choose three different loyalties—one to a government, one to a group seeking to overthrow it or to secede from its control, and one to a village that wished to be left alone by both.[34]

Again, the cause of "making the world safe for anthropology," as Adams (1971) seems to plead, is a narrow view indeed; what crimes must be swallowed in the name of preserving access to the field? Yet the claims of colleagues and the claims of a community are both serious ones. The difficulty is that we are subject to moral claims from more than one source. We enter into personal relationships in field work, but often enough with more than one group; and we cannot ignore trust in our relationships with colleagues, in and out of our profession. Nor can we ignore obligations to our families, which we might put ahead of all others. I know no calculus that does not lead persons of honesty and good will, after serious reflection, to considered judgments that conflict as to where primary duty lies in a given case. (Such people may indeed sense greater comradeship with each other than with someone whose judgment agrees with their own unreflectingly.)

I nevertheless believe that there is a direction in which one can work, and this is the ideal that Boas took the general evolution of mankind to show in process of realization (1908, p. 27): the enlarging of the moral community. The goal affects anthropology in three ways. There is the role that anthropology can play in building a world culture that is a moral community—just the old struggle against racism has far to go; there is the need to build as much of a world anthropological community as possible—a point whose importance to ethical issues has been stressed by George Appell (see Appell, 1971); and there is the relationship of ethnography.

Many, none more eloquently than Wolf (1972), rightly stress that this is not merely an instrumental relationship, but a moral one. If there is to be a future for anthropology in a democratic world, the ethnographic relationship must be developed as a mutuality not only of trust, but also of knowledge. Each person, after all, is to some considerable extent an ethnographer of his or her own world, having acquired a tacit knowledge of it that must go far beyond whatever is explicitly taught (cf. Diamond, 1972), acquisition of language being a salient example. An essential part of ethnography is to learn, and formulate, what others already in a sense know. Heretofore, the ethnographer has mediated between such specific knowledge and general knowledge usually entirely in the direction of the latter, as represented in a professional community and publications. As far as possible, the mediation must go also the other way —even primarily the other way. By helping members of a community to comprehend social reality more explicitly and generally, one may help people to employ what C. Wright Mills called "sociological imagination" (1959) and to be in greater rational control of their own destinies. Beyond this, one must follow the path urged here with respect to language by Hale and seek to help members of local communities themselves to participate in the work of anthropology. Anthropology must lose itself to find itself, must become as fully as possible a possession of the people of the world. This is a long and difficult road, but if we do not take it and keep to it, then, whatever our intentions, however much we rise above such things subjectively, our work will drift backward into the service of domination.

V

This analysis of anthropology is radical at least in this, that it accepts the contingency of anthropology and can envision a world in which it has no separate identity. One such world would be partitioned against the very possibility of the study of man as the study of others; each society's knowledge of itself would be official property, if not official secrets. Another such world would be loose and open, integrated at some levels, but comprising much diversity, part maintained from the past, part emergent, as sufficiently autonomous groups shaped their own cultural worlds. Neither world would demand a profession of anthropology, but the one might maintain it as an administrative tool, while the other might well be permeated with the grand tradition and the methodological spirit we think of as anthropological.

The first such world is possible enough. Herodotus' work survived, not because it was taken seriously as knowledge, but because of his superb style; it was only in the Renaissance, as similar reports of remarkable customs began to arrive from new travels, that Herodotus' reputation began to be vindicated (Momigliano, 1966). In recent years in Greece there has been little or no support for anthropology as the study of other cultures; there is considerable support for Laografia, the study of things traditionally Greek.

The second such world seems possible, if, as many now advocate, the goals of the eighteenth-century "science of freedom" (Gay's term) can be revitalized in the universal terms required in our own day. Anthropology has passed through the valley of colonial domination and sequestered much of its strength on departmental hilltops, but is nevertheless responding to the challenge of its time, creatively, in many ways, and moving out onto the broad plain defined by the interests of humanity.

There are many varied roles for work in the anthropological tradition. With regard to dominated cultures, there is work to help them survive, to preserve identity and dignity as part of a larger sphere; there is work to help social transformation and the emergence of new cultural forms. With regard to the cultures of power, there is work to expose them to scrutiny as careful as that which the powerless receive, to clarify the form and sources of their dominance, and again to help in social transformation and the emergence of new cultural forms. For humanity as a whole, there is the role of keeper of our secular origin myth, as discerned through prehistory and biological evolution, and as keeper in part of many truths, whose power appears only when one considers the shapes of the ignorance that would replace them. Most important of these are perhaps the evidence of humanity as maker of its own history and the evidence of human worth (cf. Wolff's paper) and value to be found in so many diverse conditions of life. That worth does not equal wealth, but depends on autonomy, on freedom to shape one's own destiny. Hunting and gathering peoples such as the Eskimos and many North American Indians had impoverished lives of material hardship, by our standards, yet it is a matter of record that many white captives preferred to stay with their Indian captors and that peoples such as the Chinook of the Columbia River had no myth of a Golden Age, but told of an earlier period in which things had been set right to prepare the lives they now led.

Theoretical and comparative work will of necessity be united with such work in other sectors of the study of man. There will be convergence in ethnographic work, too, but let me stress that good ethnography, building on the anthropological tradition, will be of perennial importance, not only for many reasons of general knowledge, but for specific reasons as well. On the one hand, there is much that ethnographers do that is wanted done by local communities, from preservation of languages and traditions (as in some American Indian communities today) to help with problems of schools. On the other hand, where social transformation is in question, Anna Louise Strong once said that if Lenin himself came to your town, he would have to know what you know about it before he could plan a revolution there.

Anthropologists themselves seem moved to three different relationships to such work—that of critic and scholar within the only institutional home provided for such in our society, the academic world; that of working for communities, movements, operational institutions; that of direct action as a member of a community or movement. There is need for all three, and no need to lay down a ukase, when talents, obligations, and opportunities vary widely. Just two or three things can be said. The critical and scholarly role is indispensable (cf. Lemisch, 1968, 1970; Wallerstein, 1971), especially given the present disarray and inadequacy of relevant knowledge.[35] Nevertheless, within the academy, a redistribution of attention and prestige from graduate to undergraduate training of anthropologists is important. Given the opportunity, undergraduates could be trained in anthropological work as well as graduate students, perhaps better; much graduate time is spent on activities required, not for training, but for induction into the hegemony of a particular department and a prospective profession. (On graduate departments, see Palson, 1970.) Undergraduates would be freer to acquire relevant training and do good work, having in mind long-range plans not under the control of their teachers. The greatest contribution of anthropology departments might be to send into the world many lawyers, historians, activists, workers for various institutions and agencies, well trained in anthropological work. This might in turn be the only way in which adequate knowledge of many sectors of society would eventually be gained. (As a step in this direction, see Spradley and McCurdy, 1972.)

Much more needs to be considered, and much can hardly be foreseen, if anthropology is to transcend its departmental stage and become more truly a study of mankind, by mankind. I have given only illustrative suggestions. The story will depend upon the community that is emerging within and around departmental shells. At this point, there is no single institutional structure or formulated doctrine that can command general respect as adequate to anthropology's situation in the world. There is a tradition on which we can draw. Its intent is liberating, and our advantage, and challenge, is to understand the limitations that have kept the tradition partial and far short of its goal. In our own lives and commitments will be determined whether the tradition shrivels or flourishes within anthropology in the United States. At the very least, we can resolve not to suffer gladly bureaucratic nonsense, time-serving, professional pettiness, and to keep attention on fundamental questions.

It should be clear that my position, intellectual and social, is more revisionist than revolutionary, regarding both anthropology and socialism, and regarding the tradition, concerned with the general problem of the evolution of mankind, in which they share. Let me end by applying words of a teacher and friend, from whom I have learned much about both (Moore, 1969, p. 44):

> What then may be expected from such revisionists? Negatively, the rejection of obscurantist verbiage and incoherent dreams, even when the verbiage and dreams are those of

Marx. Positively, an agreement to work, in the spirit of what Marx called scientific socialism, for a just society and an individualistic culture—where the free development of each is both enriched and restrained by the free development of all. . . .

They will seek no New Jerusalem. Only a time when human progress ceases to resemble that cruel god who scorned to drink the nectar, except from the skulls of the slain.

VI

The first section of this book, "The Root Is Man," presents a paper by an anthropologist who is a noted leader of efforts to revitalize American anthropology, and a humanistic sociologist, well known as a scholar of the major European sociological traditions. Berreman addresses the current malaise among anthropologists confronting the inadequacy of the status quo in the field. Wolff speaks to the twin radicalisms of a political and a humanistic bent, urging their unity in this unprecedented time.

Despite conventional images of exotic islands and remote jungles, anthropologists have been studying mostly cultures that are not autonomous, but dominated. One contribution of this book may be simply to call the situation by its right name. In the section "Studying Dominated Cultures," William Willis indicts anthropology as a servant of its own culture at the expense of others; he offers an effective operational definition of anthropology, in terms of "what anthropologists do": it is the study of the colored peoples of the world by white people. John Szwed shows that the central concept of American anthropology—that of culture —has not been applied in its own society where Afro-Americans are concerned. Anthropologists, like others, have mostly seen Afro-American life in terms of *a priori* political considerations, missing the persistence and the emergence of culture. Mina Caulfield begins with anthropology's lack of an understanding of imperialism and develops a general conception of it as domination of culture over culture. Utilizing insights from Frantz Fanon, she stresses the cultural dimensions not only of exploitation in colonial situations, but also of the struggle to overcome exploitation. Richard Clemmer analyzes yet another failure to make universal and adequate use of the concept of culture by showing that assumptions as to the assimilation of some American Indians have failed to see that their resistance is not inertia, but an active cultural process. These essays, though independent in origin, strikingly converge. In complementary ways, they highlight past and new challenges in the notion of the cultural. Conceived as emergent and as truly universal, the concept can contribute vitally to understanding and transforming the contemporary world.

In the section "Studying the Cultures of Power," the other complementary side of the world situation is explored. Eric Wolf, a leader of American anthropology, sketches the background of the failure of anthropologists to address themselves to questions of power, and the necessity for them to do so. Eugene Anderson catches the essence of the ecological crisis in the fact that great inequality of power makes it rational for both the powerful and the powerless to do ecologically destructive things. Laura Nader presents reasons why she and many students are concerned to study the organized forces that shape lives, and gives instances of this work. Norman Klein takes on a different aspect of power—interpersonal domination—and finds in the youth rebellion of the 1960s a reflection of mainstream American society. His view was opposed by a number of other contributors as one-sided, but his analysis of that side is an essential warning against unsuspected forms of ethnocentrism. It points as well to a flagrant gap—the lack of ethnographic analysis of cultural hegemony and the state in our own society. Sol Worth underscores how great is the need for such analysis, given the projected role of electronic media in the years ahead. Anthropologists are unprepared for the ethical and political issues confronting them.

The theme of the "Responsibilities of Ethnography" is taken up by Robert Jay in an exploratory, thoughtful attempt to come to terms with the personal basis of ethnographic work. Kenneth Hale has pioneered in efforts to bring "informants" fully into collaboration. He makes the case for such collaboration here in terms of language, but the argument can be extended to ethnography as a whole.

The final section returns to the theme of the first, "The Root Is Man," adding the dimension "Critical Traditions." Stanley Diamond shows the roots of anthropology in the Enlightenment, focusing on Rousseau, and brings out the relevance, in the nineteenth century, of Marx. Rejecting the depersonalization he finds entailed in the structuralism of Lévi-Strauss, Diamond calls for a renewal of the heritage represented by Rousseau and Marx, especially through the perspective on human nature and cultural adequacy that comes through knowledge of "primitive" cultures. He sees anthropology's involvement with such cultures as a permanent resource to both human and political radicalism. Where Diamond calls for a critical, dialectical, and activist anthropology, Scholte calls upon anthropology to turn criticism upon itself, through comparative study of its own traditions and their role in the shaping of anthropological knowledge; through reflection on the inescapable personal and emergent dimensions of ethnographic encounter, and through efforts to develop anthropology toward an emancipatory role.

This book is not as large as hope would have made it. Limitations of space prevented inclusion of contributions by George Appell on ethics, Roger Newman on a case study of a corporation, Charles Palson on the structural types of anthropology departments, and Trent Schroyer on the tradition of critical theory, as developed by Jurgen Habermas. I am deeply sorry for this. I am grateful to David

Aberle, Dale Fitzgerald, Bernard Fontana, David Labby, Sidney Mintz, Alfonso Ortiz, Lars Persson, David Schneider, and William Sturtevant for correspondence and discussion in the planning of the book; to Paula McGuire and James Peck for tolerant sympathy of the pace at which it became a manuscript; and to André Schiffrin, who invited me to do the book on the strength of a critical review I had written of another book he had published. Iles Minoff gave invaluable help in final preparation of the manuscript, and my wife, Virginia, much encouragement. Finally, an extra debt of thanks to John Szwed and to the Center for Urban Ethnography, who made it possible for a number of us to meet for a day's discussion in May 1971.

Notes

1. Cf. Lévi-Strauss (1966, p. 126): "Anthropology . . . is the outcome of a historical process which has made the larger part of mankind subservient to the other, and during which millions of innocent human beings have had their resources plundered and their institutions and beliefs destroyed, whilst they themselves were ruthlessly killed, thrown into bondage, and contaminated by diseases they were unable to resist. Anthropology is daughter to this era of violence: Its capacity to assess more objectively the facts pertaining to the human condition reflects, on the epistemological level, a state of affairs in which one part of mankind treated the other as an object." Cf. LeClerc (1972) and *Les Temps modernes* (1971).
2. Cf. Berreman, Gjessing, and Gough (1968); Berreman (1971a); Moore (1971); Scholte (1972); the harsh assessment by Guiart (1971), part 5, especially "L'Ethnologie utopique" (pp. 242–43) in a book for the general public; the series "Anthropologie Critique," of which LeClerc (1972) is part; Lepenies (1971); the magazine *!Kung* from the London School of Economics (1972); *Critical Anthropology* (1970–) from the New School for Social Research; and numerous discussions in the journal *Current Anthropology* and in the pages of the *Newsletter* of the American Anthropological Association. Diamond (in press) and Barnett (in preparation) complement the present book as does an anthology planned by Washington, D.C., members of Anthropologists for Radical Political Action (a group formed in 1972).
3. A word about Marx. Only a few of the contributors to this book would associate themselves with a Marxist tradition. One recognizes

in any case that to profess Marxism is not to disclose too much, since adherents of different varieties range from bureaucratic conservatives to adventurers. Just as Christians cannot fairly be held responsible for all that has been believed and done in the name of Christ, so for Marxists (and anthropologists). One is responsible for one's own use, we hope critical and creative, of a tradition. For myself, since about 1946, Marxism has been a major influence. With Sartre (1963), I think it the general tradition in which to situate one's individual talent. Social science has grown and defined itself to a great extent in relation to Marx, and we partly continue to work out implications of his thought, important portions of which have become publicly available only in the last generation or two. (On work in direct relation to ethnology, see the important monograph by Krader, and cf. Kluckhohn, 1946; Stern, 1949; Hobsbawm, 1964; Godelier, 1970.) In a sense, we are waiting for a contemporary Marx (not necessarily a single scholar) to penetrate with equal cogency our own situation. Mills (1962, pp. 91–94) and Sartre (1963, esp. pp. 26, 30, 34, 52, 56) express much of my own sense of the situation. The Marx I have learned from is mainly the historian, sociologist of knowledge, and exponent of a humanism. Admiration for him has not succeeded in blocking an affinity for the German idealism (Protestant and secular) that preceded and followed his work (cf. Hymes, 1964, pp. 18, 21). To this add an upbringing in Oregon that involved some exposure to populist attitudes, a libertarian college, and an inclination toward pacifism. So much for personal confession.

4. Becker (1971, pp. 95–100) points out the significance of the 1904 essay. I read and excerpted it as a graduate student, and it has shaped my sense of the subsequent history of anthropology, and of the difference between the "spirit" and the structure of anthropology, ever since; but Becker's treatment has made me appreciate how it implicates the prior history of anthropology as a symbolic watershed. I recommend the entire book, although I must disagree with part of Becker's interpretation. His general thesis is that, in sociology and in anthropology, a comprehensive goal—the welfare of mankind through a social science—was subverted in the twentieth century by the attempt to realize it through the building of professions. Men like Boas, and Albion Small in sociology, ironically narrowed the perspective of their successors to the furthering of a discipline. Becker appears to neglect the extent to which rejection of earlier formulations was due to scientific advance, and he seems to call upon each discipline to recapture the general goal in its own name. He speaks of Boas "demoting" anthropology to just a discipline among others; yet Boas' rejection of a "rash imperialism" for anthropology (Becker, 1971, p. 96), which Becker praises, is inseparable from his willingness to consider anthropology as an approach utilized in many disciplines. Becker writes: "But this study [of primitive culture] did not serve to illuminate any central problem, since anthropology could not

handle its central problem but had given it over to the other disciplines to share" (p. 103). Sharing is not loss; it can mean mutual illumination of the central problem. Pursuit of the general goal did decline, for a complex of reasons (postwar cynicism, falling off of the level of general culture among anthropologists, social origins and self-selection for the career of social scientist); but the return to it must be in the name, not of any one discipline, but the study of man as a whole.

5. Kroeber wrote of his quite inductive effort to discern empirical regularities in the flourishing of civilizations as something that had occupied his interest for as long as he could remember (1944), but the years of work were to be set aside condescendingly, at a session in tribute to Kroeber (Southwestern Anthropological Association, 1961), by a former student and president of the national association, as reflecting his "philosophical interests." For an introduction to substantive philosophy of history in terms of major figures, see Walsh (1960, Chs. 6–8). Danto (1968) is a lucid account of the analytical approach, relevant, like the corresponding part of Walsh's book, to general questions of methodology in anthropology; Lichtheim (1965) takes the fundamental question of philosophy of history to be that of consciousness, that is, the relation between world history and rationality. He shows the continuity of the problem from the Enlightenment to our own day, tracing different conceptions of the relation between reason, ideas, and institutions, and considering the rationalist perspective, common to both liberalism and Marxism, as creative of the possibility of a unified, peaceful world. Boas' lifelong devotion of his anthropology to these goals is evident (cf. 1904, p. 524; 1908, pp. 26–28). See the just appraisal by Stern ([1943] 1959).

6. Cf. Henry (1963, p. 146): "To think deeply in our culture is to grow angry and to anger others; and if you cannot tolerate this anger, you are wasting the time you spend thinking deeply. One of the rewards of deep thought is the hot glow of anger at discovering a wrong, but if anger is taboo, thought will starve to death." And cf. Bennett (1971, p. 9): "The *combination* of the two attitudes [commitment, objectivity] is foreign to American social science because of the generations of separation of philosophy from science—a divorce which has finally reaped the trouble so often predicted for it. What is needed is a passionate *and* dispassionate attempt to treat topics of central historical importance; to believe in these topics—as for example, desirable social innovations—and also objectively assess their social costs as well as gains."

7. Gay, whose work on the Enlightenment I admire and learn much from (see especially 1966, 1969) shows that "the metaphysical claim that progress is an inevitable process immanent in history . . . has been imputed to the [eighteenth-century] *philosophes* with great frequency and little justice" (1971, p. 271). Unfortunately, Gay describes such a claim with the term "theory of progress." That

term should be retained in reference both to the *philosophes* and our own work. Being committed to the future, major Enlightenment writers did analyze the *conditions* of progress (cf. Smith's *The Wealth of Nations,* Ferguson's *Essay on the History of Civil Society,* Robertson's *History of Charles V*). Their analytical work contributed to a theory of the nature (not the inevitability) of progress. As to the necessary function of Utopian thinking in the positive sense, cf. Finley (1967), and Kateb ([1963] 1972, pp. v–vii).

8. Note that while Danto rejects historical foreknowledge (Ch. 4), he convincingly defends narrative as a form of causal explanation (Ch. 11, esp. pp. 237, 255). He also grants rational belief as to the future (p. 197) and the prediction of events within limits (pp. 200, 255).

9. Bock (1956) provides an important critique of a long-standing conception of general evolution as divorced in principle from specific history. Such a conception has often influenced anthropologists, who have felt constrained to choose one or the other; their popular books often espouse some version of the first (cf. Moore, 1963, n. 35). Such a conception has also often been intertwined with Marxism. Nisbet (1969) is a cogent attack on a series of assumptions underlying such a conception of development throughout Western history, including its anthropological and Marxist forms. For a different conception of a Marxian approach, cf. Moore (1957, p. 123) on the dialectical method as a systematic search for the concrete; Sartre on the concrete and on LeFebvre's "regressive" methodology (1963, pp. 26, 49–52); Therborn (1970, pp. 42–3) and Balbus (1971); and, on the aspect of theory and practice, Lichtheim (1971, pp. 5, 25), and Bernstein's valuable study (1971).

10. Danto distinguishes two kinds of substantive philosophy of history: "A descriptive theory seeks to show a pattern amongst the events which make up the past, and so to make the claim that events in the future will either repeat or complete the pattern exhibited amongst events in the past. An explanatory theory is an attempt to account for this pattern in causal terms."

11. On the relevance of critical historical understanding to mankind's future, cf. Fischer (1970, pp. 317–18).

12. Cf. Boas (1904, p. 517, and 1908, p. 26): "This broader outlook may also help us to recognize the possibility of lines of progress which do not happen to be in accord with the dominant ideas of our times." Cf. Marx: "The so-called historical development amounts in the last analysis to this, that the last form considers its predecessors as stages leading up to itself and perceives them always one-sidedly, since it is very seldom and only under certain conditions that it is capable of self-criticism" (quoted from *A Contribution to the Critique of Political Economy* by Lévi-Strauss [1958, p. 337]).

13. Boas insisted that "it is impossible to exclude any part of mankind

from the considerations of anthropology" (1908, p. 9; cf. 1904, p. 522b), because of its concern with the culture of the world as a whole; concern for explanation could not be restricted to what had affected our own civilization in the past.

14. A reprint of much of the only English translation is now available in Manuel (1968). As so often with older works relevant to the history of anthropology, parts of specific interest to anthropology are omitted, but the general chapters (Herder's Books VII, VIII, and XV, reprinted as Chapters 1 and 2, "National Genius and the Environment," "Humanity the End of Human Nature") give insight into Herder's achievement. On Herder's significance, cf. Barnard (1965), Bruford (1962), and Cassirer (1950, Ch. 12).

15. In Reclus ([1885] 1891, pp. xiii–xiv) one finds already perhaps the first conscious adoption of the "ethnographic present": "These studies are drawn, for the most part, from the information given by travellers and missionaries during the first half of the century, about countries of which the social condition has since been deeply modified. . . . I shall, however, speak in the present tense." From another standpoint, the change was not simply the "influx of traders and manufacturers" of which Reclus spoke, but a new domination: "In the 1850s and after, one could be objective about the Indian as one could not have been ten, twenty, or thirty years before; one could be objective about a creature who had been reduced to the status of a specimen picked up on a field trip. One could move toward scientific analysis and away from pity and censure." (Pearce, 1953, p. 129)

16. Our present concern at loss of significance, both as to explanatory scope and as to a personal, dynamic dimension, was already expressed in the period between the two World Wars. Academic anthropology can be said to have crystallized in textbooks and paradigmatic studies about 1920. Of one of the latter, Lowie's notable *Primitive Society* (1920), Kroeber wrote (1920, pp. 380, 381) that it was

> a clear and fair representative of what modern ethnology has to offer. . . . Modern ethnology says that so and so happens, and may tell why it happened thus in that particular case. It does not tell, and does not try to tell, why things happen in society as such. . . . [but] That branch of science which renounces the hope of contributing at least something to the shaping of human life is headed into a blind alley. Therefore, if we cannot present anything that the world can use, it is at least incumbent on us to let this failure burn into our consciousness.

Lowie had earlier maintained (1917, p. 4) that kinship terminology was a subject in which Morgan was able to arouse the interest of hundreds of laymen, so he saw no reason why an up-to-date exposition should not hold their attention (in a set of public lectures); but Morgan, as Kroeber noted in his 1920 review, had related kinship to the general problem of the evolution of mankind.

Again, concerned that "anthropology must find more of a task than filling with rubble the temporarily vacant spaces in the masonry that the sciences are rearing," Kroeber (1923, p. 2) urged in the first general textbook on the subject that, in the new era, "the interpretation of those phenomena into which both organic and social causes enter" (both biological and cultural causes) provided a true scientific focus and ultimate goal for anthropology (1923, pp. 3–4). (Kroeber also mocked the idea of anthropology as [in 1920] one of the "newer sciences" [p. 379].) Concern with neglect of personal and dynamic dimensions was expressed in the period especially by Radin and Sapir (see Vidich [1966] on Radin, and Hymes [1970] on Sapir).

17. A growth predicted by MacCurdy (1902) for the beginning of the century, as a consequence of United States expansion after the Spanish-American War, but largely delayed until after two further wars.

18. The image of a world partitioned among fixed, individually named cultures has sometimes served anthropological careers more than human knowledge. By attaching one's own name to a cultural name, one secured property rights and a professional niche, while others, anthropologists and members of the culture alike, might wait indefinitely for meaningful results.

19. On the scientific success of such "objectivity," cf. as against Lévi-Strauss' apparent belief in it (1966), Macquet (1964) and P'Bitek (1972), as well as Willis in this volume.

20. On the general issue, cf. Beinfield (1970); Berman's analysis (1970) of sources of the issue in the Enlightenment with Montesquieu and Rousseau and his introduction, "The Personal is Political"; Diamond (1967, 1971) on an evolutionary perspective; and Hall (1971) on methodological perspective. Sartre (1963, p. 56) is paradigmatic here: "Valéry is a petit bourgeois intellectual, no doubt about it. But not every petit bourgeois intellectual is Valéry. The heuristic inadequacy of contemporary [official] Marxism is contained in these two sentences." Cf. also Lichtheim (1971, p. 21). The ethnographic implications of such a perspective are broached by Brown (1972) and Fabian (1971), and by Jay in this volume.

21. Of Sapir's socially oriented comments in the 1930s (closely linked to his development of a personal perspective on culture), Harris remarked (1951, pp. 332–33):

> So refreshing is this [pre-World War II] freeness and criticalness that we are brought to a sharp realization of how such writing has disappeared from the scene. In part, this was the writing of pre-administrative anthropology. . . . In part, too . . . the difference between the atmosphere of a depression

period and the atmosphere of the continuous war period
which replaced it. And in part it was Sapir.

22. Cf. Fortes (1953, pp. 1–2): "For as they [the founders of anthropology at Cambridge] insistently taught, anthropological studies
cannot flourish in isolation, either in one place or in one academic
compartment. . . . For advances in anthropological knowledge are
inseparable from advances in related human sciences." And cf.
again Tax, 1955.

23. That the problem is general to the social sciences is indicated in
many sources, e.g., Roszak (1968) and subsequent books in the
"antitext" series; Ferkiss (1971, p. 844) on the trained incapacity
fostered by professional specialization in departments in political
science; by a series of writings in sociology in the last decade (cf.
Stein and Vidich, 1963; Moore, 1963; Stein, 1963; Stein 1967; Lazarsfeld, Sewell, and Wilensky, 1967; Gouldner, 1970; Colfax and
Roach, 1971; D. Horowitz, 1971); by general analyses of departmental and disciplinary failings (Campbell, 1969; Wolfle, 1971);
that the problem is not confined to anthropology in the United
States is indicated, for example, by Worsley (1970); Banaji (1970),
by Hultkrantz' penetrating comparison (1968), and Halpern and
Hammel's interpretation of the Yugoslav situation (1969, p. 22):

> ethnography as a social science developed as a response to
> colonial pressure and followed the retreating lines of crum-
> bling empires as a major ideological contribution to the
> unification of South Slavs against non-Slavs, but . . . it was
> limited to those social goals, whatever its scientific objec-
> tives may have been. . . . the marked changes in Yugoslav
> society over the past quarter-century have left traditional
> ethnography behind. The cart has run before the faithful
> horse; ethnography and ethnology have become conservative
> and traditionalistic and are held in low repute by other
> social scientists.

Birnbaum writes with Marxist sociology in mind, and, despite
institutionalization of the subject in the Soviet Union and elsewhere, clearly the spirit of the Marxist tradition is expressed by
the leading French communist theorist, Louis Althusser, when he
remarks of intellectuals (1970, p. 7):

> With a few exceptions, they are still "dabbling'" in political
> economy, sociology, ethnology, "anthropology," "social psy-
> chology," etc. . . . Their "theories" are ideological anachro-
> nisms, rejuvenated with a large does of intellectual subtleties
> and ultra-modern mathematical techniques.

Discussing the impact of imperialism on the sector of the world
traditionally studied by anthropologists, Banaji (1970, p. 85) is
quite specific:

> Marxist anthropologists must expose the myth that anthro-
> pology has any future as an integrated discipline.

But, as Birnbaum states, Marxism itself is generally in the same boat as specific disciplines, when it comes to revitalizing "Marx's refusal to separate the different academic disciplines" (Hobsbawm, 1964, p. 16). See especially his sections on "The Analysis of Culture" and "The Marxist Anthropology."

24. Although some come near to suggesting it, e.g., Leslie White in his presidential address of 1964; see the response by Haas (1965).

25. Note the new series edited by Struever (1972–), including books by Binford (1972) and McGimsey (1972), and the new series concerned with the application of different sciences to archaeology, edited by Dimbleby (1972–). Schuyler (1970, pp. 87–88) foresees that

> just as Kathleen G. Aberle (1967) has called upon ethnography to study not only conquered non-Western cultures but also the process of imperialism itself, so Historic Sites Archaeology can make a major contribution to modern anthropology by studying the processes of European expansion, exploration, and colonization as well as those of culture contact and imperialism, that underlie one of the most dynamic periods of world history and which are reflected in both artifactual and documentary data.

The orientation of the "new archeology" is indicated in Hammond (1971).

26. Cf. Worsley (1970, p. 127): "A few anthropologists have taken the major alternative open to those who seek to assert the distinctiveness of their discipline; they define it in terms of its techniques and methods, rather than in terms of substantive subject matter. Firth, notably, has increasingly come to lay stress, over the years, on anthropology as 'micro-sociology,' rather than 'the science of primitive society.' " Note that the Boasian conception of anthropology's contribution to other fields is equivalent to the approach taken by the Anthropology Curriculum Study Project in designing educational materials (1972, p. 6):

> To the extent that anthropology had been seriously considered in the high school curriculum, the tendency had been to see it as separate from school history. The ACSP assumption was that the most (perhaps only) desirable results would come from a blending of the two, from the effect on the teaching of history of including anthropology in the curriculum. The assumption was that selected ideas and data from anthropology should be dispersed throughout the curriculum—in social studies, biology, and other courses.

27. It is encouraging to see steps within the American Anthropological Association toward greater equality of recognition and role for the three (cf. Ad Hoc Planning Committee, 1972; Executive Board, 1972).

28. See the analysis of such a pattern by Lasch (1972). There are penetrating comments by students on the bases of some calls for "unity" and "excellence," e.g., Students (1969, pp. 56–58), Selwyn (1972, p. 8). Departmental views of reality would seem to fit one or both of the two types of mystification dissected by Marx (see the parallel explications by Moore (1957, pp. 118–22) and Geras (1971, pp. 84–85).

29. Past experience with attempts to unite the social sciences from the top downward should warn us against empire-building in the name of interdisciplinary perspectives, just as much as in the name of departmental unity (and isolation). Perhaps a talisman against such things is provided by Sid Caesar:

> REPORTER: How about the fact that archaeology is a science that is very closely allied to anthropology as well as to some aspects of comparative sociology? How about the fact that these sciences overlap and complement each other and together form an overall science of mankind?
>
> LUDWIG VON FOSSIL: How about that?

30. See Horowitz, ed. (1967), and especially Sahlins, Nisbet, and Horowitz therein; and cf. Berreman (1969 and 1917b) and I. Horowitz (1971).

31. The controversy can be followed in the *Newsletter* of the American Anthropological Association from spring 1970 through early 1972; see also Wolf and Jorgensen (1970) and Jones (1971). A book on the subject is in preparation by Herbert J. Phillips.

32. Cf. resolution adopted by the International Union of Anthropological and Ethnological Sciences in 1968 (Hohenwart-Gerlach-stein, 1968); the efforts and publications of the International Work Group for Indigenous Affairs (IWGIA), founded in 1968 (Frederiksholms Kanal 4A, DK 1220, Copenhagen K, Denmark); the appointment of an international committee on genocide and forced acculturation by the IUAES (chaired by Fredrik Barth, Bergen, Norway); the incorporation of SURVIVAL by David and Pia Maybury-Lewis (Harvard University); the set of papers on ethnocide published in *Anuario Indigenista* 30 (December 1970); the motion of ethnocide adopted by the American Anthropological Association (see *Newsletter* 12, No. 6: 16 [1971]).

33. Besides papers in this volume, cf. NACLA (1970) and Africa Research Group (1971).

34. Cf. the varying choices recommended by Ellman (1972), Moore (1971), Woodburn (1972), Valentine (1972), and the discussants of Jorgensen, Adams, and Jones (all 1971).

35. Critical research on the culture itself is important; cf. the contrasting reviews of Roszak (1969) by Wolff (1971), who states that:

> Roszak may be right that our young people are fleeing from the ideal of reason, but to encourage them in their flight is to play into the hands of reaction

and by Hill (1970, p. 103):

> Roszak is not advocating a harking back to the primitive, as
> the philistine critics of Rousseau would surely chant in
> unison, rather, the drug experience, the current attraction to
> Eastern religions and the primitive all serve as antitheses
> upon which we will probably form the synthesis for times
> to come—they all represent something that is missing in our
> impoverished culture. . . . Once it is accepted that the
> disaffiliated are in fact more radical than the most radical
> Marxists because they oppose Western culture and not
> merely Western politics and economics, it is easy to expand
> this idea to all aspects of our society.

On the role of scholarship and research, cf. Bennett (1971),
Lemisch (1968, 1970), and Wallerstein (1971), who state views that
are very much my own, especially Wallerstein (1971, p. 475):

> The first need for the American left is intellectual clarifica-
> tion of the ways in which American and world society can
> and will transform itself into a socialist society.

But cf. also Dalton (1971).

References

Aberle, D. F. 1960. "The Influence of Linguistics on Early Culture and
Personality Theory." In *Essays in the Science of Culture in Honor
of Leslie A. White,* eds. G. E. Dole and R. L. Carneiro. New
York: Thomas Y. Crowell. Pp. 1–29.

[ACSP]. 1972. *Two-way Mirror: Anthropologists and Educators Ob-
serve Themselves and Each Other.* Anthropology Curriculum
Study Project. Washington, D. C.: American Anthropological
Association.

Adams, R. N. 1971. "Responsibilities of the Foreign Scholar to the
Local Scholarly Community." *Current Anthropology* 12, No.3:
335–39, 350–52.

[Ad Hoc Planning Committee]. 1972. *Annual Report 1971.* Washington, D. C.: American Anthropological Association. Pp. 30–31.

[Africa Research Group]. 1971. *Africa Report: A Tribal Analysis of
U.S. Africanists: Who they are; Why to fight them.* Cambridge,
Mass.: Africa Research Group.

Althusser, Louis. 1970. Interview with Louis Althusser. "Philosophy
as a Revolutionary Weapon." *New Left Review* 64: 3–11.

Appell, George N. 1971. "Three Cases Dealing with Dilemmas and
Ethical Conflicts in Anthropological Inquiry." *Human Organization* 30: 97–98.

Balbus, Isaac. 1971. "Ruling-Class Élite Theory vs. Marxian Class
Analysis." *Monthly Review* 23, No. 1: 36–46.

Banaji, J. 1970. "The Crisis of British Anthropology." *New Left Review* 64: 71–87.

Barnard, F. M. 1965. *Herder's Social and Political Thought: From Enlightenment to Nationalism.* Oxford: Clarendon Press.

Barnett, Stephen, ed. *We Are All Natives.* In preparation.

Becker, Ernest. 1971. *The Lost Science of Man.* New York: George Braziller.

Beinfield, Harriet. 1970. "Anomie and Alienation: Comparative Perspectives on Mass Society Ills." *Critical Anthropology* 1, No. 2: 61–85.

Benedict, Ruth. 1934. *Patterns of Culture.* New York: Houghton Miflin Co.

Bennett, John C. 1971. "Relevance and Theory." *Newsletter of the American Anthropological Association* 12, No. 2: 8–9.

Berman, Marshall. 1970. *The Politics of Authenticity: Radical Individualism and the Emergence of a Modern Society.* New York: Atheneum Publishers.

Berreman, Gerald D. 1968. "Is Anthropology Alive? Social Responsibility in Social Anthropology." *Current Anthropology* 9, No. 5: 391–96.

———. 1969. "Not So Innocent Abroad." *The Nation,* November 10, pp. 505–8.

———. 1971a. "The Greening of the American Anthropological Association." *Newsletter of the American Anthropological Association* 12, No. 1: 18–20; also, *Critical Anthtropology* 2, No. 1: 100–4.

———. 1971b. "Ethics, Responsibility, and the Funding of Asian Research." *Journal of Asian Studies* 30, No. 2: 390–99.

[Berreman, Gjessing, Gough]. 1968. "Social Responsibilities Symposium." *Current Anthropology* 9, No. 5: 391–436.

Bernstein, Richard J. 1971. *Praxis and Action: Contemporary Philosophies of Human Activity.* Philadelphia: University of Pennsylvania Press.

Binford, Lewis R. 1972. *An Archaeological Perspective.* New York: Seminar Press.

Birnbaum, Norman. 1971. "The Crisis in Marxist Sociology." In Colfax and Roach, 1971, pp. 108–31; also Dreitzel, 1969, pp. 11–42. Reprinted from *Social Research* 35 (1968): 348–80.

Boas, Franz. 1904. "The History of Anthropology." *Science* 20: 513–24.

———. 1908. *Anthropology: Lectures on Science, Philosophy and Art.* New York: Columbia University Press. Pp. 5–28.

Bock, Kenneth E. 1952. "Evolution and Historical Process." *American Anthropologist* 54: 486–96.

———. 1956. *The Acceptance of Histories: Toward a Perspective for Social Science.* Berkeley: University of California Press.

Brown, David. 1972. "A Letter from the Bush." *!Kung,* pp. 3–6. London: London School of Economics.

Bruford, W. H. 1962. *Culture and Society in Classical Weimar.* Cambridge: Cambridge University Press.

Burrows, J. W. 1966. *Evolution and Society: A Study in Victorian Social Theory.* Cambridge: Cambridge University Press.

Campbell, Donald T. 1969. "Ethnocentrism of Disciplines and the Fish-Scale Model of Omniscience." In *Inter-Disciplinary Relationships in the Social Sciences,* eds. Muzafer and Carolyn Sherif. Chicago: Aldine Publishing Co. Pp. 328–48.

Cassirer, Ernst. 1950. *The Problem of Knowledge: Philosophy, Science, and History Since Hegel.* New Haven: Yale University Press.

Chaney, Richard P. 1972. "Comparative Analysis and Retroductive Reasoning." Paper presented at the March meeting of the Southwest Anthropological Association.

Colfax, J. David, and Jack L. Roach, eds. 1971. *Radical Sociology.* New York: Basic Books.

Collingwood, R. G. 1933. *An Essay in Philosophical Method.* Oxford: Clarendon Press.

————. 1939. *An Autobiography.* London: Oxford University Press.

Dalton, George. 1971. "Reply." *Current Anthropology* 12, No. 2: 237–41.

Danto, Arthur C. [1965] 1968. *Analytical Philosophy of History.* Cambridge: Cambridge University Press.

Diamond, Stanley. 1963. "The Search for the Primitive." In *Man's Image in Medicine and Anthropology,* ed. Iago Galdston. New York: International Universities Press. Pp. 62–115.

————. 1964a. "On the Origins of Modern Theoretical Anthropology." *American Anthropologist* 66: 128–29.

————. 1964b. "A Revolutionary Discipline." *Current Anthropology* 5, No. 5: 432–37.

————. 1967. "Primitive Society in its Many Dimensions." In Wolff and Moore, 1967, pp. 21–30.

————. 1971. "The Rule of Law vs. the Order of Custom." *Social Research* 38: 42–72.

————. ed. 1972. *The Nature and Function of Anthropological Traditions.* Philadelphia: University of Pennsylvania Press.

Dimbleby, G. W., ed. 1972–. *Studies in Archaeological Sciences.* New York: Seminar Press.

Dreitzel, Hans-Peter, ed. 1969. *Recent Sociology No. 1.* New York: Macmillan Co.

Ellman, Antony. 1972. "Minorities and Cultural Diversity in Tanzania." *!Kung,* pp. 18–21. London: London School of Economics.

[Executive Board]. 1972. "Executive Board Acts for more Representative Association." *Newsletter of the American Anthropological Association* 13, No. 6: 1.

Fabian, Johannes. 1971. "Language, History, and Anthropology." *Journal for the Philosophy of the Social Sciences* 1: 19–47.

Ferkiss, Victor C. 1971. "Review of M. Surkin and A. Wolfe: An End to Political Science." *Science* 171: 883–84.

Finley, M. I. 1967. "Utopianism Ancient and Modern." In Wolff and Moore, 1967, pp. 3–20.

Fischer, David Hackett, 1970. *Historians' Fallacies: Toward a Logic of Historical Thought.* New York: Harper & Row, Torchbooks.

Fontana, Bernard L. 1968. "Savage Anthropologist and Unvanishing Indians in the American Southwest." Paper presented at annual meeting, American Anthropological Association, Seattle, Wash.

Fortes, Meyer. 1953. *Social Anthropology at Cambridge Since 1900: An Inaugural Lecture.* Cambridge: Cambridge University Press.

Galtung, Johann. "After Camelot." In Horowitz, ed., 1967, pp. 281–312.

Gay, Peter, 1966. *The Enlightenment: An Interpretation.* Vol. 1, *The Rise of Modern Paganism.* New York: Alfred A. Knopf.

———. 1969. *The Enlightenment: An Interpretation.* Vol. 2, *The Science of Freedom.* New York: Alfred A. Knopf.

———. 1971. *The Party of Humanity: Essays in the French Enlightenment.* New York: W. W. Norton & Co.

Geras, Norman. 1971. "Essence and Appearance: Fetishism in Marx's *Capital.*" *New Left Review* 65: 69–85.

Godelier, Maurice. 1970. Preface. *Sur les sociétés précapitalistes: Textes choisis de Marx, Engels, Lénine.* Paris: Éditions sociales. Pp. 19–142.

Gouldner, Alvin. 1970. *The Coming Crisis in Western Sociology.* New York: Basic Books.

Gruber, Jacob W. 1967. "Horatio Hale and the Development of American Anthropology." *Proceedings of the American Philosophical Society* 3:6–37.

———. 1970. "Ethnographic Salvage and the Shaping of Anthropology." *American Anthropologist* 72: 1289–99.

Guiart, Jean. 1971. *Clefs pour l'ethnologie.* Paris: Éditions Seghers,

Haas, Mary R. 1965. " 'Other Culture' vs. 'Own-Culture': Some Thoughts on L. White's Query." *American Anthropologist* 67: 1556–60.

Habermas, Jurgen. 1971. *Knowledge and Human Interests.* Boston: Beacon Press.

Hall, Stuart, 1971. "A Response to 'People and Culture.' " *Working Papers in Cultural Studies,* Spring, pp. 97–102. Birmingham, England: University of Birmingham, Centre for Cultural Studies.

Halpern, Joel, and Eugene Hammel. 1969. "Observations on the Intellectual History of Ethnology and Other Social Sciences in Yugoslavia." *Comparative Studies in Society* 11: 17–26.

Hammond, Allen L. 1971. "The New Archeology: Toward a Social Science." *Science,* June 11, pp. 1119–20.

Harris, Z. S. 1951. "Review of Mandelbaum 1949." *Language* 27: 288–333.

Henry, Jules. 1963. *Culture Against Man.* New York: Random House.

Hill, Brian. 1970. "Review of Roszak 1969." *Critical Anthropology* 1: 102–3.

Hobsbawm, E. J. 1964. Introduction. *Karl Marx, Pre-Capitalist Economic Formations.* London: Lawrence & Wishart. Pp. 9–65.

Hodgen, Margaret. 1964. *Early Anthropology in the Sixteenth and Seventeenth Centuries.* Philadelphia: University of Pennsylvania Press.

Hohenwart-Gerlachstein, Anna. 1968. "Resolution Accepted." *RE [Review of Ethnology,* Vienna] 9: 7–8.

Horowitz, David, ed. 1971. *Radical Sociology: An Introduction.* San Francisco: Canfield Press.

Horowitz, Irving L., ed. 1967. *The Rise and Fall of Project Camelot: Studies in the Relationship Between Social Science and Practical Politics.* Cambridge, Mass.: M.I.T. Press.

———. 1967. "Social Science and Public Policy: Implications of Modern Research." In Horowitz, 1967, pp. 339–76.

———, ed. 1971. *The Use and Abuse of Social Science: Behavioral Science and National Policy Making.* New York: E. P. Dutton & Co.

Huddleston, Lee Eldridge. 1967. *Origin of the American Indians: European Concepts, 1492–1729.* Austin: University of Texas Press.

Hultkrantz, Ake. 1968. "The Aims of Anthropology: A Scandinavian Point of View." *Current Anthropology* 9, No. 4: 289–96.

Hymes, Dell. 1964. "Directions in (Ethno-) Linguistic Theory." In *Transcultural Studies of Cognition,* eds. A. K. Romney and R. G. D'Andrade. Washington, D.C.: American Anthropological Association. Pp. 6–56.

———. 1968. "Review of Roszak 1968." *Bulletin of the Atomic Scientists* 24: 29–34.

———. 1970. "Linguistic Method in Ethnography." In *Method and Theory in Linguistics,* ed. Paul L. Garvin. The Hague: Mouton. Pp. 249-311.

———. 1972a. Introduction. In *Functions of Language in the Classroom,* eds. C. Cazden, V. John-Steiner, and Dell Hymes. New York: Teachers College Press.

———. 1972b. The Scope of Sociolinguistics." In *Sociolinguistics: State and Prospects,* ed. Roger W. Shuy. Washington, D.C.: Georgetown University Press. In press.

———. 1972c. "Restricting and Elaborating the Notions of 'Restricted' and 'Elaborated' Codes." Unpublished manuscript.

Jeffers, Robinson. [1939] 1965. "Prescription of Painful Ends." In *Selected Poems.* New York: Vintage Books. P. 65.

Jones, Delmos T. 1971. "Social Responsibility and the Belief in Basic Research: An Example from Thailand." *Current Anthropology* 12, No. 3: 347–50.

Jorgensen, Joseph. 1971. "On Ethics and Anthropology." *Current Anthropology* 12, No. 3: 321–34, 352–55.

Kaplan, Leo. 1971. "Review of Gouldner 1970." *Critical Anthropology* 2, No. 1: 85–99.

Kateb, George. [1963] 1972. *Utopia and Its Enemies.* New York: Schocken Books.

Kluckhohn, Clyde. 1946. "Review of Vernon Venable, Human Nature: The Marxian View." *Kenyon Review* 8, No. 1: 149–54.

———. 1959. "Common Humanity and Diverse Cultures." In *The Human Meaning of the Social Sciences,* ed. Daniel Lerner. New York: Meridian Books. Pp. 245–84.

———. 1961. *Anthropology and the Classics.* Providence, R. I.: Brown University Press. See review by R. Browning in *Science and Society* 27, No. 3: 347–49.

Krader, Lawrence. 1972. "The Works of Marx and Engels in Ethnology Compared." In an edition of Marx's ethnological notebooks, in preparation.

Kroeber, A. L. 1920. "Review of R. H. Lowie, *Primitive Society.*" *American Anthropologist* 22: 377–81. Reprinted in F. De Laguna, ed., *Selected Papers From the American Anthropologist,* 1888– 1920 (New York: Harper & Row, Publishers, n.d.), pp. 863–69.

———. 1923. *Anthropology.* New York: Harcourt, Brace & Co.

———. 1944. *Configurations of Culture Growth.* Berkeley. University of California Press.

———. 1959. "The History of the Personality of Anthropology." *American Anthropologist* 61: 398–404.

Lasch, Christopher. 1972. "The Good Old Days." Review of *Facing Life,* by Oscar and Mary F. Handlin. *New York Review of Books,* February 10, pp. 25–7.

Lazarsfeld, P. F., W. H. Sewell, and H. L. Wilensky, eds. 1967. *The Uses of Sociology.* New York: Basic Books.

Leacock, Eleanor. 1954. *The Montagnais Hunting Territory and the Fur Trade.* Memoirs of the American Anthropological Association, No. 78. Washington, D.C.

LeClerc, Gérard. 1972. *Anthropologie et colonialisme: Essai sur l'histoire de l'africanisme.* Paris: Fayard.

Lemisch, Jesse. 1968. "Who Will Write a Left History of Art While We Are All Putting Our Balls on the Line?" In pamphlet with S. Lynd, *Intellectuals, the University, and the Movement.* Boston: New England Free Press.

———. 1970. *What's Your Evidence? Radical Scholarship as Scientific Method and Anti-Authoritarianism, Not "Relevance."* NUC Papers, No. 2. Chicago: New University Conference.

[*Les Temps modernes*]. 1971. "Anthropologie et impérialisme." *Les Temps modernes* 27, Nos. 293–294: 1061–201; Nos. 299–300: 2345–467.

Lévi-Strauss, Claude. 1953. *Tristes Tropiques.* Paris: Plon.

———. 1963. *Structural Anthropology.* New York: Basic Books. First published, Paris: Plon, 1958.

———. 1966. "Anthropology: Its Achievements and Its Future." *Current Anthropology* 7, No. 2: 124–27.

Lichtheim, George. 1965. "The Concept of Ideology." In *Studies in the Philosophy of History,* ed. George H. Nadel. New York: Harper & Row, Torchbooks. Pp. 148–79. Also in Lichtheim, *The*

Concept of Ideology and Other Essays. New York: Vintage Books, 1967. Pp. 3–46.

———. 1971. *From Marx to Hegel.* New York: Herder & Herder.

Lowie, R. H. 1917. *Culture and Ethnology.* New York: Liveright.

MacCurdy, George Grant. 1902. "Twenty Years of Section H, Anthropology." *Science* 15: 532–34.

Macquet, Jacques. 1964. "Objectivity in Anthropology." *Current Anthropology* 5, No. 1: 47–55.

Mandelbaum, David G., ed. 1949. *Selected Writings of Edward Sapir.* Berkeley: University of California Press.

Manuel, Frank E. 1965. *Shapes of Philosophical History.* Stanford, Calif.: Stanford University Press.

———. ed. 1968. *Johann Gottfried von Herder: Reflections on the Philosophy of the History of Mankind.* Chicago: University of Chicago Press.

Marx, Karl. [1857] 1964. *Pre-Capitalist Economic Formations,* ed. E. J. Hobsbawm. London: Lawrence & Wishart.

McGimsey, Charles R., III. 1972. *Public Archeology.* New York: Seminar Press.

Mead, Margaret. 1970. *Culture and Commitment: A Study of the Generation Gap.* Garden City, N.Y.: Natural History Press.

Mills, C. Wright. 1959. *The Sociological Imagination.* New York: Oxford University Press.

———. 1962. *The Marxists.* New York: Dell Publishing Co.

Mintz, Sidney W. 1970. Foreword. In Norman E. Whitten, Jr., and John F. Szwed, *Afro-American Anthropology: Contemporary Perspectives.* New York: Free Press. Pp. 1–16.

Momigliano, A. D. 1966. "The Place of Herodotus in the History of Historiography." In *Studies in Historiography.* New York: Harper & Row, Torchbooks. Pp. 128–42.

Moore, Barrington. 1963. "Strategy in Social Science." In Stein and Vidich, 1963, pp. 66–95.

Moore, John. 1971. "Perspective for a Partisan Anthropology." *Liberation,* November, pp. 34–43.

Moore, Stanley W. 1957. *The Critique of Capitalist Democracy.* New York: Paine-Whitman.

———. 1969. "Utopian Themes in Marx and Mao: A Critique for Modern Revisionists." *Monthly Review* 21, No. 2: 33–44.

[NACLA]. 1970. *NACLA Research Methodology Guide.* New York.

Nisbet, Robert A. 1967. "Project Camelot and the Science of Man." In Horowitz, 1967, pp. 313–38.

———. 1969. *Social Change and History: Aspects of the Western Theory of Development.* New York: Oxford University Press.

Palson, Chuck. 1970. "The Desirability of Various Types of Graduate Departments." *Newsletter of the American Anthropological Association* 11, No. 8: 6–7.

P'Bitek, Okot. [1972]. *African Religions in Western Scholarship.* Kampala, Nairobi, Dar-es-Salaam: East African Literature Bureau.

Pearce, Roy Harvey. 1953. *The Savages of America*. Baltimore: Johns Hopkins Press.

Radin, Paul. 1933. *The Method and Theory of Ethnology*. New York: McGraw-Hill Book Co. Reprinted New York: Basic Books, 1966.

Reclus, Élie. [1885] 1891. *Primitive Folk: Studies in Comparative Ethnology*. London: Walter Scott; New York: Scribner & Welford.

Roszak, Theodore, ed. 1968. *The Dissenting Academy*. New York: Pantheon Books.

———. ed. 1969. *The Making of a Counter-Culture: Reflections on the Technocratic Society and Its Youthful Opposition*. New York: Doubleday & Co., Anchor Books.

Rowe, John H. 1964. "Ethnography and Ethnology in the Sixteenth Century." *Kroeber Anthropological Society Papers* 30: 1–19.

———. 1965. "The Renaissance Foundations of Anthropology." *American Anthropologist* 67: 1–20.

Sahlins, Marshall. 1967. "The Established Order: Do Not Fold, Spindle, or Mutilate." In Horowitz, 1967, pp. 71–9.

Sapir, Edward. [1927] 1949. "The Unconscious Patterning of Behavior in Society." In Mandelbaum, ed., 1949, pp. 544–59.

———. [1934] 1949. "The Emergence of the Concept of Personality in a Study of Cultures." In Mandelbaum, ed., 1949, pp. 590–97.

———. [1938] 1949. "Why Cultural Anthropology Needs the Psychiatrist." In Mandelbaum, ed., 1949, pp. 569–77.

Sartre, Jean-Paul. 1963. *Search for a Method*. New York: Alfred A. Knopf.

Scholte, Bob. 1972. "Discontents in Anthropology." *Social Research* 38: 777–807.

Schroyer, Trent. 1970. "The Tradition of Critical Theory." *Critical Anthropology* 1: 23–43.

———. 1971. "A Reconceptualization of Critical Theory." In Colfax and Roach, 1971, pp. 132–48.

Schuyler, Robert L. 1970. "Historical Sites Archaeology as Anthropology: Basic Definitions and Relationships." *Historical Archaeology* 4: 83–9.

Selwyn, Tom. 1972. "Worm's Eye-View." *!Kung*, pp. 7–9. London: London School of Economics.

Slotkin, J. S. 1965. *Readings in Early Anthropology*. Chicago: Aldine.

Smelser, Neal. 1967. "Sociology and the Other Sciences." In Lazarsfeld, Sewell, and Wilensky, eds., 1967, pp. 3–44.

Smith, Dusky Lee. [1964] 1971. "The Sunshine Boys: Toward a Sociology of Happiness." In Colfax and Roach, 1971, pp. 28–44.

Spier, Leslie. 1931. "Historical Interrelation of Culture Traits: Franz Boas' Study of Tsimshian Mythology." In *Methods in Social Science*, ed. S. Rice. Chicago: University of Chicago Press. Pp. 449–57.

Spradley, James, and David W. McCurdy. 1972. *The Cultural Experi-*

ence: Ethnography in Complex Society. Chicago: Science Research Associates.

Stein, Maurice. 1963. "The Poetic Metaphors of Sociology." In Stein and Vidich, 1963, pp. 173–82.

———. 1967. "On the Limits of Professional Thought." In Wolff and Moore, 1967, pp. 364–73.

Stein, Maurice, and Arthur Vidich, eds. 1963. *Sociology on Trial.* Englewood Cliffs, N.J.: Prentice-Hall.

Stern, Bernhard. J. [1943] 1959. "Franz Boas as Scientist and Citizen." In *Historical Sociology: The Selected Papers of Bernhard J. Stern.* New York: Citadel Press. Pp. 208–41. From *Science and Society* 7, No. 4: 289–320.

———. 1949. "Some Aspects of Historical Materialism." In *Philosophy for the Future,* eds. R. W. Sellars, V. J. McGill, and M. Farber. New York: Macmillan Co. Pp. 340–56.

Stocking, George W., Jr. 1960. "Franz Boas and the Founding of the American Anthropological Association." *American Anthropologist* 62: 1–17.

———. 1968. *Race, Culture, and Evolution.* New York: Free Press.

———. 1971a. "Animism in Theory and Practice: E. B. Tylor's Unpublished 'Notes on "spiritualism." ' " *Man* 6: 88–104.

———. 1971b. "What's in a Name? The Origins of the Royal Anthropological Institute (1837–71)." *Man* 6: 369–90.

———. 1972. "From Chronology to Ethnology: James Cowles Prichard and British Anthropology, 1800–1850." In *Researches in the Physical History of Man,* ed. James Cowles Prichard. Chicago: University of Chicago Press.

Struever, Stuart, ed. 1972–. *Studies in Archeology.* New York: Seminar Press.

[Students]. 1969. "Reports by Students on Their Participation in and Reactions to the 67th Annual Meeting of the American Anthropological Association, Seattle, November 21–24, 1968." New York: Wenner-Gren Foundation for Anthropological Research, Inc.

Tax, Sol. 1955. "The Integration of Anthropology." In *Current Anthropology,* ed. W. L. Thomas, Jr. Chicago: University of Chicago Press. Pp. 313–28.

Therborn, Göran. 1970. "Frankfurt Marxism: A Critique." *New Left Review* 63: 65–96.

Tylor, Edward. [1871] 1958. *Primitive Culture.* Vol. 2. New York: Harper & Row, Torchbooks.

Valentine, Charles. 1972. *Black Studies in Anthropology: Scholarly and Political Interest in Afro-American Culture.* Reading, Mass.: Addison-Wesley Modules.

Vidich, Arthur. 1966. Introduction. In republication of Paul Radin, *The Method and Theory of Ethnology.* New York: Basic Books.

Voget, Fred W. 1968. "Anthropology in the Age of Enlightenment: Progress and Utopian Functionalism." *Southwestern Journal of Anthropology* 24: 321–45.

————. 1969–1970. "Forgotten Forerunners of Anthropology." *Bucknell Review*, pp. 78–96.

Walker, Deward E., Jr., ed. 1972. *The Emergent Native Americans: A Reader in Culture Contact*. Boston: Little, Brown & Co.

Wallerstein, Immanuel. 1971. "Radical Intellectuals in a Liberal Society." In Wallerstein and Starr, 1971, pp. 471–77.

Wallerstein, Immanuel, and Paul Starr, eds. 1971. *The University Crisis Reader. Vol. 2, Confrontation and Counterattack*. New York: Vintage Books.

Walsh, W. H. 1960. *Philosophy of History*. New York: Harper & Row, Torchbooks.

Williams, Raymond. [1961] 1965. *The Long Revolution*. London: Pelican Books.

Wolf, Eric. 1964. *Anthropology*. Englewood Cliffs, N.J.: Prentice-Hall.

————. 1972. "The Anthropologist as Cultural Communicant: Paradox and Predicament." In Diamond, ed., *The Nature of Anthropological Traditions*. Evanston, Ill.: Northwestern University Press.

Wolf, Eric, and Joseph Jorgensen. 1970. "Anthropologists on the Warpath." *New York Review of Books*, November 19, pp. 26–35.

Wolff, Kurt, and Barrington Moore, eds. 1967. *The Critical Spirit: Essays in Honor of Herbert Marcuse*. Boston: Beacon Press.

Wolff, Robert Paul. 1971. "Reason and the Left." In Wallerstein and Starr, 1971, pp. 441–45.

Wolfle, Dael. 1971. "The Supernatural Department" Editorial. *Science* 173: 109.

Woodburn, James. 1972. "The Future for Hunting and Gathering Peoples." *!Kung*, pp. 1–3. London: London School of Economics.

Worsley, Peter. 1970. "The End of Anthropology?" *Transactions of the Sixth World Congress of Sociology* 3: 121–29.

II · The Root Is Man

"Bringing It All Back Home": Malaise in Anthropology

Gerald D. Berreman

In my recent graduate seminar on "Social Interaction" I asked that the participants introduce themselves by name and any explanatory data they thought relevant. One of the undergraduates chose to say, quite simply, "I am an undergraduate and I'm taking this seminar because I'm sick to shit of lecture courses." We are having this session on "Rethinking Anthropology" because many of us are equally sick of anthropology as it is exemplified in most of our journals, books, and courses—even those we have ourselves perpetrated.

When asked to participate, I at first declined on the grounds that I have said many times over most of what I might say here. Although I have had no reason to revise that estimate, I happened to read in the *New York Review* the series of conversations between the Jesuit priest Daniel Berrigan (then underground as an adjunct to his militant nonviolent peace activities) and the psychiatrist Robert Coles, who has worked with the poor and the black in the South and especially with their children. These appeared March 11, March 25, and April 8, 1971, under the title "A Dialogue Underground."

I was deeply moved by what these men said and what they had done, and I felt moved to say something here about the malaise that is affecting our discipline, our professional association, our department, our students, our faculty—in short ourselves—because I think that the malaise is close to the one discussed by Berrigan and Coles and close to the heart of the troubles faced by intellectuals in America today. Those troubles threaten to tear us away from each other and from any possibility of realizing the hope that many of us have cherished for a viable, responsible, and useful study of mankind.

The title of this paper, borrowed from Bob Dylan, is "Bringing It All Back Home." I turned to Dylan for inspiration because he is one of the few commentators on the human condition who has something to say, says it well, is therefore listened to, and whose theory and methodology are unassailable. On the jacket of the album sharing its title with this paper, Dylan says: "I am about to sketch You a picture of what goes on around here sometimes, tho' I don't understand too well myself what's really happening." And again: "i accept chaos. i am not sure whether it accepts me." These statements reflect my intentions and feelings regarding what I want to talk about in this paper. I might mention that I at first thought of calling the paper "Something Is Happening, and You Don't Know What It Is, Do You, Mr. Jones?" but I realized that this would raise the question among my audience: "Who is Mr. Jones *really?*" Since Mr. Jones is all of us, I decided on the present, less puzzling title.

There *is* something happening around here, and it isn't just at Berkeley. And I don't suppose it's just in anthropology, but that is where we are, so that is where we see it. It is variously described as anomie, alienation, anti-intellectualism, unscientific attitude, disrespect, laziness, know-nothingism, narcissism, being stoned, or being on the forefront of a new era. It is often described as a manifestation of radicalism, radical chic, impertinence, or a counter culture. It seems chaotic, but I don't think it is. Rather, it is coherent and comprehensible. My purpose is to try to identify its nature or at least some of its major themes. I will do so by setting forth the questions that I think are troubling those of us who are concerned about current trends in our field and who are moved to do something about them. "Us" includes students, third-world people, and those irascible others who empathize perhaps too strongly or see too clearly or think too tortuously to achieve the tranquillity which is supposed to be obtainable in the ivory tower. I do not apologize for raising questions rather than providing answers—I don't have the answers—but I take comfort in John Stuart Mill's assurance that "the next thing to having a question solved is to have it well raised." Those who are puzzled by our persistent questioning, skepticism, and dissent may find in these questions an answer to their often impatient query, "What's the matter with you? What do you *want,* anyway?"

The questions which confound so many of us are often ignored or misconstrued simply because they are ineptly worded or too harshly or passionately presented. Sometimes they are regarded as destructive or sarcastic because they question assumptions so fundamental as to cast doubt on the very legitimacy of our discipline or our lifestyle. We faculty members are in a position analogous to that of a person who has immersed himself in rigorous training to become a shaman or priest and who, after years of sacrifice and effort, steps forth to publicly perform his hard-won skills, only to find that everyone else has in the meantime become atheist. We who teach are beset by an anthropologically agnostic audience of students, leavened with a number of hard-core anthropological atheists. And even those of us with considerable investment in belief find *ourselves* beset with devilish doubts. One response by the professed believer, as Leon Festinger and his colleagues have shown in *When Prophecy Fails* (1956), is to renew the vigor of one's claims to belief and its correctness, and consequently to proselytize all the harder and demand belief from others all the more rigorously. To shift the metaphor slightly, when night closes in, one beats the drums louder and clutches more tightly the firebrand. In our case, as doubts increase, one raises standards, increases requirements, and clings more tightly to a dubious rigor. This way lies the emergence of—the regression to—an anthropological "saber-tooth curriculum" (Peddiwell, 1939). Another possible response, of course, is to reassess the situation and respond by adapting to changed circumstances with revised reactions.

The questions I will describe are fundamental ones raised in all sincerity by people who have, for the most part, thought through the implications of their work and their discipline. Whether you or I regard them as valid questions or not, they *are* real to those who raise them and hence, as W. I. Thomas would assure us, they are real in their consequences. We had better attend to them, therefore. If they are shouted in unseemly volume or vocabulary, it is because no one seems otherwise to listen; if they are repeated *ad nauseum,* it is because no one otherwise seems to attend to them. They are as troubling to me as to anyone else; I am as threatened as anyone by their implications for myself and my work. Daniel Berrigan (March 25, p. 25) struck a responsive chord in me—and I wish more of my colleagues would also feel that he spoke for them—when he said to Robert Coles, "I know that I have had to change more in the past five years than I had to change in the preceding thirty, and I know in my heart (though I dread saying it even to myself) that I am going to have to change more in the next *year* than I have in the last five." This is not an easy prospect to face; far easier to dig in one's heels and espouse the eternal verities of one's own graduate days or one's professional youth, and to judge others accordingly.

Father Berrigan gives apt and timely warning to us of the danger of being "turned into a prestigious figure who cannot be seriously questioned, least of all by those bold and impertinent youths we seem to be producing of late in America!" He goes on to say: "I've seen [it] happen again and again—so blatantly and outrageously—on our campuses, where college professors simply stand on their records, their books and articles, their capital, so to speak, and rage at anyone who questions them in a searching, face-to-face manner. And so often, those professors feel called upon to vindicate not only what *they* have won (what they have come to!) but what others have won—the system!" And he cites their doctrinaire message to the neophyte: "Conform or repent, or you are out of our guild, or you will never get in it" (March 25, p. 25).

This is what many of our students and young colleagues cannot tolerate; this stance our discipline cannot maintain if we are to survive as students of man in the contemporary world. We do not know enough to justify a claim to an exclusive truth about mankind or even to knowing how to acquire one. We can have an impact—I hope a humane impact—but it must be by the example of our honesty and humanity and by the consequences of our works; it cannot be as a result of insisting on our infallibility or the absolute nature of our discovery of truth.

In another place (March 25, p. 30) Father Berrigan comments on the modesty of Camus and the effect of his life work, for Camus worried about the implications of success, influence and "fame." "[Camus] had a certain time to live . . . and he had a certain measure of talent—and he assumed that if he spent his time wisely and worked hard, then *something* would occur. By the same token something occurs because you write, something occurs because I write, something occurs because you are who you are and have been where you have been, and the same for me." I like that statement very much and I think we students of mankind can derive inspiration from it. Perhaps the best we can hope to do is to make the results of our existence as people and as anthropologists (we must not forget that we are both—inseparably both) as positive and humane as we can. I think this is what the so-called dissidents among us are worried about, for they doubt that this is happening.

What, more specifically, are the dissidents asking? Why are some questioning the legitimacy of anthropology, of

field research, of specific studies, of our professional association, of curricula and requirements? Why have they
formed radical caucuses, nominated renegade candidates,
established renegade journals (e.g., *Critical Anthropology*),
exhibited discomfiting militance before faculty members,
demanded unconventional courses? Why have some students dropped out and others cynically fulfilled the letter
of requirements while balking at the spirit of those requirements? Why do some of us who are nonstudents find
ourselves empathizing, sympathizing, or even contributing
to these phenomena?

I think it is because they—we—are raising different questions and different issues than have conventionally been
raised heretofore in our discipline. Let me identify a few
of these with reference to some of the individuals who have
raised them in the past, in times when they fell on less
fertile ground than they now find.

1. *The humanistic aims of anthropology and the social
responsibility of anthropologists.* Ernest Becker has written
extensively on the betrayal by social scientists of the vision
out of which their disciplines grew during the Enlightenment—a vision of a humane science dedicated to the enhancement of human freedom through discovery and
critical analysis of the nature of social life. It had been
expected, he says, that this science would be utopian in
nature, its practitioners imagining, planning, constructing,
implementing, and experimenting with alternative ways of
living in society, with the goal of furthering "the progressive development of the human spirit in its earthly career"
(1971, p. 57). It seems to me that, in the broadest terms, it
is this "lost science of man," as Becker calls his book, which
those of us who today express dismay at what anthropology
has become seek to rediscover and revive. We question the
kinds of knowledge sought and the uses to which it is to
be put, and we put higher priority on these questions
than on questions of absolute truth and validity. Truth for
its own sake is not enough.

Let me quote Becker speculating on the aims and rationalizations of the scientistic, "objective" anthropologists:

> Was it possible that the science of man was conjured up to no human purpose? It was not only possible; in the first half of the twentieth century it was actual. These new men lived with an impossible fantasy; they were working for and gradually building and passing on to other new men who would gradually build and pass on a scientific picture of the human world. Of course, it was never complete. It could never be finished; therefore, they had to keep working on it, just because it was never complete and could never be finished. What use was an incomplete scientific picture? Not much use, they said. That's why we have to keep completing it. But, we retort, it will never be complete; you admit this yourself. Hence, it will never be of use. Well, they might finally answer, if we make it less incomplete it might be less useless. (1971, pp. 118–19)

So they work forever building their Tower of Babel, secure in the knowledge that it will never be finished and that it will be useless until finished.

We stand, instead, with Alvin Gouldner, who has said: "The issue . . . is not whether we know enough; the real questions are whether we have the courage to say and use what we know and whether anyone knows more" (1964, p. 205); and with Kenneth Winetrout, who says, paraphrasing Marx's last thesis on Feuerbach: "It is not enough to understand the world; one must seek to change it" (1964, p. 160). That is, we are asking that anthropologists join Robert Redfield ([1953] 1957, p. 141) in putting themselves as he did (and in his words) "squarely on the side of mankind," unashamed "to wish mankind well." As students of man, we have made a value choice for mankind, and it is inconsistent to then claim a sterile scientism which precludes the realization of the humanitarian heritage of social science.

As a corollary to this, we believe that neutrality on human issues is simply not an option open to anthropologists. To value truth over falsity in dealing with matters of social existence has political and moral consequences, as C. Wright Mills has made clear in identifying "the politics of truth" as the politics of the man of knowledge. Douglas Dowd, in an essay in Mills's honor (1964, p. 63), notes that "the alternatives are not 'neutrality' and 'advocacy.' To be uncommitted is not to be neutral but to be committed—consciously or not—to the *status quo*—to celebrate the present." The claim to value freedom, therefore, we repudiate as illusory at best, dishonest at worst.

And we go beyond that to ask if we do not have a positive responsibility, not simply to the truth, but to the courageous exposition of the truth and to acting upon the implications of that truth. Daniel Berrigan is convinced that "in view of what goes on in the world, we must each of us not only explore the world but prod it and enter into *some* kind of jeopardy." "One learns, I would hope" he says, "to discover what is right, what needs to be righted—through work, through action" (March 11, p. 23). It is this action which is now being thrown up to us scientists as the logical and necessary concomitant of our knowledge. We have a responsibility to act which derives from that knowledge.

This is the substance of the searching questions of the peoples of the third world and others: namely, "What has been the effect of your work among us? Have you contributed to the solution of the problems you have witnessed? Have you even mentioned those problems? If not, then you are part of those problems and hence must be changed, excluded, or eradicated along with their other manifestations. If you are not part of the solution, you are part of the problem."

2. *The personal accountability of anthropologists.* The Committee on Ethics of the American Anthropological Association in 1970 made a strong plea for accountability by anthropologists for their professional acts—a logical concomitant of the social responsibility discussed above (pp. 14–16). This has come clearly to the fore in the in-

stances of clandestine and secret activities by anthropologists in Thailand. The committee has asked, not that anthropologists or others make no mistakes or take no risks, or that they attain a superhuman morality, but only that anthropologists take responsibility for their acts and choices as scientists as they do for the other things they do in life as individuals. The committee has asked that anthropologists not claim immunity from responsibility in the name of science, for science grants no immunity, and to claim it only destroys the faith of others in its practitioners. Academic freedom is not license; nor is scientific freedom. As James Agee said shortly after the atomic bombs were dropped on the Japanese people: "When the bomb split open the universe and revealed the prospect of the infinitely extra ordinary, it also revealed the oldest, simplest, commonest, most neglected, and most important of facts, that each man is eternally and above all else responsible for his own soul . . ." (quoted in Matthews, 1966, p. 23). That was the end of innocence for all science, as Robert Oppenheimer recognized and devoted the rest of his life to conveying. If the implications of the bomb are not clear to anthropologists, then the work of their colleagues in Thailand and cooperation in such programs as the massive ethnographic-data retrieval system known as Project Cambridge should make the same point: that we too are accountable for our acts as scientists and as human beings (cf. Wolf and Jorgensen, 1970; Coburn, 1969). If we involve ourselves in portentous activities fateful to the lives of others, we can claim no immunity from responsibility for their consequences (Berreman, 1968). This, we radicals and dissidents want to convey to our colleagues.

3. *Relevance.* Eric Wolf has called for the creation by anthropologists of an image of man that will be adequate to the experience of our time (1964, p. 94). This is a plea for an anthropology that is relevant to the contemporary condition of man. It is a plea which has been widely

ignored—even ridiculed—but which is now being urgently revived. When "urgent anthropology" is defined as salvage ethnography, as it often has been, we know the cries of academic colonialism which come from the third world and from our internal minorities are well founded. We anthropologists are then indeed part of the problem. As we begin to study the institutions, the elite personnel, and the historical circumstances which limit human freedom, which control and repress people and societies including our own, then I think we are moving to a more viable, responsible, and relevant realm of research. Insofar as we cling exclusively to conventional studies of the remote, the exotic, and the powerless, we are contributing to the problems of people in this world and we deserve no more sympathy than we get from them. The demand for relevance, then, becomes one with the demand for social responsibility and personal accountability.

4. *The nature of truth about human social life and the kind of evidence which leads to it.* C. Wright Mills ([1959] 1961) has advocated the exercise of what he calls the "sociological imagination" in the work of all social scientists, by which he means examining and clarifying the relationship between individual experience and social issues, between private troubles and social problems—in short, the relationship between biography and history. This is close to the current plea for anthropological analyses that are not only believable but directly reflective of, and relevant to, human experience. We might call this a plea for an "anthropology of experience." Anthropology that is remote from the human experience often becomes inhumane in its consequences as well as artificial and uninteresting in content. Yet the scientism which is rampant in anthropology as well as the other social sciences, the pressure for publication and the sub-subspecialization which accompanies it, the artificial and limiting disciplinary boundaries, have had precisely this result: that much of our work bears little relationship to the

existential reality of human lives, producing what I called, in an earlier essay on the topic, "lifeless descriptions of human life" (Berreman, 1966, p. 350). An anthropology which does not reflect and convey or illuminate the human experience is no anthropology at all. Many have come to believe, as I do, that too much contemporary anthropology is this nonanthropology.

Kathleen Zaretsky has made this point strongly and cogently in a paper given at the same symposium as this one (Zaretsky, 1971). Expressing a deep and widely shared ambivalence about anthropology, she suggests that the choice facing the discipline now is between a narrowly scientific, reductionistic, positivistic definition of, and approach to, anthropological truth, and a more humanly relevant one. Clearly, anthropology as conventionally practiced exemplifies the former. "The significance of such a posture," says Zaretsky, "is inescapable: that the truth is there and that it is objectively discoverable, if only we experts look hard enough; if only we find the right models. And what about the individual men, women, and children involved? They are subsumed—vaporized—in a 'truth' which is just as absolute, if more guardedly stated, as the truth of any god. . . . The choice, then, is basically whether to look on people as things, as variables, as participants, as members, as role-takers—as robots, in short—or as persons." She, like many of her contemporaries in and recently out of graduate school (and like some of their seniors), opts for the latter: "My solution at the moment is to throw anthropology as we know it, out on its ear," and she states her own preference for an anthropology comprising a phenomenological approach to human experience.

The very nature of anthropological inquiry and description is thus being called into question. It is being revised in what may amount to a nascent "scientific revolution" in which the traditional "normal science" of anthropology will be radically altered, with new criteria used in deciding what questions will be asked, what methods will be used, what evidence will be sought, and what answers will be accepted (cf. Kuhn, 1962). The trend is toward a more humanistic, empathetic, existential brand of anthropological inquiry and communication, a trend exemplified in various ways by Castaneda (1968), Read (1965), and others, and anticipated by the writer James Agee (1941) in his classic study of the lives and circumstances of poverty-stricken Southern rural whites—a study which has attracted renewed interest in our discipline. If established anthropologists cannot respond positively to this trend, they will be left behind by it.

I am reminded here of the insight attributed to the author Marino in a story by Jorge Louis Borges: "That we may make mention or allusion of a thing and never express it at all; and that the tall proud tomes [he had authored] . . . were not—as he had dreamed in his vanity—a mirror of the world, but simply one more thing added to the universe. This illumination came to Marino on the eve of his death and, perhaps, it had come to Homer and Dante, too" (Borges, 1967, p. 83). It has come to many of our students and to some of us upon reading the tomes we have written. If it humbles us a little, it may improve our practice of the science of mankind. That could use improvement.

5. *The demand for an end to the pervasive hypocrisy in academic anthropology.* The problem of hypocrisy is so pervasive and fundamental in our society that it is difficult to exemplify briefly. Opposition to it or revulsion by it is the hallmark of the dissident counter culture exhibited by our youth, our minorities, our intellectuals, and our radicals. Its manifestation in anthropology is inseparable from its manifestation in academia, in other institutions, and in our society at large. It is found in the duplicity of our president and his advisers (and others before him and them) regarding the war in Indochina and regarding our domestic problems; it is reflected in the inconsistency of our governor's pious words on public matters and his greedy behavior

when it comes to taxes and his own pocketbook; it has to do with information management in our news; it has to do with legislators' disingenuous statements about civil rights and public education while taking away the funds which could make them possible.

But for our students and colleagues, it also has to do with the inconsistency between scientific standards and the selfish rewards of prestige, travel, and money to be derived from secret consultation and clandestine research for military ends under the guise of academic freedom and science. It has to do with the crass careerism and professional political intrigue of even our most eminent colleagues in callous pursuit of personal aggrandizement and in defense of arcane and obsolete status hierarchies having nothing at all to do with the aim or content of our discipline. It is manifest in the gentlemen's agreements which govern employment and research opportunities to the virtual exclusion of publicly communicated and democratically administered selection criteria. And these things are conveyed to our young colleagues by the requirements placed on them for success in entering and advancing within our esoteric meritocracy. They are conveyed through the fossilized system of requirements and rewards by which one becomes a certified practitioner of the science of man.

Above all, the reaction against hypocrisy is one against the sanctimonious and reactionary demand that the politics of dissent be excluded from the ivory tower so that truth can be sought and taught without distraction or interpretation—in the naive belief or cynical assertion that there is a truth independent of the human reality within which it exists.

In the context of this all-pervasive hypocrisy, simple professional honesty and humanity have come to be mistaken for courage—sometimes even *are* courageous—when in fact they should be the minimal expectations placed on any scholar.

Kingsley Widmer noted in the *AAUP Bulletin* that "dis-

sidents are much less the real problem . . . than the fradu-
lent learning and unjust social order so thoroughly, though
not yet quite completely, institutionalized in the universities" (1971, p. 143). And, I might add, in professional organizations including our own. And this is something which
accounts for dissent in anthropology as well as something
which justifies it.

What so many yearn for in our profession as in academia
generally—and some have virtually abandoned hope—is,
then, a redefinition of our aims. And we not only yearn for
it, we are committed to working for it. That redefinition entails first of all a return to the Enlightenment vision of a
social science whose aim is the enhancement of the freedom
of the human spirit, the enhancement of the quality of human life, whose practitioners and students take as a positive
responsibility the necessity to take action toward that noble
end (cf. Becker, 1971; Gay, 1959). We ask that individual
scholars be held accountable for their activities as scientists, for only thus will a humane science of man emerge
rather than one which is simply adjunct to the inhumane,
socially uninformed, and irresponsible goals of politicians,
militarists, and entrepreneurs. We ask that anthropological
work be relevant in the sense that it address the issues facing
people in their social existence, and we ask that it reflect
the quality of that social existence as it seeks to provide
foundations and practical recommendations for improving
it. And we ask that high value be placed on humanity,
originality, and freedom in the work which anthropologists
do in research and teaching.

These things sound almost trite, but they are so alien to
the experience of being an anthropologist, of being an academic, today that many of us almost despair of achieving
them, and many of our students turn away in revulsion or
sorrow rather than be assimilated into the present system.

My personal hope is that we can work—and it will be
work—for a humane, responsible, and relevant science of
man rather than abandon the attempt to the social techni-

cians who will surely replace us and may already outnumber us. I can understand and empathize with those who opt out, but I retain the tentative hope that by remaining in we can perhaps achieve some success in our pursuit of a humane discipline.

I close with a final quotation from Ernest Becker (1971, p. xi):

"As consummate realists, let us continue to work and richly to dream, lest the militarists and other bureaucrats bend our best ideas to their age-old practical nightmares."

Note

This article was first read as a paper in the session on "Rethinking Anthropology" at the 15th Annual Meeting of the Kroeber Anthropological Society, Oakland, California, May 9, 1971.

References

Agee, James (and Walker Evans). 1941. *Let Us Now Praise Famous Men*. Boston: Houghton Mifflin Co.

Becker, Ernest. 1971. *The Lost Science of Man*. New York: George Braziller.

Berreman, Gerald D. 1966. "Anemic and Emetic Analyses in Social Anthropology." *American Anthropologist* 68: 349–54.

———. 1968. "Is Anthropology Alive? Social Responsibility in Social Anthropology." *Current Anthropology* 9, No. 5: 391–96.

Berrigan, Daniel, and Robert Coles. 1971. "A Dialogue Underground." *New York Review of Books*, March 11 (pp. 19–27), March 25 (pp. 24–31), April 8 (pp. 12–21).

Borges, Jorge Luis. 1967. "A Yellow Rose." In *Jorge Luis Borges: A Personal Anthology*, ed. and trans. A. Kerrigan. New York: Grove Press.

Castaneda, Carlos. 1968. *The Teachings of Don Juan: A Yaqui Way of Knowledge*. Berkeley: University of California Press.

Coburn, Judith. 1969. "Project Cambridge: Another Showdown for Social Sciences?" *Science*, December 5, pp. 1250–53.

Committee on Ethics, American Anthropological Association. 1970. Annual Report of the Committee on Ethics, September 1970.

Newsletter of the American Anthropological Association 11, No. 9 (November): 10–16.

Critical Anthropology. 1970. Published biennially from Spring 1970, New School for Social Research, New York.

Dowd, Douglas. 1964. "Thorstein Veblen and C. Wright Mills: Social Science and Social Criticism." In Horowitz, 1964, pp. 54–65.

Dylan, Bob. 1965. "Bringing It All Back Home." Columbia Records, Album CS 9128.

Festinger, Leon, H. W. Riecken, and Stanley Schacter. 1956. *When Prophecy Fails.* Minneapolis: University of Minnesota Press.

Gay, Peter. 1969. *The Enlightenment: An Interpretation.* Vol. II, *The Science of Freedom.* New York: Alfred A. Knopf.

Gouldner, Alvin. 1964. "Anti-Minotaur: The Myth of a Value-Free Sociology." In Horowtiz, 1964, pp. 196–217.

Horowitz, Irving L., ed. 1964. *The New Sociology: Essays in Social Science and Social Theory in Honor of C. Wright Mills.* New York: Oxford University Press.

Kuhn, Thomas S. 1962. *The Structure of Scientific Revolutions.* Chicago: University of Chicago Press.

Matthews, T. S. 1966. "James Agee—Strange and Wonderful." *Saturday Review,* April 16, pp. 22–23.

Mills, C. Wright. [1959] 1961. *The Sociological Imagination.* New York: Grove Press, Evergreen Books.

———. [1955] 1963. "On Knowledge and Power." In *Power, Politics, and People,* ed. Irving L. Horowitz. New York: Ballantine Books. Pp. 599–613.

Peddiwell, J. Abner. 1939. *The Saber-tooth Curriculum.* New York: McGraw-Hill Book Co.

Read, Kenneth. 1965. *The High Valley.* New York: Charles Scribners' Sons.

Redfield, Robert. [1953] 1957. *The Primitive World and Its Transformations.* Ithaca. N.Y.: Cornell University Press.

Widmer, Kingsley. 1971. "In Reply." *AAUP Bulletin,* Spring 1971, pp. 141–43.

Winetrout, Kenneth. 1964. "Mills and the Intellectual Default." In Horowitz, 1964, pp. 147–61.

Wolf, Eric R. 1964. *Anthropology.* Englewood Cliffs, N.J.: Prentice-Hall.

Wolf, Eric R., and Joseph G. Jorgensen. 1970. "Anthropology on the Warpath in Thailand." *New York Review of Books,* November 19, pp. 26–35.

Zaretsky, Kathleen. 1971. "Anthropology and Truth." Paper read in the session on "Rethinking Anthropology," 15th Annual Meeting of the Kroeber Anthropological Society, Oakland, Calif., May 9, 1971.

This Is the Time for Radical Anthropology
Kurt H. Wolff

THE TASK of this paper is to explicate its title, thus to convey the thrust of this title. The seven words of which it is composed—"this is the time for radical anthropology" —reflect three inseparably connected concepts: *this time, radical, anthropology*. But though they are inseparably connected, their exposition, which is to tell their story, is necessarily consecutive; it begins with "anthropology."

The anthropology that is relevant at this time is radical, but the justification of this assessment must wait until we come to "this time." What radical anthropology exists is, so far as I know, either humanly radical or politically radical. Among major representatives of humanly radical anthropology (although in most other respects they are quite different from each other) are Paul Radin, Edward Sapir, Ruth Benedict (in at least one of her writings), and Dorothy Lee. A representative of politically radical anthropology is Kathleen Gough. We must find out what is common to these two radicalisms.[1]

HUMANLY RADICAL

Paul Radin, in contrast to Lévy-Bruhl, for instance, thought and felt the Winnebago—his Winnebago—to be human beings like himself; he listened in as unprejudiced a manner as he could to what Crashing Thunder (Radin,

1920, 1926) had to say and thus, incidentally, as Robert Redfield wrote in 1960 (p. 3), "stimulated the now widespread use of autobiographies"; he also found "primitive philosophers" (Radin, 1927). Joseph Campbell's observation is pertinent: whereas

> any science that takes into consideration only or even primarily the vulgar, tough-minded interpretation of symbols will inevitably be committed to a study largely of local differentiations . . . on the other hand, one addressed to the views of thinkers will find that the ultimate references of their cogitations are few and of universal distribution [will, I paraphrase, seek and come closer to what is universal, radical in man, what is the root of man]. Anthropologists, by and large (or, at least, those of the American variety), are notoriously tough-minded. . . . They have tended to give reductive interpretations to the symbols of primitive thought and to find references only in the particularities of the local scene. (1960, p. 381)

Not, of course, Paul Radin. Nor Edward Sapir, as we can see in his search for "genuine culture," which is

> inherently harmonious, balanced, self-satisfactory. . . . It would be too much to say that even the purest examples yet known . . . have been free of spiritual discords, of the dry rot of social habit, devitalized. But the great cultures, those that we instinctively feel to have been healthy spiritual organisms, such as the Athenian culture of the Age of Pericles and, to a less extent perhaps, the English culture of Elizabethan days, have at least tended to such harmony. (1919–22–24, pp. 314–15)

To be cultured, it follows, is to be honest with oneself, for spurious harmony is a contradiction in terms.

> Sooner or later we shall have to get down to the humble task of exploring the depths of our consciousness and dragging to the light what sincere bits of reflected experience we can find. These bits will not always be beautiful, they will not always be pleasing, but they will be genuine. (P. 331)

Sapir saw the implications of this view of culture and the

cultured individual for what has since been called "applied anthropology." He warns or reminds us that

> the deliberate attempt to impose a culture directly and speedily no matter how backed by good will, is an affront to the human spirit. When such an attempt is backed, not by good will, but by military ruthlessness, it is the greatest conceivable crime against the human spirit, it is the very denial of culture. (P. 328)

And from this warning or reminder follows the call for a world civilization.

> Such transnational problems as the distribution of economic goods, the transportation of commodities, the control of highways, the coinage, and numerous others, must eventually pass into the hands of international organizations for the simple reason that men will not eternally give their loyalty to the uselessly national administration of functions that are of inherently international scope. As this international scope gets to be thoroughly realized, our present infatuations with national prestige in the economic sphere will show themselves for the spiritual imbecilities that they are. (P. 329)

In other words, we have reached a stage where we must realize our "immediate ends" on a worldwide scale, precisely in order to devote our cultural activity to such "remoter ends" as we have come to envisage (cf. pp. 319–21). This argument hints at a possible connection between human and political radicalism, and we shall come back to it.

Ruth Benedict's human radicalism shows itself, above all, in her paper "Anthropology and the Humanities" (1948). Witness, for instance, her observation or insistence that the anthropologist should follow "the critic's surrender to the text itself." For he

> knows that he will succeed in his work if he takes into account whatever is said and done, discarding nothing he sees to be relevant; if he tries to understand the interrelations of discrete bits; if he surrenders himself to his data and uses all the insights of which he is capable.

Concretely, therefore (among other things), life histories should not be used so much for items of ethnographic knowledge as for

> that fraction of the material which shows what repercussions the experiences of a man's life . . . have upon him as a human being. . . . Such information, as it were, tests out a culture by showing its workings in the life of a carrier of that culture; we can watch in an individual case, in Bradley's words, *"what is,* seeing that so it happened and must have happened." (1948, p. 592)

Dorothy Lee is humanly more radical than Radin, Sapir, and Benedict. Some of the crucial elements of her position are contained in the following passage:

> I believe that it is value, not a series of needs, which is at the basis of human behavior. The main difference between the two lies in the conception of the good which underlies them. The premise that man acts so as to satisfy needs presupposes a negative conception of the good as amelioration or the correction of an undesirable state. According to this view, man acts to relieve tension; good is the removal of evil and welfare the correction of ills; satisfaction is the meeting of a need; good functioning comes from adjustment, survival from adaptation; peace is the resolution of conflict; fear, of the supernatural or of adverse public opinion, is the incentive to good conduct; the happy individual is the well-adjusted individual.
>
> Perhaps this view of what constitutes the good is natural and applicable in a culture which also holds that man was born in sin, whether in Biblical or in psychoanalytic terms. But should we, who believe that other cultures should be assessed according to their own categories and premises, impose upon them our own unexamined conception of the good, and thus always see them as striving to remove or avoid ills? It seems to me that, when we do not take this negative view of the good for granted, other cultures often appear to be maintaining "justment" rather than striving to attain adjustment. For example, for the Hopi, the good is present and positive. An individual is "born in hopiness,"

so to speak, and strives throughout life to maintain and enhance this hopiness. There is no external reward for being good, as this is taken for granted. It is evil which is external and intrusive, making a man kahopi, or unhopi; that is, unpeaceful, un-good.

In my opinion, the motivation underlying Hopi behavior is *value*. To the Hopi, there is value in acting as a Hopi within a Hopi situation; there is satisfaction in the situation itself, not in the solution of it or the resolution of tension. . . . the notion of value is incompatible with that of a list of needs, or adjustive responses, or drives; so that, wherever it is held, the list must go. (Lee, [1948] 1959, pp. 72–73)

Inasmuch as the term "value" so often smacks of, if it is not short for, "exchange value," although it is for the most part unwittingly so used, it risks contributing to the commercialization of our language and outlook, even though we may protest this commercialization by invoking "values" (Arendt, 1958, pp. 163–67; K. Wolff, 1961, pp. 94–98). Clearly, Dorothy Lee (also see Lee, [1954] 1959, p. 88) does not mean "exchange value," but rather its opposite, something inalienable, intrinsic, essential: *worth*. The student of the Hopi must seek "hopiness"; the anthropologist, in general, must seek what corresponds to "hopiness" in any "culture" he may wish to study.[2] To say that this conception of anthropology is humanly radical means to stress the injunction inferable from Dorothy Lee's writing, namely, that the student of man get at the root of man as it has grown (or grew, or is growing) in a given culture; as it is mediated by this culture, for it is never found ungrown, unmediated; and it is this grasp of a *unique* growth which is the grasp of man's root, that is, of the *universally* human. This view, on which cultures and culture are relative to man—the absolute —is thus the opposite of that cultural relativism for which cultures are relative and monadic and culture itself is absolute (cf. Gibson, 1966, p. 56).

Dorothy Lee does not examine the relation between man's or an individual's worth and his religiosity. But she writes:

"To describe a way of life in its totality is to describe a religious way of life" ([1952] 1959, p. 165). The paragraph that ends with this sentence reads as follows:

> In these societies [Wintu, Kaingang, Arapesh, Tikopia, and presumably other "primitive" societies], where religion is an ever-present dimension of experience, it is doubtful that religion as such is given a name; Kluckhohn reports that the Navaho have no such word, but most ethnographers never thought to inquire. Many of these cultures, however, recognized and named the spiritual ingredient or attribute, the special quality of the wonderful, the very, the beyondness, in nature. This was sometimes considered personal, sometimes not. We have from the American Indians terms such as *manitou,* or *wakan,* or *yapaitu,* often translated as power; and we have the well-known Melanesian term *mana.* But this is what they reach through faith, the other end of the relationship; the relationship itself is unnamed. Apparently, to behave and think religiously, is to behave and think. [Hence:] to describe a way of life in its totality is to describe a religious way of life.

The relation between man's worth and the power experienced in religious experience is a topic for particular studies. Dorothy Lee's message is to remember both "powers" or at least one or the other, if we would come into them—our heritage. Implied in this message is a contrast between primitive and contemporary society. For instance, with reference to freedom:

> As a concept or as a recognized value, freedom is rarely if ever present in non-Western cultures; but the thing itself, freedom, is certainly often present and carefully implemented—as autonomy, or otherwise as a dimension of the self. In this country, on the other hand, we do have the notion of freedom, and an ideal image of ourselves as "free." Ours is the "land of the free," we are born "free and equal," and certainly, when these phrases were originally used, *free* referred to something of value beyond price, worth fighting and dying for.

A few years ago, with this in mind, I proceeded to find out how we use the term *free* in the mid-twentieth century. . . . I came reluctantly to the conclusion that the term *free* was almost never used, except by people whose function it was to evoke or facilitate freedom, or to remind people about freedom, or to prod people into being concerned about it, that is, by people such as social scientists, politicians, psychoanalysts, and educators. Otherwise, the term *free* was not applied to the freedom of the self. When used at all, it was used occasionally to refer to freedom from entanglement, and more frequently, to free time and free objects, that is, objects which could be acquired or enjoyed without being paid for, such as free lectures or free cigars. *Free* here referred merely to a condition of the situation, a negative condition, to something that was not there. It referred to a welcome lack of requirement, to an absence of *have to*. I *do not have to* pay for the cigars, or for a ticket to attend the lecture; my time is free because I *do not have to* do anything now. (Lee, [1958] 1959, pp. 53–54)

This passage does more than contrast primitive and contemporary society; it implies a historical judgment ("when these phrases were originally used, *free* referred to something of value beyond price"; when Dorothy Lee made her observations, "free" "referred merely . . . to an absence of *have to*"). To explicate "This Is the Time for Radical Anthropology," a historical judgment of the kind must be developed. For the moment, let us only realize that Dorothy Lee's idea of worth/*mana*/ power has close kinship with Hannah Arendt's concept of power. For Hannah Arendt:

Power and violence are opposites; where the one rules absolutely, the other is absent. Violence appears where power is in jeopardy, but left to its own course its end is the disappearance of power. (1969, p. 27)

Perhaps we might add already that we men today have gained in violence what we have lost in power.

POLITICALLY RADICAL

Before we venture more forthrightly into such manner of historical judgment—before we come to "this time"—we turn to the politically radical anthropologist Kathleen Gough.

Kathleen Gough (1967–1968) sees the tasks of anthropology in a political perspective in which four "new proposals for anthropologists" emerge (Gough, 1968; Gough, 1967, for an earlier version; and Gould, 1968, for a sharp critique of her political perspective; also see "Comments" by various authors on Gough, 1968, appended there): (1) a comparison between "capitalist agricultural production in underdeveloped countries" and "socialist production," to ascertain which is better; (2) "comparisons of the structure and efficiency of socialist and capitalist foreign aid"; (3) "comparative studies of types of modern inter-societal political and economic dominance which would help us to define and refine such concepts as imperialism, neo-colonialism, etc."; (4) comparisons of "revolutionary and proto-revolutionary movements for what they can teach us about social change" (Gough, 1968, pp. 406–7). "I may be accused," Kathleen Gough adds,

> of asking for Project Camelot, but I am not. I am asking that we should do these studies in *our* way, as we would study a cargo cult or kula ring, without the built-in biases of tainted financing, without the assumption that counter-revolution, and not revolution, is the best answer, and with the ultimate economic and spiritual welfare of our informants and of the international community, rather than the short run military or industrial profits of the Western nations, before us. (P. 407)

Such proposals, it would appear, are in response to the question about its purpose and its beneficiaries that science, including anthropology, must "periodically" ask itself, lest its practitioners cease being "fully social" and fully "human" intellectuals (cf. Gough, 1967, pp. 148–49). Gough also sees her proposals as contributions to the maturing of anthropology

> into an interconnected body of empirical knowledge and theory, continually being revised, about the total process and main directions of the evolution of human societies and cultures, geared ultimately, although not at every point directly and immediately, to a search for the enhancement of human happiness and dignity.
>
> Such a view of the ultimate goals of anthropology [she adds] does lead to criteria of relevance or, as I would prefer to put it, significance. (Gough, 1968, "Replies," p. 429)

"THIS TIME": RECONCILING RADICALISMS

Now, then, to "this time." Although Edward Sapir wrote the essay from which I quoted earlier almost fifty years ago, and although *that* time is, indeed, not *this,* much of Sapir's paper still applies to *us.* I repeat a passage:

> Sooner or later we shall have to get down to the humble task of exploring the depths of our consciousness and dragging to the light what sincere bits of reflected experience we can find. These bits will not always be beautiful, they will not always be pleasing, but they will be genuine.

Sapir continues: "And then we can build." He meant to build "culture," but the last half-century has shown this to be a historically inadequate formulation. Since Sapir launched his plea, we have experienced—witnessed, contributed to, fought, turned away from, been enthused, terrified, victimized, or killed by—fascism, Stalinism, Nazism, an incomparably vaster world war than the first (at the end of which Sapir wrote), nuclear explosion, and much else that is unprecedented and as yet impossible radically to come to terms with. "Impossible radically to come to terms with" means that we have to go deeper than culture if there is to be any hope that we *can* come to terms with it. Sapir, we saw, envisaged something of the sort in his idea of "international organizations" and his judgment of "infatuations with national prestige" as "spiritual imbecilities." Without explicating the concepts needed for distinguishing "international organizations" from "culture" and for relating "international organizations" to "culture," he paid attention to them and separated their discussion from that of culture.

Today, and indeed already yesterday, something, however, seems even more promising and urgent than to engage in the conceptual clarification of these phenomena. This is that our time is so unprecedented that we cannot hope to do justice to it by relying on, as it were, precedented concepts, on received notions. Instead, we must suspend or bracket received notions as best we can, for only in this way—by not relying on them—can we hope to come upon a conception and upon concepts that may be less inadequate (cf. K. Wolff, 1964, 1967). This is what to be "radical," what seeking the "root of man," now means.

In this view it appears that the humanly radical anthropologists we have recalled are more radical than the one politically radical anthropologist we have considered. If their position were carried to its logical consequence, the former would in their study suspend their received notions as much as possible, whereas Kathleen Gough has rejected, rather than suspended, the received notions that make up capitalist-bourgeois ideology (and not without replacing them by a strong dose of equally received neo-Marxism).

The decisive difference between the two radicalisms, however, is not this matter of degree. Instead, the difference lies in what our authors do not even perceive as relevant to their tasks, hence in what they neither work with in traditional fashion nor suspend. This—greatly oversimplified—is politics in the case of the humanly radical anthropologists, with which Gough, on the contrary, is concerned; and in Gough's case, the relation of the student to the people he studies, which is in the forefront of Radin's, Sapir's, Benedict's, and above all Dorothy Lee's attention. Yet again, for one who seeks an anthropology more adequate to this time, more commensurate with it, neither difference is nearly as pertinent as is the fact that both radicalisms, variously and unevenly indeed, do go beyond received notions: this is what humanly radical and politically radical anthropology share. To become aware of it calls for pleading with the former that it recognize the relevance of politics; with the latter, that it recognize that of the relations between student and persons studied; and with both, that they practice the maximal suspension of received notions. Both kinds of anthropologists would then come closer to the root and to perhaps unsuspected roots of man; hence closer to doing right by our unprecedented time.

A given anthropologist may well find it impossible to be radical in both senses. For instance, the investigation of a particular group may so draw the explorer into political problems, if not into politics, that he cannot remain true to his goal, which is to come as close as possible to the people he studies. Vice versa, one may be so concerned with the clarification of a given political problem as to find it irrelevant if not frivolous to be "humanly radical" ("What poetry after Auschwitz?"). Thus the two radicalisms have complementary limitations. Their complementarity may be expressed by saying that to explore while being moved only by the desire to get at the root of man, failing to analyze his social setting with its institutions and arrangements that diminish him, is to engage in *political* mystification, while the analysis of a social setting without the endeavor to "surrender to" the people involved in it is an exercise in *human* mystification. Once more, to say this cannot imply that one must be expected to be both humanly and politically radical; it only invites one to be aware of the difficult if not impossible demand to be both, and to do one's best within the difficulties this demand imposes.[3]

Underlying the difference between the two radicalisms

may be different attitudes toward our time—the "humanly radical" faith and hope in man's worth and the "politically radical" insistence on the compelling need for great change. This is a very serious difference, but it is as nothing compared with what the two attitudes have in common, with what distinguishes both from the attitudes of social scientists and other men who have not "examined life" critically as both kinds of radicals have. It is in the light of our time that the two radicalisms appear far more similar than different, or, one might say, that it is much more pertinent to stress what they have in common than what separates them.

THE CHARACTER OF "THIS TIME"

To understand our time, we must realize that "unprecedented" refers to our experience of it, here, now; "unprecedented" cannot mean that our time has not developed in time. In fact, if we would understand it, we must consider the processes that have brought it about.

Among social scientists, Max Weber was probably the most devoted and farsighted explorer of those processes. One of many passages in his writings, dating from about the same year as Sapir's essay, may serve to illustrate his reading of this time and the historical processes at work in it:

> The fate of our times is characterized by rationalization and intellectualization and, above all, by the "disenchantment of the world." Precisely the ultimate and most sublime values have retreated from public life either into the transcendental realm of mystic life or into the brotherliness of direct and personal human relations. It is not accidental that . . . today only within the smallest and intimate circles, in personal human situations, in *pianissimo*, that something is pulsating that corresponds to the prophetic *pneuma,* which in former

times swept through the great communities like a firebrand, welding them together. (Weber, [1918] 1946, p. 155)

For our purposes, we may omit the "prophetic" from "*pneuma*" (in view of Weber's fascination with prophecy) and add "*pneuma*" to Dorothy Lee's "worth/*mana*/power" and Hannah Arendt's "power" as characteristics of "primitive societies" or of "earlier times"—which, of course, remain to be specified; or we may, with similar intent, concentrate on Weber's insistence on "disenchantment," which marks our time, as does the *absence* of worth/*mana*/power/*pneuma*. Long before all of these authors, Rousseau, in 1755, expressed a similar idea:

> The savage lives within himself, while social man lives constantly outside himself and only knows how to live in the opinion of others, so that he seems to receive the consciousness of his own existence merely from the judgment of others concerning him. (Rousseau, [1755] 1941, p. 237)

Indeed, Rousseau held that advances beyond the "savages"

> have been apparently so many steps towards the perfection of the individual, but in reality towards the decrepitude of the species. (P. 214)

> And inequalities and men's obsession by them may lead to such flagrant despotism that all private persons return to their first equality, because they are nothing: and, subjects having no law but the will of their master, and their master no restraint but his passions, all notions of good and all principles of equity again vanish. There is here a complete return to the law of the strongest, and so to a new state of nature in its first purity, while this is the consequence of excessive corruption. (P. 235)[4]

This vision leaves no hope, in stark contrast with most of the Enlightenment philosophy of history, or Hegel's, or Marx's. It may strike us as all the more plausible for its bleakness and tempt us to succumb to it. But we know that this can be only a mood of desperation. Indeed, we can read another text, far less well known in the English-speaking world, less desperate and more realistic, perhaps, thus bearing more directly on the historical diagnosis in which we are engaged.

In 1810, Heinrich von Kleist (a year, it must be said, before his suicide at the age of thirty-four) published a story, "On the Puppet Theater." It relates a conversation between the narrator and a dancer who praises the excellence of puppets, even their superiority to dancing human beings.

". . . What advantage would this puppet have over living dancers?"

"What advantage? First of all, a negative one, my excellent friend, namely this one, that it would never give itself airs. For airs, as you know, appear when the soul (*vis motrix*) finds itself at any point other than the point of gravity of the movement. Since the puppeteer, simply by means of the wire or thread, holds no other point in his power but this one, all other limbs are what they ought to be—dead; pure pendula; and follow the mere law of gravitation; an excellent quality, which one seeks in vain among most of our dancers." . . .

"Such mistakes [as human dancers make]," he added, stopping short, "are unavoidable ever since we have eaten from the tree of knowledge. But paradise is bolted, and the cherub is behind us; we must make the trip around the world and see if it is perhaps somehow open again at the back." . . .

"We see that in the measure in which in the organic world reflection becomes darker and feebler, grace appears ever more radiant and dominant. . . . when knowledge has gone through an infinitude, as it were, grace re-emerges, so that it appears in its purest form in that frame of the human body which has either no consciousness at all or an infinite consciousness—that is, in the puppet or in the god."

"Thus," I said, a bit distracted, "we should have to eat once more of the tree of knowledge to fall back into the state of innocence?"

"Exactly," he answered. "That is the last chapter in the history of the world." (Kleist, [1810] n.d., IV, pp. 136–37, 140; cf. Kleist, [1941] 1947, pp. 69–70, 72)

It may be worthwhile reading this story, written more than a century and a half ago, as a parable that refers to *us*, people of the most advanced historical consciousness, living in the industrially and technologically most advanced societies. Laboring, working, acting (for these three activities, cf. Arendt, 1958), creating, experiencing, enjoying, despairing, in short, being, and leading lives (cf. K. Wolff, 1967), for tens of thousands of years, we and our predecessors have produced an unmastered artifice.[5]

We have traded our "worth/*mana*/power/*pneuma*" (and, to add Kleist's word, our "grace"—whether read as "gracefulness" or as "gift," as in *charisma*) for a struggle with "disenchantment" and "alienation," for compulsive domination, for an indifferent or cynical or hypocritical or desperate play with life and death, for, when we feel driven to it, a global sneer.[6] We must emerge from this condition into such "innocence" as man is capable of, through whatever "opening at the back" human and political radicalism can jointly discover.

Thus seen, we are not at the end; but if we can become conscious of it and act on our consciousness—if, as Kleist put it, we realize that we must once more eat of the tree of knowledge and have the courage to do so—we may become able, in Marx's terms, to leave our prehistory and begin our history. For we have reached a time when we can hardly bear our failure to master our disenchantment, because this failure has resulted in masks, machines, and deceptive substitutes whose character reveals itself to us by their capacity and threat to destroy us even physically. The great inventions of science and technology have seduced us to use them also for controlling, manipulating, exploiting, and destroying ourselves and everything else. The liberal glory has become bankruptcy, destitute either in its continued insistence on tolerance at all costs, even of hate-mongering and racism, or in its untutored and fearful casting about for grounds on which to qualify it (R. Wolff, Moore, and Marcuse, 1965); the epistemological and ethical companion of the liberal bankruptcy is cultural and moral relativism (Mannheim, [1946] 1959, for a moving illustration).

In his effort to define "primitive societies," which he intends "as a means of furthering our critical understanding and, hopefully, our humane shaping of the processes of civilization" (Diamond, 1967, p. 22), Stanley Diamond writes that

> the sanguine and terrifying aspects of primitive life, which civilized individuals could hardly sustain, precisely because of the immediate personal contexts in which they occur, do not begin to compete with the mass, impersonal, rationalized slaughter that increases in scope as civilization spreads and deepens. . . . Certain ritual dramas or aspects of them acknowledge, express, and symbolize the most destructive, ambivalent, and demoniacal aspects of human nature; in so doing, they are left limited and finite; that is, they become self-limiting. For this, as yet, we have no civilized parallel, no functional equivalent. (P. 26)

To generalize from this, we have not learned to civilize, or sublimate without loss, the primitive oneness of confrontation and harmony. There is a largely instinctive effort to re-enact this oneness in contemporary young men-and-women-hippie-flower-children's "confrontations" of "war" by "love," as if they believed in Freud's conviction that "all that brings out the significant resemblances between man calls into play this feeling of community, identification, whereon is founded, in large measure, the whole edifice of human society" (Freud, [1932] 1964, p. 78). They correspond, outside the academy, although many are or were students, to the humanly radical anthropologists with their attention to their relations with the people they study, and they act out or live much of what radical philosophers —existentialists, including for many the "early Marx," and phenomenologists—have thought, and think. And the other chief group of critics of our society—the militant blacks and representatives of the third world—corresponds, outside the academy (and fewer of them are or were students), to the politically radical anthropologists with their attention to the injustices of the status quo.

These two groups constitute, on this diagnosis of our time, the main hope for us of entering history, of realizing in knowledge, rather than in primitive innocence of it, worth, *mana*, power, grace, *pneuma*. By virtue of their education and attendant experience, radical anthropologists have a better chance than sheer individual talent to acquire a consciousness that would make them ally themselves with these two groups and make them seek allies also among comparably favored individuals, such as philosophers, theologians, historians, and other social scientists—and make them seek allies anywhere at all. This alliance, that is to say, *we*, we constitute the vanguard of history and must diffuse the worth that we remember so that others, too, remember their own, lest all that they, all that we, are left with be violence. This proposition, obviously, resolves none of our excruciating political problems; but it is prepolitical to the extent and in the sense that "the maximal suspension of received notions" is the precondition of knowing what we must do—*whatever* this may be. Men of critical mind and good will, we everywhere, must unite, for we realize that we may very well have "nothing to lose" but our lives.

Notes

This paper was written in 1969 as a contribution to a *Festschrift* for Dorothy Lee. The *Festschrift* did not materialize, but *Reinventing Anthropology* is at least as good a place in which to honor her.

I wish to thank Dell Hymes for criticisms and suggestions based on an earlier draft of this paper.

1. To avoid misunderstandings, I want to stress that all authors referred to throughout this paper are referred to, not as private individuals, but as types construed from their conceptions of study as gleaned from some of their writings. I make no statement whatever concerning their personal interaction or lack of it with the people they study or report on.

Kurt H. Wolff · 116

2. If "hopiness" is the exclusively human as exemplified in the Hopi, its study does not exhaust the student's task, which also includes aspects of man he shares with other contents of the cosmos, because he is a "mixed phenomenon." In passing, it may be pointed out that this conception of man as a mixed phenomenon militates against the romanticization of "primitives" inasmuch as it invites attention, among other things, to dismal aspects of them and their conditions (cf. Wolff, 1964, especially pp. 244–46; for the examination of some community studies in regard to their adequacy to "exclusive" and "shared" human features, pp. 251–61).

3. Much in this paragraph was stimulated by comments on an earlier draft of this paper that I was fortunate to receive from Paul Riesman and Kewal Motwani, to whom I am grateful.

4. In "Rousseau, Father of Anthropology" (1963), Claude Lévi-Strauss celebrates Rosseau as, among other things, the father of what here is referred to as humanly radical anthropology. Also cf. Chomsky, 1966, pp. 91–93, n. 51.

5. This view is compatible with, if not a variant of, Stanley Diamond's position in "What History *Is*": "the spectacle of a people forming out of their natural, material, and spiritual resources, their 'fate' " (1964, p. 45).

6. A comparable process of disenchantment or degeneration may be found if we move from *ratio* to "race" in the eighteenth- and nineteenth-century use of this term: the former appears to be the etymon of the latter (Spitzer, 1948; Partridge, [1958] 1959, p. 546a, v. *race* [2]).

References

Arendt, Hannah. 1958. *The Human Condition*. Chicago: University of Chicago Press.
———. 1969. "Reflections on Violence." *New York Review of Books*, February 27, pp. 19–31.
Benedict, Ruth. 1948. "Anthropology and the Humanities." *American Anthropologist* 50: 585–93.
Bramson, Leon, and George W. Goethals, eds. 1964. *War: Studies from Psychology, Sociology, Anthropology*. New York: Basic Books.
Campbell, Joseph. 1960. "Primitive Man as Metaphysician." In Diamond, 1960, pp. 380–92.
Chomsky, Noam. 1966. *Cartesian Linguistics: A Chapter in the History of Rationalist Thought*. New York: Harper & Row, Publishers.
Diamond, Stanley, ed. 1960. *Culture in History: Essays in Honor of Paul Radin*. New York: Columbia University Press for Brandeis University.
———. 1964. "What History *Is*." In Manners, 1964, pp. 29–40.

———. 1967. "Primitive Society in its Many Dimensions." In Wolff *et al.*, 1967, pp. 21–30.

Freud, Sigmund. 1932. "Why War?" In Bramson and Goethals, 1964, pp. 71–80.

Gerth, H. H., and C. Wright Mills, trans. and eds. 1946. *From Max Weber: Essays in Sociology.* New York: Oxford University Press.

Gibson, Mickey. 1966. "The Image of Man in Social Anthropology." *Review of Existential Psychology and Psychiatry* 6: 51–62.

Gough, Kathleen. 1967. "New Proposals for Anthropologists." *Economic and Political Weekly* (Bombay), September 9, pp. 1653–58.

———. 1967. "World Revolution and the Science of Man." In Roszak, 1967, pp. 135–58.

———. 1968. "New Proposals for Anthropologists." *Current Anthropology* 9: 403–7.

Gould, Harold A. 1968. "New Proposals for Anthropologists: A Comment." *Economic and Political Weekly* (Bombay), April 27, pp. 682–85.

Gross, Llewellyn Z., ed. 1959. *Symposium on Sociological Theory.* Evanston, Ill.: Row, Peterson & Co.

Kleist, Heinrich von. [1810] n.d. "Über das Marionettentheater." *Werke*, Vol. 4. Pp. 133–41. Leipzig: Bibliographisches Institut.

———. [1941] 1947. "Essay on the Puppet Theater," trans. Eugene Jolas. *Partisan Review* 14: 67–72.

Lee, Dorothy. 1948. "Are Basic Needs Ultimate?" In Lee, 1959, pp. 70–77.

———. 1952. "The Religious Dimension of Human Experience." In Lee, 1959, pp. 162–74.

———. 1954. "Symbolization and Value." In Lee, 1959, pp. 78–88.

———. 1958. "What Kind of Freedom?" In Lee, 1959, pp. 53–58.

———. 1959. *Freedom and Culture.* Englewood Cliffs, N.J.: Prentice-Hall, Spectrum Books.

Lévi-Strauss. Claude. 1963. "Rousseau, Father of Anthropology." *UNESCO Courier* 16, No. 3: 10–14.

Mandelbaum, David G., ed. 1949. *Selected Writings of Edward Sapir in Language, Culture, and Personality.* Berkeley: University of California Press.

Manners, Robert A., ed. 1964. *Process and Pattern in Culture: Essays in Honor of Julian H. Steward.* Chicago: Aldine Press.

Mannheim, Karl. 1946. "Letter." In Wolff, 1959, pp. 571–72.

Partridge, Eric. [1958] 1959. *Origins: A Short Etymological Dictionary of Modern English.* New York: Macmillan Co.

Radin, Paul. 1920. *The Autobiography of a Winnebago Indian.* University of California Publications in American Archaeology and Ethnology, Vol. 16, pp. 381–473. Berkeley, Calif.

———, ed. 1926. *Crashing Thunder: The Autobiography of an American Indian.* New York: D. Appleton & Co. (Commercial publication of Radin, 1920.)

————. 1927. *Primitive Man as Philosopher*. Foreword by John Dewey. New York: D. Appleton & Co.

Redfield, Robert. 1960. "Thinker and Intellectual in Primitive Society." In Diamond, 1960, pp. 3–18.

Roszak, Theodore, ed. 1967. *The Dissenting Academy*. New York: Pantheon Books.

Rousseau, Jean-Jacques. 1755. A Discourse on the Origin and Foundations of Inequality among Men. In Rousseau, pp. 155–238.

————. [1755] 1941. *The Social Contract and Other Writings,* trans. G. D. H. Cole. London: J. M. Dent & Sons, Everyman's Library.

Sapir, Edward. 1919–22–24. "Culture, Genuine and Spurious." In Mandelbaum, 1949, pp. 308–31.

Spitzer, Leo. 1948. *"Ratio* > Race." *Essays in Historical Semantics.* New York: S. F. Vanni. Pp. 147–69.

Vidich, Arthur J., Joseph Bensman, and Maurice R. Stein, eds. 1964. *Reflections on Community Studies*. New York: John Wiley & Sons.

Weber, Max. 1918. "Science as a Vocation." In Gerth and Mills, 1946, pp. 129–56.

Wolff, Kurt H. 1959. "The Sociology of Knowledge and Sociological Theory." In Gross, 1959, pp. 567–602.

————. 1961. "On the Significance of Hannah Arendt's *The Human Condition for Sociology." Inquiry* 4: 67–106.

————. 1964. "Surrender and Community Study: The Study of Loma." In Vidich, Bensman, and Stein, 1964, pp. 233–63.

————. 1967. "Beginning: In Hegel and Today." In Wolff *et al.,* 1967, pp. 72–105.

Wolff, Kurt H., and Barrington Moore, Jr., with the assistance of Heinz Lubasz, Maurice R. Stein, E. V. Walter, eds. 1967. *The Critical Spirit: Essays in Honor of Herbert Marcuse*. Boston: Beacon Press.

Wolff, Robert Paul, Barrington Moore, Jr., and Herbert Marcuse. 1965. *A Critique of Pure Tolerance*. Boston: Beacon Press.

III · Studying Dominated Cultures

Skeletons in the Anthropological Closet

William S. Willis, Jr.

Do you not see how facts change their aspects, their meaning, under the pressure of oppression? So strong and widespread is this tendency for facts to be seen by the oppressed from a special point of view that I've called this a Metamorphosis of Facts.

—Richard Wright

ANTHROPOLOGY is in trouble, especially since World War II. The trouble arises essentially from the emergence of black and other colored peoples around the world. This emergence demands drastic changes in anthropology; even if such changes are made, the survival of anthropology is not ensured. To meet the crisis, we need to know the actual conditions in which anthropology has developed and to know what anthropology has been. This knowledge is only partially attained from the perspectives of white people (Maquet, 1964). We must also view anthropology from the perspectives of colored peoples, from Richard Wright's "frog perspectives" of looking upward from below (1957, pp. 27–29). When we do this, the importance of color erupts, and the world of E. B. Tylor, Franz Boas, and A. R. Radcliffe-Brown becomes articulated with the world of W. E. B. Du Bois, Richard Wright, and Frantz Fanon. The "frog perspectives" reveal surprising insights about anthropology, and these insights are the skeletons in the anthropological closet.

A MINIMAL DEFINITION OF
ANTHROPOLOGY

At the end of the fifteenth century, whites in Europe began expanding all over the world. They conquered, dominated, exploited, and humiliated colored peoples in America and Asia, in the South Seas, and in Africa. They established their rule by force and maintained it by force: this expansion is steeped in violence, bloodshed, and deceit. The military defeat of the colored world enhanced self-confidence among white people. This confidence and the pillage of the colored world brought new prosperity and power to the white world. White superiority in technology has been increased, and superiorities have developed in other institutions in white societies. On the other hand, white rule has brought death and distress to colored peoples; some colored societies have been destroyed, while others have been pathologically distorted. White rule has simplified the colored world by reducing its diversity and has complicated this world by creating these pathological distortions. It has simplified this world in another way: white rule has created a new generalization of worldwide inequality of colored peoples. One explanation for this inequality has been the postulation of innate biological inferiorities of colored peoples, and this explanation has achieved an uncritical acceptance that is remarkable (Worsley, 1964, pp. 1–49; Lévi-Strauss, 1966; Gough, 1968).

White rule with its color inequality is the context in which anthropology originated and flourished, and this context has shaped the development of anthropology. The formalization of anthropology in the nineteenth century coincided with the shift from "booty" colonialism to imperialism, which stressed profit from the control, exploitation, and preservation of cheap colored workers and consumers. The persistent distinction between "primitive" and "civilized" has been made falsely to coincide with the pervasive color bar. This distinction has ignored colored individuals and societies that satisfy the criteria of civilization; on the other hand, this distinction has ignored white individuals and societies not meeting these criteria. That these flaws existed was a major defect in the racist explanation.

The context of white rule provides a conception of anthropology that emphasizes what it actually has been. *To a considerable extent, anthropology has been the social science that studies dominated colored peoples—and their ancestors—living outside the boundaries of modern white societies.* This minimal definition of anthropology avoids key deficiencies in prevailing descriptions of anthropology as the science of man, as the science of culture, and as the science that employs field-work methodology. At best, these descriptions are aspirations of contemporary anthropologists seeking design in a historical development; at worst, they are ways to avoid admitting that anthropology has been an instrument of white rule. This minimal definition reveals the hyperbole in the assertion by anthropologists that their discipline is the science of man. Indeed, realization of the preoccupation with the dominated colored world should shake this self-image and reduce confidence in the "global" visions of anthropology. This minimal definition avoids the dilemma posed by nineteenth-century anthropologists, and many British social anthropologists, who did not subscribe theoretically to the concept of culture. Similarly, this definition does not exclude anthropologists, such as Fraser, Spencer, and Tylor, who did not engage in field work. Further, by recognizing the division of labor among the social sciences of the white world, this definition separates anthropology historically from sociology and other social sciences. These latter sciences deal diachronically and synchronically with sociocultural data of individuals and groups in white societies. In this context, sociology is seen as the study that concentrates on the poorer segments in white societies. Therefore, the tortuous distinction between human society and human culture becomes unnecessary in order to distinguish sociology from anthropology.

ANTHROPOLOGICAL
PERCEPTIONS AND PROJECTIONS

The concept of primitive is a construction created by white people from their racist perceptions of contemporary colored peoples. It is a sad fact that this concept has been accepted uncritically by many white anthropologists and used extensively in studying the colored world. Stanley Diamond is one of the few anthropologists to examine the primitive concept as a construction, but he does not then challenge the ethnographic validity of anthropology (1964). Since distortion by white rule preceded anthropologists into the colored world, it follows inexorably that no anthropologist has ever seen a real primitive. Many anthropologists disagree with this conclusion. For instance, even Marvin Harris declares that it is "undeniable" that primitive cultures have survived into the contemporary world (1968, p. 154). But I stress that the perceptions that anthropologists have of contemporary colored peoples as primitive peoples are mainly projections of two long-standing needs among white people. One need is to approve the conditions that have developed in white societies in the wake of capitalist industrialism and to approve the actions of white people as they dominated colored peoples around the world. The other need is to condemn some conditions in white societies and some aspects of white domination of the colored world.

In principle, the need for approval leads to negative perceptions of colored peoples and their cultures, whereas the need for disapproval leads to positive perceptions. In reality, these opposing needs coexist in most anthropologists, and contradictory perceptions are the rule. (The diachronic projection of this dilemma is analyzed by Diamond, 1964.) The emphasis on one kind of perception or the other varies among anthropologists, especially according to the century in which they live. The perceptions were more negative among nineteenth-century evolutionists than among Boasian anthropologists, although Tylor made some comparisons favorable to colored peoples, whereas even Boas believed that colored peoples were less sensitive to suffering, more cruel, and less forgiving than white people (Tylor, 1891, 1: 29, 31; Boas, 1928, pp. 223–24; Stocking, 1968a, pp. 110–32). Apart from the exploitation of some white people by other white people, white exploitation of colored peoples has been crucial to the prosperity of white societies. This cruciality is the key to the persistence in anthropology of negative perceptions of colored peoples, and it has ensured that positive perceptions have seldom, if ever, been devoid of some kind of negativism—for instance, paternalism. In addition, it helps explain the limited acceptance of positive perceptions among white people outside of anthropology. This cruciality has operated especially in perceptions of black people, since the exploitation of these people has been cumulatively more profitable—and more crushing—than the exploitation of other colored peoples. This being the case, a worldwide racial hierarchy has developed under white rule, in which black people are placed consistently at the bottom, and the black man has seldom been regarded as the "noble savage."

The projection of the needs of white people means that realities in the colored world are often distorted by anthropologists. Since the effects of white rule were often ignored in seeking aboriginal conditions, the subjective distortion by anthropologists has compounded the objective distortion created by colonialism and imperialism. This compounding of distortions within the racist organization of the modern world has prevented most—if not all—white anthropologists from seeing contemporary colored peoples as real human beings enmeshed in their intricate depths. Instead, anthropologists have constructed imaginary counter cultures to serve white needs and thereby obtained reaffirmations. In the nineteenth century, anthropologists used an explicit racist ideology to make colored peoples into different human beings than white people. Later, when scientific racism became less popular, anthropologists achieved almost the same result with the concepts of culture and of cultural relativism. The enculturation inherent in the culture concept was seen as having the power to mold most human beings into accepting and internalizing almost any kind of sociocultural arrangement. These arrangements, whatever their nature and political and economic basis, were then justified by the "dignity" that was accorded them by cultural relativism. Thus, colored peoples, having been construed as simply culturally different, could be manipulated as things in the "laboratory" of the colored world. Hence, Du Bois described the black man as the "football of anthropology" (1939, p. ix).

This sleight of hand, whatever the liberal intent involved in the culture concept, avoids the distress and misery of colored peoples, cringing and cursing at the aggressive cruelty of white people. This avoidance helps explain the lack of outrage that has prevailed in anthropology until recent years, and this lack of outrage made neutral inaction more tenable. This intellectual exploitation by anthropologists parallels the economic exploitation by imperialists. Indeed, anthropologists have been "penny" imperialists in making modest profits from studying dominated colored peoples (Deloria, 1969, pp. 97–100). Finally, the compounding of distortions suggests that ethnographic monographs are simply novels and that theoretical concepts are but daydreams.

Anthropologists have been worried about methodological inadequacy for a long time; they have usually seen this inadequacy in the same simple way. Both Tylor and Boas held that reporting by untrained persons led to erroneous concepts and that improved reporting by trained persons must precede theorizing (Tylor, [1889] 1931, pp. 464–71; Lowie, 1937, pp. 131–42). Many anthropologists have been unaware of subjective distortion via projected perceptions on the part of even trained persons, but hope now appears that intensive methodological re-examination will overcome this pitfall (cf. Scholte in this volume). The goal of Boasian anthropology to see a culture as its members see it was indeed an impossible dream, since the differences in specific enculturations precluded anthropologists from viewing the world now as an adult Crow Indian, now as an adult Blackfoot Indian. In recent years, Harris has insisted upon an outsider's ("etic") approach as a correction to the distortion inherent in an exclusive pursuit of the Boasian goal (1968, pp. 568–604). However, another kind of "inside view" at a different level of enculturation is possible, although difficult, and it is essential: the "inside view" that has arisen from being colored under white rule and is shared by Blackfoot, by Crow, and by Ibo alike. White anthropologists, guided by their colored colleagues, should be able to project their own humanity into this transtribal milieu created by white rule everywhere in the colored world and thereby achieve a new empathy with the oppressed. In addition, there is an equal need for anthropologists to reject the posture of neutral scientists and accept that social scientists cannot avoid "leaning to one side." Until these steps are taken, an observer's approach is premature and runs the dangerous risk of rationalizing white chauvinism.

More anthropologists now recognize the distortion by white rule; for instance, Charles Wagley now sees most Latin American Indians as peasants and not as primitives (1968, pp. 84–90). The tradition of ignoring white rule dies hard, as shown by Robert Redfield's belief that real primitive societies can be re-created after centuries of white rule (1953, pp. 48, 70–72). However, some anthropologists are beginning to reappraise themselves and the history of their discipline, and a major stimulus to this reappraisal is provided by liberation movements among contemporary colored peoples. This reappraisal should end in a general recognition of the ways in which white rule and its effects have been distorted in representations commonly found in the works of anthropologists.

THE USES OF
ANTHROPOLOGY (ABROAD)

That anthropology has been used for the benefit of white societies is shown by persistent efforts of anthropologists to aid imperialism (Foster, 1969, pp. 180–217).[1] Early, and throughout the nineteenth century, some British anthropologists tried to convince imperialists of their usefulness, stressing that knowledge of sociocultural differences among colored peoples was important to imperialist success. However, imperialists then felt too secure to need anthropologists. About the beginning of the twentieth century, the structure of imperialism began to change—and perhaps it began to weaken. Then imperialists responded to the pleas of anthropologists, and this response played a big role in the development and present organization of anthropology. In addition to collecting data on temporary assignments, some British anthropologists became permanent employees of imperialism as government anthropologists. Money from imperialists meant not only more anthropological societies and journals, but the establishment of anthropological institutes and the introduction of anthropology into many university curricula. There was a mutual understanding that anthropologists had one essential service as repayment: to provide data that might assist the imperialists.

The story in the United States is about the same. The vast majority of anthropologists in the late nineteenth and early twentieth centuries concentrated on North American Indians, defeated victims of white expansion now placed in reservations. A tiny minority of anthropologists turned to Pacific islands acquired after the Spanish-American War. United States anthropologists generally gave less assistance to imperialism than British anthropologists, since the United States was not then a major imperialist power, but World War II reversed this situation as the United States replaced Britain as the imperialist behemoth. Acquiring big grants from government and private foundations, anthropologists flocked to Latin America, then to Asia, and finally to Africa. They were enthusiastically following the new imperialist priorities of the United States government. In addition to collecting sociocultural data on colored peoples, they served as diplomats, most often in an unofficial capacity, and as public relations experts. Moreover, an indeterminate number engaged in espionage. Finally, some anthropologists cooperated with the United States government in its relocation program that placed the Nisei in detention camps during World War II. This enthusiasm at mid-century for aiding imperialism contrasts with the diminished enthusiasm appearing among some British anthropologists, but it coincides neatly with the shifting imperialist roles of the United States and Britain.

Until mid-century, most anthropologists accepted the inevitability of the imperialist system even when they did not accept its legitimacy and permanency. Whatever their attitudes, they certainly operated within the framework of imperialism, and they did not agitate for the overthrow of imperialism. Indeed, nineteenth-century evolutionists and then British social anthropologists subscribed to imperialism as the "white man's burden." Since colored cultures were seen as lacking competitive innovative potential, the Boasian anthropologists also subscribed—although more covertly—to imperialism as the "white man's burden." Perhaps the acceptance of this function of imperialism is one deep reason for diffusionism in twentieth-century anthropology (see below, pages 137–38), which also served as a way of masking from liberal social scientists their underlying evolutionary biases. Moreover, numerous twentieth-century anthropologists were satisfied with their participation in one-shot, piecemeal projects sponsored by their governments in the colored world. Their satisfaction in particular was in conflict with some theoretical concepts that prevailed generally in anthropology—namely, the continuity of culture, the interrelationship of culture, and the integration of culture. George Foster has concluded that the goal of "efficient and humane" administrations was one main reason for employing anthropologists in the British colonies of Africa (1969, p. 193). In addition to the significant precedence of efficiency, making imperialism a more efficient and humane system was merely a desire for an imperialism without atrocities. This aim was consistent with the aim of imperialism: after initial subjugation via terrorization, imperialists wished to preserve colored peoples as producers and consumers. Since nineteenth-century anthropologists were racists (cf. Harris, 1968; Haller, 1971), they had no quarrel with the color bar. Indeed, the main annoyance of twentieth-century anthropologists with imperialism was that they were relegated to being technicians, devoid of initial decision-making functions.

Toward the mid-century, some anthropologists began condemning the color bar. Then there was some advocacy of more sharing of the wealth of the colored world with colored peoples, and this new posture was consistent with scientific antiracism. It was also consistent with new imperialist aims adopted to parry the threat posed by colored liberation movements. Put another way, as these anthropologists were subscribing to a policy of partnership between colored and white peoples in the colored world, the imperialists were adopting a similar policy in order to salvage white economic interests in a revolutionary colored world. But these anthropologists and the imperialists were out of step with colored nationalists: Malinowski offered partnership via peaceful negotiation, whereas Fanon demanded replacement via violence (Harris, 1968, pp. 556–58; Fanon, 1968, pp. 35–41, 46).

Anthropologists in the United States are now losing their enthusiasm for aiding imperialism. This diminished enthusiasm might mean that the militant opposition of the United States government to intensified colored liberation movements has made clearer the moral bankruptcy of serving imperialism. This interpretation flatters anthropologists and augurs well for the future of their profession. But is this the whole story? Perhaps the diminished enthusiasm is a convenient way to avoid painful confrontations of political liberals, and sometimes even radicals, with anthropology operating under the umbrella of white rule.

THE USES OF
ANTHROPOLOGY (AT HOME)

To anthropologists, the study of dominated colored peoples was not merely exoticism nor even only service to imperialism. The ultimate aim of anthropology was the improvement of white societies everywhere. Indeed, anthropologists have boldly proposed solutions to social problems in white societies. I will give attention first to Tylor, the so-called "father" of British anthropology, who has been praised by Boasian anthropologists, and then to Boas, the so-called "father" of modern anthropology in the United States. In doing so, I will consider the scientific functions of their views on racism.

TYLOR AND THE USE OF
SCIENTIFIC RACISM

To Tylor, anthropology was relevant to many problems besetting white societies in the late nineteenth century. Tylor believed that reconstructing white history provided general laws that were essential for guiding sociocultural change in white societies. Hence, he explained that anthropology was an "important practical guide to the understanding of the present and the shaping of the future" and that the study of "savages and old nations [is] to learn the laws that under new circumstances are working for good or ill in our own development." That Tylor was not equally concerned with providing similar assistance to contemporary colored peoples is shown by his candid admission that "for matters of practical life these people may be nothing to us."

Since progress in white societies meant eliminating some old customs as well as adding new ones, Tylor was greatly concerned with the persistence of survivals in these societies. These survivals were seen as resembling sociocultural patterns found in the colored world. Tylor advocated the selective elimination of these survivals; specifically, he advocated the elimination of those that failed the logical and functional tests of anticlerical middle-class Englishmen like himself. Thus, Tylor declared that the "practical office of ethnography [is] to make known . . . what is but time-honoured superstition in the garb of modern knowledge [and] to mark these out for destruction." These survivals were widespread in white societies and impeded the clear thinking that was necessary for progress. Indeed, survivals were especially dangerous since they might suddenly develop into active revivals, as had happened with witchcraft and spiritualism (Tylor, 1891, 1: 2, 16–17, 24, 159; 2: 445, 453; Harris, 1968: pp. 137, 140–79). That Tylor's anthropology was a frank intellectual exploitation of colored peoples for the benefit of white people is shown by his arrogant couplet: "Theologians all to expose, 'Tis the mission of Primitive Man" (Kardiner and Preble, 1963, p. 68).

The danger from religious survivals was one main reason that Tylor studied the animistic religions of colored peoples, Christianity being predominantly animistic. He declared that it was "with a sense of attempting an investigation which bears very closely on the current theology of our own day, that I have set myself to examine systematically, among the lower races, the development of Animism" (Tylor, 1891, 1: 23). This danger gave to Tylor a sense of urgency toward his work, since he believed that the "oft-closed gates of discovery and reform stand open at their widest [in late nineteenth-century England]. How long these good days may last, we can not tell" (Tylor, 1891, 2: 452). Indeed, this urgency was an additional reason for using sociocultural data from the colored world, especially "innocuous" sports, games, and popular sayings. Tylor hoped that their apparent remoteness and insignificance would make his advocacy of reform, especially religious reform, more palatable (Tylor, 1891, 1: 23, 158; 2: 452). Advocating religious reform was necessary and even courageous in view of the resurgence of the theological fundamentalism that had occurred earlier in the century. Nevertheless, it was political timidity in approaching social problems; it avoided the crucial problem of the private ownership of the means of production and provided an alternative prescription to the Marxian solution via class struggle. Finally, Tylor's preoccupation with trivia to avoid provocation helped establish a dissemblance that prevails too frequently in twentieth-century anthropology.

The desire to improve white societies guided decisively Tylor's research strategy and was one main reason for the importance of historical reconstruction. It was another main reason for using so much sociocultural data from the colored world, since white peasants and ancient whites provided insufficient evidence for early white history and for the general progressive interpretation of human cultural history which Tylor was concerned to establish as a basis for his critical analysis of his own culture.

This led to the comparative method, and to equating contemporary colored peoples with white ancestors. This equation required the concept of psychic unity as modified by scientific racism: colored peoples shared only the "more elementary processes" with white people. This version of psychic unity established *just the right amount of pertinency* of colored peoples. Since it established the humanity of colored peoples, the comparability of their customs was acceptable; indeed, the need to fix this comparability sometimes led Tylor to make statements that approximate the scientific antiracism of Boasian anthropology. Nevertheless, scientific racism was predominant in Tylor's thinking. Indeed, scientific racism was essential to Tylor in order to establish the mental inferiority of colored peoples and thereby explain the progress of the white world over the colored world. That Tylor's scientific racism had this heuristic origin does not deny that racism had important uses as a justification for imperialism as well as for class exploitation and national aggrandizement.

BOAS AND THE USE OF "SCIENTIFIC ANTIRACISM"

The improvement of white societies was as much the aim of Boas as it was of Tylor, although the mature Boas rejected the comparative method, general laws, and scientific racism while adopting a more thoroughgoing cultural relativism (cf. Harris, 1968). Believing that anthropology illuminated contemporary social processes, Boas prescribed solutions to many social problems in the white world (Boas, 1928, [1925] 1945). Since he posed as a neutral scientist, these prescriptions are masked in his scholarly publications beneath an apolitical surface. For instance, anti-Marxism is behind the emphasis on irrational customs among colored peoples and the incongruity between their technology and sociology. These prescriptions are explicit in his popular writings; but anthropologists read his *Race, Language, and Culture* and not his *Anthropology and Modern Life*.

The basic prescription of Boas was the extension of individual freedom, unrestricted by the "shackles" of tradition and the merging of individuals into social categories (Boas, 1938a)—hence the high premium on deviant individuals and the opposition to class, racial, and religious discrimination. Socio-economic changes were necessary to allow a degree of social participation in white societies that matched the participation that had been observed in small communities in the colored world. Moreover, these changes were necessary to provide more constructive leisure and to provide much more than existed in these small colored communities (Boas, 1928, pp. 218–20). The need for these socio-economic changes became so compelling that the elderly Boas, despite his long-standing anti-Marxism, moved ever closer to the communist movement (Rohner, 1969, p. 296).

Since individual freedom was at odds with the nationalism in the white world, Boas became increasingly anti-nationalistic and advocated pluralism within white societies and pacific internationalism among them. Indeed, his ideal prescription was world federation as the ultimate extension of the in-group ethic of brotherhood, but he compromised for the more practical federation of white nations (Boas, 1928, pp. 97–101). This compromise is an old dream of white Europe: the dream of Napoleon, Kaiser Wilhelm, Hitler, and De Gaulle. Imagine what this white federation would do to nationalist aspirations in the colored world! Thus, instead of calling for the liberation of colored peoples living in imperialist colonies in 1919, Boas saw the "true solution of the colonial problem" in a direct and kindly governance by an international organization of the nation states (1919). Finally, pluralism and pacific internationalism are distinctive of a segment of Jews living in Europe and the United States in the nineteenth and twentieth centuries.

In the Boasian strategy, diversity among colored peoples permitted an objective appraisal of white societies, and this objectivity was crucial for the rational solutions of social problems. In 1939, Boas stated that "conditions of life fundamentally different from our own can help us to obtain a freer view of our own lives and of our own life problems" (1940, p. vi). The desire for objectivity is another main reason for field work, since emancipation from ethnocentric blindness was obtained by immersion in an unfamiliar colored society. This meant that field work was for the immediate benefit of anthropologists and the ultimate benefit of white societies. It was not an experience to help colored peoples. On the contrary, there was one aspect of field work that was dangerous to colored peoples living under white rule: except for protecting the anonymity of individual informants, anthropologists were expected to report fully to the white world on what they had seen and heard while visiting among these colored peoples. Moreover, conversion to colored life-styles was not a goal of field work, since anthropologists were expected to return to white societies and live again as middle-class white people. Some Boasians were opposed to full participation in the lives of colored peoples while engaged in field work; thus, Alexander Goldenweiser believed that such participation should be only "on the surface," while Paul Radin considered it a "delusion and a snare" (Paul, 1953, p. 438). Melville Herskovits' position coincided with the worldwide racial hierarchy established by white rule when he admitted that "going native" might be feasible in the South Seas but that it was "neither possible nor of benefit among West African Negroes and their New World descendants." Indeed, his reason was similar to one frequently advanced by segregationists in the Southern United States: the failure to observe "caste" distinctions will offend blacks and subject the white anthropologist to ridicule (Herskovits, 1937, pp. 326–27). Finally, field work is always a calculated experience, and it is sometimes superficial and transient as well. Therefore, it probably does not provide emancipation from ethnocentrism, and it might confirm cultural bias.

Diversity among colored peoples constituted alternative answers to some social problems in white societies. However, the Boasians seldom, if ever, advocated that white societies borrow the particular answers found in the colored world.[2] Instead, the Boasians used this diversity to show that socio-cultural change was feasible in white societies. To do this, they needed to show that cultural behaviors were not determined by biology. Since they were committed to change, they needed to show that change was both rapid and widespread. These needs account for the Boasian preoccupation with human nature vis-à-vis cultural conditioning and for pushing cultural conditioning as far as possible, as against an immutable human nature. These needs help explain why scientific antiracism replaced the racial determinism of nineteenth-century anthropology, and account for the emphasis on cultural relativism. These needs were crucial in establishing the centrality of the culture concept in Boasian anthropology. Finally, these needs required the adoption of an anti-evolutionist position in order to deny also the inevitability of sociocultural patterns, and so that psychic unity should become a perfunctory concept, similarities in culture being minimized.

This strategy posed a considerable dilemma. Enculturation led to the belief in the tenacity of culture—hence Herskovits' African survivals among New World blacks. Logically, the tenacity of culture placed unacceptable limits on the feasibility and rapidity of sociocultural change, although less than scientific racism. Therefore, the need arose to restrict the power of enculturation in order to provide more leeway for change. The first step was to show that extensive and rapid change did occur, and this was done by diffusionism and historical reconstruction. The second step was to show how change occurred. This was done by the shift to studying individuals in relation to their societies, thereby underscoring the inevitability of deviation. Inventors as deviant individuals produced new cultural traits and opened the way to sociocultural change via individual free will. This is one main reason for the antideterminism in Boasian anthropology.

Since colored solutions were seldom recommended to

white people, diffusionist studies were concerned with the transmission of culture among colored peoples. Acculturation studies were similarly concerned with the impact of white culture on colored peoples, however incompletely this impact was conceived. *The transmission of culture from colored peoples to white people was largely ignored, especially when studying North American Indians.* Indeed, the main exception to this generalization was the study of the diffusion of Chinese cultural traits into the white world. To Boasians, improvement in white societies depended overwhelmingly—if not completely—on deviant individuals who were white people. The implication is clear: white societies deserved something better from their deviant individuals than was offered in the colored world.

Historically, scientific antiracism was *not* conceived primarily to defend colored peoples. As applied to these peoples, scientific antiracism has been really misnamed. This intellectual tradition increasingly minimized—but never completely excluded—the possible influence of racial factors on the sociocultural behavior of colored peoples, especially the black people. In fact, Boas consistently entertained the hypothesis that the smaller average brain size of black people precluded them from producing as many "men of highest genius as in the other races." There is a need to recognize that scientific antiracism has been a heuristic device, sometimes used by nineteenth-century evolutionists, but especially by Boasians, to increase the pertinency of colored sociocultural patterns. Also, Boasians used scientific antiracism to attack racial discrimination among white groups, especially Nordicism and anti-Semitism. Intermingling, as well as internal variation, overlapping, and instability of physical traits among white populations in Europe and the United States, was used to establish the irrelevancy of race as an explanation for the differing sociocultural patterns existing among these white groups. The minimal role assigned to race in regard to sociocultural patterns among colored peoples was used to establish *a fortiori*, as it were, the irrelevancy of racial explanations in regard to white groups. Hence, Boas concluded, "there is no need of entering into a discussion of alleged hereditary differences in the mental characteristics of various branches of the white race" (1911, p. 268; 1934, p. 34; 1938b, pp. 135, 226–31, 238, 240). Since Boasians were mostly European Jews, they suffered anti-Semitic discriminations first in Europe and then in the United States, and they were outraged by Hitler's atrocities. Indeed, Boas emigrated from Germany to esccape anti-Semitism, and he admitted that most scientific antiracism was an "effort to combat the anti-Semitic drift" in the white world (Rohner, 1969, p. 295; Boas, 1925, p. 21). Since most native-born white Protestant anthropologists were racist and anti-Semitic, scientific antiracism was used by Boasians as an intellectual weapon in their struggle for the domination of anthropology in the United States, especially against those anthropologists centered in Washington (Stocking, 1969a, pp. 270–307).[3]

Scientific antiracism was concerned only secondarily with colored peoples. Yet it was strategic to use them and their sociocultural patterns—another exploitation of colored peoples for the benefit of white people. This helps explain why Herskovits' initial work with New World blacks dealt with problems in physical anthropology: it was designed to confirm antiracist conclusions in the physical anthropology of Boas, who had dealt mainly with white immigrants (Herskovits, 1928). It helps explain the detachment of many Boasians from the civil rights movement—even Herskovits as late as 1951 excluded the ending of discrimination against New World blacks as a goal of Afro-American studies (Herskovits, 1951, p. 32). Scientific antiracism has shifted more to colored peoples in recent years. This shift coincides with the muting of racism between white groups under the shock of Hitler's crimes and the remarkable economic and political advances of white Catholics and Jews. It also coincides with the increasing threat from black and other colored liberation movements.

Scientific antiracism does not mean the absence of color prejudice and discrimination. "No inherent connection between race, language, and culture" often becomes a mere catechism, devoid of personal commitment. Malinowski's secret diary shows that scientific antiracism can coexist with vicious color antipathies and suggests that color prejudice is more prevalent than white anthropologists admit (Malinowski, 1967). Hence, the futile attempt to explain away Malinowski's racism as well as the silence and even hostility to this revealing diary (Firth, 1967, Introduction; Hogbin, 1968, p. 575; Stocking, 1968b). Manuscripts of other dead white anthropologists and life histories of the few black anthropologists will reveal additional evidence. These revelations should not be surprising: white anthropologists are members of racist societies, and color prejudice and discrimination must be incorporated into any history of anthropology. This evil helps explain the lily-white composition of anthropology, the lack of recruitment of colored anthropologists until very recently—and continuing resistance to any special effort to do so. Even Herskovits did not develop a program to train United States blacks as professional anthropologists and utilize them in African and Afro-American research. It helps explain why Boasians so largely avoided the study of United States blacks (Willis, 1970). In view of the long-standing partisanship for white interests, color prejudice is one main reason for the present outcry against some forms of "relevant" anthropology.

With more information about field experiences, it becomes clear that anthropologists have not practiced what they preached, and color prejudice is one reason why. Malinowski exaggerated his separation from white people while in the field as well as his participation in Melanesian life. His periodic vacations were as much an escape from annoying colored people as an escape from aggravating customs; in fact, he confessed a "need to run away from the niggers" (Malinowski, 1967, p. 167). A double standard clearly pervaded field procedures. For instance, Boas robbed graves for skeletons and commandeered Indian prisoners for anthropometric measurements (Rohner, 1969). These deceptions and bullying tactics would have been unthinkable toward white people in New York City. Color prejudice in even Boas (so hard to believe!) becomes a distinct possibility.

The tiresome professions of friendship for colored informants now become suspect. Real friends are not treated in such unjust ways. Moreover, the concealment of color prejudice now appears as one reason for the puzzling secrecy of anthropologists about their field experiences. Indeed, their discussions of methodological difficulties concentrate on intercultural problems and neglect interracial problems (Freilich, 1970; Pelto, 1970). This concealment is shortsighted: white anthropologists cannot operate successfully among angry and suspicious colored peoples unless racial arrogance is purged, and the first step is candor.

ANTHROPOLOGY AS AN ENTERTAINMENT

That anthropology has been for the benefit of white societies is also shown by its use to provide education and recreation for white people, and these functions were prominent in Boasian anthropology. Ethnographic museums served these functions earlier than that of teaching, and the demand for the possessions of colored peoples played a crucial role in the development of the profession and its structure in university curricula. Recreation has been at least as important as serious education, perhaps more so. This is obviously true of museums, especially on idle Sundays. Thus, Boas declared that the "museum as a resort for popular entertainment must not be underrated" and estimated that the "majority [of museum visitors] do [*sic*] not want anything beyond entertainment" (1907, p. 1). Since anthropologists have generally presented harmless "aboriginal" customs while avoiding the frightful contemporary realities, recreation has been prominent in the teaching of anthropology, especially at the undergraduate level. This entertainment of white people at the expense of colored peoples has been widened as the teaching of anthropology now occurs in primary and secondary schools as well as on television. Anthropology for pleasure also applies to many professional anthropologists: the distant colored world is often perceived as an exotic place offering temporary escape from the familiarity and monotony of middle-class society in the white world. In the nineteenth century, considerable satisfaction with middle-class society existed among anthropologists; therefore, most anthropologists then were able to ease their discontent by reading accounts of the faraway colored world. However, disenchantment with middle-class society deepened in the twentieth century, and this disenchantment is one main reason for the popularity of field work in twentieth-century anthropology. In this way, field work is a kind of tourism—West Indian nationalists now decry tourism as whorism.

ANTHROPOLOGY AND THE ASPIRATIONS OF THE COLORED WORLD

Bona fide political freedom through viable national consolidation and rapid economic development is the main nationalist aspiration in the colored world. There is need then for strong governments, but the persisting Boasian premium on individual freedom and the position of anti-nationalism oppose the development of such governments. Moreover, strong governments and violence go together. Terrible violence is predictable in the emergence of colored peoples, since this emergence is comparable to white expansion around the world and dwarfs modern revolutions in white societies. Some colored nationalists now advocate violence as a positive good, politically and psychologically; and violence has been the stock-in-trade of imperialists (Fanon, 1968, pp. 35–106). However, anthropologists have been generally committed to progress via reason and opposed to sociocultural change through violence. Since the vast majority of anthropologists are white people, they are especially opposed to colored peoples using violence to overthrow white rule. Despite fascination with tribal warfare, anthropologists neglect brutal conquests by white people and desperate resistance by colored peoples. If understanding leads to social control, then anthropologists are derelict in not studying violent interracial conflicts. Moreover, they have missed a decisive chance to help repair the damaged self-image of colored peoples, for there is heroism in the struggle against white rule.

Some important theoretical concepts in twentieth-century anthropology are inimical to the nationalist aspirations of the colored world. The ahistoricism of functionalism simply ignores the very existence of white rule and thereby absolves white people of their crimes. The model of the isolated society does more than evade: by stressing sociocultural differences, it facilitates the imperialist policy of divide and rule. In addition, it provides colored peoples with an easy excuse for failure: they can readily point to insurmountable tribal differences. In conjunction with the search for aboriginal cultures, this model precludes the discovery of sociocultural links wider than tribal allegiance and more realistic than Pan-Africanism. Similarly, functional ahistoricism precludes the discovery of wider links in a past more meaningful than near-forgotten medieval kingdoms. Yet the discovery of these wider links is essential to viable national consolidation and rapid economic development. To an African nationalist, tribalism is heresy.

There is now some recognition that cultural relativism is logically incompatible with advocacy of sociocultural change and that it complements Lord Hailey's "Indirect

Rule" (Bidney, 1967; Hartung, 1954; Northrup, 1955; Kluckhohn, 1955). Significantly, the initial impetus to this recognition was the dilemma posed by Hitler's Germany and the Soviet Union, and not the evil of imperialism. Since relativism is applied only to "aboriginal" customs, it advises colored peoples to preserve those customs that contributed to initial defeat and subsequent exploitation. It is really advising them to preserve the crippling distortions that white rule has made of traditional customs. By applying relativism in this way, new sociocultural patterns that arise in urban settings have been frequently ignored as worthless; like imperialists, anthropologists have condemned these new patterns and warned against "detribalization." Hence, relativism defines the good life for colored peoples differently than for white people, and the good colored man is the man of the bush. But the demand for liberation and modernization originates among the new men of the towns. Colored nationalists want so much more than pleasant words about traditional customs; indeed, they are suspicious that white men bearing these words are condemning colored peoples to eternal poverty and powerlessness (Wright, 1957, p. 93; Fanon, 1968, p. 224). In revolutionary situations, the realities of fighting for liberation and modernization supersede the opiate in negritude.

Most anthropologists are at best committed only to gradual sociocultural change. Since institutions are considered interrelated, anthropologists believe that innovations may have unforeseen consequences, some of which could be harmful. This being the case, prolonged investigation must precede innovation. The meaning of "taking social factors into consideration" is clear: wisdom is to proceed slowly (Foster, 1969, pp. 73–89, 108). Is the anticipation of harm from unforeseen consequences so justified? If harm is in disturbing traditional patterns, then I remind that these patterns are already crippling and pathological distortions of an older way of life that countenanced defeat. If harm is in upsetting colored peoples psychologically, then I remind that nothing has upset colored peoples more than white rule. Moreover, trauma is an inevitable concomitant to change. Perhaps the real harm is in disturbing imperialist domination and thereby upsetting white people.

It is clear that anthropology postpones the end of imperialism to the distant future. But there is something more: a strong bias against sociocultural change is persistent in anthropology, and some concepts defend the status quo (Myrdal, 1956, 171–73). This defense is now recognized in the equilibrium model of functionalism Harris, 1968, pp. 516–17). The model of the isolated society locates the causes of change inside artificial boundaries of small communities and not in the worldwide system of capitalist imperialism. This misplacement of causation in less significant conditions means that anthropology has provided an inadequate guide to change, and inadequacy is no way to achieve anything. Moreover, the premium on individualism means that sociocultural change is dependent upon previous changes in the thinking of individual persons. Even if valid, the priority on changes in individuals has been historically a conservative doctrine. Finally, the Boasian position that culture is complex and that causation is fortuitous means that causes cannot be found and that the search for them is a useless procedure. The failure to seek and to find causes means the absence of any scientific basis for a program of sociocultural change.

THE END OF ANTHROPOLOGY?

The end of anthropology is an old fear. Anthropologists have always been afraid of the disappearance of "aboriginal" cultures in the wake of depopulation and sociocultural change, and this fear helps explain the priority of data-collection over theory and the recent shift to studying development (Worsley, 1970). Ironically, anthropologists have feared the increasing specialization that has arisen with the expansion of ethnographic information (Mead, 1964, p. 7). Finally, they have feared totalitarian repression in white societies (Linton, 1936, p. 490). These fears have been unrealistic. Many colored populations are increasing, and their enlarged sociocultural inventories can now be studied from the point of view of development. Increased specialization has not so far disturbed the formal organization of anthropology. Finally, totalitarian success in white societies is not incompatible with the study of dominated colored peoples. Yet there is now real reason to fear for the future of anthropology.

The end of imperialism is a probable contingency. Its end will mean the end of what has been anthropology, since this anthropology has been based on the subordination of colored peoples. Imperialist domination has now been overthrown in some parts of the colored world, and it has been weakened in other parts. In many places, anthropologists are having a hard time with the new outward anger and suspicion of colored peoples. Moreover, most conventional anthropological preoccupations are irrelevant in solving the increasing poverty in the colored world, and colored nationalists in the early years of independence have turned to economists for help (Onwichi and Wolfe, 1966; Myrdal, 1968, pp. 8–10). It seems now that colored nationalists are becoming disenchanted with the economists. Will they now turn to the anthropologists? Whatever happens, anthropologists no longer have the colored world to themselves.

There is still some hope for anthropology. The present disarray among colored peoples and the still immense power of the imperialists mean that the end of imperialism is only a probability. Even if the end of imperialism is certain, it will not end quickly nor at the same time around the world. Even if imperialism does not end everywhere, new conditions in the colored world mean that anthropologists cannot proceed in the old way. It is time for anthropologists to make drastic changes. If they make these changes, then perhaps a new kind of anthropology can survive in a new world in which colored peoples enjoy bona fide freedom and equality.

WHAT IS TO BE DONE?

Urban ethnography is one crucial proving ground for forging this new kind of anthropology. White anthropologists must get along with black and other colored peoples of the ghettos, and these peoples are now angry, literate, and politicized. Moreover, they are no longer awed by the mystique of the white man. The new terrorism in the ghetto is not only dangerous but plays upon deep-seated fears and guilt feelings, the legacy of slavery and slave revolts. It is clear that color prejudice has no place in the ghetto. If anthropologists succeed in the ghetto, then they can probably succeed with colored peoples anywhere. This requires a new kind of anthropologist, one for whom old standards of professionalism are impediments.

The ghetto will not tolerate only white anthropologists. There is an immediate need to develop active and creative programs to recruit, train, and employ many young black and other colored anthropologists. If these programs are successful, then the new colored anthropologists will become articulated with the ghetto poor. They will not be so isolated in white academia as the few colored anthropologists of the past and therefore not as derivative in their anthropology. The numerical increase and the new articulation will encourage colored anthropologists to initiate distinctive approaches (Jones, 1970).[4] Perhaps they and white anthropologists working together in the ghetto can achieve a new identity in political ideology that can overcome the divisiveness of the uniform of color. But white anthropologists must make the first moves, and one such move is to refrain from any kind of demand for ideological subservience. Perhaps even then, this new kind of identity is a pipe dream.

Successful urban ethnographers will become a separate force in anthropology, distinctive in personality, race, and especially politics. Sociopolitical significance will become the main criterion in selecting research problems. Out of the crucible of the ghetto, a new perspective of black people as real human beings will emerge. This new perspective is consistent with the emergence of a new kind of partisanship, one that advances the political demands of the ghetto poor. Since urban blacks are structurally the most revolutionary segment in United States society, political radicalism must then replace the older liberalism. If this is not the path of urban ethnography, then it will wither away, sooner rather than later.

Some innovations are already occurring. Urban ethnographers are realizing that the holistic concept of culture, developed from the model of the isolated "primitive" society, does not fit ghetto sociocultural institutions. They are realizing that field work must be changed—frankness instead of deception, courtesy instead of insult, and participation in partisan politics instead of only in pathetic ceremonies. The ghetto demand for continuous accountability of outside institutions requires periodic publications while the ethnographers are still living in the ghetto instead of their publishing only when safely home from the field. (In actual fact, urban ethnographers are never safely home, since the ghetto is so near academia.) Finally, self-censorship replaces the conceit of total investigation: urban ethnographers must agree readily to the boundaries of investigation as decided by ghetto nationalists (Valentine, 1970).

What else is to be done? Anthropologists can revaluate the development of their profession from new perspectives, exposing skeletons as I have attempted.[5] Using ethnographic data already collected, exposing skeletons can emphasize the total impact of white rule on colored peoples (Fried, 1967, pp. 52–107).[6] Like Harris, they can seek more adequate theories of sociocultural change and more rigorous methodologies. These two endeavors are closely linked. Exposing skeletons provides clues for developing better theories and methods, and both endeavors derive crucial momentum from urban ethnography and from the ferment in the colored world. Exposing skeletons has one immediate advantage: it supplies effective propaganda to colored nationalists in their fight against white rule. In view of the atrociousness of this rule, exposing skeletons for this kind of propaganda poses no great threat to objectivity. However, developing better theories of sociocultural change has the potential advantage of enabling colored peoples to improve their levels of living as they move toward bona fide freedom and equality. This advantage is only a potentiality, since colored peoples might reject these theories for valid or invalid reasons. In any case, anthropologists must not try to force their theories upon colored peoples. At the same time, they must not let appeasement of colored peoples influence the development of theory, except to the extent that the goal of anthropology is the end of poverty and powerlessness among colored peoples. In correcting white middle-class bias, urban ethnographers must not romanticize ghetto patterns; instead, they must evaluate these patterns by the criterion of this goal of anthropology. Finally, anthropologists must give no credence to the vicious theory that poor people are responsible for their poverty.

Urban ethnography, exposing skeletons, and developing better theories are less expensive than the old field trips to distant colored peoples. Therefore, big grants from the United States government and the foundations are not needed. Also, there is less need to get involved in international politics. All this means more freedom to pursue the goal of anthropology, a goal inimical to the present foreign policy of the United States. One final point: urban ethnography, exposing skeletons, and better theories must incorporate a new sensitivity toward black and other colored peoples everywhere. This sensitivity will make anthropology more acceptable among colored peoples, even in Africa and Asia; but more importantly, it will help colored peoples accept themselves as equal human beings and thereby help undo the damage of centuries of white rule.

Notes

This is a small part of a larger investigation in which I am now engaged. For essential help, I thank Morton H. Fried, Robert F. Murphy, and my students: Shirley Achor, Joi Anne Garrett, Ashley Marable, Maria Luisa Urdaneta, and David M. White. However, the responsibility for any infelicities of style or errors in content is mine.

1. The evidence for this discussion of anthropologists and imperialism can be found in Foster (1969). However, my interpretations are not necessarily identical with those of Foster.
2. It is possible that polygyny has been recommended by some male anthropologists.
3. The "power struggle" is one of the major research problems in the history of United States anthropology, and anti-Semitism has yet to disappear entirely from anthropology even at some leading institutions.
4. Jones presents a stimulating discussion of some problems facing black anthropologists.
5. The skeleton of racism in nineteenth-century anthropology has been exposed by Harris (1968) and Stocking (1968a). Morton H. Fried is revealing racism in twentieth-century anthropology in *The Study of Anthropology* (1972).
6. Fried exposes some fictions about small egalitarian societies.

References

Bidney, David. 1967. *Theoretical Anthropology.* Introduction to 2nd ed. New York: Schocken Books.
Boas, Franz. 1907. "Some Principles of Museum Administration." *Science* 25: 921–33.
———. 1911. *The Mind of Primitive Man.* New York: Macmillan Co.
———. 1919. "Colonies and the Peace Conference." *The Nation* 108: 247–49.
———. [1925] 1945. "What Is a Race?" in *Race and Democratic Society,* ed. Ernst Boas, New York: J. J. Augustin. Pp. 20–27.
———. 1928. *Anthropology and Modern Life.* New York: W. W. Norton & Co.
———. 1934. "Race." *Encyclopaedia of the Social Sciences,* Vol. 13, pp. 25–36.
———. 1938a. "An Anthropologist's Credo." *The Nation* 147: 201–4.
———. 1938b. *The Mind of Primitive Man.* Rev. ed. New York: Free Press.

———. 1940. *Race, Language, and Culture.* New York: Macmillan Co.

Deloria, Vine, Jr. 1969. *Custer Died for Your Sins: An Indian Manifesto.* New York: Macmillan Co.

Diamond, Stanley. 1964. *Primitive Views of the World.* Introduction. New York: Columbia University Press.

Du Bois, W. E. B. 1939. *Black Folk: Then and Now.* New York: Henry Holt.

Fanon, Frantz. 1968. *The Wretched of the Earth.* New York: Grove Press.

Firth, Raymond. 1967. Introduction to *A Diary in the Strict Sense of the Term,* by Bronislaw Malinowski. New York: Harcourt, Brace & World.

Foster, George M. 1969. *Applied Anthropology.* Boston: Little, Brown & Co.

Freilich, Morris, ed. 1970. *Marginal Natives: Anthropologists at Work.* New York: Harper & Row, Publishers.

Fried, Morton H. 1967. *The Evolution of Political Society.* New York: Random House.

———. *The Study of Anthropology.* New York: Thomas Y. Crowell.

Gough, Kathleen. 1968. "New Proposals for Anthropologists." *Current Anthropology* 9: 403–7.

Haller, John S., Jr. 1971. "Race and the Concept of Progress in Nineteenth-Century American Ethnology." *American Anthropologist* 73, No. 3: 710–24.

Harris, Marvin. 1968. *The Rise of Anthropological Theory: A History of Theories of Culture.* New York: Thomas Y. Crowell Co.

Hartung, Frank. 1954. "Cultural Relativity and Moral Judgments." *Philosophy of Science* 21: 118–26.

Herskovits, Melville J. 1928. *The American Negro: A Study in Racial Crossing.* New York: Alfred A. Knopf.

———. 1937. *Life in a Haitian Valley.* New York: Alfred A. Knopf.

———. 1951. "The Present Status and Needs of Afro-American Research." In *The New World Negro,* ed. Frances S. Herskovits. Bloomington: Indiana University Press. Pp. 23–41.

Hogbin, Ian. 1968. Review of *A Diary in the Strict Sense of the Term,* by Bronislaw Malinowski. *American Anthropologist* 70: 575.

Jones, Delmos J. 1970. "Toward a Native Anthropology." *Human Organization* 29: 251–59.

Kardiner, Abram, and Edward Preble. 1963. *They Studied Man.* New York: New American Library.

Kluckhohn, Clyde. 1955. "Ethical Relativity: Sic et Non." *Journal of Philosophy* 52: 663–77.

Lévi-Strauss, Claude. 1966. "Anthropology: Its Achievement and Future." *Current Anthropology* 7: 124–27.

Linton, Ralph. 1936. *The Study of Man.* New York: D. Appleton-Century Co.

Lowie, Robert H. 1937. *The History of Ethnological Theory.* New York: Farrar & Rinehart.

Malinowski, Bronislaw. 1967. *A Diary in the Strict Sense of the Term.* New York: Harcourt, Brace & World.

Maquet, Jacques J. 1964. "Objectivity in Anthropology." *Current Anthropology* 5: 47–55.

Mead, Margaret. 1964. *Anthropology: A Human Science.* Princeton, N.J.: D. Van Nostrand Co.

Myrdal, Gunnar. 1956. *An International Economy.* New York, Harper & Brothers.

————. 1968. *Asian Drama.* Vol. 1. New York: Pantheon Books.

Northrup, F. S. 1955. "Ethical Relativity in the Light of Legal Science." *Journal of Philosophy* 52: 649–62.

Onwichi, P. Chike, and Alvin W. Wolfe. 1966. "The Place of Anthropology in the Future of Africa." *Human Organization* 25: 93–95.

Paul, Benjamin D. 1953. "Interview Techniques and Field Relationships." In *Anthropology Today,* ed. A. L. Kroeber. Chicago: University of Chicago Press. Pp. 430–51.

Pelto, Pertti J. 1970. *Anthropological Research: The Structure of Inquiry.* New York: Harper & Row, Publishers.

Redfield, Robert. 1953. *The Primitive World and Its Transformations.* Ithaca, N.Y.: Cornell University Press.

Rohner, Ronald P., ed. 1969. *The Ethnography of Franz Boas.* Chicago: University of Chicago Press.

Stocking, George W., Jr. 1968a. *Race, Culture, and Evolution.* New York: Free Press.

————. 1968b. "Empathy and Antipathy in the Heart of Darkness: An Essay Review of Malinowski's Field Studies." *Journal of the History of the Behavioral Sciences* 4: 189–94.

Tylor, E. B. [1889] 1931. "On a Method of Investigating the Development of Institutions: Applied to Laws of Marriage and Descent." In *Source Book of Anthropology,* eds. A. L. Kroeber and T. T. Waterman. New York: Harcourt, Brace & Co. Pp. 464–71.

————. 1891. *Primitive Culture.* 3rd ed. 2 vols. London: John Murray.

Valentine, Charles A. and Betty Lou. 1970. "Making the Scene, Digging the Action, and Telling It Like It Is: Anthropologists at Work in a Dark Ghetto." In *Afro-American Anthropology: Contemporary Perspectives,* eds. Norman E. Whitten, Jr., and John F. Szwed. New York: Free Press. Pp. 403–18.

Wagley, Charles. 1968. *The Latin American Tradition.* New York: Columbia University Press.

Willis, William S., Jr. 1970. "Anthropology and Negroes on the Southern Colonial Frontier." In *The Black Experience in America: Selected Essays,* eds. James C. Curtis and Lewis L. Gould. Austin: University of Texas Press. Pp. 33–50.

Worsley, Peter. 1964. *The Third World.* Chicago: University of Chicago Press.

————. 1970. "The End of Anthropology?" *Transactions of the Sixth World Congress of Sociology* 3: 121–29.

Wright, Richard. 1957. *White Man, Listen!* Garden City, N.Y.: Doubleday & Co.

An American Anthropological Dilemma: The Politics of Afro-American Culture

John F. Szwed

"Harlem was never like this!"
—Mantan Moreland, in the film King of the Zombies

I

It is more than obvious that anthropology has from its beginnings had some pleasant advantages not available to the other social sciences. Working in distant places, largely with nonliterate peoples, anthropologists have seldom had to face their informants as critics of their published work; and having luxuriated in a sparsely populated discipline, they have often been able to avoid even the critical assessments of colleagues who have worked with the same people. In this comfortable situation anthropology developed smoothly, free to move at its own rate, with subjects of its own choice. Perhaps only in times of national upheaval, such as periods of economic instability or war, have its purposes and findings been seriously questioned. When answers to urgent problems are sought in the society as a whole, anthropology comes under pressure to supply answers, to speak to its time and its people's problems, to be, as they say, relevant. Moreover, it is difficult to avoid these challenges, for the anthropological perspective has already had its effects on American thinking; and reciprocally, the country's particular concerns have had their effects on the kinds of problems that anthropology undertakes and the manner in which it undertakes them.

Unfortunately, it is precisely when societal needs are most pressing that the difficulties of doing research and communicating its results are most pronounced. In recent days, such problems have produced an anxiety and desperation that fill professional meetings and shadow research projects. There is concern with spies among scientists, with malign forces behind research projects. In addition, the exacerbated class, racial, sexual, and political divisions in American society have become confused with the more vulgar facts of professorial competition, so that critical areas of concern are even more difficult to approach. Faced with such strains, some have a tendency to "ghettoize" research and teaching and to demand that anthropologists work only with their "own" people;[1] others, to withdraw in despair from research altogether; and still others, to become mere propagandists.

But in addition to spies, hidden motives, and withdrawal from research, there is loose in anthropology a sense of purposelessness, a lack of direction, and even a growing skepticism about the vision of man that anthropology developed. It is thus a need to restore purpose and personal commitment to anthropology that has lately prompted a variety of impassioned suggestions, perhaps the most appealing of which is a call for anthropology to become involved in the defense of the oppressed peoples of the world and to abandon illusory scientific objectivity: in short, a demand for anthropology to undertake committed, partisan research (Wolf and Jorgensen, 1970; Willis in this book). This is a serious proposal and it deserves serious consideration. As a beginning, I would like to briefly review in this essay one area of anthropological work of great contemporary relevance—the study of Afro-American peoples in the United

States—and to argue that in at least this area just such a proposal has in fact been accepted and acted upon for the last forty years, but with rather dismal results. And I will further suggest that in these respects cultural anthropology's contemporary problems are even more complex and plaguing than we have dared think.

II

We can begin by observing that American anthropologists have done almost no research in the usual sense among Afro-Americans in the United States. Why? Several commentators have addressed themselves to this subject and have agreed that the "impure," "acculturated" nature of American blacks made them poor subjects for a cultural anthropology originally bent on reconstructing the ethnographic past of isolated societies (Mintz, 1970, pp. 13–14; Willis, 1970, pp. 35–36; Fischer, 1969). Less charitable but equally important is the fact that Afro-Americans were geographically too close and of too low status for professional prestige in American society. William S. Willis, Jr. (1970, p. 36), calls attention to other political constraints on the study of Afro-Americans, especially the uncomfortable fit of imported ex-slaves to the usual anthropological image of a proper subject—that is, natives defeated and dominated by imperialistic enterprise on their home soil. Ann Fischer (1969), in addition, suggested that field work among lower-class Afro-Americans lacks the exoticism that so appeals to anthropologists. Further, she argued that love of informant and anthropologist for each other is a prerequisite for sound anthropological research and one that is difficult to achieve among Afro-Americans. Quoting Margaret Mead, she insisted that it would be impossible for an anthropologist to convince ghetto residents that he has any respect for their way of life. However, there seem to me to be more fundamental factors restricting and circumscribing this research, factors discoverable first in the beginnings of American anthropology, in the ideas of Franz Boas during the early 1900s.

Boas was of course the most influential professional anthropologist of his time, and he also became the chief scientific spokesman on the subject of race and its social implications. Viewing race as a statistical range of a given population, he argued for cultural influences on physique and introduced new evidence on the plasticity of the human organism. In addition, by insisting on the study of particular cultures as functional responses to universal needs, rather than as unique expressions of "racial genius," Boas created an intellectual framework and a body of evidence to support the central premise lying behind all of his work: the necessity for keeping race and culture conceptually distinct.

When Boas encountered arguments for racial determination of culture, he chose to oppose them by using the ethnographic facts of exotic societies such as the Eskimo and by placing these facts in a relativistic framework. But Afro-Americans—certainly the chief object of racist speculation at the time—seem not to have appeared to him to provide good evidence for this kind of argument, as illustrated by a comment in *The Mind of Primitive Man* ([1938] 1963, p. 240):

> The traits of the American Negroes are adequately explained on the basis of his history and social status. The tearing-away from the African soil and the consequent complete loss of the old standards of life, which were replaced by the dependency of slavery and by all that it entailed, followed by a period of disorganization and by a severe economic struggle against heavy odds, are sufficient to explain the inferiority of the status of the race, without falling back upon the theory of hereditary inferiority.

Similarly, when at W. E. B. Du Bois's request Boas addressed the graduating class at Atlanta University in 1906, he urged black students to become aware of the many cultural accomplishments of Africa and directed the class to confront those who argued for the innate inferiority of Afro-Americans with this reply:

> . . . that the burden of proof lies with them, that the past history of your race does not sustain their statement, but rather gives you encouragement. . . . say that you have set out to recover for the colored people the strength that was their own before they set foot on the shores of this continent.[2]

Though this was an astonishingly strong statement of negritude for a white *or* a black man of the period, it is also remarkable in its evasion of the issue of the existence and nature of an Afro-American culture.

Boas' political liberalism is evident in his involvement with Du Bois on many ventures, such as the founding of the National Association for the Advancement of Colored People in 1910, in which he became part of the opposition to the accommodationist strategies of Booker T. Washington. Boas had completed numerous anthropometric studies of both whites and blacks, and having discovered the non-exclusive and overlapping nature of racial statistics, he argued eloquently against the reliability of racial identity as a means of predicting cultural capacity. But when he dealt with Afro-American culture, he was equivocal. It is as if the "hard" data of physical anthropology misled Boas into confusing race and culture in a manner opposite to that of the usual confusion of his era—in other words, the overlapping statistics of the physical features of the two races together with overlapping scores on intelligence tests may have led Boas to infer that blacks, as a group, simply "overlapped" white American culture, if only imperfectly.[3]

Much the same argument appears in Boas' student Ruth Benedict's *Race: Science and Politics* ([1940] 1959, pp. 86–87):

> Their patterns of political, economic, and artistic behavior were forgotten—even the languages they had spoken in Africa. Like the poor whites of the South, they gathered to-

gether instead for fervent Christian revivalist camp meetings; they sang the hymns the poor whites sang, and if they sang them better and invented countless variations of great poignancy, nevertheless the old forms which they had achieved in Africa were forgotten. Conditions of slavery in America were so drastic that this loss is not to be wondered at. The slaves on any one plantation had come from tribes speaking mutually unintelligible languages, and with mutually unfamiliar arts of life; they had been herded together like cattle in slave ships and sold at the block in a strange and frightening world. They were worked hard on the plantations. It is no wonder that their owners remarked on their lack of any cultural achievements; the mistake they made was to interpret the degradation of the slave trade as if it were an innate and all-time characteristic of the American Negro. The Negro race has proud cultural achievements, but for very good reasons they were not spread before our eyes in America.

In *Patterns of Culture* ([1934] 1959, p. 26), too, she argued that in Northern cities as well Afro-Americans had come to "approximate in detail that [culture] of whites in the same cities."

Meanwhile, other anthropologists, such as Ashley Montagu (e.g. 1942), attempted to exorcise both the folk and the scientific concepts of race. And as such arguments developed over the years, there was a tendency for scientists to deny the existence of *both* racial differences in capacity *and* any significant cultural differences between members of the two different "races." It is important to reiterate that these anthropologists arrived at their conclusions, not on the basis of ethical neutralism, but through a deep commitment to the need for social change. Indeed, it was in their very zeal to refute genetic racism for general audiences and to demonstrate a universal capacity for culture that they argued that Afro-Americans shared essentially the same culture as white Americans, and where they differed, the differences were to be accounted for exclusively as the result of environmental deprivation or cultural "stripping," but certainly not as the result of any normal cultural processes.

Launched and reinforced by these anthropological conceptions, sociologists took up their own version of the same arguments; they soon went much further, bolstering their position with statistical surveys, while still lacking any ethnographically based insights into black life. The chief work in sociology was done at the University of Chicago, where Robert E. Park and E. Franklin Frazier developed what Charles Valentine (1968, pp. 20–24) has called the "pejorative tradition": the use of social pathologists' data to describe black communities as disorganized and culturally nonadaptive. Frazier (1934, p. 194), for example, in commenting on the significance of Afro-American culture, said:

> To be sure, when one undertakes the study of the Negro he discovers a great poverty of traditions and patterns of behavior that exercise any real influence on the formation of the Negro's personality and conduct. If . . . the most striking thing about the Chinese is their deep culture, the most conspicuous thing about the Negro is his lack of a culture.

But perhaps the key contribution of the sociological approach was the work done by Gunnar Myrdal and his associates, who developed their arguments on the basis of an extensive examination of the degree of damage done to black Americans by racism and slavery. Typical was the section of *An American Dilemma* that deals with the Negro community: Myrdal argued (1944, p. 928) that the Negro is "characteristically American" and is "not proud of those things in which he differs from the white American." Following this, he lists features of Negro life which are a "distorted development, or a pathological condition, of the general American culture." The list includes the "emotionalism" of their churches, the "insufficiency and unwholesomeness" of their recreational activity, "the plethora of Negro sociable organizations," "the cultivation of the arts to the neglect of other fields," and so on (pp. 928–29).

One might have thought that such views were doomed to easy refutation, since lower-class Afro-Americans continued to manifest patterns of behavior in many domains of activity which were distinctively their own, with a historical and comparative basis in Africa and elsewhere in the Americas. However, these "culturally different" behaviors (i.e., different from white middle-class culture) continued to be treated as evidence of deviance, as social pathology, as failures on the part of individual black people in the face of oppression; and if these behaviors became recognized as patterned and normative, they were nonetheless treated as part of a deficit culture,[4] a kind of negative culture existing in the absence of a real one. Afro-American culture was—in Ralph Ellison's phrase—nothing more than the sum of its brutalization (quoted in Bennett, 1971, p. 56).

By the 1950s and 1960s such views had assumed the status of orthodoxy, and were nowhere better summarized than in Glazer and Moynihan's *Beyond the Melting Pot,* where it is said that in America the Negro "has no values and culture to guard and protect."[5] If there was some grumbling over Glazer and Moynihan's straightforwardness, there was, and is, very little objection to, say, Kenneth B. Clark's (1965) portrayal of Harlem as nothing more than a cultural hell; or Christopher Lasch's (1969, pp. 125–26) easy dismissal of "ghetto culture" as "thin" and chiefly characterized by "despair and self-hatred"; or Michael Harrington's (1968, p. 80) or Lee Rainwater's (1968, pp. 41–42) reading of black expressive culture as self-destructive or detrimental to development; or Grier and Cobb's (1968, pp. 114–29) suggestion that black dialect and speech events are evidence of mental disorder among black males; or Kardiner and Ovesey's (1962, pp. 333–34) diagnosis of black dancing as a product of pure rage.

If prophets of deficit culture were simply unaware of a counter position on these matters, they might be dismissed as naive and ignorant. But a quick scanning of the literature will show that everyone from Frazier forward has known of the kind of distinctive culture argument mounted by Melville J. Herskovits (see below), and most feel compelled to dismiss Herskovits out of hand. Stanley Elkins, for example, in *Slavery,* after wondering "how it was ever possible that all this [West African] native resourcefulness and vitality could have been brought to such a point of utter stultification in America," dismisses Herskovits' position as concerned with "esoteric vestiges of a suspiciously circumstantial nature" (1959, pp. 93, 107). Milton Gordon is more systematic in his dismissal of Herskovits and Afro-American culture, when, in *Assimilation in American Life* (1964, p. 179), he curiously divides ethnic culture into *intrinsic* ("essential and vital") elements such as ethics, religion, music, language, and history, and *extrinsic* (situationally adaptive) elements such as dress, "manner," "emotional expression," and dialect. In this way, he can suggest that Yiddish and Italian as well as Judaism and Catholicism are intrinsic elements for Jews and Italians, while black dialects and the "frenzy" and "semicoherence" of fundamentalist black churches are extrinsic. ("Were the argot . . . to disappear, nothing significant for Negro self-regard as a group or the Negro's sense of ethnic history and identity would be violated" [Gordon, 1964, p. 79]. One could, alas, go on at length extending this list, but in all the diagnosis is the same: lower-class Afro-Americans have no distinctive culture or subculture of their own and what they do have is a nonsupportive or pathological version of "mainstream" American culture. Only on the question of remedy is there disagreement.

Again, the terms of this matter are just those in which anthropologists have some expertise, and it is surprising to see how much has been left to laymen and other social scientists. The fact is that most anthropologists seem themselves to have accepted the conventional wisdom on these matters, especially as it was an unpleasant experience to enter into a field of inquiry in which laymen had preceded them and had given racist interpretations to the same kinds of data the anthropologist is interested in. Anthropologists also avoided the issue of gathering or analyzing data on other ethnic groups that might challenge the assumption of a melting-pot society, except where the "culturally different" groups could be shown to have behaviors clearly positive in white middle-class terms. Consequently, we have dozens of articles in anthropological journals on Japanese-Americans, whose enterprise, thrift, and cleanliness are stressed.

Thus, in the main, anthropologists and other social scientists have taken a very special position toward Afro-Americans: they have either ignored them, or, abandoning their most sacred dogmas—value-free methods and the necessity for firsthand empirical evidence—they have proceeded to pronounce on black people in a thoroughly nonrelativistic manner, presumably excusing their departure in the name of social justice. Politicos to the contrary, research in black communities by white or black social scientists has hardly begun, unless, of course, one is willing to grant ethnographic status to studies of "culture at a distance," reminiscent for all the world of those carried out on the enemy in World War II.[6]

If the pathologists' approach were simply a matter of professional in-fighting, it could perhaps be ignored. But I think that the evidence is that the noncultural and deviance orientations of the social sciences toward Afro-Americans have taken hold broadly across the society, and that it is this view that is hardening as the racial stresses of the society increase. Witness the wide popularity of the notion of "cultural deprivation" among politicians, educators, and social workers by which, in an irony cruel to anthropology, material poverty is grossly confused with ideological poverty, culture now being given a remarkably restricted definition. (One recent study suggested that multipurpose room use in crowded slum housing prevents residents from developing "normal" middle-class kinship relations; or, in other words, house type determines kinship patterns!)

Thus, black Americans, having survived the cruel discrediting of slavers and segregationists and the curiously ambivalent stereotypes of abolitionists, must now confront a new bizarre reading of their lives and traditions. It is startling to realize that in the following quotation Ralph Ellison (1966, pp. 129–30) is objecting not to the crude renderings of traditional racists, but to those of the contemporary left:

> Many of those who write of Negro life today seem to assume that as long as their hearts are in the right place they can be as arbitrary as they wish in their formulations. . . . They have made of the no man's land created by segregation a territory for infantile self-expression and intellectual anarchy. They write as though Negro life exists only in light of their belated regard, and they publish interpretations of Negro experience which would not hold true of their own or for any other form of human life.
>
> Here the basic unity of human experience that assures us of some possibility of empathetic and symbolic identification with those of other backgrounds is blasted in the interest of specious political and philosophical conceits. Prefabricated Negroes are sketched on sheets of paper and superimposed upon the Negro community; then when someone thrusts his head through the page and yells, "Watch out there, Jack, there's people living under here," they are shocked and indignant.

But perhaps most disturbing is the fact that many black political activists now find it increasingly impossible to press their case for social justice without evoking this social-science fiction monster. Now the jargons of the social worker, the psychiatrist, and the anthropologist have been correctly divined as something, at last, to which the white middle class will respond (Szasz, 1970, pp. 67–77). (Let no one say that the War on Poverty produced no results!)

III

Yet there is an alternative view of Afro-Americans to that of the pathologists, one which begins by examining the distinctive culture history of black people in the United States. It appeared almost forty years ago in the folkloristics of Boas' student Zora Neale Hurston (e.g., 1935), and later in the research of linguist Lorenzo D. Turner (1949), themselves black Americans. And Paul Radin ([1945] 1969, pp. vii–xiii) and Hortense Powdermaker (1939), too, followed the cultural tradition of American ethnography in their studies of Afro-Americans. But it was Melville J. Herskovits who undertook the most serious and systematic study of Afro-American culture in the United States. After years of field work in Haiti, Trinidad, Brazil, and West Africa, Herskovits formulated a comprehensive view on the culture history of Afro-Americans in the United States, which he published in 1941 as *The Myth of the Negro Past*. In this work he chose to oppose the consensus of virtually all of the white and black intellectuals and laymen of his time by presenting an outline of the African cultural background of American blacks and by developing a theory of cultural change that would argue for the persistence and continuity of some aspects of this culture.

Soon after publication of this book, however, interests in anthropology shifted heavily toward the ahistoricism of social structural studies, and as a result the weakest features of the book were dwelled upon critically[7] while its strengths were ignored. And, most unfortunately, Herskovits' *handling* of cultural facts was assailed, while the *facts* themselves were discarded. With hindsight, however, one senses that perhaps the primary objection to *The Myth* stemmed from the fear that Herskovits' conclusions might be used by racists and the ethnocentrically inclined to build a case against integration and social equality. Perhaps if a person with lesser antiracism and civil rights credentials than Herskovits had attempted this work, he might have been labeled a racist.[8]

It appears certain that Herskovits was fully aware of the political implications of Afro-American cultural studies. Early in his career he had rejected the possibility of any African-derived or independent Negro cultural reality (1925, pp. 359–60). Later, once he began to work in what he called the "cultural laboratory" of comparative Afro-American cultures across the New World and reversed his argument ([1930] 1966, p. 6), he seems to have been concerned with the impact that his data might have on a white society which already asserted racial-cultural differences from a folk perspective of genetic racism; consequently he chose to present his findings in such an oblique manner as to put the white American reader on the defensive. First, he tried to show that Afro-American cultural behaviors had an honorable and, from the standpoint of cultural relativism, valid basis in African culture; and second, he argued that American whites had already been acculturated to the point that they had unknowingly absorbed a great deal of African culture, even in some of the most sacred of white American domains (Herskovits, 1935, pp. 92–96). But by the time Herskovits wrote *The Myth* there was no questioning his political assumptions and goals: they were ([1941] 1958, p. 32), (1) "to give the Negro an appreciation of his past" and "to endow him with the confidence in his own position in this country and in the world which he must have," and (2) "to influence opinion in general concerning Negro abilities and potentialities, and thus contribute to a lessening of interracial tensions."

After publication of *The Myth*, a few scholars such as the black historian Carter Woodson welcomed it as a great breakthrough, but most of them followed E. Franklin Frazier in rejecting it as misguided or exaggerated. Ironically, now, thirty years later, there is something of a drift of black ideology in the direction of Herskovits' thesis, so that those who reject the cultural approach must again at least address themselves to Herskovits. Now, for example, arguing that contemporary Afro-American culture is nothing more than a culture of poverty, Christopher Lasch (1969, pp. 121–22) must complain that "unfortunately the whole question of African survivals has now become involved in the politics of cultural nationalism, and it is hard to argue against Herskovits without being accused of wishing to subvert the cultural identity of black people."

Over the last thirty years no one has dared to attempt a

work of the scope of Herskovits's, but scattered through a half-dozen disciplines there is a body of Afro-American cultural data that has been accumulating nonetheless. Though there is less interest in African origins, we now have a sizable literature that provides evidence for the existence of the following distinctive Afro-American cultural domains: aesthetics, including plastic arts, crafts, architecture, music, verbal lore, and dance[9]; speech (Dillard, 1972; Dalby, 1970; Reisman, 1970a; Abrahams, 1970b; Kochman, Stewart, 1970; Labov, Cohen, Robins, and Lewis, 1968); oral history (Stuckey, 1969, 1971; Montell, 1970; Levine, 1969; Blauner, 1970); religion (Marks, 1969); and the vaguely defined but vitally important areas of style and interpersonal behavior (Lomax, 1968; Ellison, 1966; Reisman, 1970b). The literature on the slave and the slavery experience has been renewed as improved data on the slave trade appeared (Curtin, 1969; Harding, 1969; Bryce-Laporte, 1968). Even though thoroughly muddled by lack of facts, the issue of Afro-American kinship is also being reopened (Hannerz, 1969). And the lessons learned among other Afro-Americans in the Caribbean and South America are assuming fresh meaning for the United States, especially as Cubans and Puerto Ricans begin to become major revitalization forces in urban centers (Bastide, 1967; Marks, 1970; Narvaez, 1970). There are even hints that Afro-American data may offer new insights for the understanding of Africa itself (Greenberg, 1957; Thompson, 1970a, b).

None of these Afro-American cultural studies is satisfactorily comprehensive, but seen together they offer a substantively alternative view of black people in America. First, they all assert that from the beginnings of slavery Afro-Americans exercised the capacity to perpetuate and create means of comprehending and dealing with the natural and social worlds surrounding them—they were culture bearers and creators as well as receivers and learners. In other words, although slavery, poverty, and racism have severely circumscribed the exercise of this capacity, even sometimes driving it underground, these constraints can in no way be seen as the sufficient cause of Afro-American behavior. All of this is borne out by both the continuities and the discontinuities that exist between black people in North and South America and in Africa. Nor do these studies see Afro-American culture as being exclusively negative, "thin," nonsupportive, or "reactive." Far from seeing black Americans as having "no values and culture to guard and protect," they cumulatively suggest that in some respects Afro-Americans have guarded and protected their culture better than any other ethnic or national group in the United States. In fact, they additionally argue that blacks have elaborated some cultural domains in such a rich and vital manner that they have been the source of a huge portion of unacknowledged American culture. Finally, these studies indicate that one cannot set about describing and measuring black cultural incapacity, pathology, and deprivation by simply crudely comparing and contrasting black and white behaviors and institutions to see how closely black approximates white (whites forever the "control group"), suspending, all the while, a century of Euro-American criticisms of the pathology of Western behaviors and institutions.

But there are counterarguments raised in anthropology against the notion that Afro-Americans have a distinct cultural heritage and a distinct subculture. Briefly, the first is that the harshness of the slavery experience wiped out all vestiges of African culture and that that experience, followed by segregation and racism, acted to create a deficit or poverty culture. One need only note in objection here that *no one* arguing this point has used any quantity of primary data on slavery or the slave trade; in addition, very few undertaking this argument have been familiar enough with West African cultures to be able to recognize such cultural elements in operation in the New World if they saw them. It is significant that the most serious and competent critic of the African survival thesis, M. G. Smith, set standards for such research that virtually assured that no proof could be established. One such was that "traits re-garded as evidence of the persistence of African cultural forms must be formally peculiar and distinct from the customs or institutions characteristic of all other cultural groups within the society of their location" (1960, p. 45). In other words, when in doubt, assume that Africans always turn Euro-American.

Less sophisticated counterarguments simply say that if one suggests that any African cultural elements did survive slavery, or became transmuted, then one is saying that slavery was really not such a bad experience after all; or that if African cultural traditions did persist, they were of a superficial nature (music, folk tales, language, religion, and the like) and not substantive—that is, institutional. Thus, the obsessive concern with the nature of the black family.

The problem with these arguments is clearly evident. At root, they suffer from a lack of ethnographic data on Afro-Americans and an ignorance of existing historical materials on slavery and racial contact in the American South and elsewhere, as well as a refusal to effectively use the second basic tool of cultural and social anthropology: the comparative method. Secondly, they are unabashedly ethnocentric, not only in their bias toward institutions and institutional relationships at the expense of culture, but also in their preoccupation with questions of black-white interaction with no concern whatsoever for black-black interaction.

IV

But, having heard all of this, some will insist that there have nonetheless been gains from politically committed research which stressed the destructive aspects of being black in a society built on racist principles. Doubtless such research has played an important role in "unmasking" the social structure of the United States and in demonstrating the massive human costs of such a society. This should not be gainsaid. But even at this pragmatic level there is reason to doubt the long-run utility of the exclusivity of this approach and the wholesale selection and distortion of Afro-American life which accompanied it.

To take an example, virtually all of the race-relations literature of the last thirty years argued that the way out of the American racial dilemma was clear: integration must be implemented in all areas and changes effected in the life-style of the poor and black—toward white middle-class "enrichment" aspirations.[10] It was on the crest of this re-search and its policy actualization that a counter movement toward separation and withdrawal from integration began among black people. Many (e.g. Tumin, 1969, pp. 256–59) have argued that this was clearly the result of a distrust of white people's willingness to make basic changes in Amer-ica, and certainly such distrust is massively justified. But might it not also have been that a significant number of black people—especially those poor who were on the re-ceiving end of the change process—also began to tire of the stigmatization and forced change that were attached to these programs? Is it not possible that the rejection of one's whole life-style was simply too dear a price to pay, espe-cially when the reasons for doing so were so spurious and the rewards so remote? Was the rejection of whites from posi-tions of leadership in the civil rights movement merely a matter of a wish to assert black control, or was it in addition a move to resist unreasonable and irrelevant white cultural models of change? The answers to these questions are frankly not certain, for social scientists have not been used to doing this kind of thinking.

But whatever the causes, we are now faced with a situation in which interracial politics are intertwined with social science such that current changes in political strategy and style instantly reverberate through social science. Now research begins to appear that "confirms" that racial separation rather than integration is *the* answer. In this liminal confusion of failure and inadequacy some social scientists call for an end to all research with the black poor, asserting that we "know enough." It would be one thing to recognize that long-distance studies of degradation have begun literally to exhaust their subject, but it is altogether another to arrogantly acclaim a sufficiency of knowledge and at the same time to assume a posture of heroic self-denial! Other social scientists call for a moratorium on Afro-American research by whites in order to establish black hegemony in the field with the expectation that black social scientists' work will be more satisfactory than that of the whites. But thus far most black social scientists have bought the same methods and conceptual approaches which rendered their white nonbrothers incapable of dealing with a major portion of lower-class Afro-American life and culture. (One need only contrast the treatment of black culture by black artists and fiction writers with that of black social scientists to sense the inadequacy.)

Yet another variant of such arguments has it that *any* research on black people—even that of the highest quality done by either black or white with the best of intentions—may be used to further oppress and control with greater efficiency, and thus should not be done. But this is a simplistic and dreamlike argument, one that presupposes the possibility of controlling information about the "black community" and that ignores the everyday interracial contacts through which information passes. It ignores, too, the fact that *where a people lacks sufficient information about another people, the blanks are filled in by fantasy*—as indeed has been happening these many years in social science. Finally, it denies the possibility of research ever being of use to its subjects; even though this appears to have typically been the case of Afro-Americans in the United States, anthropology has been of some importance to Afro-Americans elsewhere in the Americas where it has been pursued in less restricted, politically limited fashion.[11]

V

I have been arguing by example that a politicized and partisan approach to anthropology is not in and of itself an answer to the kinds of dilemmas in which anthropology finds itself today. In short, mere commitment, advocacy, and explicit rejection of injustice are by no means sufficient to make anthropology relevant to the problems of the contemporary world. *In the absence of descriptive honesty and imagination, such a position serves as a smoke screen for simple failure and inadequacy.* Worse, perhaps, in the Afro-American case, the radical position comes to little more than that of the reactionaries.

Political positions are easy to take in research, especially when the causes are popular among one's peers, but it is another thing to be aware of how one's research relates to one's cause. It was my intention here to show how a veneer of partisanship has allowed shabby research on Afro-Americans in the United States to persist in the face of a continuing racial crisis. Afro-Americans as people, as human, cultural creators, have been sacrificed to serve as causes, as ciphers in an anthropology of pathos.

In my insisting on a cultural approach as a specific corrective to the Afro-American dilemma in anthropology, it should be clear that I am not calling for a period of "benign neglect" of the hard realities of American social structure and racial separation—only a scoundrel or a fool could ignore the country's need to deal swiftly and directly with the poverty and injustices brought on by its racial policies and attitudes. Yet at the same time I would insist that social scientists have also escaped this task by merely preaching, pointing fingers, and using "racism" in a simple-minded explanatory fashion—this, instead of defining and describing racism and the mechanisms and institutions which maintain it, delineating the nature and transmission

of racist attitudes, or showing the broad linkages that underlie and support racist thought and policy (Marx, 1970, pp.
82–84).[12]

For those who would suggest that a concern for Afro-
American culture is an evasion of the real issue—racism
and the larger American social structure—I can only insist
that the ascription of culturelessness and partial humanness
to Afro-American peoples is basic to both racism and the
social system. In exploring the order and kind of influence
of Afro-American culture on the various black and white
populations of America, we not only move a step closer to
the working of "the system," but we also lay a basis for
attaching a humanistic conception of man to efforts at
social and economic change.

I am asking, then, that we "desegregate" anthropology,
giving Afro-Americans the best we can as observers of
human cultural capacity and achievement. If we treat Afro-
Americans without political posturing, the hidden assumptions and the smuggled motives, I am convinced that their
cultural accomplishments will not need the spurious de-
fenses and the eleventh-hour apologies that we have been
in the habit of offering in the name of research. Lastly, I
am of course not arguing that commitment and political
partisanship have no place in social science, merely that
the links between advocacy and research be clearly articulated, related, and executed. If this is done, it will not be
necessary to belabor the obvious—that partisanship and
bias are by no means the same thing.

Beyond all of this, anthropologists should be concerned
with the need for what Alan Lomax calls *cultural equity*,
the rights of a people to maintain, choose, and create
cultural alternatives. To do this, it is necessary to develop
and make known the kind of descriptive and historical
materials which anthropologists can provide, especially to
those colonized peoples who have for so long been cut off
from their own histories and traditions, and from each
other. It should be remembered that cultural stripping was

by no means limited to slavery days, but still continues in
the classroom and on television, as well as in anthropological journals—in fact, wherever a narrow vision of man
and his creative, expressive power is held.

It might be inserted that a cultural approach to Afro-
Americans will not be without its own rewards to anthropology as a discipline. By coming to terms with the spurious
characterizations of diverse cultural behavior—those which
explain cultures as being "reactive," or as nothing more
than those of poverty, or of the oppressed—the role of the
individual in society can emerge with greater clarity here
in our midst than it ever did abroad. Basic anthropological
concepts such as acculturation can also take on new meaning
when applied here at home. It was, after all, Malinowski,
nowadays increasingly dismissed as an imperialist, who, in
a discussion of the acculturation of Afro-Americans,
warned that the concept was ethnocentric and fraught with
moral connotations ([1940] 1947, pp. viii–ix).

> The immigrant has to *acculturate* himself; so do the natives,
> pagan or heathen, barbarian or savage, who enjoy the benefits
> of our great Western culture. . . . The "uncultured" is to
> receive the benefits of "our culture"; it is he who must change
> and become converted into "one of us."
>
> It requires no effort to understand that by the use of the
> term *acculturation* we implicitly introduce a series of moral,
> normative, and evaluative concepts which radically vitiate
> the understanding of the phenomenon. . . . Every change of
> culture . . . is a process in which something is always given
> . in return for what one received . . . a process in which both
> parts of the equation are modified, a process from which a
> new reality emerges, transformed and complex, a reality that
> is not a mechanical agglomeration of traits, not even a
> mosaic, but a new phenomenon, original and independent.

With the exception of some brief comments by Herskovits and a few literary critics, the influence of Afro-
Americans on American "mainstream" culture remains
mysteriously unwritten, a part of our own "preliterate"

period. It may be difficult to bring middle-class academics, those who find so little meaning in their own ethnicity and traditions, to the point where they can see that others may have seen their own lives in a different manner. But the task is necessary, and it grows more necessary every day, particularly as we must now begin to think of the influence of Afro-American culture and history on the entire world, as mediated by the influence of the United States.[13]

The dilemma comes to this: Despite their clearly recognized non-European source and their unique history of enforced isolation from the rest of society, some 25,000,000 American people are not subject to understanding by anthropologists in any terms except as dependents or appendages of a vaguely defined white social structure. And the justification for this is the power and dominance of the economic and social systems of the United States. But since most of the non-Western world is in the process of coming within a similar relationship with the United States and the other developed nations, just such logic means that the anthropology of the immediate future will be nothing more than a particularly narrow and sterile sociology and the study of antiquities.

One could feel comfortably *au courant* if the inability of anthropologists to come to terms with Afro-American life could be dismissed as simple ethnocentrism or worse. But there remains an uneasy feeling that the Afro-American dilemma is merely a special case of a much larger problem. It is no accident that the closer the anthropologist comes to his own society the more culture escapes him as a viable concept. In knowing, or rather believing he knows, the sources and processes of his culture, he loses interest in it and readily abandons its study to the hegemony of the sociologist. The apparent demystification of our own culture—a demystification evidenced in the explanations implicit in concepts such as "mass culture"—easily leads to dismissing it as unimportant, unreal, or even externally provided. It thus becomes paradoxically remystified. It is then not only Afro-American culture that is escaping our grasp, but American culture.

Notes

The preparation of this essay was accomplished with the support of the National Institute of Mental Health, U.S. Public Health Service, Grant No. MH–17216. It has also benefitted from discussions with my colleagues Erving Goffman, Dell Hymes, and Dan Rose.

1. See for example Katznelson 1970, pp. 47–48.
2. Quoted in Herskovits, 1953, p. 111. It is incidentally worth noting that the details of Boas' involvement with black leaders and causes are generally missing from his numerous biographers' writings.
3. Cf. the following statement from *The Mind of Primitive Man* (Boas, [1938] 1963, p. 238):

   > We have found that no proof of an inferiority of the Negro type could be given, except that it seemed barely possible that perhaps the race would not produce quite so many men of highest genius as other races, while there was nothing at all that could be interpreted as suggesting any material difference in the mental capacity of the bulk of the Negro population as compared with the bulk of the white population. There will undoubtedly be endless numbers of men and women who will be able to outrun their white competitors, and who will do better than the defectives whom we permit to drag down and retard the healthy children of our public schools.

   It is possible that Melville J. Herskovits also confused anthropometric and cultural data in the same way early in his career. William Stewart has suggested that it was this earlier seductive encounter with "science" that later led Herskovits to be so wary of the use of physical science as a model for anthropology. See Herskovits, 1960, pp. 559–68.
4. For a critique of the concept of deficit culture, see Baratz, 1970.
5. Glazer and Moynihan, 1963, p. 53. A recent revised edition of this work renounces this statement, however.
6. Given all the pronouncements over the years, it is shocking to realize that in 1969 an anthropologist could truthfully claim to be publishing the first ethnographic, community-based study of black lower-class child-training practices in the United States. See Young, 1970.

7. For a discussion of the criticism of Herskovits, see the introduction to Whitten and Szwed, 1970, pp. 28–30.

8. Herskovits published and lectured extensively on racist policies and practices; his articles appeared in the liberal political journals of the 1920s and 1930s and in the NAACP and Urban League magazines. And, like his mentor Boas, he was involved with W. E. B. Du Bois in such ventures as the Fourth Pan-African Congress in 1927.

9. Recent literature includes the following: plastic arts, crafts, and architecture (Thompson, 1969; Abrahams, 1970a); verbal arts (Abrahams, 1970b, 1970c; Rosenberg, 1970); music (Jones, 1963; Schuller, 1968; Keil, 1966; Oliver, 1970; Lomax, 1970a; Szwed, 1970); dance (Stearns, 1968).

10. The fact that "cultural deprivation" of the black poor should have become an issue just at the point where many white middle-class and upper-class youths were finding their own culture meaningless is a sad commentary on social scientists' sense of paradox.

11. Two examples are: (1) the successful efforts of Andrew Pearse and Melville J. Herskovits in support of the Spiritual Baptists of Trinidad against repressive government legislation; and (2) Jean Price-Mars's and others' use of voodoo and folk culture as a basis for nationalism during the United States occupation of Haiti.

12. Cf. Sartre's analysis of a priori and "schematizing" responses to the second Soviet intervention in Hungary in 1956 (1963, pp. 29–30, n. 8):

> . . . it matters little a priori that the Communist commentators believed that they had to justify the Soviet intervention. What is really heartbreaking is the fact that their "analyses" totally suppressed the originality of the Hungarian fact. Yet there is no doubt that an insurrection at Budapest a dozen years after the war, less than five years after the death of Stalin, must present very particular characteristics. What do our "schematizers" do? They lay stress on the faults of the Party, but without defining them. These indeterminate faults assume an abstract and eternal character which wrenches them from the historical context so as to make of them a universal entity; it is "human error." The writers indicate the presence of reactionary elements, but without showing their Hungarian *reality*. Suddenly these reactionaries pass over into eternal Reaction. Finally, those commentators present world imperialism as an inexhaustible, formless force, whose essence does not vary regardless of its point of application. They construct an interpretation which serves as a skeleton key to everything. . . . In short, nothing new has happened. That is what had to be demonstrated.

13. For a discussion of the influence of Afro-American political style

on other parts of the world, see Freyre, 1966, pp. 18–21. A specific example of this influence is Vallières, 1971, on the Front de Libération du Québec.

References

Abrahams, Roger D. 1970a. "Social Uses of Space in an Afro-American Community." Paper presented at the Conference on Traditional African Architecture, Yale University, May 7–9, 1970.
———. 1970b. *Positively Black*. Englewood Cliffs, N.J.: Prentice-Hall.
———. [1964] 1970c. *Deep Down in the Jungle . . . Negro Narrative Folklore from the Streets of Philadelphia*. Chicago: Aldine Press.
———. 1970d. "Black Uses of Black English." Paper read at the Social Science Research Council Conference on Continuities and Discontinuities in Afro-American Societies and Cultures, Mona, Jamaica, April 2–4, 1970.
Ashley-Montagu, M. F. 1942. *Man's Most Dangerous Myth: The Fallacy of Race*. New York: Harper & Brothers.
Baratz, Stephen S. 1970. "Social Science's Conceptualization of the Afro-American." In Szwed, 1970b, pp. 55–66.
Bastide, Roger. 1967. *Les Amériques noires*. Paris: Payot.
Benedict, Ruth. [1934] 1959. *Patterns of Culture*. New York: New American Library, Mentor Books.
———. [1940] 1959. *Race: Science and Politics*. New York: Viking Press, Compass Books.
Bennett, Lerone, Jr. 1971. "The World of the Slave." *Ebony* 26 (February): 44–56.
Blauner, Robert. 1970. "Black Culture: Myth or Reality?" In Whitten and Szwed, 1970, pp. 347–66.
Boas, Franz. [1938] 1963. *The Mind of Primitive Man*. New York: Macmillan Co.
Bryce-Laporte, Roy S. 1968. "The Conceptualization of the American Slave Plantation as a Total Institution." Unpublished Ph.D. dissertation, University of California, Los Angeles.
Clark, Kenneth B. 1965. *Dark Ghetto*. New York: Harper & Row.
Curtin, Philip D. 1969. *The Atlantic Slave Trade: A Census*. Madison: University of Wisconsin Press.
Dalby, David. 1970. *Black Through White*. African Studies Program, Indiana University. Bloomington: Indiana University Press.
Dillard, J. L. 1972. *Black English*. New York: Random House.
Elkins, Stanley M. 1959. *Slavery: A Problem in American Institutional and Intellectual Life*. Chicago: University of Chicago Press.
Ellison, Ralph. 1966. *Shadow and Act*. New York: New American Library, Signet Books.

Fischer, Ann. 1969. "The Effect upon Anthropological Studies of U.S. Negroes of the Professional Personality and Subculture of Anthropologists." Paper presented at the annual meeting of the Southern Anthropological Association, New Orleans, March 13–15.

Frazier, E. Franklin. 1934. "Traditions and Patterns of Negro Family Life in the United States." In *Race and Culture Contacts*, ed. E. B. Reuter. New York: McGraw-Hill Book Co. Pp. 191–207.

Freyre, Gilberto. 1966. *The Racial Factor in Contemporary Politics.* Occasional Papers of the Research Unit for the Study of Multi-Racial Societies, University of Sussex. London: MacGibbon & Kee.

Glazer, Nathan, and Daniel P. Moynihan. 1963. *Beyond the Melting Pot.* Cambridge, Mass.: MIT Press.

Gordon, Milton. 1964. *Assimilation in American Life.* New York: Oxford University Press.

Greenberg, Joseph H. 1957. "An Application of New World Evidence to an African Linguistic Problem." In *Les afro-américains*, Mémoire 27. Dakar: Institut français d'Afrique noire. Pp. 129–31.

Grier, William H., and Price M. Cobbs. 1968. *Black Rage.* New York: Basic Books.

Hannerz, Ulf. 1969. *Soulside: Inquiries into Ghetto Culture and Community.* New York: Columbia University Press.

Harding, Vincent. 1969. "Religion and Resistance Among Ante-Bellum Negroes, 1800–1860." In *The Making of Black America*, eds. A. Meier and E. Rudwick. Vol. 1. New York: Atheneum Publishers. Pp. 179–97.

Harrington, Michael. 1968. *Toward a Democratic Left.* New York: Vintage Books.

Herskovits, Melville J. 1925. "The Negro's Americanism." In *The New Negro*, ed. A. Locke. New York: Charles and Albert Boni. Pp. 353–60.

———. 1935. "What Has Africa Given America?" *New Republic* 84, No. 1083: 92–96.

———. 1953. *Franz Boas.* New York: Charles Scribner's Sons.

———. [1941] 1958. *The Myth of the Negro Past.* Boston: Beacon Press.

———. 1960. "The Ahistorical Approach to Afroamerican Studies." *American Anthropologist* 62: 559–68.

———. [1930] 1966. "The Negro in the New World: The Statement of a Problem." In *The New World Negro*, ed. Frances S. Herskovits. Bloomington: Indiana University Press. Pp. 1–12.

Hurston, Zora Neale. 1935. *Mules and Men.* Philadelphia: J. B. Lippincott Co.

Jones, LeRoi. 1963. *Blues People.* New York: Wiliam Morrow & Co.

Kardiner, Abram, and Lionel Ovesey. 1962. *The Mark of Oppression.* New York: World Pub. Co., Meridian Books.

Katznelson, Ira. 1970. "White Social Science and the Black Man's

World: The Case of Urban Ethnography." *Race Today*, February, pp. 47–48.

Keil, Charles. 1966. *Urban Blues*. Chicago: University of Chicago Press.

Kochman, Thomas. 1970. "Toward an Ethnography of Black American Speech Behavior." In Whitten and Szwed, 1970, pp. 145–62.

Labov, William, *et al.* 1968. *A Study of the Non-Standard English of Negro and Puerto Rican Speakers in New York City*. Vol. 2. Final Report, Cooperative Research Project No. 3288. Washington, D.C.: Office of Education.

Lasch, Christopher. 1969. *The Agony of the American Left*. New York: Vintage Books.

Levine, Lawrence W. 1969. "Slave Songs and Slave Consciousness: An Exploration in Neglected Sources." Paper presented at meetings of the American Historical Association, December 28.

Lomax, Alan. 1968. *Folk Song Style and Culture*. Washington, D.C.: American Academy for the Advancement of Science.

————. 1970. "The Homogeneity of African-Afro-American Musical Style." In Whitten and Szwed, 1970, pp. 181–201.

Malinowski, Bronislaw. [1940] 1947. Introduction to *Cuban Counterpoint*, by Fernando Ortiz. New York: Alfred A. Knopf, 1970.

Marks, Morton. 1969. "Trance Music and Paradoxical Communication." Paper read at the American Anthropological Association meetings, New Orleans, November.

————. 1970. "El santo en Nueva York." Paper presented at the meetings of the American Anthropological Association, San Diego, November 22.

Marx, Gary T. 1970. "Two Cheers for the National Riot Commission." In Szwed, 1970b, pp. 78–96.

Mintz, Sidney. 1970. "Foreword." In Whitten and Szwed, 1970, pp. 1–15.

Montell, William L. 1970. *The Saga of Coe Ridge*. Knoxville: University of Tennessee Press.

Myrdal, Gunnar. 1944. *An American Dilemma: The Negro Problem and Modern Democracy*. New York: Harper & Row.

Narvaez, Alfonso A. 1970. "Where Religion and Superstition Mix in the City." *New York Times*, September 15, p. 41.

Oliver, Paul. 1970. *Savannah Syncopators*. New York: Stein & Day.

Powdermaker, Hortense. 1939. *After Freedom: A Cultural Study in the Deep South*. New York: Viking Press.

Radin, Paul. [1945] 1969. "Status, Fantasy, and the Christian Dogma." In *God Struck Me Dead*, ed. C. H. Johnson. Philadelphia: Pilgrim Press. Pp. vii–xiii. (Originally issued: Nashville, Fisk University Social Science Institute, 1945, from a typescript written before 1930.)

Rainwater, Lee. 1968. "The American Working Class and Lower Class: An American Success and Failure." In *Anthropological Backgrounds of Adult Education, Notes and Essays on Educa-*

tion for Adults 57, eds. S. Tax *et al.* Boston: Center for the Study of Liberal Education for Adults. Pp. 29–46.

Reisman, Karl. 1970a. "Cultural and Linguistic Ambiguity in a West Indian Village." In Whitten and Szwed, 1970, pp. 129–44.

————. 1970b. "Contrapuntal Communication." Mimeo. Austin, Texas: Penn-Texas Working Papers in Sociolinguistics.

Rosenberg, Bruce A. 1970. *The Art of the American Folk Preacher.* New York: Oxford University Press.

Sartre, Jean-Paul. 1963. *Search for a Method,* trans. Hazel E. Barnes. New York: Vintage Books.

Schuller, Gunther. 1968. *Early Jazz.* New York: Oxford University Press.

Smith, M. G. 1960. "The African Heritage in the Caribbean." In *Caribbean Studies: A Symposium,* ed. V. Rubin. Seattle: University of Washington Press. Pp. 34–46.

Stearns, Marshall and Jean. 1968. *Jazz Dance.* New York: Macmillan Co.

Stewart, William. 1970. "Towards a History of American Negro Dialect." In *Language and Poverty: Perspective on a Theme,* ed. F. Williams. Chicago: Markham Publishing Co. Chap. 7.

Stuckey, Sterling. 1968. "Through the Prism of Folklore: The Black Ethos in Slavery." *Massachusetts Review* 9: 417–37.

————. 1971. "Twilight of Our Past: Reflections on the Origins of Black History." In *Amistad 2,* eds. John A. Williams and Charles F. Harris. New York: Vintage Books, Pp. 261–95.

Szasz, Thomas S. 1970. "Blackness and Madness: Images of Evil and Tactics of Exclusion." In Szwed, 1970b, pp. 67–77.

Szwed, John F. 1970a. "Afro-American Musical Adaptation." In Whitten and Szwed, 1970, pp. 219–27.

————, ed. 1970b. *Black America.* New York: Basic Books.

Thompson, Robert Farris. 1969. "African Influence on the Art of the United States." In *Black Studies in the University,* eds. A. L. Robinson *et al.* New Haven, Conn.: Yale University Press. Pp. 122–70.

————. 1970a. "The Sign of the Divine King." *African Arts,* Spring, pp. 8–17.

————. 1970b. "From Africa." *Yale Alumni Magazine,* November, pp. 16–21.

Tumin, Melvin M. 1969. "Some Social Consequences of Research on Racial Relations." In *Recent Sociology No. 1,* ed. H. P. Dreitzel. New York: Macmillan Co. Pp. 242–62.

Turner, Lorenzo D. 1949. *Africanisms in the Gullah Dialect.* Chicago: University of Chicago Press.

Valentine, Charles. 1968. *Culture and Poverty: Critique and Counter-Proposals.* Chicago: University of Chicago Press.

Vallières, Pierre. 1971. *White Niggers of America.* New York: Monthly Review Press.

Whitten, Norman E., and John F. Szwed, eds. 1970. *Afro-American Anthropology.* New York: Free Press.

Willis, William S., Jr. 1970. "Anthropology and Negroes on the Southern Colonial Frontier." In *The Black Experience in America*, eds. James C. Curtis and Lewis L. Gould. Austin: University of Texas Press. Pp. 33–50.

Wolf, Eric R., and Joseph G. Jorgensen. 1970. "Anthropology on the Warpath in Thailand." *New York Review of Books*, November 19, pp. 26–35.

Young, Virginia H. 1970. "Family and Childhood in a Southern Negro Community." *American Anthropologist* 72: 269–88.

Culture and Imperialism: Proposing a New Dialectic

Mina Davis Caulfield

THE MOST IMPORTANT FORCE for culture change in the history of man to date almost certainly has been the Western expansion that has matured in the pattern we call "imperialism." Beginning with the racial and evolutionary issues of the nineteenth century, a definition of problems in anthropology has been shaped by the need to explain the relation of dominated to dominating people (cf. Haller, 1970 and 1971, and Willis in this volume). Anthropologists have largely studied societies and cultures existing under some form of colonial or neocolonial domination by which the natives were, so to speak, made safe for ethnography. The very rise of interest in exotic customs, peoples, and races that lies at the root of anthropology was part of the initial phase of expansion that brought members of the Western European and American educated elite into close contact with such customs and peoples. It might seem too facile or Machiavellian to suggest that the discipline itself developed because Western expansion made knowledge of such cultures important for efficient exploitation of lands and labor, but it could well be argued that the social need for such research was translated into the sincere and disinterested fascination which we now identify as our own.

In these respects, anthropology, as Kathleen Gough has pointed out (1968), is the "child of imperialism." It seems extraordinary, then, that anthropology has no general theory dealing with imperialism. Of course, one of the most easily observed facts about socialization is that children find it difficult to question the implicit assumptions of their parents. From this perspective, perhaps it is less amazing that anthropology has largely accepted a more or less imperialistic structure to its world and has failed to develop a consistent, critical body of theory on imperialism, or even, for all its study of cultural change, on the simple process of exploitation.

BOAS AND AFTER: LIMITATIONS OF ANTHROPOLOGICAL APPROACHES

I want to emphasize that I do not mean to say that anthropologists are imperialists, or that they favor exploitation; the vast majority are not and do not. In fact, the emergence of anthropology as an academic discipline in America was ushered in with a concerted attack on theories of racial and cultural superiority, the classic pillars of ideological justification for the imperialist structure. The Grand Scheme of unilinear cultural evolution as it was developed in the nineteenth century, placing Western European and American civilization at the pinnacle of humanity, was vigorously attacked by the Boasian school, and the theory of cultural relativism was forged in the heat of many long theoretical battles in the discipline. Simultaneously, the Boas school attacked the fundamental tenets of white supremacy by showing with solid empirical studies that race, language, and culture were not coextensive entities and that there was no innate racial inheritance guaranteeing the white man's natural right (or duty) to rule.

The attack on race prejudice and ethnocentrism, however, never led to an all-out attack on exploitation of subject peoples, to an interest in the modes of oppression and their cultural consequences, or even to scholarly acknowledgment of the fact of exploitation. In fact, the Boas school never showed any real interest in studying the *situation* of conquest and exploitation as such. On the contrary, the doctrine of equal respect for all varieties of cultural configuration seems to have led American anthropologists to seek out the most "pure," "uncontaminated" cultures they could find as objects of study. In the case of the North American Indians—the major focus of interest for American anthropologists in this period—the "pure" cultures were assumed to be *only* the aboriginal ones, which anthropologists apparently thought were fast disappearing by a sort of natural process. The brutality of Indian colonization, the dynamic culture change as land was stolen from existing groups, and the fact that the anthropologist himself was a member of a conqueror group in relation to his subjects were all ignored. Interestingly enough, such anthropological treatment as there was of America's other internal colony, the blacks, departed from the prevalent social scientific view and stressed cultural distinctiveness, but again only insofar as blacks retained aboriginal (i.e. African) culture traits (Herskovits, 1941).[1] Boas' concern over the rapid extinction of the aboriginal languages and cultures of American Indians, then, was not translated into any significant intellectual or political interest in the material exploitation, even genocide, practiced against the *peoples* concerned. The romantic humanism of the configurationists turned away from the social problems of the present and recent past and attempted to capture for humanity the vanishing puzzles and beauties of former cultures (cf. Fontana, 1968).

The two major new foci of American anthropology in the period before and after World War II—acculturation and culture-and-personality—approached cultures which had clearly undergone change in historical times, but sidestepped, or at best underplayed, the material facts of colonialism. Studies such as those of Lewis (1942), Secoy (1953), and Leacock (1954) have been exceptional. With the process of change defined in terms of traits and patterns rather than the actual social and ecological experiences of people, material exploitation was seen as secondary at best. Degradation and impoverishment were essentially irrelevant to theories of cultural dynamics. Culture and personality studies were virtually ahistorical; since culture was conceived as molding and shaping the psyches of all its members in childhood, there was no logical place for change to enter the equation except through "imperfect enculturation," as if experiences and perceptions throughout the life span had no effect in changing world view or social consciousness (see Harris, 1968, Chaps. 15 and 16). Even the more recent psychological studies of revitalization, dealing directly with social protest movements, couch their interpretations in ideal terms: "reformulation of the mazeway" follows cognitive dissonance between traditional and modern world views, and there is little reason to investigate the social and economic realities which lead people to listen to a prophet (Wallace, 1961). In virtually every case, the relationship of exploitation to culture is either ignored or made completely subsidiary to the study of "culture" as abstracted from the exploitative reality.

The functionalist school, though its principal adherents studied primarily in colonial countries, has likewise not dealt directly with the situation of exploitation. The imperialist frame has been taken for granted as a stable background, and society has been analyzed as a smoothly integrated mechanism, functioning virtually without need of historical context. From this point of view, any form of extreme or sudden change is dysfunctional, and the presence within one society of directly opposing interests, or struggle between them, is almost a contradiction in terms. It is consensus that binds societies together, not force, and temporary imbalances are erased through a natural tendency toward homostasis. The only way such an interpretation can be adhered to in a study of a colonial society is by simply ignoring the colonial presence, especially the conflicts and contradictions of exploitation.

The work of the self-styled Marxist and neo-evolutionist

Leslie White might be expected to deal directly with class struggle and imperialism, but White's "Marxism" is of a different order. White's universal "Culture" is virtually the same as Kroeber's "superorganic," in spite of the antagonism between the two men. The only difference is that White's Culture evolves through regular stages, and since White sees the cause of change to be the advance of technology, he calls himself a materialist; but there is no hint in his works of a dialectical process, or indeed of any social process at all (White, 1959, *passim*). According to this theory, Culture evolves by its own laws; human beings, exploitation, protest, contradictions resolved through action, are beside the point. This is not Marxism, or even materialism, in my understanding of those terms.

There has been, however, an important offshoot of the neo-evolutionist theory in the work of Steward, Wolf, Mintz, Geertz, and Sahlins—the cultural ecologists. All of these anthropologists have produced excellent studies of colonial situations (see especially Geertz, 1963), dealing more or less directly with the facts of imperialist exploitation in historical context, with emphasis on economic relations. Thus the focus on the material base of society, which is the most important aspect of White's approach adopted by the ecologists, when applied to concrete situations rather than abstractions, inevitably exposes the problems of economic exploitation and cultural adaptations to colonialism; just as inevitably, it necessitates a historical rather than an ideal evolutionary approach. Focus on ecological relations, crucial as it is for an understanding of the colonial situation, is not, however, sufficient in itself for the development of a body of theory covering the relationship between culture and imperialism. As I shall develop below, there are aspects of culture change, interaction, and the development of consciousness under exploitation which are essential to a comprehensive theory, and which are largely bypassed in these works.

Another approach is found in studies of social and cultural pluralism which focus mainly on the structural peculiarities of colonial societies and societies with minorities or pariah groups. These studies, such as those of M. G. Smith in the West Indies (1965), Despres in British Guiana (1967), and Benedict in Mauritius (1961), deal with the total society in colonial or immediate postcolonial times. Even when the focus is on a small community, such as Van den Berghe's *Caneville* (1964), the larger colonial and even world context is made explicit and relevant. Ecological relations and the facts of economic exploitation, though frequently underplayed in my opinion (especially in the works of M. G. Smith), are impossible to ignore in such studies, and the role of systems of imperialism in establishing and maintaining social and cultural plural hierarchies is dealt with explicitly by Van den Berghe and Benedict. Van den Berghe in particular makes a number of essential theoretical points about plural societies which relate racist ideology and "economic interdependence" (i.e., control of resources by the dominant racial and cultural group) with the structure of pluralism. A crucial contribution of this school is the concept of societies held together by coercion rather than consensus. Van den Berghe goes so far as to suggest a process which I shall develop at some length below:

> A dialectic of group conflict frequently sets in, which, in turn, leads to a polarization of ideology and values or at least to a widely discrepant interpretation of common values. (1967, p. 144)

In general, however, anthropologists concerned with pluralism concentrate on structural categories such as institutional autonomy or incompatibility. Processes of change are dealt with in terms of acculturation and assimilation, or the lack of it, and consciousness, conflict, and struggle as factors of social or cultural change are ignored or de-emphasized. Kuper, in dealing with "Conflict and the Plural Society" (1969), stresses the importance of economic interdependence in *reducing* the possibility of polarization and violence. He asserts that Frantz Fanon's characterization of African societies as extremely polarized (1963) "represents revolutionary ideology rather than sociological analysis" and that "its closest approximation is to be found in the early stages of conquest and the consolidation of power" rather than in the present period (Kuper, 1969, p. 161).

As I shall show below, Kuper misreads Fanon, and in a way that is representative of the difficulty inherent in the structural approach of the plural society model when confronted with the realities of the colonial situation. Fanon speaks of problems of identity and cultural consciousness in an exploitative situation. Fanon's "simple dichotomy," though it may indeed function as revolutionary ideology, is fundamentally neither sociological analysis nor ideology, but rather psychological and *cultural* analysis of a dynamic that is there to be observed. Thus, when Kuper maintains that Fanon's "polarized society" represents "a dialectic without possibility of synthesis, without possibility of higher unity" (p. 156), he does not seem to realize that the dialectic he conceives within an analytical framework of parallel social structures is very different from the dialectic which Fanon poses in quite other terms, and for which Fanon develops an eloquent and involved synthesis (see the second section of this paper). The plural society model, while it contributes to an understanding of the ecological relations, structural characteristics, and institutional forms of colonial societies, fails to deal with the cultural dynamics of imperialist exploitation because it bypasses the locus of change, which is in the manifold psychological and social responses and actions of individuals.

IMPERIALISM: MODES OF CONTROL AND OF EXPLOITATION

Ever since publication of Thomas Kuhn's *Structure of Scientific Revolutions* (1962), social scientists of various persuasions have been suggesting that their disciplines are in need of a new "paradigmatic focus," on the grounds that the old ones have come up against irreconcilable anomalies. At the risk of seeming trendy, I would suggest that anthropology, too, is faced with an anomaly which necessitates the creation of a new paradigm. This anomaly is not a case of pattern exhaustion, or failure of old paradigms for internal reasons, but rather the problem which I have outlined in the previous section: Theoretical approaches up to the present have failed, in one respect or another, to deal adequately with the phenomenon of imperialism and its relationship to culture change, in particular the dramatic and urgently important changes evident in current liberation struggles throughout the third world.

With all due immodesty, then, I shall propose my conception of a Marxist anthropological theory of culture and imperialism, with the hope that, even if it does not generate a host of new hypotheses and directions for research, at least it will generate useful disagreement and debate.

At the outset, some definitions should be clarified. Since anthropologists have not been in the habit of thinking in terms of imperialism and exploitation, and since the main thesis of my paper is that they should and must, some kind of technical definitions would seem to be in order here.

Imperialism, then, I shall use as a broad term covering an extremely wide range of situations, including direct political control, indirect political control, and economic control. The central characteristic uniting these situations is that key decisions on the disposition of resources and benefits in a community are made by members of another ethnic or cultural group, and that the purpose of such decisions is, ultimately, the extraction of profit from the community and its resources for the capitalistic enterprises of the dominant group. This definition, then, would include not just the "old colonialism" of the European empires, but also the multitudinous forms of neocolonialism of the present period.

The Guianese sugar workers, both black and East Indian, are thus victims of imperialism, even though their nation has been granted independence by Britain, for their economy is directed and controlled by British, Canadian, and American interests; likewise, the American Indians, whose land was stolen in a previous imperialistic period, remain a subject people whose tribal councils, even where they are representative of the community, wield only minimal control over lives on the reservations. Of course, there is an important distinction to be made between these two types of victims of imperialism: the first are incorporated as underpaid workers into the empire, and the second are largely left in the backwaters. There are strong analogies between them—for example, the Africans in the kraal are a reserve labor force for the gold mines, and the unemployed blacks and Puerto Ricans (including those still in Puerto Rico) are a reserve labor pool for United States employers. There are also complications in making such a distinction: for example, many old colonies such as the smaller West Indian islands are backwaters relative to modern capitalism but still preserve an older mode of exploitation. Nonetheless, the distinction is a real one, and the two types of relation to the empire may be seen to have had different social and ideological concomitants. An important characteristic of the present period is the lessening of these differences, as consciousness of exploitation and solidarity of interest between these two types of victim increase.

It is important to note that incorporation of a few members of the oppressed group into the ruling circles of a colonial or neocolonial system does not alter the status of the group under this definition. As an extreme example of such a token elite, the Cherokee in Oklahoma have a tribal "chieftain" who is a top executive of Phillip's Petroleum Company, one of the most powerful interests in the American imperialist elite. However, Chief Keeler was appointed to his tribal post by President Truman, and furthermore he is *culturally* white upper class; the decisions he makes "for the good of the Cherokee nation" can be shown to be more in the interests of white culture and the white upper class than in those of the community he allegedly represents (Collier, 1970). The crucial factor of cultural as well as class identity will, I hope, be made clearer in the main body of my argument.

Imperialist *exploitation* takes many forms. (My use of the term is an extension of the conventional Marxist usage.) Since the main body of this article is concerned with this extended definition, I shall make only one definitional comment here. Following Marx, when I use the term "exploitation of land and natural resources," I intend the meaning that the original users of these resources have been deprived of their right to make their own cultural use of them, rather than the economist's meaning that the resources have simply been utilized. Although Marx used exploitation to refer primarily to labor power, I think my extension of usage to other aspects of social, economic, and cultural existence is valid for at least the colonial situation.

Marxist, or self-styled Marxist, theories have of course been held in very low esteem in American anthropology. Both Balandier and Van den Berghe, whose treatments of the colonial situation I consider among the most exciting and theoretically fruitful in the field, take pains to reject the standard Marxist approach, or rather their conception of it. Balandier complains of the primacy given to economic (he seems to mean economic class) aspects of colonialism, citing Stalin's dogmatic insistence that colonial revolutions take place under the direction of the proletariat (Balandier, 1966, p. 40). Van den Berghe, on the other hand, rejects the Marxist "or Machiavellian" view of power, because it "fails to account for the role of ideas in human behavior" (1964, p. 251).

Balandier's objection seems to be well taken. Many Marxists have tried to fit the facts of imperialist exploitation into the model of class exploitation which Marx outlined for a capitalist society, in spite of the fact that Lenin (1939) showed clearly that the system of imperialism specifically inhibited the growth of industry and an industrial proletariat in colonial countries. Thus, communist parties in underdeveloped countries have tended to pin their hopes for revolution on the development of *class* consciousness, even to the extent of ignoring national liberation movements originating in rural areas, as in the case of Cuba (see Wolf, 1969, pp. 267–69).

Van den Berghe's objection, on the other hand, appears almost incomprehensible, given the central importance which Marx assigned to the role of ideas in social action. Marx made it very clear that socialist revolutions would *not* occur automatically out of the contradictions of capitalist economic and social structure; he specified that only with the growth of awareness of these contradictions, and the conscious social action of men and women which follows from this growth, would a new form of society arise (1924).

Had Van den Berghe phrased his objection in terms of a failure of many Marxists to account for the role of culture in human behavior (and judging from the context, it is possible that this is closer to his meaning), his comments would be very much to the point. American Marxists have not followed the lead of British Marxists like Hobsbawm and Worsley in applying a historical materialist approach to problems of cultural process, perhaps owing to a recognition of the pitfalls in the pseudo-Marxist Culturology of Leslie White. I hope that the paradigm which I shall outline will deal adequately with both of these objections, which I consider extremely serious ones.

As I have indicated above, Marx's analysis of the dialectics of change from capitalism to socialism is not applicable to the colonial situation, because the underlying contradiction of capitalism—that between private ownership of the means of production and the social mode of production in industrial technology—is not the same as the underlying contradiction of imperialism. Marx specified that the basis for the emergence of class consciousness, the agent of social change, was the exploitative relation between classes, that is, between the bourgeoisie and the proletariat, and that the qualitative leap to revolutionary consciousness would come about through the social transformations and economic crises inherent in capitalist society.

In the colonial situation the basic contradiction, the opposing interests, the social and economic transformations, and the changes in consciousness all take different forms; in short, a qualitatively different dialectic is at work, and the nature of the ensuing synthesis is likewise different. *It is my thesis that the underlying form of exploitation under imperialism is not that of class over class, but rather of culture over culture.* As expanding capitalism, with its industrial base in the home country, encountered and engulfed nonindustrial cultures, the dominant system developed modes for exploiting not just the labor power of these subject peoples, but their entire cultural patterns. As Balandier puts it, "colonialism was literally at times an act of social surgery" (1966, p. 37); Wolf notes that "the contact between the capitalist center, the metropolis, and the precapitalist or noncapitalist periphery is a large-scale cultural encounter, not merely an economic one" (1969, p. 278).

EXPLOITATION IN ECONOMY

Much has been written of the economic exploitation of colonized peoples: exploitation of land, labor power, and natural resources as sources of the "primary accumulation" which made possible the rapid expansion of the industrial technology of Western Europe and North America under capitalism (see, e.g., Eric Williams, 1961). It is not simply that these factors of human culture were transformed into commodities, as Polanyi (1957) and Heilbroner (1962) have noted, but also that they were directly expropriated and consistently exploited, with the consequence that the material elements of the previous culture were radically distorted or even destroyed. The massive depopulation of whole villages in Africa due to the slave trade, for example, not only meant exploitation of the labor power of those deported, but the virtual destruction of the economic basis of the African cultures involved. Plantation systems, whether based on slave labor or superimposed on pre-existing agricultural forms as in Java (Geertz, 1963), various forms of migrant and forced labor, in addition to the expropriation of land and resources, rendered subject populations to one extent or another dependent on the forms of labor and ownership of the dominant culture (see Harris, 1966). And this dependence applied to *all* classes in the exploited culture, certainly in differential degrees, but nonetheless across the board. The "cultural exploitation" in the economic sphere, while fundamental to the exploitation of other elements of the culture, was exploitation not simply of the economic *resources* of colonized peoples, but of the total economic *organization*, and the subordination of traditional elites as well as peasant and laboring classes to the interests of the imperial power. What is important here is not just that there was rapid and drastic "culture change" in the ecological relations of subject peoples, but that their formal cultural arrangements in this realm were destroyed, distorted, and made subservient to the cultural arrangements of the imperialists. The economic culture, not just control over economic surplus, was subject to exploitation.

IN SOCIAL STRUCTURES

In addition to the exploitation of the ecological base of nonindustrial cultures, the kind of whole-culture exploitation I am suggesting also exploits the pre-existing social and political structures. Again, traditional roles and statuses are distorted and made to serve the interests of the new dominant culture. It is evident that this process is not simply the substitution of a new ruling class, or the imposition of a set of superordinate statuses for the representatives of the conquering power; the transformation of traditional bases of power has led to the *use* of social organization for the benefit of the dominant culture as a whole. The end result has been the plural society, with parallel sets of roles and institutions, one set dominant over the other, *in toto.*

Eric Wolf has described this process in terms of a "crisis in the exercise of power" brought about by the advent of the capitalist market-principle.

> Tribal chief, mandarin, landed nobleman—the beneficiaries and agents of an older social order—yield to the entrepreneur, the credit merchant, the political broker, the intellectual, the professional. . . . The managers of fixed social resources yield to the managers of "free-floating" resources. Groups oriented toward subsistence production diminish, and groups committed to commodity production or to the sale of labor power grow in size and social density. (1969, p. 282)

While Wolf's analysis is in many respects very cogent and insightful, one must distinguish between imperialist and nonimperialist settings. A "crisis of power" is characteristic of both settings, but in a colonial country the total socio-cultural system of the imperialist power, already relatively well integrated, technologically advanced, and bureaucratically organized, is placed in a dominant position over the total system of the subject peoples: there is not only a "dual economy," but a dual social system. Thus, at the same time as the traditional social structure is transformed by the advent of the market-principle, the *entire set* of roles and statuses held by natives, *whether transformed or not,* is subordinated to the *entire set* held by the colonialists. While holding up its own social system as superior and ultimately the only mode for the exercise of real power, the imperialist cultural section effectively denies access to positions of substantive power or control to anyone not of its own race and culture. The native social organization is not only transformed, it is debased and exploited for the benefit of the imperialist culture as a whole. This is the peculiarity of the "advent of the capitalist market-principle" in the colonial situation, and makes it qualitatively different from the development of capitalism in Europe and North America.

The difference between the spread of capitalism in colonial countries and in countries untouched by this type of exploitation can be made clear through a closer examination of the process as outlined by Wolf. Continuing the discussion cited above, Wolf speaks of the dislocations wrought by the rapid change characteristic of the advance of capitalism.

> Commitments and goals point in different directions: the old is not yet overcome and remains to challenge the new; the new is not yet victorious. . . . Traditional groups have been weakened, but not yet defeated, and new groups are not yet strong enough to wield decisive power. (1969, pp. 283–84)

In this situation of "weak contenders," says Wolf, the tendency is for centralization of executive power in a dictator-type political structure, playing one power group off against another. (He cites the examples of Mexico, Russia, China, Vietnam, Algeria, and Cuba, in the period before their respective revolutions.) It is possible, however, he points out, to avoid the "weakness" such a power structure entails, and he cites the cases of Germany and Japan, where the "executive allied itself not with new groups, but with a section of the traditional feudal aristocracy which provided the backbone of an efficient centralized bureaucracy."

> The commercial and professional groups, rather than striving for independent ends, accepted the feudal values as their own, thus consenting to guidance by the aristocrats. The peasantry was similarly held fast to the inherited cultural ceremonial of obligations between social superiors and inferiors, and by the development of a national ideology of kinship or kinship-based *Gemeinschaft*. (1969, pp. 284–85)

The significance of these cases, which Wolf fails to point out, lies in the rapid introduction of capitalism in Germany and Japan *without* the imperialist element. In these countries, then, the transformation of economic relations and the restructuring of the social system were *not* accompanied by whole-culture exploitation; land, labor, and resources were transformed into commodities, but they were not exploited for the profit of an alien nation. Capitalism developed from within, and the advent of the market-principle led to the growth of national industrialization, in contrast to the colonial situation, where inhibition of industrial technology is an essential component of the maintenance of imperialism. The transformation of the peasantry into the entrepreneur-farmer in Japan, which Steward (1959) has suggested is a normal, "evolutionary" development, can also be seen to be "normal" only in the noncolonial setting. Furthermore, in Germany and Japan the advent of capitalism certainly entailed a new kind of exploitation and social hierarchy, but there was no pan-class subordination of one sociocultural section by another; there was no dual economy, no dual set of social institutions, no plural culture. Thus the "unique conditions" which Wolf suggests account for the exception of these two countries can be seen as the simple absence of imperialism and of the cultural exploitation I am suggesting is its characteristic.

IN CULTURAL IDENTITY

Wolf's stress on the role of values, "inherited cultural ceremonial of obligation," and "national ideology" in the passage above leads to the last and probably the most controversial element in my analysis of cultural exploitation. Perhaps owing to the ubiquity of the market-principle in our own value system, the concept of "exploitation" is generally considered to apply only to economic factors, and its extension into other realms of cultural being may raise objections—and eyebrows. I have tried to show that in the colonial setting it is appropriate to apply this concept to the social structure; now I would like to suggest that it is applicable to the entire field of internalized values, ethos, ethnic or cultural identity itself.

The ideologies of white supremacy and cultural superiority have been generally regarded in the literature as rationalizations for economic and political domination and as mechanisms by which such domination is exercised. For the anthropologist, they must be regarded as something more: they are cultural expressions, parts of a cultural value system and important items in the cultural self-definition of West Europeans and North Americans. In the colonial setting—and here I include the "internal colonies" of Indians and blacks in the United States (see Blauner, 1969)—it is clear that they operate not only to partially define the dominant cultural identity, but, by the same token, they define the "other"—by exclusion, negation, by opposition to all that is held in high esteem or given value. Fanon expresses the process of definition and the good-bad dichotomy it imposes on the nonwhite native:

> I begin to suffer from not being a white man to the degree that the white man imposes discrimination on me, makes me a colonial native, robs me of all worth, all individuality, tells me that I am a parasite on the world, that I must bring myself as quickly as possible into step with the white world, "that I am a brute beast, that my people and I are like a walking dung-heap that disgustingly fertilizes sweet sugar cane and silky cotton, that I have no use in the world." (1967, p. 98; included quotation from Césaire, 1956)

Thus when students of "plural societies" speak of autonomous, incompatible sets of institutions characterizing the different cultural sections of colonial societies, it is understood (though not always stated) that these sets of institutions, through which values are expressed, are ranked hierarchically: one set is higher, the other lower; one is advanced, the other backward; one is Christian, the other heathen; one is civilized, the other savage; one is refined, the other crude, and so on and so on. At the same time, access to the presumptive superior set of attributes and behavior is effectively denied to the holder of the debased set, on the assumption that he is racially incapable of understanding them. As Balandier points out, the characteristic social hierarchy of a colonial country is "a distinction and a hierarchy based, first of all, on criteria of race and nationality, implying as a sort of postulate the excellence of the white race and more especially of that fraction which is the colonial power." Thus, through racism and ethnocentrism, the very cultural identity of the colonized individual, even his humanity, is exploited to the aggrandizement of the cultural identity of the colonizer.

It is important to note here that in the cases of Germany and Japan noted earlier, though industrialization and modernization were certainly accompanied by a hierarchical social system, the traditional culture, far from being devalued, was actively *idealized*—at the same time as it was being altered—by the native commercial elites, as part of the consolidation of their power. Although peasant and laboring classes were assuredly exploited and assigned low status, they did not suffer from wholesale derogation of their cultural values or their physical characteristics.

The equation of race and culture, and the old evolutionary hierarchies based on it, have not been laid to rest by liberal social-scientific theory; they are alive and kicking throughout the third world and in every "mother country" in Europe and America. Seen in the context of their effective operation in imperialist exploitation, ethnocentric and racist assumptions have been relatively little affected by liberal anthropology's intellectual attack on their scientific validity and the analysis of the "psychology of prejudice." Racism and ethnocentrism are integral parts of a total exploitative system, and will only be really destroyed in the course of the social action which will destroy the total system and give rise to a new social consciousness of affirmation and dignity on the part of the colonized man, who will redefine himself in the course of the struggle.

Many writers have dealt with the effects of colonization on the colonized, suggesting that the results have been various forms of social and psychological "pathology" (e.g., Myrdal, 1944; Elkins, 1959; Mannoni, 1964). It seems clear that pathological effects are also to be found in the personalities and social structures of the colonizers, as Memmi's study *The Colonizer and the Colonized* (1965) describes. The whole-culture exploitation I have been describing has far wider effects, however, than the distortion of the personalities of those overt racists most directly involved. Just as all classes in the colonized cultures are exploited by the system of imperialism, so all classes in the mother country "benefit" by that exploitation. It has been argued that the superprofits extracted by imperialism have raised living standards in the industrialized nations to such an extent that the working classes are effectively blinded to the fact that their own labor is being exploited. In like manner, I would argue that the aggrandizement of cultural self which goes with membership in an imperial culture blinds us all to the fact of our basic alienation—alienation from our work, from each other, from ourselves—and thus operates to "prop up" the irrational, exploitative system of monopoly capitalism. That total consciousness of exploitation and alienation which Marx predicted would lead to the creation of the New Man (see Fromm, 1961, *passim*; Marx, pp. 93–109 in the same volume) has been a long time coming; but Marx, as I have suggested, did not see the complications which imperialism would present to his analysis. How can one become conscious of alienation when one's cultural identity is the "best" in the world, when we are carrying the American Way of Life (or the British, or the French, or the "civilized" way of life) to the "backward nations"? What is the ideology behind the Peace Corps?

THE DIALECTIC OF CULTURAL EXPLOITATION AND REVOLUTION

I have deliberately refrained up to this point from discussing the effects of cultural exploitation on the colonized culture, because it is a question of some complexity, and I want to treat it as a conceptual whole. If we conceive of the pre-colonial culture as the thesis, and the system of cultural exploitation as antithesis, then the end point in the dialectic, the synthesis, is the coming into being of a new cultural entity. Given the extreme and violent nature of the basic contradiction itself, which permeates virtually every aspect of the human existence of the colonized individual, the ultimate struggle leading to the qualitative leap into new cultural existence can be assumed to be violent and cathartic, that is, revolutionary. The small, incremental, quantitative changes preceding this qualitative leap, however, should concern us first.

What then are the consequences of cultural exploitation in terms of the colonized culture and the individuals sharing it? Fanon describes the psychological pathologies of the colonized personality and suggests that the inhibition of native culture by imperialism leads to an effective "withering away" of that culture itself:

> After a century of colonial domination we find a culture which is rigid in the extreme, or rather what we find are the dregs of culture, its mineral strata. (1963, p. 238)

Peter Worsley equates Fanon's "colonized personality" with Stanley Elkins' "infantilized slave" personality and suggests that this is the same process: the *deculturation* of colonial peoples (Worsley, 1964, pp. 30–31). But Worsley has missed a crucial distinction between Fanon's concept and Elkins's. Elkins speaks of the slave as a person who has been deprived of "significant others" in his own culture and therefore made dependent upon the master's definition of his very identity (1959, pp. 128–29). Fanon speaks rather of active response to inhibition:

> The negation of the native's culture, the contempt for any manifestation of culture whether active or emotional, and the placing outside the pale of all specialized branches of organization contribute to breed aggressive patterns of conduct in the native. (1963, p. 238)

"Aggressive"—not helplessly dependent. Fanon's stress is on the *creation* of cultural expressions in the process of struggle against oppression. But let us consider for a moment the "deculturated" man.

In the first place, I doubt that anyone would seriously

argue that actual, complete deculturation of any person or group is possible. Man is a cultural animal, and no matter how distorted, constricted, or exploited his cultural context, he cannot live without one. Perhaps the most nearly complete destruction of cultural continuity was that perpetrated on the North American slaves, who were brought to this country and placed in situations where their cultural forms had very little meaning and had to be rapidly and drastically reformulated. Robert Blauner, in speaking of this "forced deculturation," suggests:

> But at the same time, beginning with slavery, the group- and culture-*building* process began among the black population, and the development of an ethnic group identity and distinctive culture has been going on ever since. (1969, p. 422; my emphasis)

Other peoples may not have undergone such drastically destructive experiences, but as I have indicated above, the characteristic effects of imperialism have included serious distortion of the economic bases, the social structures, and ethos of colonized peoples generally. It is my contention that Blauner's process of "culture-building," developing in adaptation to, and in protest against, the social experiences of the colonial situation, can be discerned in the group lives of most if not all culturally exploited peoples.

While it is true, then, that the "traditional" culture is eroded by exploitation, it is not true that colonized peoples were simply stripped of their old cultural baggage and gradually re-equipped with European or American values, nor that the "mineral strata" of old cultures were the only self-identifying mechanisms. As Fredrik Barth has pointed out, for colonized or outcast groups that are effectively barred from "passing," strategies tending to maximize ethnic boundaries may be adopted in order to maintain a degree of security, both psychological and social (1969, Introduction). In other words, the social experience of segregation, economic discrimination, and prejudice creates a consciousness of the importance of the segregated community as a social base and leads to the emphasizing of group distinctiveness. These boundary-maintaining mechanisms may be in fine details of behavior, interactional innuendos, gestures, ways of speaking, body movements, as well as in significant institutional activities—the establishment of separate churches, mutual aid societies, or cooperative work groups such as the "morning sport" in Jamaica (cf. Reisman, 1970). I am suggesting that "boundary maintenance" and other means of cultural self-definition should be viewed as basically the same type of interactional process, essentially creative and individual as well as traditional and group-determined. These expressions of ethnic identity and group solidarity are retained in part from precolonial traditions, but they are also reshaped, altered, and created anew, sometimes using selected elements of the dominant culture. The process of "culture-building" and affirming cultural identity is a never-ending, ever-changing, innovative process, and it involves not just the withering away of some elements, but the addition of new ones from a variety of sources.[2]

Different strategies are adopted by different individuals in different social situations or historical periods—there is nothing steady or sure about the culture-building process. It is possible to maximize boundaries at one time or place while minimizing them at others. Thus a Jamaican peasant may affirm cultural bonds, participating in his village work group, and still feel awe and admiration for the economic institutions of the whites in the town. The exalted economic and political statuses of the European rulers lend powerful support to their assertions of cultural superiority, and many members of the derogated group have attempted to identify with the aggressor by adopting his cultural attributes. Yet it is one's social experience that molds one's social consciousness, and there have been certain very important developments in the social facts of colonial life that have forcefully maximized affirmation of independent cultural values and also extended the scope of the exploited group with which the native identifies. In order to make this point properly, I would have to detail the social transformations wrought in each colonial country separately, for there is a tremendous range of variation. Nonetheless, one can discern a few common factors with similar effects.

The introduction of plantation systems, mining enterprises, and so on has radically altered not only ecological relations but demographic distributions. In plantation colonies, where peasant economies exist side by side with large estates, labor patterns of seasonal migration have developed, and longer-term migrant labor is a common pattern in African mining. Furthermore, as Wolf notes, imperialism has everywhere engendered an "ecological crisis."

> Where in the past the peasant had worked out a stable combination of resources to underwrite a minimal livelihood, the separate and differential mobilization of these resources as objects to be bought and sold endangered that minimal nexus. . . . Paradoxically, these processes of containment, subversion, and forced withdrawal of the peasantry [from their land] coincided with a rapid acceleration of population growth. . . . The peasant thus confronted a growing imbalance between population and resources. (1969, pp. 280–81)

Wolf goes on to suggest that this imbalance forced men to "seek new social forms which would grant them shelter" and that the peasant revolutions in the countries he is considering were the "outcome of such defensive reactions, coupled with a search for a new and more human social order" (1969, p. 282). I think that this analysis is essentially correct, but in this form it telescopes the whole process of development of revolutionary consciousness, the highly significant cultural side to national liberation struggles, and reduces the causal process to a need-fulfillment mechanism. I am suggesting a *long* process of redefinition of cultural identity, widening in scope from narrow village or tribal identification to larger and larger groups, coupled with a growing awareness of the commonality of exploitative situations and of solidarity in the face of oppression.

For example, when Mozambique males left their villages in large numbers for years-long labor in the Rhodesian mines, they not only altered the domestic and ecological pattern of subsistence farming (Harris, 1966); they also came into contact with similarly affected males from other areas, forming bonds and shared cultural identities. Similarly, as pressures on peasant land in Jamaica forced fathers to send their children to seek domestic work in the towns, the new social experiences, coalitions, and consciousness of the urban migrants were brought back to the villages when the children returned. Geographic mobility and the multiplication of part-time or temporary survival strategies in the face of exploitation and population increase, plus the demographic concentrations occasioned by that increase itself, have created a variety of new social groupings and a vastly increased range of communication and identification. With the growth of urban populations, clustered around commercial and administrative centers, former peasants and part-time peasants have come in contact with other classes as well. The recognition that even the Westernized native elites were objects of derogation by whites has led to pan-class identification of interests and culture, and new elites have arisen that are more in tune with the developing consciousness of the masses.

Geographic mobility and urbanization have led to new social groupings and communication between formerly unfamiliar groups. In addition, mass communications techniques, in particular the radio, have introduced the colonized peoples of the world to each other on a very broad scale; cross-cultural identification between exploited peoples very widely removed in space and tradition, news of the growth of revolutionary consciousness in all parts of the world, have had an electrifying effect on the processes of cultural affirmation. The qualitative leap in consciousness from boundary-maintaining mechanisms to positive affirmation of cultural and racial worth and dignity is the final step in the dialectic of imperialism.

Of course, there has been an almost endless number of complications, permutations, and combinations to the rather simple scheme I have suggested. For example, an important part in self-definition has been played by native literary elites, and their role has been far from consistent. The use of Western-educated natives as civil servants, professionals, and so on has been common, and in most cases a relatively affluent commercial bourgeoisie has developed, profiting from the increased flow of goods but denied access to the sources of real power and profit. Where a degree of administrative control is allowed to such elites, as in the British West Indies, competition for the limited number of favored positions can lead to factional squabbling between the "ins" and the "outs" (see Singham, 1967). In muticultural societies, such in-and-out fighting may move the elites of separate cultural sections to mobilize the developing cultural consciousness of the masses into disputes along racial or cultural lines, often with the connivance of the imperial power. The case of Guiana illustrates this process: in spite of efforts by Jagan to unify Africans and Indians against the British, Burnham's racial appeal succeeded in polarizing the society between the oppressed groups, much to the satisfaction of the British (Despres, 1967).

The tendency for a portion of the disaffected intellectual elite to turn away from European culture and to look to their own "common people" for inspiration and self-identification has produced other interesting effects. The literary and philosophical movement championing "negritude," or African personality, was the product of such a Western-educated elite—a rather self-conscious attempt to make their new-found identity "respectable" to Western eyes.

> Their program is to create the missing African great tradition from above through refined, synthetic restatement of indigenous cultural materials, hopefully extant and widespread, but still waiting to be identified. (Marriott, 1963, p. 49)

The trouble with this attempt at literary expression is that it looks backward, to a precolonial mythical golden age, rather than to the future, where the aspirations of the people lie. Fanon has stated the case with characteristic fervor:

The native intellectual nevertheless sooner or later will realize that you do not show proof of your nation from its culture but that you substantiate its existence in the fight which the people wage against the forces of occupation. . . . You will never make colonialism blush for shame by spreading out little-known cultural treasures under its eyes. At the very moment when the native intellectual is anxiously trying to create a cultural work he fails to realize that he is utilizing techniques and language which are borrowed from the stranger in his country. He contents himself with stamping these instruments with a hallmark which he wishes to be national, but which is strangely reminiscent of exoticism. . . . Sometimes he has no hesitation in using a dialect in order to show his will to be as near as possible to the people; but the ideas he expresses and the preoccupations he is taken up with have no common yardstick to measure the real situation which the men and the women of his country know. . . . He wishes to attach himself to the people, but instead he only catches hold of their outer garments. And these outer garments are merely the reflection of a hidden life, teeming and perpetually in motion. That extremely obvious objectivity which seems to characterize a people is in fact only the inert, already forsaken result of frequent, and not always very coherent, adaptations of a much more fundamental substance which itself is continually renewed. . . . When a people undertakes an armed struggle or even a political struggle against a relentless colonialism, the significance of tradition changes.

All that has made up the technique of passive resistance in the past may, during this phase, be radically condemned. In an underdeveloped country during the period of struggle traditions are fundamentally unstable and are shot through by centrifugal tendencies. (1963, pp. 223–25)

I have quoted from this passage at some length because it expresses far better than I am able to do the continuous, creative process I have called "culture-building"—"adaptations of a fundamental substance which itself is continually renewed." Further, Fanon here makes clear the qualitative difference between this process and the revolutionary change in consciousness which accompanies the act of violent liberation itself, when "the significance of tradition changes." Culture, in this view, is a continual creative act; the qualitative leap into awareness and affirmation takes place in the struggle to resolve the contradictions of man's existence. Another black spokesman for an emerging cultural consciousness has likewise emphasized the self-creation process:

> But can a people (its faith in an idealized American Creed notwithstanding) live and develop for over three hundred years simply by *reacting*? Are American Negroes simply the creation of white men, or have they at least helped to create themselves out of what they found around them? Men have made a life in caves and upon cliffs, why cannot Negroes have made a life upon the horns of the white man's dilemma? (Ellison, 1953, p. 301)

ANTHROPOLOGY AND LIBERATION

The passage from Fanon is instructive in another way, one which brings us back to the problems which anthropology has had in dealing with imperialism. Try reading the first three sentences of the passage again, in the context of what follows them, substituting "anthropologist" for "native intellectual" and, to bring out the point, "concern for a nation," for "your nation," "scientific" for "cultural," and "relevant" for "national." Possibly a radical renewal of our own self-definition is in order. When we understand "native intellectual" as comprising "anthropologist," in a world in which the profession of anthropology is no longer the monopoly of citizens of colonial and imperial countries, no substitutions are even necessary.

What I am suggesting for my profession, then, is not that

we should turn sociologist, historian, or economist and deal with the phenomena of imperialism in terms of another discipline, but rather that we should become more truly ourselves and try to understand imperialism in its cultural aspects. As I have tried to show, this demands that we treat culture change in a new way, a way which incorporates the data of related fields and at the same time focuses on the real locus of change: the culture-creating individual and his actions and interactions. Whether or not the dialectic I propose appears adequate as a general paradigm for further work, I think it is time that American anthropologists recognized their past failure to deal with the questions raised, and recognized that these questions surround them in their own country.

During the upsurge of cultural consciousness (Red Power) which led to the invasion of Alcatraz, I was engaged in carrying supplies and Indians back and forth on my boat, and the thought occurred to me that the little help I was contributing probably amounted to more real aid to liberation for those people than any amount of anthropologizing I might conceivably do in my lifetime. On the other hand, the need for a body of revolutionary theory which deals with the questions of consciousness, culture, and social action so evident in today's world is a need which I feel for my *own* liberation; the future transformation of American society and culture is intimately bound up with liberation struggles everywhere. I feel confident that anthropology, with all its shortcomings, has a potential contribution to make to the understanding—and the attainment—of liberation for us all.

Notes

I want to thank Professors Dell Hymes, Horace B. Davis, Robert Blauner, Chandler Davis, and Gerald Berreman for their helpful criticisms and suggestions in preparing this paper.

1. The notable exception to this generalization is the excellent ethnography by Hortense Powdermaker, *After Freedom* (1939), a study which has been largely ignored by anthropologists. Szwed (in this volume) shows how inadequate has been anthropological attention to Afro-American culture.

2. Norman Klein, in a review article (1966) on Fanon's *The Wretched of the Earth,* has noted many forms of expression of group consciousness peculiar to colonial peoples, emphasizing those forms which are specifically prerevolutionary—ranging from "cultural codes," or systems of communication, to full-blown millenarian movements. I would include all of these as expressions of "culture-building" in an imperialist setting. Many aspects of Afro-American culture, cited by Szwed in this volume, must also be interpreted in terms of "culture-building" in a context of exploitation.

References

Balandier, Georges. 1966. "The Colonial Situation: A Theoretical Approach." In *Social Change: The Colonial Situation,* ed. I. Wallerstein. New York: John Wiley & Sons.

Barth, Fredrik. 1969. *Ethnic Groups and Boundaries: The Social Organization of Cultural Difference.* Boston: Little, Brown & Co.

Benedict, Burton. 1961. *Indians in a Plural Society: A Report on Mauritius.* London: HMSO.

Blauner, Robert. 1969. "Internal Colonialism and Ghetto Revolt." *Social Problems* 16: 393–408.

———. 1970. "Black Culture: Myth or Reality?" In *Americans from Africa,* ed. Peter Rose. Vol. 2, New York: Atherton Press. Pp. 417–40.

Césaire, Aimé. 1956. *Cahier d'un retour au pays natal.* Paris: Présence Africaine.

Collier, Peter. 1970. "The Theft of a Nation: Apology to the Cherokees." *Ramparts* 9: 35–50.

Despres, Leo. 1967. *Cultural Pluralism and Nationalist Politics in British Guiana.* Chicago: Rand McNally & Co.

Elkins, Stanley M. 1959. *Slavery: A Problem in American Institutional and Intellectual life.* Chicago: University of Chicago Press.

Ellison, Ralph. 1953. "An American Dilemma: A Review." In *Shadow and Act,* ed. R. Ellison. New York: New American Library, Signet Books. Pp. 290–302.

Fanon, Frantz. 1963. *The Wretched of the Earth.* New York: Grove Press.

———. 1967. *Black Skins, White Masks: The Experience of a Black Man in a White World.* New York: Grove Press.

Fontana, Bernard L. 1968. "Savage Anthropologists and Unvanishing

Indians in the American Southwest." Paper read at the annual meeting of the American Anthropological Association, Seattle, Wash.

Fromm, Eric. 1961. *Marx's Concept of Man.* New York: Frederick Ungar.

Geertz, Clifford. 1963. *Agricultural Involution: The Processes of Ecological Change in Indonesia.* Berkeley: University of California Press.

Gough, Kathleen. 1968. "Anthropology: Child of Imperialism." *Monthly Review* 19, No. 11: 12–27.

Haller, John S., Jr. 1970. "The Species Problem: Nineteenth-Century Concepts of Racial Inferiority in the Origin of Man Controversy." *American Anthropologist* 72: 1319–29.

———. 1971. "Race and the Concept of Progress in Nineteenth-Century American Ethnology." *American Anthropologist* 73, No. 3: 710–24.

Harris, Marvin. 1966. "Labour Emigration Among the Mozambique Thonga: Cultural and Political Factors." In *Social Change: The Colonial Situation,* ed. I. Wallenstein. New York: John Wiley & Sons. Pp. 91–106.

———. 1968. *The Rise of Anthropological Theory: A History of Theories of Culture.* New York: Thomas Y. Crowell Co.

Heilbroner, Robert. 1962. *The Making of Economic Society.* Englewood Cliffs, N.J.: Prentice-Hall.

Herskovits, Melville J. 1941. *The Myth of the Negro Past.* Boston: Beacon Press.

———. 1964. *Cultural Dynamics.* New York: Alfred A. Knopf.

Klein, Norman. 1966. "On Revolutionary Violence." *Studies on the Left* 6: 62–82.

Kroeber, A. L. 1917. "The Superorganic." *American Anthropologist* 19: 163–213.

Kuhn, Thomas S. 1962. *The Structure of Scientific Revolutions.* Chicago: University of Chicago Press.

Kuper, Leo. 1969. "Some Aspects of Violent and Non-Violent Political Change in Plural Societies." In *Pluralism in Africa,* eds. Leo Kuper and M. G. Smith. Berkeley: University of California Press. Pp. 153–94.

Leacock, Eleanor. 1954. *The Montagnais Hunting Territory and the Fur Trade.* Memoirs of the American Anthropological Association, No. 78. Menasha, Wis.

Lenin, V. I. 1939. *Imperialism, the Highest Stage of Capitalism.* New York: International Publishers.

Lewis, Oscar. 1942. *The Effects of White Contact Upon Blackfoot Culture with Special Reference to the Fur Trade.* Monographs of the American Ethnological Society, No. 6. Seattle: University of Washington Press.

Mannoni, O. 1964. *Prospero and Caliban: The Psychology of Colonization.* New York: Praeger Publishers.

Marriott, McKim. 1963. "Cultural Policy in the New States." In *Old Societies and New States,* ed. Clifford Geertz. New York: Free Press. Pp. 27–56.

Marx, Karl. [1850] 1924. *The Class Struggle in France.* New York: New York Labor News.

Memmi, Albert. 1965. *The Colonizer and the Colonized.* New York: Orion Press.

Myrdal, Gunnar, 1944. *An American Dilemma: The Negro Problem and Modern Democracy.* New York: Harper & Row.

Polanyi, Karl. 1957. *The Great Transformation: The Political and Economic Origins of Our Times.* Boston: Beacon Press.

Powdermaker, Hortense. [1939] 1968. *After Freedom: A Cultural Study in the Deep South.* New York: Russell & Russell.

Reisman, Karl. 1970. "Cultural and Linguistic Ambiguity in a West Indian Village." In *Afro-American Anthropology,* eds. Norman E. Whitten and John F. Szwed. New York: Free Press. Pp. 120–44.

Secoy, Frank R. 1953. *Changing Military Patterns on the Great Plains.* Monographs of the American Ethnological Society, No. 21. Seattle: University of Washington Press.

Singham, A. W. 1967. "Legislative-Executive Relations in Smaller Territories." In *Problems of Smaller Territories,* ed. Burton Benedict. London: Athlone Press. Pp. 134–48.

Smith, M. G. 1965. *The Plural Society in the British West Indies.* Berkeley: University of California Press.

Steward, Julian H. 1959. "Perspectives on Plantation." In *Plantation Systems of the New World.* Washington, D.C.: Pan-American Union. Pp. 5–12.

Van den Berghe, Pierre. 1964. *Caneville: The Social Structure of a South African Town.* Middletown, Conn.: Wesleyan University Press.

———. 1967. *Race and Racism.* New York, John Wiley & Sons.

Wallace, A. F. C. 1964. *Culture and Personality.* New York: Random House.

White, Leslie A. 1959. *The Evolution of Culture.* New York: McGraw-Hill Book Co.

Williams, Eric. 1961. *Capitalism and Slavery.* New York: Russell & Russell.

Wolf, Eric R. 1969. *Peasant Wars in the Twentieth Century.* New York: Harper & Row.

Worsley, Peter. 1964. *The Third World.* Chicago: University of Chicago Press.

Resistance and the Revitalization of Anthropologists: A New Perspective on Cultural Change and Resistance

Richard O. Clemmer

Hell is Truth seen too late; a Duty neglected in its Season.
—Tyrone Edward

I

WITH THE ADVENT of the 1970s, it appears that anthropology is soon to become an academic discipline as entrenched in college education as its more prestigious sisters, sociology and psychology. Provided, of course, that academia, the social system of the United States, and the world in general survive the effects of many changes that will take place and the consequences of those that will not. Change is the anthropologist's specialty, particularly when change involves two or more cultural systems. And much of the change that captures the attention of journalists, newscasters, politicians, commentators, writers, activists, and laymen directly involves either emergent or resurgent cultural systems.

A surprising development for Anglo-European America

/

has been the change of attitude among American "Indians."[1] A decade ago, it seemed that most American Indians would either be assimilated into the dominant Euro-American society of the United States, or would retain some of their cultural identity as members of societies that were definitely little more than slightly special subunits of the larger and dominant social system. Yet suddenly, things changed. Indians became "militant," and before most anthropologists knew what had happened, journalists were writing about "Red Power" (cf. Steiner, 1968).

Such changes on the American Indian scene have caught anthropologists with their theoretical cupboards bare. Although native peoples of this continent have been subjects of anthropological research for a hundred years, anthropological theory does not seem to have changed quickly enough or purposively enough to explain or even account for the sudden development of "Red Power." Actually, the development is neither sudden nor new. In the context of present-day circumstances, the development is completely consistent with certain aspects of native culture that simply were not recognized for what they were.

Anthropological studies of culture change among the native peoples of this continent have become wedged in a rut, and this stagnation has been caused primarily by the treatment of resistance to acculturation. *Resistance*, if discussed at all, is usually treated as a phase of acculturation, and in a theoretical framework that may explain the acculturation, but not the resistance to it. Resistance movements are analyzed either as tension-relieving mechanisms whose prime function is to ease the strain of the acculturative process, or as simple unwillingness by a particular group of people to abandon the security of preciously encultured behavior patterns. Such analysis may disclose something valid, but it is only half the picture; the dynamics and significance of resistance are lost.

In losing the significance of resistance, anthropologists have lost a major key to the revolutionary changes affecting the relationship between United States society and the societies of native peoples. This is not the result simply of intellectual myopia or careless research. Rather, it is the result of a subtle but significant bias that permeates anthropology and has especially dominated research on the native peoples of this continent.

The bias is pure ethnocentrism, a natural component of most cultural systems and particularly evident among members of societies that are, so to speak, on the winning side. Kathleen Gough (1967, p. 12) has characterized anthropology as a "child of Western imperialism," and Mina Davis Caulfield, in another paper in this volume, discusses anthropology's lack of theory for dealing with the politicoeconomic system that "made the natives safe for ethnography." Although few anthropologists may actually have been sympathetic to imperialism, and although many have sincerely sympathized with their subjects of study, it is not difficult to see why many subjugated people regard anthropologists as the rear guard of the conqueror's invasion force. Whenever the United States Army defeated a band of native people in battle, anthropologists from the Bureau of American Ethnology usually followed close behind and quickly set about doing salvage anthropology. Their goal was to gather as much information about the "dying" cultures as possible and to trundle away as many ethnographic artifacts as they could.

Undoubtedly, since anthropologists were on the winning side, most of them believed that they were witnessing the demise of aboriginal culture in what they called North America, shattered and bruised as native societies were by the onslaught of a technologically superior and ceaselessly aggressive force of invaders. But in the 1930s, anthropologists began to realize that while native societies had been subjected to severe pressures, native culture had not disappeared; rather, it had changed, and was still changing.

Resistance to acculturation has obviously been responsible for preventing the expected demise. The subtle bias continues to prevent anthropologists from assessing its significance. To illustrate this point, I shall discuss concepts from the culture-change literature that can be very useful in analyzing resistance movements if they are applied from a new vantage point. I shall then present a theoretical framework which establishes such a perspective, and detail a case of resistance with reference to it.

II

The first systematic attempt to bring together a number of concepts useful for the study of acculturation was made by Redfield, Linton, and Herskovits (1936, p. 149). They carefully distinguished between acculturation, which is a phase of culture change, and assimilation, which in turn is "at times a phase of acculturation." But they did not include resistance to acculturation as an equally important component of culture change. Nevertheless, many researchers noted that resistance was indeed a component of culture change, and a perplexed Linton (1940, p. 503) wondered if non-assimilation of the gypsies in Europe could be treated as a "result" of acculturation. He seemed to feel that a crucial factor in a group's assimilation was the existence of "directed culture change," in which "one of the groups in contact interferes actively and purposefully with the culture of the other" (1940, pp. 501–2).

In 1953 the Social Science Research Council Summer Seminar devoted some discussion to boundary-maintaining mechanisms as the means by which the autonomy of a cultural system might be perpetuated in the face of "directed culture change." They defined an autonomous cultural system as "one which is self-sustaining—that is, it does not need to be maintained by a complementary, reciprocal, subordinate, or other indispensable connection with a second system," and boundary-maintaining mechanisms as including "the relative presence or absence of devices by which the knowledge of customs and values is restricted to in-group members and thus shielded from alien influences" (Broom *et al.*, 1954, pp. 974, 976). It remained for Spicer to emphasize the coercive nature of directed culture change in sharpening Linton's definition.

Spicer substituted "contact" for "culture change" and proposed the following two diagnostic characteristics of directed contact (1961, pp. 520–21):

1. Definite sanctions—which may be political, economic, supernatural, or even moral—are regularly brought to bear by members of one society on members of another.

2. Members of the society applying the sanctions are interested in bringing about changes in the cultural behavior of members of the other society in particular ways.

Spicer also brought into use the words "superordinate," to characterize the society applying the sanctions, and "subordinate," to characterize the society to which sanctions are applied.

Thus his culture-change theory identified the following essential components of a directed contact situation: (1) Existence of a superordinate-subordinate relationship between two originally autonomous cultural systems; (2) employment of sanctions by the superordinate system to force changes; and (3) employment of boundary-maintaining mechanisms by the subordinate system to resist those sanctions. Yet the most important component of directed contact situations, which would have immediately clued anthropologists in to the importance of resistance, had not been discovered. This component is *ideology*.

Although researchers noted that fundamental beliefs, or values, influenced behavior patterns and could cause persistence of certain cultural traits, they failed to note exactly how their subjects of study responded to specific situations in terms of those beliefs or values. They failed to look for the existence of a set of guiding ideological principles that influenced behavior in a systematic manner and that could turn the persistence of cultural traits into a source of group mobilization for action to promote the group's self-interest. They also failed to look for the set of ideological principles that the superordinate society used to justify the sanctions it brought against the subordinated groups.

As long ago as 1951 Edward Dozier pointed out the importance of resistance as a phenomenon of culture in his article "Resistance to Acculturation and Assimilation in an Indian Pueblo." This study is the only one of which I am aware, however, that documents resistance to acculturation as the definite and systematic goal of a particular group. Dozier, himself a Tewa, discusses the success of the Hano-Tewa of First Mesa in perpetuating their own autonomous cultural system despite residence among the Hopi since the early 1700s, when they left the Gallisteo Basin to escape Spanish reprisals against rebellious Pueblos.

Despite the fact that the Hopi themselves consist of a number of different peoples who migrated to Hopi country from various now-ruined pueblos and were assimilated by the original dwellers of the country, the Tewa have retained their identity by developing countersanctions against possible Hopi pressure to either adopt Hopi culture or move back to their home. Although Tewas speak Hopi fluently, they speak Tewa when they do not want Hopis to know what they are saying. Although they participate in Hopi religious ceremonies, they often perform their own ceremonies according to their own rules. And while the Tewas tacitly recognize the authority of the Walpi village chief, the Tewa village also has its own chief and its own independent social organization.

Dozier concludes that the Tewas' success in perpetuating their cultural autonomy lies primarily in their use of psychological techniques to maintain a cultural boundary between themselves and the Hopi.

By the repeated assertion that the Hopi were unable to learn the Tewa language, a psychological "set" was created among the Hopi that prevented them from acquiring that knowledge. It is very curious that Hopi men who marry into Tewa Village, and live there most of their lives, never speak the language. Any attempt at uttering Tewa words is met with immediate mocking laughter. (Dozier, 1951, p. 63)

This lingual barrier is the manifestation of what Dozier calls a "curse," which the Tewa put on the Hopi of First Mesa when the Hopi purportedly refused to fulfill a promise they had made to supply the Tewas with payment for the Tewas' help in repelling Navajo, Ute, and Spanish invaders. The "curse" prevents Hopis from understanding or speaking Tewa, but allows the Tewas a perfect understanding as well as an ability to speak it.

Of course, Hopi pressure to assimilate the Tewas cannot be equated with Anglo-European pressure to assimilate the native peoples of the continent they conquered. Never did the Hopis threaten or attempt to exterminate the Tewas. Nevertheless, the case illustrates an aspect of resistance to acculturation that most researchers seem to have overlooked: *the positive, creative aspect.* What appeared to the Hopis as a negative rejection of the Hopi way of life was for the Tewas a positive affirmation of their own cultural traditions, heritage, and identity. What appeared to the Hopis as resistance to accepting their hegemony and their own way of doing things was for the Tewas a revitalization of Tewa culture in a harsh and barren land hundreds of miles from their home. The Hopis accepted the boundary-maintaining mechanism, and they continue to respect the Tewas' perpetuation of what must have been a mild revitalization movement.

A revitalization movement is, in Wallace's words, a "deliberate, organized, conscious effort by members of a society to construct a more satisfying culture" (1956, p. 65). If constructing a more satisfying culture in the face of assimilative pressure entails collectively erecting a boundary-maintaining mechanism that preserves cultural autonomy, then resisting acculturation and assimilation can be regarded as revitalization as well as resistance. It is impossible to move back in time, of course, to prove the assertion that the Tewa resistance began as a revitalization movement. But the creative aspects of Hano-Tewa resistance (which included adoption of Hopi unilineal and unilocal rules of marriage and residence—forms of "assimilation" which had precisely the effect of maintaining autonomy) and the uniqueness and vitality of Hano-Tewa culture today would seem to support the inference that resistance has been a positive cultural force, exhibiting some important elements of revitalization. The Tewa case shows that a successful resistance movement requires a deliberate ideology and a conscious effort, just as a revitalization movement does.

Wallace includes what Linton (1943) calls "nativistic" movements in his discussion of revitalization, but he also includes such successful social movements as the Russian Revolution. Few people would see a similarity between a "nativistic" movement such as Handsome Lake's Longhouse Religion and a class conflict between the oppressed and their oppressors, yet Wallace argues cogently that the psychological processes generating the two movements were quite similar. Although Wallace elaborates his discussion by referring to prophets, visions, and hysterical seizures, he also states that "there is a tendency, which is implicit in the earlier discussion of stages, for movements to become more political in emphasis and to act through secular rather than religious institutions, as problems of organization, adaptation, and routinization become more pressing" (1956, p. 277).

Furthermore, "if the group action program in nonritual spheres is effective in reducing stress-generating situations, it becomes established as normal in various economic, social, and political institutions and customs" (Wallace, 1956, p. 275). Thus, a revitalization movement that begins as a religious movement or as the dream or vision of several individuals can become a purely political movement, as did the Taiping Rebellion (Wallace, 1956, p. 275). It is possible, then, for a revitalization movement, aimed at constructing a more satisfying culture by resisting subjugation under another cultural system, to evolve in a steady state of cultural resistance employing boundary-maintaining mechanisms, as in the Tewa case, or to culminate in rebellion or revolution, if the movement is forced to adopt increasingly more pragmatic strategies in the face of pressures from an encroaching oppressor.

I am suggesting that, because of its ideological basis, resistance to acculturation can be a force as potentially significant for anthropological analysis of culture change as are the forces pressuring for acculturation. With its revitalistic qualities, a resistance movement can become a revolutionary movement if the correct circumstances obtain. Youths professing adherence to Handsome Lake's Longhouse Religion, a revitalization movement that has become an organizational force for Iroquois resistance to acculturation, were leaders of the Iroquois who ousted Canadian customs officials from Cornwall Island in spring 1969; they also led the colonization of Alcatraz in the fall of the same year.

III

The failure to recognize the relationship of resistance to acculturation, cultural revitalization, and revolution results from anthropological theory having become stranded in the quagmire of ethnographia and "objectivity" salvaged in anthropology's heyday as a "child of Western imperialism." While the formerly docile subjects of anthropological research accuse anthropologists of being part of the problem because they are not part of the solution, the accused wring their hands, form ethics committees, and start radical caucuses.

More fruitful directions for significant action might emerge from establishing an entirely new perspective on the nature of directed contact. To illustrate this point, I propose applying the following theoretical framework to the analysis of culture change in situations of directed contact.[2] The new and important aspect of this framework, as has been stressed, is emphasis on ideology and treatment of resistance behavior as systematic phenomena.

There are three components of this theoretical framework: fundamental beliefs, ideology, and behavior. Fundamental beliefs are those convictions of what constitutes reality that are most important for the self-identification of the particular group adhering to the beliefs; they are most conveniently articulated as a set of suppositions. Action, or behavior, is the readily observable activity by which a collective effort to accomplish goals is manifested. Apter (1964, p. 17) notes that ideology is the very important transitional link between fundamental belief and action.

Ideology must not be confused with fundamental belief, for ideology, when articulated—usually as a set of goals—is a statement of the moral superiority of fundamental beliefs and applies to specific situations rather than to all situations, as do fundamental beliefs. Ideology transforms fundamental beliefs from the passive, cognitive level to the active, behavioral level in particular situations and thus sanctifies behavior with the same moral superiority attributed to the fundamental beliefs. Ideology, then, presents a moral imperative compelling individuals ascribing to certain beliefs to validate and affirm the moral superiority of those beliefs by engaging in certain behavior; it binds those individuals together on a behavioral as well as on a cognitive level.

Ideology is the basic component of an active response by any particular group of people to new circumstances that require some kind of collective effort on their part. Ideology represents an emerging self-consciousness and is the motivating factor in resistance movements and revolutions, as well as in wars of conquest and manifest destiny. As I shall attempt to show, it is the most important component of a concerted effort to force acculturation on a subordinate society and is equally crucial for the concerted movement to thwart that effort, whether that movement is resistance to acculturation, revitalization, or revolution. An ideology of resistance is formed when the behavior of one group of people causes certain fundamental beliefs to become the focal point for a social movement by another group of people—dissatisfied people.

IV

Let me now describe a resistance effort by a group of native people to illustrate application of the theoretical framework to a real situation. The resisters in this case constitute approximately two-thirds or more residents of the small Hopi village of Hotevilla, on Third Mesa. Although Hotevilla's population probably does not exceed eight hundred,[3] Hotevilla, like all other Hopi villages, is a complete and autonomous social unit. Traditionally, there is no indigenous structure uniting all the Hopi villages, nor is there a chief representing them all. Each village is a functionally independent social unit, and the village chief is, according to tradition, the sole spokesman for his village. Should all Hopi villages but one suddenly disappear from the face of the earth, that one remaining village could carry on by itself as an autonomous nation.

Hotevilla is one of twelve Hopi villages that feel the effects of sanctions directed against them in the form of acculturative pressures. Four of the villages were formed as direct results of these acculturative pressures, and three of these are generally regarded by the Hopi themselves as "Christian" and "progressive" towns. Although the resistance movement has some adherents in all villages, even among ostensibly "progressive" segments, resistance is centered in five strongholds of traditional culture and is particularly potent at Hotevilla.

The sanctions which United States society levies against the Hopi and therefore against Hotevilla are manifold;

some are levied in very subtle ways, others in more overt ways. Explicitly stated rules, regulations, and laws emanating from the United States government applying to the Hopi must be regarded as overt sanctions, since Indian reservations are defined and ultimately controlled by the federal government. Examples of such overt sanctions are those laws and regulations now in force requiring compulsory standardized education for Indian children in United States schools; requiring male Indians to join the armed forces of the United States; requiring Indians to accept unilateral agreements decreed in congressional acts, executive orders, executive agreements, and so on. Thus the conflict arising from directed contact is largely between Hotevilla resisters and the institutions of the federal government.

Probably the most significant institution for levying sanctions was originally the Bureau of Indian Affairs. The federal government established the Hopi Indian Reservation in 1882 along with an agency of the Bureau of Indian Affairs to administer the reservation. Located eleven miles from First Mesa in the traders' settlement of Keams Canyon, the BIA today operates six day schools, one boarding school, and one junior high; supervises installation of public works; builds roads on the reservation; negotiates boundaries and land-use claims between the Navajo and Hopi tribal councils; approves all money-making ventures undertaken by the council; and operates a Hopi-manned police force. Through the Bureau of Indian Affairs, the federal government implements policies established by Congress.

Three of the most important of these policies were contained in the Citizenship Act of 1924, the Indian Reorganization Act of 1935, and House Concurrent Resolution 108 of 1953. Extension of the rights and obligations of United States citizenship in 1924 resulted in various states according voting rights to previously disenfranchised Indians between 1924 and 1953. But it also resulted in all Indian males, including Hopis, becoming eligible to the draft under Selective Service regulations, and gave unscrupulous missionaries and agency superintendents an excuse to suppress native culture. It was not uncommon in the 1920s for public religious ceremonies and dances to be prohibited on the pretext that such performances were pagan and not proper for people who were now citizens of the United States.

Religious persecution was firmly stopped, however, when John Collier instituted his "New Deal for Indians" in 1933. The pros and cons of Collier's policies are still being argued (cf. Steward, 1969), but it cannot be denied that his policies had profound effects on reservation life, and those effects are emerging most dramatically today. A significant portion of the New Deal's philosophy was contained in the Indian Reorganization Act of 1935. Originally drawn up as the Wheeler-Howard Act, the IRA proposals were submitted for approval to all Indian groups living on reservations that did not already have a governmental structure considered to be adequate for dealing officially with the United States government. Among other things, the bill proposed social and political reorganization for those Indian groups that approved the bill in a special reservation referendum. According to Commissioner of Indian Affairs John Collier (1936), voters on the Hopi Reservation accepted the Wheeler-Howard Bill by a vote of 519 to 299, the total votes cast amounting to 45 percent of the eligible voters. A number of Hopis maintain, however, that voters were told they were voting for retention of their land, not for reorganization, that registration papers were falsified, and that votes were fabricated. Congress subsequently passed the bill in amended form as the amended Indian Reorganization Act of 1935.

To those groups accepting reorganization, the Bureau of Indian Affairs presented constitutions establishing a system of government which followed a general pattern on all reorganized reservations: determination of policy was invested in an elected tribal council which became the legal representative of the group in question and governed the group in accordance with the group's constitution and the rules and regulations established by the Secretary of Interior within the bounds of the Indian Reorganization Act. Oliver La Farge wrote the "Constitution and By-laws of the Hopi Tribe, Arizona" for the Bureau of Indian Affairs, and on October 24, 1936, it was submitted to Hopis and approved by a vote of 651 to 104, with 42 percent of the eligible voters participating in the referendum. The Hopi Agency of the BIA was given the responsibility of forming a Hopi tribal council and setting it in motion, which it did not permanently succeed in doing until 1955.

Over the years, the tribal council has become a major subject of criticism and opposition from resistant Hopi factions. Some of its more controversial actions have been the hiring of a tribal lawyer to settle a land dispute with the Navajo tribe; granting leases to oil companies to drill test wells on Hopi land; and granting Peabody Coal Company of St. Louis a lease to strip-mine coal on a part of the Hopi Reservation that is disputed with the Navajos. As far as the United States government is concerned, however, the council is the only legal representative of the Hopi people, including the Hotevilla people, who refuse to appoint their two allotted representatives to it and refuse even to acknowledge the council's validity.

For the BIA, the existence of the council has greatly reduced the complexity of dealing with the Hopi. Before it was created, the BIA had to contact each village chief if it wished to consult the official representatives of the Hopi people. The village chief (*kikmongwi*) is installed according to heredity, clan affiliation, and other qualifications—not by popular election—and in theory he controls all land belonging to his village, although in practice these lands are held and farmed by groups of matrilineally related clansmen. The *kikmongwi* is regarded as the protector of his people, and he is more an interpreter of Hopi tradition than an executive, since there is no mechanism by which a *kikmongwi* can enforce his decisions or punish dissenters (Titiev, 1944, p. 65). In claiming the power to make decisions binding on all the Hopi people, the council has in large part usurped the position of village spokesman formerly held by the village chiefs, and it is easy to see why villages adhering to the traditional form of social and political organization oppose it as a *de facto* institution of the United States government.

Although application of the provisions of the Indian Reorganization Act has brought tremendous pressure on Hopis to change their aboriginal social organization and conform to Anglo-European conceptions of sociopolitical structure, implementation of congressional intent as articulated in House Concurrent Resolution 108 would totally eliminate the special status of reservation-based native nations and would increase acculturative pressures on individual Hopis even more. H.C.R. 108, passed by both houses of Congress in 1953, states in part:

> Whereas it is the policy of Congress, as rapidly as possible, to make the Indians within the territorial limits of the United States subject to the same laws and entitled to the same privileges and responsibilities as are applicable to other citizens of the United States, to end their status as wards of the United States. . . .

And:

> Whereas the Indians within the territorial limits of the United States should assume their full responsibilities as American citizens. . . .

The meaning of this resolution for Bureau of Indian Affairs activity was expressed to me in 1969 by a BIA official:

> The Indians don't like termination, but eventually it's going to have to come. District Six is all tribal land, and when termination comes, it'll be divided up into so many acres per person and every Hopi'll have a plot of his own. It's going to have to come eventually.

As the official noted, termination would result in reservation lands being divided and allotted to individuals. Such a situation would create opportunities for outsiders to pur-

chase these lands on the real-estate market or lease them
from individuals who decided that they would rather have
money than land; it would mean the end of the closed,
corporate community (cf. La Farge, 1957, p. 45; Watkins,
1957, p. 53). For the United States, termination would mean
more consumers for the economy and more candidates for
the mythical melting pot. For the Hopis, it would mean the
end of cultural autonomy and the end of their identity as a
distinct group.

FUNDAMENTAL BELIEFS AND IDEOLOGY: UNITED STATES

Despite the fact that "the Indians don't like termination,"
it is clear that the general purpose of important legislation
and policies regarding native peoples since 1924 has been
to create circumstances that would pressure them to assimilate. Although the Nixon administration has repudiated
termination of special status as official policy, H.C.R. 108
remains the official policy of Congress despite many bills
introduced into the Ninety-first Congress to repeal it. The
most recent campaign for assimilation came in 1967 when
President Lyndon Johnson announced a new package of
plans, and his Commissioner of Indian Affairs, Robert Bennett, submitted the "Omnibus Bill" to the House and Senate
Indian Affairs subcommittees.

Selected parts of the "Omnibus Bill" as well as testimony
of the Indian Affairs subcommittees' hearings and from
policy announcements of the Johnson administration provide insight into the fundamental beliefs of United States
society as well as that current ideology which compels
transformation of the beliefs into action undertaken by the
institutions set up to deal with subordinate aboriginal
societies. Below are selected quotations for proposed legislation of 1967, President Johnson's policy statement, testimony on the "Omnibus Bill" to the House Subcommittee

on Indian Affairs, and an official Bureau of Indian Affairs publication.

From "Statement of Purpose" of H.R. 15035, "A BILL to Provide for the Economic Development and Management of the Resources of Individual Indians and Indian Tribes, and for Other Purposes":

> Sec. 2. Congress recognizes that, notwithstanding the significant social and economic advances the American Indian has made, his progress has not been sufficient to enable him to share fully in our national life.

From "The President's Message to the Congress on Goals and Programs for the American Indians," March 8, 1968:

> Our goal must be:
> —A standard of living for the Indians equal to that of the country as a whole.
> —Freedom of choice: An opportunity to remain in their homelands, if they choose, equipped with the skills to live in equality and dignity.
> —Full participation in the life of modern America, with a full share of opportunity and social justice.

From *Answers to Your Questions About American Indians*:

> 33. What are the basic aims of the Bureau of Indian Affairs? Briefly stated they are: 1) higher Indian standards of living; 2) assumption by Indians and Indian tribes of the responsibility for managing their own funds and other resources; and 3) political and social integration of Indians.

From testimony before the House Subcommittee on Indian Affairs on H.R. 15035, the "Omnibus Bill," entitled "The Indian Resources Development Act of 1967":

> SECRETARY UDALL: . . . I would think this type of legislation [the "Omnibus Bill"], which I think would encourage decision-making, would develop the capacity of Indian groups and leaders to make decisions, and would move us down the road toward the right kind of ultimate independence that I think the Indian people want.

REPRESENTATIVE ASPINALL: By "ultimate independence" do you mean the doing away with Reservations as such?
SECRETARY UDALL: I think this is undoubtedly the ultimate result, yes.

As a participant-observer of the superordinate society, I would identify the fundamental beliefs represented in these statements, policies, and legislation, and in the history of the development of the United States in general, as follows:

1. The people of the United States have earned the right to occupy and use their land because they developed it from an unproductive wilderness into a productive area supporting the highest standard of living in the world.
2. This development has been achieved because government has allowed and encouraged private enterprise, which has been free from governmental fetters to develop the nation's resources—both natural and human.
3. All men are created equal; therefore each person has the right to live as he pleases according to his own beliefs as long as he does not interfere with the rights of others to do the same.
4. All Americans have the right to an opportunity to share in the productivity.
5. The principles of democracy—including the right to vote and determination of policy by elected representatives—ensure that government is the servant of its people, not their master.

The ideological principles compelling transformation of these fundamental beliefs from the cognitive to the behavioral level speak directly to the problem posed to United States society of unassimilated native groups. They are:

1. The United States government is obligated to improve the living standards of native peoples.
2. The government is obligated to encourage native peoples to allow private enterprise to develop the resources of their land and to guide them in doing so, in

order that their living standards may be raised and in order that they may legally and morally retain rights to those lands.

3. The government is obligated to assimilate native peoples into the mainstream of Euro-American life by terminating their special status and to thereby grant them the dignity that automatically accrues from being wage-earning citizens of the United States.

4. The federal government is obligated to establish and ensure the operation of representative government for native groups.

These fundamental beliefs and ideological principles produce a logical chain of reasoning culminating in actions by United States government institutions, and often by tribal governments acting under supervision of the Bureau of Indian Affairs, which are almost certain to produce resentment and noncooperation among people who do not share the fundamental beliefs of the superordinate society. This chain of reasoning goes something like this:

Since all men are created equal, it is paradoxical that the Indian is "an alien in his own land," and he must therefore be assimilated into the mainstream of Euro-American life. Native peoples are subject to *de facto* discrimination in that the reservation system encourages persistence of old ways and concomitant high unemployment and low standards of living, and thus prevents them from assuming the rights and obligations due them as American citizens. Since the United States government is responsible for the reservations, it must supervise assimilation. But since democracy ensures that government is the servant and not the master of its people, democratic, representative "tribal" government must determine the exact course of assimilation at each reservation.

"Tribal" governments must be persuaded to accomplish much of this assimilation by being shown the economic benefits of cooperating with the BIA in attracting private enterprise to the reservation and preparing members of the tribe for eventual alienation from their land. If tribal councils legally own land for their people, or if each individual himself owns lots, instead of clans claiming acres of land by right of tradition, tribal land can be developed in accordance with the principles of private enterprise, and thus moral and legal rights to occupy the land may be retained. Developing resources will alleviate poverty by providing wage jobs and attracting more goods and services to reservations. But since the federal government is the servant of the people within the territorial boundaries of the United States, it must temporarily provide some of these jobs as well as health facilities and basic public works such as electricity, piped water, and sewage disposal in order to fulfill its commitments to raising standards of living. The BIA must also do its best to instill American values and expectancies as well as elementary skills in children through standardized curricula in all BIA schools.

THE BEGINNING OF A RESISTANCE MOVEMENT

Whereas Euro-American fundamental beliefs, ideology, and behavior are clearly rooted in an expansionist and achievement-oriented life-style, Hopi beliefs, ideology, and behavior are rooted in a life-style of domiciliary continuity and role-fulfillment. Hopi resistance to acculturative pressure from United States society has been almost constant from the time of original contact between the two cultural systems, but it did not manifest itself as a movement with a clearly articulated ideology until 1948. In that year six *kikmongwi* from all three mesas met together with other Hopi religious leaders for several days and produced the nascent ideology of the resistance movement.

At the meeting, it was determined that younger Hopis were not fulfilling their proper roles in Hopi social and ceremonial activities and that Hopi culture was suffering deterioration as a result. The war had indeed forced many young men into the armed forces, thus leaving performance of traditional religious ceremonies and social functions largely to older men. It was decided at the meeting that the chiefs and religious leaders would make concerted efforts to fulfill their own roles as social and religious pace-setters and revitalize Hopi culture. Results of these efforts were an increase in initiates to religious societies; the passing on of secret knowledge to younger people; the assured continuation of religious ceremonies that were about to disappear; and the start of a countercampaign to the white man's acculturative pressures that would articulate resistance in political language and action that the white man would understand.

Part of the development of a motivating ideology for resistance consisted in the systematic divulgence of prophecies made forty to sixty years previously that seemed to be coming true and the interpretation of these prophecies in light of current world events. Probably the most influential interpreter of these prophecies was the spokesman from Hotevilla. In the years since the first chiefs' meeting, this man has, through popular mandate of his villagers, become *kikmongwi* of Hotevilla. Despite his unorthodox attainment of that position, he is generally acknowledged by Hopi and BIA alike as village chief, and he continues to be the most outspoken Hopi opponent of the United States government. He clearly has a vision of a future world in which Hopi will be the spiritual leaders of a revitalized North American continent, where native peoples will again be keepers of the natural order as they were in the past, and where white men will live the native way or not at all. The statements below indicate this man's vision, and were made by him in a public meeting which he held in Hotevilla, August 5–6, 1956 (Hotevilla, 1956).

> The Hopi have, in following that Life Pattern ever since the Great Spirit gave it to us, obtained many prophecies. One of the things that was told to us was that the white man will

come and be a very intelligent man, bringing to us many things that he will invent. . . . Then they told us . . . that there would be a road in the sky. How could anyone build a road in the sky? we wondered. But when we see airplanes going back and forth over us we know what they were talking about.

These signs all tell us that we are nearing the end of our Life Patterns, that man will soon have to be judged. We call that Great Day the Purification Day; the white man calls it the Judgment Day. We look forward to it with great joy and the white man with horror and fear; and rightly so, for both of us know that on that day each will be dealt with according to what he justly deserves.

When our brother comes on the Purification Day it will be found that many of us have created much hardship for other people. The Hopi, for instance, will identify many people who have beaten us up, put us into jail, taken our land, starved us. Those people will of course be punished.

If, when He [the Purifier] comes, it will be found that the white man has done the best he can to right the wrongs he has committed, some of the white people in the U.S. may be saved. If he will *not* do what he is supposed to do, it will be doubtful if the white race will be allowed to live on any of this land after the Purification Day. This is as it was told by our forefathers.

Although the vision of purification, punishment of the Anglo-European invader, and eventual ascendency of native peoples fits the standard conception of the visionary prophet of a revitalization movement as outlined by Wallace (1956), activities of the movement are quite pragmatic. A year after the first chiefs' talk, village chiefs from Mishongnovi, Shungopavi, and Hotevilla held another meeting along with twenty-two Hopi religious leaders and addressed a letter to President Truman expressing strong opinions on a number of federal government programs that epitomize Euro-American conceptions of their relationship to native peoples. The letter was the first overt declaration of the resistance movement and spoke to the following points:

1. A request by the Land Claims Commission for Hopis to file claim to any land to which they felt entitled was rejected: "We will not ask a white man, who came to us recently, for a piece of land that is already ours."

2. A request from the Hopi Indian Agency for Hopis to decide whether they should lease land to oil companies to drill for oil was rejected on the grounds that the soil is sacred and must not be disturbed at this time.

3. The appropriations proposed under the Navajo-Hopi Bill and "the new theories that the Indian Bureau is planning for our lives under this new appropriation" were rejected.

4. The motives of the United States government inherent in the Hoover Commission's proposal to turn American Indians into "full taxpaying citizens" (in accordance with the legislation of 1924) were questioned on the grounds that since its establishment the United States has usurped Indian possessions "either by force, bribery, trickery, and sometimes by reckless killing, making himself very rich. . . . There is something terribly wrong with your system of government because after all these years, we the Indians are still licking on the bones and crumbs that fall to us from your table."

5. The North Atlantic Treaty Organization was rejected on the grounds that the Hopi are an independent nation and are not bound by such a treaty, since all the laws under the United States Constitution were made without Hopi consent, knowledge, or approval. "We will not go with you on a wild and reckless adventure which we know will lead us only to a total ruin."

The Navajo-Hopi Bill mentioned above would have allotted close to $1,000,000,000 to the Navajo and Hopi agencies of the Bureau of Indian Affairs to be spent on various reservation projects over a ten-year period. It was the target of a special protest made by the Hotevilla spokesman to the 1949 meeting of the National Congress of American Indians. After several unsuccessful attempts to gain the floor, the spokesman was eventually given permission to speak. Through an interpreter, he surprised the delegates to the placid meeting by vociferously condemning the Navajo-Hopi Bill, maintaining that it should not be forced on Hotevilla because the *kikmongwi* had not requested the money and did not want his village to be obligated to the United States for accepting benefits accruing from it.

Hotevilla's protest was ignored, of course. The bill passed in 1950, and $88,500,000 was allotted to the two agencies. But when the BIA tried to implement the "new theories" which it had indeed planned under the appropriation, Hotevilla again protested. The plans for Hotevilla included a new school building, a sewer system, and a water line complete with water tower. The bureau, in keeping with its obligation to ensure the operation of representative government, held a meeting at Hotevilla on the eve of February 11, 1957, to ascertain the opinion of the citizenry. Most of the citizenry of Hotevilla, however, wanted nothing to do with the Bureau of Indian Affairs and most of them did not attend the meeting. The results of balloting procedures which ostensibly conformed to the principles of Euro-American democratic process approved the bureau's proposals 49 to 2.

When the Hotevilla spokesman learned of the results of the votes, however, he immediately took action. Having attained the position of *kikmongwi* by this time, he was able to quickly circulate a petition to his villagers expressing extreme dissatisfaction with plans to proceed with the improvements. A letter of February 14, 1957, addressed to the superintendent of the Hopi Agency and signed by eighty-three Hotevillans explained the situation as follows:

> We do not recognize the results of the vote counted during the meeting in Hotevilla Day School on the night of February 11, 1957. As expected, only the ballots of the Hopi Govt. Employees and a small group of women folks who favored it and with whom Mr. ———, a schoolteacher, had been meeting with prior to issuance of the ballots, were counted. . . .

The majority of the people and leaders did not vote one way or another due to the fact that we have always adhered to our ancient custom of first freely discussing over any matter at hand with our leaders before making any decisions. We do not vote in our general meetings on any matter.

. . . It has been found that one of the Government Employees went from house to house getting signatures, using undue influence, on ballots. Some of the women folks did not know or quite understand why or what they were voting for. Some of them changed their minds since. . . .

. . . We know this new project is another way of destroying our culture and religion; therefore we are determined to live our way of life by raising our children along the lines of our religious principles. . . . If any one Hopi is dissatisfied with Hopi life he or she is free to go where white man's life is, and stop creating trouble among the Hopi people who wants to live the Hopi way.

Hotevilla's protest was ignored, of course. The new school was built, the sewer system was installed, and the well was drilled. Hotevilla Day School now sports a tall, silvery water tower shaped rather like an upside-down rocket, visible on the Hotevilla horizon from miles around, and a sewer system with an open-air settling basin enclosed by a barbed wire fence and a sign proclaiming, "Danger! Contaminated water." But the next protest against bureau-backed modernizations was not ignored.

It began one morning in May 1968, when the acting superintendent of the agency, together with the local supervisor of the Arizona Public Service Company and several white and Hopi workmen, brought a hole-digger, graders, utility poles, and other equipment to the outskirts of Hotevilla. Their objective was to install power lines in the village. When the *kikmongwi* and a few curious villagers assembled and asked him to justify this action, the acting superintendent proffered a petition signed by ninety people requesting that an electric power line be installed in Hotevilla.

The *kikmongwi* argued strenuously against the power line

on the grounds that, in spite of the petition, he had not given his permission, and that his villagers did not want public works; a number of Hotevilla residents joined him in protesting. The protestors maintained that the petition listed names of persons living outside Hotevilla—some in other villages, some living off the reservation entirely. The *kikmongwi* argued with the acting superintendent through an interpreter, and other arguments ensued among the Arizona Public Service supervisor, BIA officials, Hopi workmen, the *kikmongwi's* representatives, and Hotevilla residents. Despite the arguments, some utility poles were placed, but opposition was so strong that the acting superintendent took his men and equipment away. He promised to return, however, declaring to the uncooperative citizens that their protests were overridden by the pro-utility petition with ninety names on it.

In the meantime, the pro-utility and anti-utility Hotevillans took head counts, each group circulating a petition stating its position. The pro-utility group gathered 98 signatures, the anti-utility group led by the village chief gathered 130. Anti-utility Hotevillans also pulled down several utility poles, and the chief sent telegrams of protest to Secretary of the Interior Udall, Commissioner of Indian Affairs Bennett, various senators and representatives, and to presidential candidate Dick Gregory.

A few days later, the acting superintendent returned with his men and equipment, reinforced with several members of the Hopi police force from the agency and a number of county sheriff's deputies. Both petitions were shown to the acting superintendent. In spite of the majority opposing the public works, he ordered his workmen to begin operations. They immediately met with resistance. Anti-utility Hotevillans, swelled in numbers and prepared for action, jumped into post holes to prevent poles from being placed. Police dragged them out, and anti-utility Hotevillans scuffled with police and pro-utility Hotevillans. In the midst of the sit-ins and struggling, however, the utility poles were installed by sunset. The resisters report that the acting superintendent had live wires strung on the poles and again left, warning that anyone attempting to dislodge the poles would risk danger of electrocution. But this time the *kik-mongwi* and his resisters, aided by pressure exerted as a result of publicity, prevailed. Within a week the poles had been removed, and all attempts to force public works into Hotevilla were stopped. Before summer was over the acting superintendent was transferred to another reservation.

FUNDAMENTAL BELIEFS AND IDEOLOGY: HOPI

Although the unaesthetic appearance of power poles and the economic burden of monthly electricity bills were real issues in the opposition, the showdown at Hotevilla was primarily a symbolic action. It symbolized the basic ideological conflict between the superordinate and aggressive United States and subordinated and manipulated Hotevilla. It was an act of defiance against the ideology and hegemony of a foreign power, and an affirmation of the fundamental beliefs which Hotevilla resisters feel are characteristic of the Hopi as a nation.

1. The Great Spirit entrusted certain land to the Hopi as a shrine to be used wisely for the perpetuation of life and gave the Hopi instructions for the care of this land.
2. The Great Spirit gave the Hopi a Life Plan which prescribes the kind of life that is morally and practically best for the Hopi; other ways of life are not suited to the Hopi on Hopi land.
3. Each traditional Hopi village is an independent social unit, whose inviolability is guaranteed by the religiously sanctioned methods by which it was formed and the religious ceremonies that are performed for its continued prosperity.

The ideological principles generated from these fundamental beliefs speak to the kinds of actions by the federal government and the tribal council which the resisters feel have violated Hopi sovereignty. They are as follows:

1. The United States government has no legal right of authority over Hotevilla; Hotevilla is an independent village and never signed a treaty acknowledging the sovereignty or even the existence of the United States as a nation.
2. The United States government has no moral right to pressure Hopis to assimilate.
3. Neither the Hopi Tribal Council nor any other agency can represent or act for Hotevilla or for any Hopi village; there is no place in the Hopi Life Plan for a "tribal council" or a "Bureau of Indian Affairs."
4. Neither the United States government nor the Hopi Tribal Council has the right to promote or allow the lease, sale, disposal, mineral exploration, or exploitation of Hopi land or the resources under that land.
5. Public works and other development or welfare projects which would benefit Hotevilla residents materially cannot be accepted; to accept the privileges of Euro-American life would mean accepting the obligations and suicidal life-plan of the United States and its government.

With the glaring differences in fundamental beliefs between Hotevilla and the United States government, it is not surprising that operation of United States government ideology should stimulate behavior that has resulted in the counterideology and counterbehavior of the Hotevilla resistance. The government encourages private enterprise to develop the economic resources of the nation, because private enterprise has made the United States great. But to Hotevillans, private enterprise is a foreign intrusion that threatens to exploit their labor as well as their land, and economic development only means profit for industry and destruction of the Hopi way of life. The government considers standardized education equal to nonreservation education to be important for assimilation because it instills Anglo-European values in children and teaches them the basic skills necessary for participating in Euro-American life; but to the Hotevilla resisters, who want neither assimilation nor the rights and obligations that go with it, schools are straitjackets that usurp parents' opportunity and responsibility to bring their children up in their own way and fail to inculcate those skills and values that are important for present Hopi life.

The government's effort to bring democracy to the Hopis is regarded, not as an opportunity for self-determination, but rather as an effort to abrogate the sacred sovereignty of the independent Hopi villages and to create a puppet institution committed to the government's ideology. Thus the kind of independence which Secretary Udall saw in the termination of the reservations is the kind which Hotevilla resisters dread. Termination would give them independence only if they converted to the fundamental beliefs of the government about land, economic enterprise, and the most desirable form of political organization. This independence would give them all the obligations of American citizenship, including the privilege of paying property taxes, but would take away their sacred sovereignty and force them to give up title to a large part of what they consider to be already a fraction of their sacred lands. Welfare, public works, and other material benefits offered by the government are regarded as bribes for forcing Hopis into the wage-earning economy and making them dependent on the United States government and the way of life it proselytizes and defends.

V

Of course, much more could be said about Hotevilla and the Hopi resistance movement in general. But my point in discussing the Hotevilla resistance has been to illustrate the utility of a theoretical framework consisting of fundamental belief, ideology, and behavior for establishing a new perspective on resistance to acculturation. It is significant that the twenty-two-year-old Hopi resistance has been the object of little anthropological research. Aside from a short journal article and a lengthier pamphlet on the subject published obscurely in the 1950s (Yamada, 1952, 1957), little mention of it has been made in published works.[4] Although this fact may reflect a matter of choice by individual researchers more than anything else, it may also reflect an inadequacy of culture change theory to account for resistance to acculturation.

The framework presented here is not intended to be a new theoretical *Wunderkind* capable of transforming heretofore unintelligible data into a computer print-out of anthropological sense and order. It is not very useful in causative analysis. But the perspective it establishes makes the isolation of resistance to acculturation as a focal point of a culture-change study much easier than does the standard acculturation perspective. It may also provide a perspective that regards resistance to acculturation as a systematic and potentially creative phenomenon in situations of directed contact, and the element of ideology provides continuity for analysis of movements that begin as religious and cultural revitalizations, but end as rebellions or revolutions.

Although the Hopi resistance shows no imminent signs of a revolutionary character, especially in view of the Hopi abhorrence of conflict and warfare, other resistance movements with similar beliefs and ideologies have demonstrated that resistance to acculturation can become an overt and painful challenge to the authority of the conqueror. Since the fundamental beliefs of a resistance movement can exist for many years as the "mazeways" of unassimilated members of a subordinate society and can even be passed from generation to generation through the enculturation process, the occurrence of certain events or the existence of certain circumstances may be sufficient to suddenly generate a resistance movement, complete with ideology and a plan of action that has many revivalistic characteristics.

With a perspective that encourages analysis of resistance to acculturation as a potential "culture-building" phenomenon in Caulfield's sense (see her contribution to this volume), it is to be hoped that anthropologists will be motivated to undertake more studies of cause and effect in situations of culture contact. If this is done, more studies of revolutionary change or attempts at revolutionary change may be incorporated into the culture-change literature; they would provide anthropology with a much more balanced and useful body of theory.

Likewise, a perspective acknowledging that culture change in one society can result from deployment of sanctions against it by a superordinate society should motivate anthropologists to correct the unfortunate effect of the "bias of objectivity." As I noted earlier, this bias is a natural one for people who are on the winning side in a confrontation between two cultural systems.

Among anthropologists, the winners' ethnocentric bias has been manifested as a purported concern with scientific objectivity that would yield the almighty but elusive Truth; it has also been a preventive mechanism that kept anthropologists from identifying too strongly with the subordinate societies they were studying. If they did identify too strongly, they "went over the hill" and lost their objectivity, their identification with the superordinate society, and their standings as proper anthropologists and purveyors of Truth. The classic example of the anthropologist who went over the hill and lost his objectivity concerns a man who spent many years trying to learn the religious secrets of a particular society. When he was finally initiated into one of the society's religious cults and learned the secrets, he refused to divulge them. He maintained that because he was a member of that cult, he was as bound to secrecy as the other members and could not break the bond even in the name of science.

This example illustrates the difference between an anthropologist who identifies with the subordinate society he is studying and an anthropologist who sympathizes with his subjects but retains his identification with the basic position of the society of his origins. Many sympathizers have performed valuable services for the people they have studied, and their efforts to help the victims of Anglo-European expansion are a hopeful sign for those who would like to expunge some of the more barbarous elements of Euro-American culture. But sympathizers still retain their primary identification with the superordinate position, and their concern should serve as groundwork for more penetrating efforts, not as excuses for smug assertions of anthropology's righteousness or as an object of scorn from those motivated to greater action by the crises of a more insane era.

Native peoples of this continent are in a structural position vis-à-vis the United States that is quite similar to the structural positions of colonial peoples with relation to their masters. With a new perspective on culture contact, anthropologists might mitigate their bias enough to identify their own position with that of the oppressed rather than with the oppressors. They might comprehend what it is like to actually be a member of a "subordinate cultural system" and an oppressed society, and at the same time might see some relationship between the causes of distress in some societies and the spectacular material progress of their own. They might elucidate the nature of such structural relationships among societies and probe their causes.

Some might also comprehend a duty, now in its season, that should not long be neglected. For when members of subordinated societies begin to identify the anthropologist per se as one of their oppressors rather than as one of their liberators, as an exploiter rather than an enlightener, as a spy rather than a scientist, and as part of the problem rather than part of the solution, anthropologists as individuals should consider undertaking a visionary quest of their own that might lead them to their own personal revitalizations.

Neither ethics committees nor radical caucuses can dictate what that duty is nor how the revitalization should proceed. Anthropologists are as subject to the effects of worldly events as their fellow non-anthropologists and are equally capable of making their own individual decisions and their own personal commitments. Just as no single strategy can guarantee to the discipline of anthropology a "piece of action" or "relevance to the real world," no single set of actions can guarantee to an anthropologist his continued access to a favorite "ethnographic laboratory" or his discovery of "God's Truth." Only his perception of the trend of world events and the relationship of conjunctive cultural systems can guide him into actions that are as helpful to the oppressed of his studies as they are to himself and to the people who read them.

Notes

1. The term "Indian" is at best a misnomer. The Indian Research and Development Association, Ottawa, Canada, expresses its sentiments on the term as follows:

   > For almost 500 years the word "Indian" has been used to describe the original inhabitants of this continent, who are in no way related to the people of India. . . . Many generations of subjection to the invaders' error has brought about a general acceptance of the name by the native people. This mistaken identity is significant of the thorough manner in which the original people have been divested of every shred of human dignity. . . . (*Akwesasne Notes,* October 1970, p. 48)

2. I first presented this theoretical framework and most of the accompanying data in a paper presented at the 49th Annual Meeting of the Central States Anthropological Society (cf. Clemmer, 1969). Although the theme of that first paper is pursued herein, some new dimensions are presented on what is a highly important yet complex problem, in a thoroughly revised version.

3. Accurate census data on Hotevilla do not exist; Hotevillans refuse to give information to census-takers.

4. Shuichi Nagata refers to the traditionalists in his book *Modern Transformations of Moenkopi Pueblo* (1970), as does Bruce Cox in his papers "Information Management and Hopi Factions" (1970) and "Ecology and Inter-Societal Conflict on the Hopi Reservation" (manuscript). Nagata has written two papers analyzing aspects of the traditional movement (1968a,b), but both are in manuscript form.

References

Akwesasne Notes. 1970. "Are You an Indian?" *Akwesasne Notes* 2, No. 6 (October). Roosevelt-town, New York. P. 48.

Apter, David. 1964. "Ideology and Discontent." In *Ideology and Discontent,* ed. David Apter, pp. 15–46. New York: Free Press.

Broom, Leonard, Bernard S. Siegel, Evon Z. Vogt, and James B. Watson. 1954. "Acculturation: An Exploratory Formulation." *American Anthropologist* 56: 973–1000.

Bureau of Indian Affairs. 1968a. *Indian Record.* Special Issue, March: President Johnson presents Indian message to Congress: "The Forgotten American."

———. 1968b. *Answers to Your Questions About American Indians* (May). Washington, D.C.: Government Printing Office.

Clemmer, Richard O. 1969. "The Fed-Up Hopi: Resistance of the American Indian and the Silence of the Good Anthropologists." *Journal of the Steward Anthropological Society* 1, No. 1: 18–40.

Collier, John. 1936. Letter to Secretary of the Interior, September 16. In Ref. Exhibit 221 of Healing vs. James, United States District Court, Arizona, Civil 579, Prescott.

Congress of the United States. 1934. Indian Reorganization Act, June 18. S. 3645, 73rd Cong., 2nd sess., chs. 575–77.

———. 1968. A Bill to Provide for the Economic Development and Management of the Resources of Individual Indians and Indian Tribes, and for Other Purposes, February 1 (H.R. 15035).

Cox, Bruce A. 1970. "What is Hopi Gossip About? Information Management and Hopi Factions." *Man* 5, No. 1: 88–98.

———. n.d. "Ecology and Inter-Societal Conflict on the Hopi Reservation." Unpublished manuscript.

Dozier, Edward. 1951. "Resistance to Acculturation and Assimilation in an Indian Pueblo." *American Anthropologist* 53: 56–66.

———. 1954. *The Hopi-Town of Arizona. University of California Publications in American Archaeology and Ethnology,* Vol. 44, No. 3. Berkeley, Calif. Pp. 259–376.

———. 1966. *Hane, a Tewa Indian Community in Arizona.* New York: Holt, Rinehart & Winston.

Gough, Kathleen. 1967. "Anthropology: Child of Imperialism." *Monthly Review* 19, No. 11: 12–27.

Hotevilla Village. 1956. "Hopi Meeting of Religious People." Hotevilla, Arizona.

La Farge, Oliver. 1957. "Termination of Federal Supervision: Disintegration and the American Indian." *Annals of the American Academy of Political and Social Science* 311: 41–46.

Linton, Ralph. 1940. "The Distinctive Aspects of Acculturation." In *Acculturation in Seven American Indian Tribes,* ed. Ralph Linton. New York: D. Appleton-Century Co. Pp. 501–20.

————. 1943. "Nativistic Movements." *American Anthropologist* 45: 230–40.

Nagata, Shuichi. 1968a. "Political Socialization of the Hopi 'Traditional Faction.'" Unpublished manuscript.

————. 1968b. "Constituency of Moenkopi Factionalism." Unpublished manuscript.

————. 1970. *Modern Transformations of Moenkopi Pueblo.* Illinois Studies in Anthropology, No. 6. Urbana: University of Illinois Press.

Redfield, Robert, Ralph Linton, and Melville Herskovits. 1936. "A Memorandum for the Study of Acculturation." *American Anthropologist* 38: 149–52.

Spicer, Edward H. 1961. "Types of Contact and Processes of Change." In *Perspectives in American Indian Culture Change,* ed. Edward H. Spicer. Chicago: University of Chicago Press. Pp. 516–44.

Steiner, Stan. 1968. *The New Indians.* New York: Harper & Row.

Steward, Julian H. 1969. "The Limitations of Applied Anthropology: The Case of the Indian New Deal." *Journal of the Steward Anthropological Society* 1, No. 1: 1–17.

Titiev, Mischa. 1944. *Old Oraibi: A Study of the Hopi Indians of Third Mesa.* Papers of the Peabody Museum of American Archaeology and Ethnology, Harvard University, Vol. 22, No. 1. Cambridge, Mass.

Wallace, A. F. C. 1956. "Revitalization Movements." *American Anthropologist* 58: 264–81.

Watkins, Arthur V. 1957. "Termination of Federal Supervision: The Removal of Restrictions over Indian Property and Person." *Annals of the American Academy of Political and Social Science* 311: 47–55.

Yamada, George. 1952. "The Great Resistance." *Indigenista* 12, No. 2: 142–51.

————, ed. 1957. *The Great Resistance: A Hopi Anthology.* New York: Yamada.

IV · Studying
The Cultures of Power

American Anthropologists and American Society
Eric R. Wolf

I SHALL ARGUE that in the period of the last hundred years there have been three major phases of American anthropology, and that these three phases in the development of our discipline correspond largely to three phases in the development of American society. Such a triadic scheme represents, of course, an oversimplification, but the oversimplification will serve its purpose if it leads us to think about problem-setting in our discipline, not merely in terms of the truth and falsity of answers to questions asked, but about our whole intellectual enterprise as a form of social action, operating within and against a certain societal and cultural context. I must also caution that in this attempt I cannot help but be idiosyncratic, though common acquaintance with our professional literature renders my idiosyncrasy intersubjective, that is, amenable to discussion by others who, in turn, hold their own idiosyncratic positions. My purpose in this presentation is not to defend a new interpretation of American anthropology, but to generate an interest in the sociology of anthropological knowledge.

The oversimplified periods into which I want to break down the development of American society during the last century are, first, the period of Capitalism Triumphant, lasting roughly from the end of the Civil War into the last decade of the nineteenth century; second, the period of intermittent Liberal Reform, beginning in the last decade of the nineteenth century and ending with the onset of World War II; and third, the America of the present, characterized by what President Eisenhower first called "the military-industrial complex" in his farewell address of January 17, 1961. Each of these periods has been characterized by a central problem and a central set of responses to that problem. There were, of course, numerous subsidiary and peripheral problems and subsidiary and peripheral responses to them; and there were more often than not divergent and contradictory responses. But I want to argue that even the divergent and contradictory responses possessed a common denominator in that they addressed themselves to the same central issue of the day and that they were marked by a common intellectual mood, even when directly opposed to each other in suggesting possible solutions.

The phase of Capitalism Triumphant witnessed the construction of American industry by our untrammeled entrepreneurs; its dominant mode of intellectual response was Social Darwinism. The period of reform was marked by the drive to democratize America; the dominant mode of intellectual response was to explain and justify the entry of "new" and previously unrepresented groups into the American scene and to adumbrate the outlines of a pluralistic and liberal America. The period of the present is marked by the extension into all spheres of public life of a set of civil and military bureaucracies, connected through contracts to private concerns. I shall argue that the dominant intellectual issue of the present is the nature of public power and its exercise, wise or unwise, responsible or irresponsible.

To each of these three phases American anthropology has responded in its own way: it responded to the intellectual mood of Social Darwinism with the elaboration of evolutionist theory; it responded to Liberal Reform with theories which stressed human flexibility and plasticity; and it responds to the present phase with uncertainties and equivocations about power. Intellectual responses fed theory, and theory, in turn, fed practice; concern with the central issues of each period did not mean that anthropologists abandoned their technical tasks. Under the impetus of an evolutionist philosophy, Lewis Henry Morgan studied the Iroquois and collected the data which underwrote *Systems of Consanguinity and Affinity* (1870), just as John Wesley Powell embarked on a vast effort to study Indian languages, institutions, arts, and philosophies (cf. Darrah, 1951; and on both men, Hallowell, 1960, pp. 48–58). The emphasis on human plasticity and flexibility similarly prompted numerous technical investigations, especially in the field of culture and personality, a mode of inquiry which made American ethnology distinct from the ethnological efforts of other nations. Nor does the character of the present inhibit technical skill and cumulation; indeed, I shall argue that it is the very character of the present which causes us to emphasize technique and to de-emphasize ideas or ideology. Yet in no case could American anthropology escape the dominant issue of the time, and its intellectual responses could not and cannot help but direct themselves to answering it, or to escaping from it. To that extent, at least, the problems of the day enter into how we construct the picture of reality around which we organize our common understandings. As that reality shifts and changes, so our responses to it must shift and change.

Of Social Darwinism, the intellectual response of the first phase, its historian, Richard Hofstadter, has written that

> Darwinism had from the first this dual potentiality; intrinsically, it was a neutral instrument, capable of supporting opposite ideologies. How, then, can one account for the ascendancy, until the 1890's, of the rugged individualist interpretation of Darwinism? The answer is that American society saw its own image in the tooth-and-claw version of natural selection, and that its dominant groups were therefore able to dramatize this vision of competition as a thing good in itself. Ruthless business rivalry and unprincipled politics seemed to be justified by the survival philosophy. As long as the dream of personal conquest and individual assertion motivated the middle class, this philosophy seemed tenable, and its critics remained a minority. (1959, p. 201)

To the extent that American anthropologists were primarily concerned with the Indian, this general view also informed their own. It was anthropology, above all, which had contributed the realization that "savagery is not inchoate civilization; it is a distinct status of society with its own institutions, customs, philosophy, and religion," but "all these must necessarily be overthrown before new institutions, customs, philosophy, and religion can be introduced" (John Wesley Powell, quoted in Darrah, 1951, p. 256).

Such an overthrow of one status of society by another involves numerous processes—the process of power among them—but it is a hallmark of Social Darwinism that it focused the scientific spotlight, not on the actual processes —the fur trade, the slave trade, the colonization of the Plains—but on the outcome of the struggle. This allowed Americans—and American anthropologists among them— to avert their eyes from the actual processes of conflict both morally and scientifically. Hence the problem of power, of its forms and their exercise, remained unattended. Unattended also remained the problem of the power relationship which would link victor and defeated even after savagery had yielded to civilization. This basic paradigm did not change even when it was extended from Indians to Negroes, immigrants, Mexicans, or Filipinos by equating the spread of civilization with the spread of the Anglo-Saxons. When Theodore Roosevelt exclaimed (quoted in Hofstadter, 1959, pp. 171–72) that "the Mexican race now see in the fate of the aborigines of the north their own inevitable destiny. They must amalgamate or be lost in the superior vigor of the Anglo-Saxon race, or they must utterly perish," he was merely elaborating an already familiar argument. The civilized are more virtuous than the uncivilized; the Anglo-Saxons are the most capable agents of civilization; *ergo*, the non-Anglo-Saxons must yield to their superior vigor. Here moral judgment masked, as it so often does, the realities of power, and Americans, including American anthropologists, emerged into the next phase of their intellectual endeavors with appreciably less concern and understanding of power than their British confreres. The victim could be censured, or he could be pitied (Pearce, 1953, p. 53), but as an object of censure or pity he was merely an object lesson of history, not an object himself.

We have said that the next stage in American history was the movement toward reform. It began around the turn of the century and found its most substantial expression in the New Deal. On the one hand, it asserted the claims of society as a whole against the rights of the untrammeled and individualistic entrepreneur. On the other hand, it sponsored the social and political mobility of groups not hitherto represented in the social and political arena. On the wider intellectual scene, the assertion of a collectivity of common men against the anarchistic captains of industry was represented by Beard, Turner, Veblen, Commons, Dewey, Brandeis, and Holmes; in American anthropology, the reaction against Social Darwinism found its main spokesman in Franz Boas. Boas' work in physical anthropology furnished some of the initial arguments against a racism linked to Social Darwinist arguments. In his historical particularism he validated a shift of interest away from the grand evolutionary schemes to concern with the panoply of particular cultures in their historically conditioned setting. If we relate these anthropological interests to the tenor of the times, we can say that the renewed interest in cultural plurality and relativity had two major functions. It called into question the moral and political monopoly of an elite which had justified their rule with the claim that their superior virtue was the outcome of the evolutionary process; it was their might which made their right. If other races were shown to be equipotential with the Caucasians in general and the Anglo-Saxons in particular, if other cultures could be viewed as objects in themselves and not merely as object lessons in history, then other races and other cultures could claim an equal right to participate in the construction of an America more pluralist and more cooperative in its diversity. For the intellectual prophets of the times the pre-eminent instruments for the achievement of this cooperative participation among new and diverse elements were to be scientific education and liberal reform achieved through social engineering. The major protagonist of this faith in education as a means of liberating men from the outworn canons of the past was John Dewey, who saw in the union of education and science the basis for a true association of equals, sustained through the freely given cooperation of the participants. In anthropology, this concern found its expression in the variety of approaches to culture and personality. These celebrated the malleability of man, thus celebrating also his vast potential for change; and they pointed to the socialization or enculturation process as the way in which societies produced viable adults. Each culture was seen, in fact, as one large schoolhouse instead of a little red one; the plurality of cultures constituted a plurality of educational institutions. The tool for the discovery of the manifold educational processes—and hence also for a more adequate approach to the engineering of pluralistic education—was science, that is, anthropology. The faith in social engineering and in the possibility of a new educational pluralism also underwrote the action programs among American Indians, who by means of the new techniques were to become autonomous participants in a more pluralistic and tolerant America.

But like the anthropology of Social Darwinism before it, the anthropology of Liberal Reform did not address itself, in any substantive way, to the problem of power. Humankind was seen as infinitely malleable, and the socialization processes of personalities in different cultures as enormously diverse in their means as well as in their ends. But only rarely—if at all—did anthropologists shift their scientific focus to the constraints impeding both human malleability and malleability in socialization from the outside. At the risk of overstating my case, I would say that the anthropology of the period of Liberal Reform placed the burden for change on freely volunteering participants, drawn from both the culture under consideration and from among their neighbors. It might no longer deal with a given culture as an object lesson in history, but as an object in itself. Yet just as the Social Darwinists had made a moral paradigm of the evolutionary process, so the culture-and-personality schools of the thirties and forties made a moral paradigm of each individual culture. They spoke of patterns, themes, world view, ethos, and values, but not of power. In seeing culture as more or less of an organic whole, they asserted some of the claims of earlier intellectual predecessors who had seen in "political economy" an organic model for the explanation of a vast range of cultural phenomena. But where "political economy" explicitly emphasized the processes by which an organization of power is equipped with economic resources as central to the organic constellation to be explained, the anthropologist's culture of the thirties and forties was "political economy" turned inside out, all ideology and morality, and neither power nor economy. Neither in the nineteenth century nor in the first half of the twentieth century, therefore, did American anthropology as such come to grips with the phenomenon of power. It is with this legacy of unconcern that we enter the period of the present, a period in which the phenomenon of power is uppermost in men's minds.

This period, it seems to me, is characterized by two opposing and yet interconnected trends. The first of these is the growth of a war machine which is becoming the governing mechanism of our lives. Whether we are radicals or liberals or conservatives, we have a prevailing sense that knowledge is not sufficient to put things right; we have come up against institutional restraints which may have to be removed before changes can occur. Gone is the halcyon feeling that knowledge alone, including anthropological knowledge, will set men free. On the other hand, the pacific or pacified objects of our investigation, primitives and peasants alike, are ever more prone to define our field situation gun in hand. A new vocabulary is abroad in the world. It speaks of "imperialism," "colonialism," "neocolonialism," and "internal colonialism," rather than just of primitives and civilized, or even of developed and under-developed. Yet anthropology has in the past always operated among pacified or pacific natives; when the native "hits back" we are in a very different situation from that in which we found ourselves only yesterday. Thus the problem of power has suddenly come to the fore for us; and it exists in two ways—as power exerted within our own system and as power exerted from the outside, often against us, by populations we so recently thought incapable of renewed assertion and resistance.

Yet neither the intellectual endeavors of Social Darwin-ism nor the period of Liberal Reform has equipped us to deal with the phenomenon of power. In these matters we are babes in the woods, indeed, "babes in the darkling woods," as H. G. Wells entitled one of his last novels. We confront the problem of understanding power at a time when the very signposts of understanding are growing confused and irrelevant.

This is not only our own situation. Stillmann and Pfaff, political scientists, write of this as an age in which

> the world practices politics, originated in the Western histori-cal experience, whose essentially optimistic and rationalistic assumptions fail utterly to account for the brutality and terror which are the principal public experiences of the twentieth century. . . . neither tragedy nor irrationality are to be under-stood in terms of the political philosophies by which the West, and now the world, conducts its public life. (1964, p. 238)

Daniel Bell, in a similar vein of ambiguity, entitles a book of essays *The End of Ideology*, and subtitles it *On the Ex-haustion of Political Ideas in the Fifties*; and John Higham summarizes the mood of present-day American historians by saying:

> Most of the major postwar scholars seem to be asking, in one way or another, what (if anything) is so deeply rooted in our past that we can rely on its survival. This has become, per-

haps, the great historical question in a time of considerable moral confusion, when the future looks precarious and severely limited in its possibilities. (1965, p. 226)

Yet where some are lost in doubt, others assert a brutal return to Machiavellianism, to a naked power politics, abstracted from the social realities which underlie it. "The modern politician," write Stephen Rousseas and James Farganis,

> is the man who understands how to manipulate and how to operate in a Machiavellian world which divorces ethics from politics. Modern democracy becomes, in this view, transformed into a system of techniques sans *telos*. And democratic politics is reduced to a constellation of self-seeking pressure groups peaceably engaged in a power struggle to determine the allocation of privilege and particular advantage. (1965, pp. 270–71)

On the international plane, this has meant recourse to a "new realism," most evident in the application of game theory to what the Germans so charmingly call the international *"Chickenspiel."* This new realism emphasized technique over purpose, the *how* of political relations over their *whys* and *wherefores*. Where opponents of this approach argue that such a new emphasis sacrifices the hope of understanding the causes of such politics, its defenders argue, as true American pragmatists, that what matters is the world as given, and what counts is the most rational deployment of our resources to respond to present-day dilemmas. What counts in Vietnam is not how "we" got there, but that "we" are there. Two kinds of rationality thus oppose each other: a substantive rationality, which aims at a critical understanding of the world, and perhaps even at critical action; and a formal or technical rationality, which understands the world in terms of technical solutions.

In this argument social scientists find themselves heavily involved. Some feel, with Ithiel de Sola Pool (1967, pp. 268–69):

The only hope for humane government in the future is through the extensive use of the social sciences by government. . . . The McNamara revolution is essentially the bringing of social science analysis into the operation of the Department of Defense. It has remade American defense policy in accordance with a series of ideas that germinated in the late 1950's in the RAND Corporation among people like Schelling, Wohlstetter, Kahn, and Kaufmann. These were academic people playing their role as social scientists (whatever their early training may have been). They were trying to decide with care and seriousness what would lead to deterrence and what would undermine it. While one might argue with their conclusions at any given point, it seems to me that it is the process that has been important. The result has been the humanization of the Department of Defense. That is a terribly important contribution to the quality of American life.

Others will echo C. Wright Mills when he described the selfsame set of social scientists as

crackpot realists, who, in the name of realism, have constructed a paranoid reality all their own and in the name of practicality have projected a utopian image of capitalism. They have replaced the responsible interpretation of events by the disguise of meaning in a maze of public relations, respect for public debate by unshrewd notions of psychological warfare, intellectual ability by the agility of the sound and mediocre judgment, and the capacity to elaborate alternatives and to gauge their consequences by the executive stance. (1963, pp. 610–11)

Anthropologists, like other social scientists, cannot evade the dilemmas posed by the return to Machiavellian politics. Yet our major response has been one of retreat. This retreat is all the more notable when we realize that wholly anthropological ideas have suddenly been taken over and overtaken by other disciplines. Political scientists have appropriated the anthropological concept of "tradition" and used it to build a largely fictitious polarity between traditional and modern societies; Marshall McLuhan has made use of largely anthropological insights to project the outlines of the communication revolution of the present and future. In contrast to the thirties and forties when anthropology furnished the cutting edge of innovation in social science, we face at the moment a descent into triviality and irrelevance. This descent into triviality seems to me, above all, marked by an increasing concern for pure technique. Important as our technical heritage is for all of us, it cannot in and of itself quicken the body of our discipline without the accession of new ideas. Technique without ideas grows sterile; the application of improved techniques to inherited ideas is the mark of the epigone. This is true regardless of whether anthropologists put themselves at the service of the new realists, or whether they seek refuge in an uncertain ivory tower.

Someone who diagnoses an illness should also prescribe remedies. If I am correct in saying that anthropology has reached its present impasse because it has so systematically disregarded the problems of power, then we must find ways of educating ourselves in the realities of power. One way I can think of to accomplish this is to engage ourselves in the systematic writing of a history of the modern world in which we spell out the processes of power which created the present-day cultural systems and the linkages between them. I do not mean history in the sense of "one damned thing after another"; I mean a critical and comprehensive history of the modern world. It is not irrelevant to the present state of American anthropology that the main efforts at analyzing the interplay of societies and cultures on a world scale in anthropological terms have come from Peter Worsley (1964), an Englishman, and from Darcy Ribeiro (1968), a Brazilian. Where, in our present-day anthropological literature, are the comprehensive studies of the slave trade, the fur trade, of colonial expansion, of forced and voluntary acculturation, of rebellion and accommodation in the modern world, which would provide us with the intellectual grid needed to order the massive data we now possess on individual societies and cultures engulfed by these phenomena? We stand in need of such a project, I believe, not only as a learning experience for ourselves, but also as a responsible intellectual contribution to the world in which we live, so that we may act to change it.

Note

This essay was originally published in Stephen A. Tyler, ed., *Concepts and Assumptions in Contemporary Anthropology*, Proceedings of the Southern Anthropological Society, No. 3 (Athens: University of Georgia Press, 1969), pp. 3–11.

References

Bell, Daniel. 1960. *The End of Ideology*. Glencoe, Ill.: Free Press.
Darrah, William C. 1951. *Powell of the Colorado*. Princeton, N.J.: Princeton University Press.
Hallowell, A. Irving. 1960. "The Beginnings of Anthropology in America." In *Selected Papers from the American Anthropologist, 1888–1920*, ed. Frederica de Laguna. Evanston, Ill.: Row, Peterson & Co. Pp. 1–90.
Higham, John. 1965. *History*. Englewood Cliffs, N.J.: Prentice-Hall.
Hofstadter, Richard. 1959. *Social Darwinism in American Thought*. New York: George Braziller.
Mills, C. Wright. 1963. *Power, Politics, and People: The Collected Essays of C. Wright Mills*, ed. Irving L. Horowitz. New York: Ballantine Books.
Morgan, Lewis Henry. 1870. *Systems of Consanguinity and Affinity of the Human Family*. Smithsonian Contributions to Knowledge, No. 16. Washington, D.C.
Pearce, Roy Harvey. 1953. *The Savages of America*. Baltimore: Johns Hopkins Press.
Pool, Ithiel de Sola. 1967. "The Necessity for Social Scientists Doing Research for Government." In *The Rise and Fall of Project Camelot*. ed. Irving L. Horowitz. Cambridge, Mass.: M.I.T. Press. Pp. 267–80.

Ribeiro, Darcy. 1968. *The Civilization Process*. Washington, D.C.: Smithsonian Institution Press.

Rousseas, Stephen, and James Farganis. 1965. "American Politics and the End of Ideology." In *The New Sociology*, ed. Irving L. Horowitz. New York: Oxford University Press. Pp. 268–89.

Stillmann, Edmund, and William Pfaff. 1964. *The Politics of Hysteria*. New York: Harper & Row, Colophon Books.

Worsley, Peter. 1964. *The Third World*. London: Weidenfeld & Nicholson.

The Life and Culture
of Ecotopia
E. N. Anderson, Jr.

I

HUMAN ECOLOGY has always been a concern of anthropology, though not always under its present name.
Recently, interest in human ecology has increased parallel
to the rising concern with the environment that has followed
on the massive insults thereto during the past few years.
Ecology is a popular cry in professional and nonprofessional
circles; everyone has become an advocate of, or at least
student of, man's relationship with nature.

In spite of this, the world ecological situation is deteri-
orating at an accelerating rate. At least four million people
starve to death each year, and uncounted millions more die
with malnutrition and undernourishment as contributing
causes (Ehrlich, 1968; Pyke, 1970). Pollution continues to
increase and to take new and ever deadlier forms (Still,
1967; *Environment* magazine, *passim*). World population
and resource-use increase and put more and more pressure
on the food base (Borgstrom, 1969)—a food base steadily
declining as a result of soil erosion, overfishing, overhunting, overgrazing, deforestation, urbanizing of cultivable
land, pollution of food-producing areas, and increased pest
and disease incidence due to new agricultural techniques.
Most of the world lives in abject poverty, if not indeed on
the edge of starvation; the rest lives in a polluted environ-

ment, and chokes itself to death on its own overconsumption. In spite of detailed assessments and proposals (notable are: Calder, 1967; Murphy, 1967; Committee on Resources and Man, 1969; Pirie, 1969; President's Science Advisory Committee, 1967), the world situation, particularly in regard to food and the food base, worsens more rapidly than before.

Anthropologists have been slow in awakening to this problem. Surprising as this is in view of the traditional anthropological concern with the weak, human ecologists in the field have paid little attention to such problems as the world food crisis. The standard reader in cultural ecology (Vayda, 1969) has many articles about primitive food habits —hardly a new concern in the field, and at least as well covered by the first ethnographers (e.g. Cushing, 1920) as by those in the Vayda book—but nothing about modern food problems and, indeed, only one article about pollution. By contrast, the standard collection of readings in *biological* human ecology is entirely problem-oriented and well titled *The Subversive Science* (Shepard and McKinley, 1969). The anthropological belief that a culture's importance is inversely correlated with its population[1] could not be better shown. Socially conscious human ecologists remain trapped in a social framework even when they denounce it. Thus Marvin Harris, in *The Rise of Anthropological Theory* (1968), sets up a techno-environmental framework for considering cultures; yet his book contains no mention of the world ecological crisis, but rather some discussion of racism, colonialism, and other traditional social concerns. These are intimately related to ecology, as Harris shows, but they are not the whole problem. In contrast to the brilliant works produced in economics (Murphy, 1967), systems-analysis biology (Watt, 1968), and other fields, anthropologists have been surprisingly poor at applying their analytical tools to the world's most serious problem.

This is particularly unfortunate in view of the unique position of anthropologists. Most of us live in two worlds: the starving, depleted villages of our field situations and the overconsumption-poisoned cities where we teach. No other professionals so regularly shuttle back and forth between the two foci of the problem. Moreover, anthropology is notable in bridging the gap between the biological and the social sciences, and has a long and honorable tradition of concern with man's management of his resources. It is perhaps excusable for sociologists to ignore the ecological crisis, for their sights are set on other targets; and for biologists to come out with the embarrassing and pathetic folk social science they derive from Ardrey (1966), Lorenz (1966), and studies of overcrowded rats. It is not excusable for anthropologists to ignore the problem or to continue to allow biologists to speak in ignorance of social science findings.

The myth of "value-free" social science is now thoroughly dead, and we must take responsibility for our actions. In anthropology, this will mean on the one hand an expansion of applied anthropology from its present rather *ad hoc* shape to a synthesizing discipline at least as powerful as economic development theory, and on the other a concern by human ecologists with applied anthropology and with the wider context of the world crisis. It will mean a broader focus of research. The problems raised here cannot possibly be considered at the small-community level. Regarding the community or the culture as an isolated unit, comparable in cross-cultural studies with other units, misses the worldwide nature of the problem: its roots in colonialism and world trade (among other places), its universality, its transcendence of national boundaries as seen in the distribution of pollution to Antarctica and the mid-ocean regions. It will also mean research oriented toward genuine solutions of the problem. The present "environmental crisis literature" is dismally devoid of suggestions, with exceptions noted above, and frequently shows all too obviously that the authors were afraid of rocking the boat by proposing any. This has allowed a myth to arise, both in the establishment and among radicals, that the ecological cause is a cop-out.

The reverse is more likely true: ecology is part of the radical movement (Slater *et al.*, 1970), but its implications have not been followed up because of their very radicalness. Anthropologists are faced with the duty of finding genuine analyses of the problem and solutions to it. Human and cultural ecology should focus on this task.

Exhortation being of value only if one puts up the goods, I shall devote the rest of this chapter to attempting to set up some guidelines for analysis. This is in no sense the analysis and solution called for above, but rather an idea of the necessary groundwork.

II

The ecological crisis is one result of exploitation. Overuse of resources, whether by a rich nation consuming too much or by a poor nation driven to overdraw its resource base or starve, is a result of a world economic system that does not include the necessary balances to protect the resource base through sustained-yield management and recycling. Tremendous overdraft on the base is matched by tremendous waste and inefficiency in resource use—the use-once-and-throw-away economy, the economy in which up to half the food is lost in storage and distribution and processing, the throughput economy. We are fishing out the oceans faster than the fish breed, cutting trees faster than new ones grow, and mining metal rather than reusing it. Urban sprawl, erosion, war, and mismanagement are costing us thousands of square miles of farmland every year. Now, in energy cost, and obviously in ecological cost, it is better to be efficient and conservationist than to be wasteful and destructive. Under what circumstances is it more economical to be uneconomical? Under what circumstances can the wasters afford to go on, and the economy become based on throughput, while conservers are unable to compete? Obviously this occurs when real ecological costs of production are *much* greater than economic costs, or at least those economic costs reckoned on the balance sheets.

Now, ecological costs are ultimately going to show up as economic costs, at least insofar as real resource-base depletion or destruction is involved. Thus the reckoning, the cost accounting, is clearly sick. But whether the costs are reckoned as ecological or economic, they are real, and somebody will suffer in paying them. The economic costs specified on the producer and consumer are low; the ultimate ecological costs are high. Who pays the difference?

The answer, of course, is that the slack is taken up by those least able to resist. The real costs of production (and consumption) are passed off on the general public; on the poor and the politically weak; or on those conveniently voiceless unfortunates, the future generations—including today's young people, not old enough to be politically visible. This is the classic exploitation: X gets the profits by forcing Y to pay the real costs. In modern industrial economy, the whole system runs on profits that simply would not exist if this did not happen. The corporations, nations, and individuals who benefit from wrecking the ecosystem can benefit only insofar as they can make others pay the cost.

Such a situation can exist when certain groups are extremely powerful in relation to others. The rich nations vis-à-vis the poor ones, the energy suppliers such as oil and power companies, who have a stranglehold on the economy because they supply the energy that runs it, and the governments of very highly centralized economies (capitalist or communist) are such groups. These are the leading destroyers of the environment, because they can most successfully pass the costs down the line.

Consider a few cases in point. Peru is overfishing its anchovy stocks. This is leading to the death of the guano birds, which depend on the anchovy schools, and of course to the ultimate destruction of the entire Peruvian fishery. The fish is ground to meal and almost all of it exported to the United States, where it is fed to chickens. Peru's population, especially in the highlands, is (to put it mildly) short of protein. Yet they get no fish meal; the United States can afford to pay more. The real costs of production here are passed off on the poorer Peruvians, who have their protein source removed, and the guano industry that once sustained Peru is also taken away. The benefits, however, accrue to the United States—at least the chicken farmers there. Similarly, Africa has lost nearly all its large fauna; the game herds outside the few national parks are almost gone. This has occurred because of "white hunters" and other features of colonialism, as well as the wide dissemination of guns, often through colonialistic wars. The end of the game has led to a catastrophic decline in the protein base in Africa, where cattle are notoriously less productive than game, and in many environments quite unable to exist at all (see Brown, 1967). Much of the *kwashiorkor* and general protein shortage in modern Africa is the direct result of game depletion due to overhunting and habitat destruction, and for these colonialism must take much of the blame (though also some credit for establishing parks and reserves). The white hunters got the trophy heads, but the African people get the *kwashiorkor*.

Bringing it within the confines of one country, we can observe the real costs being passed off by the corporations on the poor of their own polity. Freeways, reservoirs, and stream-channeling (despite this so-called "flood control," floods have worsened) projects displace the poor or expose them to maximal danger, because, on the cost-benefit accounting, the poor are more vulnerable. Their homes are cheaper and thus less expensive to destroy, less expensive to expose to maximum flood danger. Also very noteworthy is the fact that the most polluted areas of cities are the slums, if only because everyone not poor has moved out because of the pollution. The pollution problems of the rich nations would no doubt end in a week if the rich had to live where the poor now do, instead of residing in remote, tree-shaded suburbs and exurbs. In agriculture, the rich agribusiness corporations use the pesticides, but the poor farm workers, being the ones who actually contact them in the field, are the ones who die from them. Cesar Chavez's group has hotly protested this, and in the course of protest fully documented it.

The economic structure that underlies and causes this specifying of real costs on the weakest members of society, rather than on the beneficiaries, has never been well analyzed. Economics is limited by unawareness of ecological costs, and ecology by a similar lack of knowledge of economics, though the connection of the two was specifically made by Haeckel in coining the word "ecology"! But a groping through conventional economics to this realm has been made by a few radical economists, hampered by Marxian (pre-ecological) theory in some cases, but adding their own ideas which are more suited to the present case. Notable analyses are those of Baran and Sweezy (1966), Magdoff (1969), Jalée (1968), and, from quite a different perspective, Murphy (1967). The union of ecology and economics must be effected through mutual accommodation by those disciplines, but anthropologists must mediate—both to combat the myths and folk social science that keep them separate now and to provide a holistic framework for the inputs.

Now observe some causes and effects. *The cause, or more exactly the maintaining factor, in this modern industrial economy is the very unequal distribution of power in the world.* Only when the division of powerful and weak is really inordinately great can so much real cost be passed down. It is noteworthy that the concentration of political power in the hands of a few economy-running bureaucrats in the communist countries has had the same effect as concentration of economic and political power in the hands of giant corporations in the rest of the world. The Soviet Union has polluted its sturgeons out of existence and is slowly getting concerned (see, most recently, Abelson, 1970); even Mao's China, agriculturally more or less responsible, is featuring pollution-belching industries in its magazines. Evidently the economic-political disequilibrium that is at the heart of modern industrial society is the same, whatever the other differences between the various rich nations. (Not that the poor nations are free from such disequilibrium!) The solution, similarly, cannot rest with capitalism or communism; these have been tried and have failed to deal with the basic problem. If the goal is to maximize short-term production at the expense of the general public, or the poor nations, or future generations, then it matters not whether the maximizer be a corporation magnate, a commissar, or a welfare-state bureau head.

As to effects, the following most concern us:

1. Extraction becomes cheaper than recycling and overdraft cheaper than sustained yield. This is true especially of *very* large endeavors with great power to pass off costs and of small, undercapitalized units which must maximize short-term profits (at the expense of long-term) to survive at all. The typical case is seen in the lumber industry, where such giant firms as Boise Cascade have almost abandoned tree-farming and taken to stripping the land to get capital to go into more lucrative fields like land development, while small firms must cut inefficiently and waste wood because they are too inadequately capitalized to install expensive equipment or to plan for long-term payoffs. Almost as interesting is the situation in the countryside of many former colonies, where colonialism led to a separation of plantations so big they could safely wreck the land and smallholders so small they could do nothing but maximize in the short run, whatever the long-term costs. This did not produce a "dual economy" with two sectors unrelated to each other, but a vicious cycle in which the two sectors reacted on each other to produce what Geertz has brilliantly described as "agricultural involution" in what is perhaps the best study yet written in cultural ecology (Geertz, 1963).

2. Single use becomes more economic than multiple use

—for the same reasons. Monocropping displaces the mixed-farming-with-aesthetic-benefits of peasant agriculture and of Bucks County's traditional landscape. Ecologically, multiple use makes more sense, and it also does economically if the system is not unbalanced, as shown in a study by Guest (1968).

3. Population explosions occur. This is really a special case of point 1. If the rich are so rich that they cannot damage heir position no matter how many children they have, but can rather build up dynasties by doing so, and the poor cannot get any economic power at all other than homemade manpower, one has a population explosion. The examples of Haiti, Madagascar, and the like prove that no negative forces, no crowding, expense, cultural freedom, or problems of having children, can stop this. Given social equity, or even a rough chance of a widespread belief in the hope of it, population curves level off fast (see Frederiksen, 1969, and Slater *et al.*, 1970, for more and better discussion of this). This is *not* to say that we should not worry about population, for social equity is, among other things, concerned with providing free birth control and abortion as a natural right and with eliminating natalistic ideas; but it *is* saying that neither "family planning" nor Davis-style population control will work in a society of such economic structure.

III

If this analysis is correct, the ecological crisis is largely a result of the political and economic structure, specifically of the balance of power. This thesis runs against the conventional wisdom, notably the folk social science of biologists. Man is not territorial in the biological sense, that is, he does not defend a territory *exclusively* (we all allow guests in), nor does he remain on territory nor hold territories with all the resources he needs. Aggression is no doubt a human universal, but the forms it takes and the way it is channeled are obviously conditioned by economic factors. Crowding is simply not relevant as a way of understanding human behavior, at least in the simplistic way biologists do in coffee and cocktail conversation; the immensely crowded Oriental cities are not proportionally more pathological than American ones, and American rural slums are as sick as urban ones, if not sicker, while rich urban wards have quite different problems from poor ones in spite of roughly equivalent crowding (at least as compared with the rural slums).

More important is the belief that ideology and religion (not economics and politics) condition ecological behavior. This belief is found almost universally in Shepard and McKinley's readings. Much of it stems from White's paper included in that volume (pp. 341–50), or at least uses White as an authority. The belief in the priority of ideology seems to stem, originally, from a misunderstanding or oversimplification of Max Weber's sociology; in any case, it is now well entrenched among biologists. The Western "growth and progress" ideology, or the "Judeo-Christian tradition" with its belief in "man's mastery over nature," is held guilty— presumably or explicitly in contradistinction to those wonderful, remote Oriental ideologies that stress "man's harmony with nature."

Disposing of this belief is absurdly easy: one has only to point to the incredible Oriental record of pollution, erosion, deforestation, and wreckage, most recently exemplified in Japan's rapid rise to the dubious distinction of the world's most polluted nation (or at least a competitive stance in that regard)—a rise thoroughly explicable in terms of economic-political structure (see Abegglen's excellent analysis, 1970). The reasons are clear in my research in Hong Kong also. My informants did indeed have a religion and belief structure stressing man's harmony with nature, but they were engaged in wholesale damage to the ecosystem due to pure economic necessity, in explicit, self-admitted violation of their norms and their knowledge of final effect. This was particularly true of my boat-people informants in the highly overfished coastal fishery. But the overfishing went on, because no one would stop simply because of ideology, and because the places of those that *did* stop (for whatever reason) were immediately filled by the expansion of other fishermen's activity. The "tragedy of the commons" (Hardin, 1968; Crowe, 1969) is not a problem limited to the Judeo-Christian tradition. Moreover, as White points out in that oft-cited article, the Judeo-Christian lore includes plenty of sound ecology; if we have ignored it, the fault is ours, not the tradition's. In practice, an appeal to "ideology" often equals a failure to face the need for socioeconomic and political change, or, in short, a cop-out. Anthropologists should be particularly vigilant about this, since we, presumably, are the most knowledgeable workers in the field of cross-cultural ideology and religion research.

A *caveat* here is that we may ignore the more down-to-earth, yet still values-connected, matter of effective demand for actual goods. If the broad, general principles of ideology are always flexible and adaptable to economic motives—not for nothing is the British royal motto *Dieu et mon droit* cynically rendered, "I'm all right, Jack, shove off the boat" —the more are hard and day-to-day transactions of the economy determined in great measure by what people want. Harris (1968) has effectively dispelled the view that people's desires are simply irrational and not related to ecological or economic rationality. The whole existence of the advertising industry proves that demand can be created (see Baran and Sweezy, 1966; Slater *et al.*, 1970), but the failure of so many of its campaigns proves that the public is not quite the blind herd of sheep that certain items in the literature imply. Exercising control on day-to-day market decisions—whether to buy a little more gasoline or another packaged good, whether to throw away a jar or reuse it for canning—would seem importantly involved in the whole process of making the economy run. Anthropologists have rarely considered this sort of question, and when they have they have usually done so in the context of *ad hoc* applied anthropology: how to get the farmers to buy improved seed, and so on. The dynamic relationship between the economic structure, advertising and the synthetically created demand it leads to, and the public wants and effective demands is in much more need of anthropological research. Note also the difference between demand and effective demand. Americans successfully demand wilderness conservation in the political arena, but they don't pay much for it in the market-place, since the actual saving is mostly financed from tax-dollars payments, and thus wilderness gets less attention than many a less serious want or need.

The role of anthropology in ecology certainly should run heavily to combatting the myths of vague instincts and ideologies with hard data on exactly what really does determine behavior in a given context. Research directed specifically at counteracting folk social science, or ethnoanthropology of the ecological community, is particularly needed.

IV

This, of course, raises the central question of this paper: What should we be doing? Research and training in the whole field of restructuring the world as an "ecotopia" (eco-, from *oikos*, household; -topia from *topos*, place, with implication of "eutopia"—"good place") will presumably be the goal. Applied anthropology is already committed to this goal, but in practice tends to take the dominant structures as given and to adapt its strategies to helping a given village or peasant family to live with them. (Which, of course, is why applied anthropology has been known to fail on occasion—even to be repelled by the people to whom it is applied. This is especially true when military ends are involved.) Expanding it so that all anthropology is directed toward a similar goal should eliminate this drawback, given the existing almost obsessive concern with professional ethics in this field.

Groundwork in the form of research on actual existing human ecology is needed. We still do not know much about the actual energy-flow and resource-management strategies in non-Western societies, though the Columbia group is rapidly changing this (cf., notably, Rappaport, 1967). Peasant agricultural techniques should be at least as interesting as peasant crop strains. Yet the latter are a matter of considerable concern because of their value in providing new genetic material (Konzak and Dietz, 1969). The former include many techniques of ecological sophistication, as the Columbia group has shown (Harris, 1968; Rappaport, 1967; *et al.*), and these should be fully documented.

But in addition to the documentation, anthropologists should concern themselves with planning for the world. Planning, as the phrase goes, is too important to be left to the planners, and social scientists in other fields are already highly involved. Anthropologists can contribute to this, especially in such fields as cultural ecology and cultural content—future patterns of taste and preference, future structures of organization. Perhaps even kinship can play a role, if the more extreme utopians are right in saying that family structure must be changed if the world is to go on (*Modern Utopian* magazine, *passim*).

Some of the constraints on planning—constraints unfortunately not often remarked by economic development experts—are already clear.

In the first place, the present growth of population and consumption will stop. Neither can expand to infinity, nor indeed, very much more than they have already done. By the time growth stops, many resources will be more or less depleted. Clean water, clean air, fish, and forests are in imminent danger; helium, wildlife and wilderness, genetic stocks of crop strains, and tin ore are among other things that should fall short by the year 2000 or so (see Committee on Resources and Man, 1969). Most important of all, we are running out of places to dump the heat that the second law of thermodynamics tells us we must have if we use so much energy. Thermal pollution is getting critical; energy consumption—and thus all production—must level off.

In this situation, labor will probably become cheaper in relation to material goods, but not necessarily in relation to services; extraction will be less economical, and for some resources, like tin, it may become very much less economical than recycling.

In such a case, one of two things can happen. The existing power disequilibrium may intensify fantastically as material poverty spreads and the existing middle class is wiped out. (Few seem to realize how much of America's "growth" in recent years has been at the expense of the working man, whose real wage has declined because of inflation and whose life has been impoverished by the wreck of his environment; and how much "growth" is merely a matter of making people pay for formerly free goods, like clean air, water, and open space.) This would lead to a situation rather like that found in preindustrial society (Sjoberg, 1960): a tiny elite with great control over resources, and a vast majority with almost none. This leads to high birth rates, high death rates, destructive land use (notably deforestation and soil erosion), and a falling away from technical progress or change, as the record of preindustrial civilization shows.

On the other hand, if the power gap closes, and the world's people are able to share the poverty equally, we may expect a culture rather like that of the more fortunate preindustrial elite, but extended to everyone. Labor being cheap in relation to goods, a great deal of service, craftsmanship, remaking and reuse, multiple use, and art would be expended in managing given articles and production systems. Mass production and the use-once-and-throw-away model would be replaced by an essentially service economy. It is highly significant that the American economy is doing exactly this. Spending on services, recreational activity, and education is increasing faster than spending on material goods. In a sense, this is temporary, since one of the reasons for it is the artificially low price of the goods. But it may be a sort of preadaptation for the "steady-state" world of the future (Dubos, 1969). Moreover, efficiency of allocation will tend to increase. Consider the management of space. Urban sprawl would be impractical, because a rise in the price of energy for transportation would draw people back to the city, while a rise in agricultural prices and therefore in the value of farmland would prevent the present insane and wanton destruction of farmland for cities (1,000,000 acres annually in the United States alone).

Under these constraints, anthropologists can speculate on how the balance of power can be redressed (a united front of minorities and other oppressed groups with conservationists and ecologists seems the best hope) and on how the balance can be maintained in a dynamic society. The organizational framework that will maintain equilibrium in a complex postindustrial society is difficult to imagine at this time. Possible organizational strategies can be formulated and computer-simulated, as ecological ones are today (Watt, 1968). Integrating new market demands with new political behaviors and new organizational developments would be clearly a job for anthropologists and others in related fields. Some form of ecological regulation—worldwide zoning, restrictions of take to sustained-yield levels in the fishing and logging industries, and so forth—is obviously indispensable and will materialize if the human race is to survive at all. The administration and enforcement of this must be controlled against human lives and against the natural environment; anthropological skills are needed to coordinate these.

The way of life in ecotopia begins to emerge from these patterns. It would be a relaxed place of efficiency and material simplicity. People would probably not work very much of the time. Leisure and status consumption would not be a matter of amassing the most of the most expensive commodity, in the style of that prototypical capitalist Diamond Jim Brady. It would rather be concerned with amassing a great deal of intangible commodities—education, recreation by walking and observing, festivals, arts, crafts, skills, and services of all kinds. In an industrial society, there is pressure to show difference and status by amassing ever more material goods (as some business firms now buy paintings by the square foot). In ecotopia, the same communicated material would be coded in terms of difference in kind of service rather than amount of goods. The most important service would necessarily be education, since only through a positive demand therefor would the polity be able to maintain equilibrium in a dynamically changing system. Education, research, and planning would be integrated into one establishment. Also important in consumption and effective demand would be appreciation of nature, and perhaps religion would return to such concerns. (Sun worship has been advocated to me, and White advocates a return to Saint Francis of Assisi's teachings.) The hippie movement has rather self-consciously drifted in this direction, but a deeper and more broadly appealing contact seems needed: a genuine and widespread revival of commitment to the world. Alienation and failure of will are notoriously characteristic of industrial society, and much of our ecological crisis is the result of a failure of will—people just don't care enough about the world to save it, perhaps because they have so small and specialized a stake in it. Rivival of commitment—through religion, education, love, interest, or whatever channel—to the human and nonhuman world will be a cause and an effect of ecotopian developments.

V

Now, to bring all this back down to earth, I think anthropologists should allocate their own efforts in certain directions:

1. When we do research, we should make it relevant to at least some aspect of planning. We should try to get into the planning sector. An eventual amalgamation of research,

teaching, and planning (artificially separated by the down-fall of the "apprentice" attitude toward, and among, students and its replacement by the factory style of lecture-and-exam "teaching") is expected, and should be sought. This is not unknown today (cf. the Vicos project), and it should be done on a broader and more fearless scale.

2. When we do a study, we should find out the relation-ship of production in the community to the world market. No community is isolated any more, if any ever were. The corollary is that applied anthropologists should try to change the world as well as their village, and, given that they have even vaguely humanistic goals, this should eliminate any tie-ins with military and governmental subversion.

3. We should then figure out how to maximize local control of the relationship, or at least local benefit from it—*not* in short-term profits but in long-term ecological payoffs. There are necessary trade-offs here. Consider, for instance, the debate about whether to grow plantation crops for ex-port or food crops for the home. Ecologically, the latter is best, since it keeps soil nutrients at home and tends to check monocrop culture and destructive soil and forest use. The former, however, yields more short-term profit, though not generally for the people who really need the profits and who would be helped more by food.

4. From these limited, local-interest strategies of perfec-tion, we should look toward the design of a new culture on a worldwide scale. What, exactly, are the laws and market relationships that we should try to effect? What can we actually get away with effecting? Where are the points at which applied pressure could change the system in the direction of maximizing rational control of the ecosystem? What cultural and ideological changes are really needed? Can we get the public to change effective demand and to become less alienated toward the world and especially the natural world?

5. Some establishment of priorities is needed. Is cross-cousin marriage really a more vital issue than the world

food problem? If not, then why do we not change editorial and instructional policies that imply this?

6. Organizational changes can begin at home. Anthropologists are supposed to know about human organization, yet we do not try to change the appalling and obviously failing structure in which most of us work: the universities and other educational establishments. Here, a reintroduction of the planning function and of the concept of student as apprentice (not victim) is needed, as well as redirection to make the schools less obviously dedicated to maintaining an elite and weeding out others (however defined in different countries). If the balance of power cannot be redressed in this system, it cannot be redressed anywhere.

7. Last, because almost too obvious to state, is the need for anthropologists to learn from and cooperate with workers in biology and other relevant fields and to do more integrated research in the problems outlined. Biological planning for ecotopia is beginning (Todd and McLarney, 1970). Our help is needed in combatting myths and providing our own ideas.

The world ecological crisis is a facet of world exploitation. It is a particularly destructive facet: it will exterminate us unless we do something fast. The ivory-tower approach and the dream of pure science will not survive; either we abandon them and work for preservation, or we shall be destroyed. To these nonviable alternatives we must oppose a viable one.

Notes

An earlier and shorter version of this chapter was read at the Kroeber Anthropological Society's annual meeting, 1970, and subsequently broadcast over Radio KPFA.

My personal research was felt to be relevant then, and a word on it requested. The same may apply here. I have done research in Tahiti and in rural California, but primarily in Hong Kong, where

I studied the fishery—primarily the sea fishery, but with accumulation of data on aquaculture, which provided a fascinating contrast, since while the former was destroying its stocks via the commons situation, the latter was building up its stocks, because the real costs were specified on them as producers (see Murphy, 1967).

My interest in ecology and in conservation became militant because of Hong Kong experience. Living with people whose children were malnourished or downright starving and observing the effects of thousands of years of land misuse were the major causes. A contributing factor was observing the process of rapid ecological decline in the United States on my return, coupled with the knowledge and personal experience of the eventual results of such decline.

1. Purely the biased statement of one whose field is China.

References

Abegglen, James C. 1970. "The Economic Growth of Japan." *Scientific American* 222, No. 3: 31–37.

Abelson, Philip H. 1970. Editorial: "Shortage of Caviar." *Science* 168, No. 3928:199.

Ardrey, Robert. 1966. *The Territorial Imperative.* New York: Dell Publishing Co.

Baran, Paul, and Paul Sweezy. 1966. *Monopoly Capital.* New York: Monthly Review Press.

Borgstrom, Georg. 1969. *Too Many.* New York: Macmillan Co.

Brown, Leslie. 1967. "To Save an Eden, Wildlife Must Pay." *Audubon Magazine,* September–October: 43–49.

Calder, Nigel, 1967. *Eden Was No Garden.* New York: Holt, Rinehart & Winston.

Committee on Resources and Man, National Academy of Sciences and National Research Council. 1969. *Resources and Man.* San Francisco: W. H. Freeman.

Crowe, Beryl. 1969. "The Tragedy of the Commons Revisited." *Science* 166, No. 3909: 1103–7.

Cushing, Frank H. 1920. *Zuni Breadstuffs.* Indian Notes and Monographs, No. 8, Museum of the American Indian, New York.

Dubos, René. 1969. Editorial: "A Social Design for Science." *Science* 166, No. 3907: n.p.

Ecology Action: The Journal of Cultural Transformation. 1970–. Ecology Action Educational Institute, Box 3895, Modesto, Calif.

Ehrlich, Paul. 1968. *The Population Bomb.* New York: Ballantine Books, for Sierra Club.

Frederiksen, Harold. 1969. "Feedbacks in Economic and Demographic Transition." *Science* 166, No. 3907: 837–47.

Geertz, Clifford. 1963. *Agricultural Involution*. Berkeley: University of California Press.

Guest, B. Ross. 1968. "The Cimarron National Grassland: A Study in Land Use Adjustment." *Journal of Range Management* 21, No. 3: 167–70.

Hardin, Garrett, 1968. "The Tragedy of the Commons." *Science* 162, No. 3859: 1243–51.

Harris, Marvin. 1968. *The Rise of Anthropological Theory: A History of Theories of Culture*. New York: Thomas Y. Crowell Co.

Jalée, Pierre. 1968. *The Pillage of the Third World*. New York: Monthly Review Press.

Konzak, C. F., and S. M. Dietz. 1969. "Documentation for the Conservation, Management, and Use of Plant Genetic Resources." *Economic Botany* 23, No. 4: 299–308.

Lorenz, Konrad. 1966. *On Aggression*. New York: Harcourt, Brace & World.

Magdoff, Harry. 1969. *The Age of Imperialism*. New York: Monthly Review Press.

Murphy, Earl. 1967. *Governing Nature*. Chicago: Quadrangle Books.

Pirie, N. W. 1969. *Food Resources: Conventional and Novel*. Hardmondsworth, Middlesex: Pelican Books.

President's Science Advisory Committee. 1967. *The World Food Problem*. Washington, D.C.: Government Printing Office.

Pyke, Magnus, 1970. *Man and Food*. New York: McGraw-Hill Book Co., World University Library.

Rappaport, Roy A. 1967. *Pigs for the Ancestors*. New Haven, Conn.: Yale University Press.

Shepard, Paul, and Daniel McKinley. 1969. *The Subversive Science*. Boston: Houghton Mifflin Co.

Sjoberg, Gideon. 1960. *The Pre-Industrial City*. Glencoe, Ill.: Free Press.

Slater, R. G., Doug Kitt, Dave Widelock, and Paul Kangas. 1970. *The Earth Belongs to the People: Ecology and Power*. San Francisco: Peoples Press.

Still, Henry. 1967. *The Dirty Animal*. New York: Hawthorn Books.

Todd, John, and William O. McLarney. 1970. *The New Alchemists*. New Alchemy Institute, San Diego, Calif.

Vayda, Andrew, ed. 1969. *Environment and Cultural Behavior*. New York: American Museum of Natural History and Doubleday & Co.

Watt, Kenneth E. F. 1968. *Ecology and Resource Management*. New York: McGraw-Hill Book Co.

Up the Anthropologist— Perspectives Gained from Studying Up

Laura Nader

IN THIS ESSAY I shall describe some opportunities that anthropologists have for "studying up" in their own society, hoping to generate further discussion of why we study what we do (Nader, 1964). Anthropologists have a great deal to contribute to our understanding of the processes whereby power and responsibility are exercised in the United States. Moreover, there is a certain urgency to the kind of anthropology that is concerned with power (cf. Wolf, 1969), for the quality of life and our lives themselves may depend upon the extent to which citizens understand those who shape attitudes and actually control institutional structures. The study of man is confronted with an unprecedented situation: never before have so few, by their actions and inactions, had the power of life and death over so many members of the species. I shall present three reasons for "studying up": its energizing and integrating effect for many students; scientific adequacy; and democratic relevance of scientific work. Finally, I shall consider some frequent obstacles and objections, and try to answer them.

INDIGNATION AS MOTIVE

Many of our brighter students look at the anthropology journals of recent times and conclude that anthropology appears to be phasing out, content to make a living for the most part by rediscovering what has been discovered or by selling our wares to other disciplines and professions. The audience is too narrow, the nitpicking too precious. Making a living by selling one's wares is not an inappropriate way to subsist; it is however, in this case, symptomatic that a talent, the perspective of a *Mirror for Man,* is being under-used.

Today we have anthropology students who are indignant about many problems affecting the future of *Homo sapiens,* but they are studying problems about which they have no "feelings." Some think this is the only appropriate stance for a science. Yet the things that students are energetic about they do not study. I think we are losing something here. The normative impulse often leads one to ask important questions about a phenomenon that would not be asked otherwise, or to define a problem in a new context. A rapid growth in civil rights studies is directly attributable to activities whereby the victims of the system made their victimization visible. By a process of contagion, this visibility spread moral indignation into the law schools and the legal profession, which in turn led to research into civil rights questions and the related area of poverty law. In anthropology we have the example of Ruth Benedict's *The Chrysanthemum and the Sword* (1946), an effort to understand opponents in war. The normative impulse here, generated by patriotism and loyalty, considered appropriate in World War II, was responsible for an insightful book and the development of new techniques for studying culture at a distance.

Looking back to an early founder of American anthropology, L. H. Morgan (the first anthropologist to become president of the AAAS), we discover that he broke new ground in science as a result of having been interested in a social problem (Resek, 1960). Throughout his career, Morgan was indignant at how American Indians were being treated, at how they were being pushed off the land. It was his initial indignation which led him to study American

Indians, and his indignation preceded his curiosity about kinship systems and social structure. In Morgan's case, indignation had an energizing effect.

As Jules Henry put it:

> To think deeply in our culture is to grow angry and to anger others; and if you cannot tolerate this anger, you are wasting the time you spend thinking deeply. One of the rewards of deep thought is the hot glow of anger at discovering a wrong, but if anger is taboo, thought will starve to death. (Henry, 1963, p. 146)

I see among young students at Berkeley an energizing phenomenon in studying major institutions and organizations that affect everyday lives, such as the California Insurance Commission, the Better Business Bureau, air pollution agencies, and the like. The following extended excerpts illustrate something about what motivated these students to study what they did:

> I chose to study the insurance industry primarily because it is one of those "things" (there is no term) which is made of vast networks of people who have effects on many aspects of the lives of all people in California. Most are affected in a direct way, by owning an insurance policy. All are affected in other ways, such as by the vast political influence of the "insurance industry" and its tremendous economic influence over our personal lives.
>
> For example, one drives to the market in one's car, which is itself insured. The market one arrives at is insured for loss, theft, damages and liability. The food was delivered by trucks which were insured for the cargo they carry, which is also protected against various problems. The price of these coverages also affects the price of your food. Incidentally, the factories where the truck and your auto were manufactured are insured with various policies (as are all the employees). One of these, termed "pollution insurance," protects the company for liabilities incurred if they are sued for pollution damages. The price of this affects other prices, as mentioned, but the ownership of the insurance permits the factory or the

network of people who control the factory to pollute the air without economic risk to themselves. To extend this further, the auto company is probably owned in large part by insurance companies. To get an idea of the tremendous wealth of the insurance industry, consider that California owners of insurance policies paid over $6 billion in insurance premiums in 1970, which is over $300 per person in the State of California. This is greater than the per capita income of most of the world's population. As a matter of fact, the annual amount of premiums taken in the U.S. by the insurance industry is greater than the gross national product of all but five nations in the world. (Serber, 1971, pp. 2–3)

Another student had the following to say about her study of the Oakland Better Business Bureau:

In our complex society, we obtain many goods and services in a prepackaged state. Like the proverbial city child who grows up believing that milk grows in paper cartons, most consumers know little about what their purchases are made of, how they work, how to evaluate their potential before buying them, and how to repair them if they break down. This ignorance is not limited to goods but extends to services, investments, charities, to say nothing of the legal and medical professions. We rely on [Pacific Gas and Electricity] to install gas equipment, to check it for safety, even to relight the pilot if we cannot locate it when it is accidentally extinguished. We take our special garments to a dry cleaner. When the transmission on an automobile doesn't work, the car must be towed to a transmission specialist. Goods are ordered by telephone or through the mail. Appointments at a photographer's studio, cosmetics, magazine subscriptions, and investments may be sold and contributions to charities collected by door-to-door solicitors. When a carpet is desired, the consumer depends on a salesman to explain the qualities of the constituent fibers, to calculate the number of yards needed to cover a given area, and to make sure that incidentals like matting, tacks, and labor are included in the quoted installation cost. We depend upon specialists to provide services and often even to give us the criteria by which we are to judge their work. Many of our transactions take place infrequently, which means that the consumer may be totally inexperienced in evaluating what he pays for when he buys a large appliance, an insurance policy, or a vacation trip.

Likewise he may find himself incapable of obtaining redress of his grievances when he thinks he has been misled or cheated. Most contacts with businesses are limited to the disembodied voice of the switchboard operator, to the secretary or public relations representative in the front office, or to the salesman who happens to be on the floor when the customer walks into the store. The consumer phones the company to see what it will do for him, or he writes to a newspaper complaint column or a broadcasting station's "hotline" program. The services of these expediters are also "packaged": the complainant sends in his story and waits for the machinery to grind out an answer. This situation extends even to the law enforcement and consumer aid organizations to which the irate customer may eventually refer his problem. . . .

I began this project on the BBB in total ignorance of what it is, what it does and does not do, and why. Like the typical citizen, I began with the simple knowledge that there is a business-supported organization called the Better Business Bureau and that it is customarily contacted by telephone when a person has a question about the dependability (or existence!) of a firm or has a complaint against a business that has failed to give satisfaction. Few people go beyond these facts to ask who the voice on the other end of the line is, where she gets her information, or what actually happens to the complaint form which arrives, is returned, and whose results are relayed back to the consumer by mail. And yet thousands of people use the BBB every year. (Eaton, 1971, pp. 2–3)

Maybe these are attempts to get behind the facelessness of a bureaucratic society, to get at the mechanisms whereby faraway corporations and large-scale industries are directing the everyday aspects of our lives. Whatever the motivation, the studies raise important questions as to responsibility, accountability, self-regulation, or on another level, questions relating to social structure, network analysis, library research, and participant observation.

SCIENTIFIC ADEQUACY

If we look at the literature based on field work in the United States, we find a relatively abundant literature on the poor, the ethnic groups, the disadvantaged; there is comparatively little field research on the middle class and very little first-hand work on the upper classes. Anthropologists might indeed ask themselves whether the entirety of field work does not depend upon a certain power relationship in favor of the anthropologist, and whether indeed such dominant-subordinate relationships may not be affecting the kinds of theories we are weaving. What if, in reinventing anthropology, anthropologists were to study the colonizers rather than the colonized, the culture of power rather than the culture of the powerless, the culture of affluence rather than the culture of poverty?

Studying "up" as well as "down" would lead us to ask many "common sense" questions in reverse. Instead of asking why some people are poor, we would ask why other people are so affluent? How on earth would a social scientist explain the hoarding patterns of the American rich and middle class? How can we explain the fantastic resistance to change among those whose options "appear to be many"? How has it come to be, we might ask, that anthropologists are more interested in why peasants don't change than why the auto industry doesn't innovate, or why the Pentagon or universities cannot be more organizationally creative? The conservatism of such major institutions and bureaucratic organizations probably has wider implications for the species and for theories of change than does the conservatism of peasantry.

If, in reinventing anthropology, we were principally studying the most powerful strata of urban society, our view of the ghetto might be largely in terms of those relationships larger than the ghetto. We would study the banks and the insurance industry that mark out areas of the city to which they will not sell insurance or extend credit. We would study the landlord class that "pays off" or "influences" enforcement or municipal officials so that building codes are not enforced. Slums are technically illegal; if building codes and other municipal laws were enforced, our slums would not be slums (if enforcement were successful), or they might be called by another name which would indicate that they were results of white-collar crime. One might say that if business crime is successful, it will produce street crime. With this perspective on white-collar crime, our analysis of gang delinquency might be correspondingly affected, and in developing theories of slum-gang behavior we might ask: Is it sufficient to understand gangs as products of the value systems of that subculture alone? We might study the marketing systems or the transportation system which, as in Watts, makes virtual islands of some ghetto areas. We might study the degree to which legal practices, or the kind of legal services, mold the perceptions of law that are present in the ghettos.

The consequences of not studying up as well as down are serious in terms of developing adequate theory and description. If one's pivot point is around those who have responsibility by virtue of being delegated power, then the questions change. From such a perspective, one notices different facets of culture—the ghetto may be viewed as being without law, lawless. The courts are not geared to the complaints of the poor (which would fall in the $20 to $80 range); furthermore, they are not geared for cheap and quick resolution of conflict—crucial features for the poor. From this perspective, ghetto communities may be said to be shut out of the legal system except as defendants, and indeed they are often shut off from other municipal services ranging from garbage-collecting to police protection. From this orientation, then, the question may be raised again: In our studies of delinquency, is it sufficient to understand gangs as products of the value systems of that subculture alone?

Let's ask another question: What have been the consequences of social science research on crime? By virtue of our concentration on lower-class crimes, we have aided in the public definition of the "law and order problem" in terms of lower-class or street crimes. Let's assume that the taxpaying public in a democracy, after listening to a presidential speech calling for more tax money for enforcement and protection from street crimes, decides to see for itself. No matter what library they went to, the most they could get is some information on crimes committed by the lower class. They would have no way of evaluating, given present descriptive materials, whether, in a situation of limited money, they would do better to put their money on street crime or on white-collar crime, both of which, after all, imperil the lives of all taxpayers every day in many ways.

As Clyde Mitchell has noted, it was with such problems in mind that anthropologists first introduced the concept of "social field."

> The classical anthropological study takes a unit—a "tribe" or "society" or "community"—and presents the behavior of its members in terms of a series of interlocking institutions, structures, norms, and values. It is not only anthropologists working in urban areas who have found this sort of assumption difficult to maintain, but also those who have been conducting "tribal" studies in modern Africa (and presumably also elsewhere). They have found that the effect of groups and institutions not physically present in the tribal area influences the behavior of people in it. The unit of interacting relationships, in other words, is larger than the tribe. (Mitchell, 1966, p. 56)

Lowie may have studied the Crow, Llewellyn and Hoebel the Cheyenne, as if they were "islands" unrelated to the wider society and even unrelated to the policies and actions of the Bureau of Indian Affairs, but there has raged a whole literature since the fifties challenging the limited ethnographic community view of the world, and a recognition of methodological need has been, as Mitchell noted, what has perhaps stimulated the development of network theory and the development of nation state studies (Adams, 1970).

If anthropology were reinvented to study up, we would sooner or later need to study down as well. We are not dealing with an either/or proposition; we need simply to realize when it is useful or crucial in terms of the problem to extend the domain of study up, down, or sideways. If we become interested in the determinants of family patterns (rather than the poor or the rich as such), then studying this problem across class, or at least on a vertical slice, would be a way to test hypotheses regarding whether certain aspects of lower-class or upper-class plight are somehow due to a particular kind of family pattern (serially monogamous, matrifocal, father-absent), whether poverty, for example, is generated by certain types of employment patterns or external factors. At least posing the problems in a comparative frame would help improve our chances for understanding the forces that generate excessive poverty or affluence and the origins of those forces, whether intrusive from the larger society or "determined by cultural transmission within the group." Depending on one's view of the processes that generate behavior, one would seek solutions to social problems either by a policy directed to reforming the society as a whole or by one directed to modifying the behavior of the subculture, or both (Valentine, 1969; Gladwin, 1969).

On the basis of such work in our own society,[1] we could rewrite the books on American Society, whose indexes make no mention of the advertising, insurance, banking, realty, or automobile industries, which most people on the street know have played a major role in forming modern American society. Ethnographic reports would describe the communications industries, the agencies which regulate them, the institutions that undergird the industrial sector, such as the legislative bodies, the universities and professional organizations, and such descriptions would be from the point of view of the *users* as well as the managers. It is appropriate that a reinvented anthropology should study powerful institutions and bureaucratic organizations in the

United States, for such institutions and their network systems affect our lives and also affect the lives of people that anthropologists have traditionally studied all around the world.

It is particularly appropriate that anthropologists should lead the way in this work by virtue of a number of characteristics of our discipline. The study of man has had to be eclectic in its methods, broad in its vision of what it takes to understand man—his past, his present, his culture, his biology. We have specialized in understanding *whole* cultures in a cross-cultural context. We should, for example, be at home in studying the law firm as a secret society, in finding and analyzing the networks of power—which on paper may not be there—in describing those unwritten customary behaviors that are completely indispensable for understanding, for example, what makes Congress tick. The anthropologist should, above all, by virtue of his understanding of the principle of reciprocity, be able to analyze why it is that decisions of Federal Communications Commissioners may not be "rational," or the cultural dimensions involved in the failure of national programs ostensibly geared to reintegrate society. It is the anthropologist who, by virtue of his populist values, may be able to define the role of citizen-scholar—a science of man for man.

DEMOCRATIC RELEVANCE

"Studying up" seems to be one track for integrating paramount social concerns with the goals and aims of the science of man. The service function we have performed in the past could be amplified to include another service, social as well as scientific, that is, writing ethnographies for the "natives." A monograph that should be taken into account by managers for the benefit of people concerned is Colson's recent (1971) book on *The Impact of the Kariba Resettlement upon the Gwembe Tonga*.

Massive technological development hurts. This is a fact
largely ignored by economic planners, technicians, and
political leaders. In planning drastic alterations in environment that uproot populations or make old adjustments impossible, they count the engineering costs but not the social
costs. After all, they do not think of themselves as paying the
latter. . . . This book is a study in the impact of forced
change upon some of its victims.

Another example is Spradley's *You Owe Yourself a Drunk*,
an ethnographic description of the interaction and the consequences of the interaction that drunks have with the
legal and enforcement systems. This monograph is already
serving to educate managers of that system about the
consequences of specific legal decisions and procedures.
This is not a novel role for social scientists to play, and
unfortunately our findings have often served to help manipulate rather than aid those we study. Another role, however, is related to the concept of citizenship in a country
that is to be run on a democratic framework and the control
that citizens must have to harness managerial manipulation.
We cannot, as responsible scientists, educate "managers"
without at the same time educating those "being managed."
A democratic framework implies that citizens should have
access to decision-makers, institutions of government, and
so on. This implies that citizens need to know something
about the major institutions, government or otherwise, that
affect their lives. Most members of complex societies and
certainly most Americans do not know enough about, nor do
they know how to cope with, the people, institutions, and
organizations which most affect their lives. I believe that
anthropologists would be surprisingly good at applying
their descriptive and analytical tools to a major problem:
How can a citizenry function in a democracy when that
citizenry is woefully ignorant of how the society works and
doesn't work, of how a citizen can "plug in" as a citizen, of
what would happen should citizens begin to exercise rights
other than voting as a way to make the "system" work for

them? But first, as we know, we have to describe the bureaucracy and its culture.

Love and Eaton (1970) began their study of the Bay Area Air Pollution Control Agency with questions about the functions of the agency: How does the agency perceive itself? Who uses it? How do the users perceive the agency? Public access was a key question.

> Our approach was, at first, guarded due to our doubts. We pretended innocence, and in fact found out that we really were innocent. We then began to realize that we were "outsiders." We were the public who did not understand the professional language being spoken. The avenues we approached were those the public generally approached. Gradually, a picture of the agency and its position in the legal system emerged.
>
> Its structure, the personalities of the decision-makers, the limitations reality places on any ideal system, and finally the kinds of uses made of it became clearer. . . . (Pp. 2–3)
>
> When the citizen goes to the agency, he is translated into statistical data which separate him from the actual procedure or use of the agency. . . . Assumed in this is the notion that since the agency is supposed to protect the public interest, the public will seek access to it. The reality of the situation is very different. The agency acts as autonomously as possible to combat air pollution and in so doing, comes into close contact with the industry officials who speak the same technical and legal language. It is industry which has the greatest access to the agency, especially at the legislative level. It is industry which makes the greatest *use* of the agency to protect *its* interests. (Pp. 32–33)

This same study notes that, in the legal division of the agency, violation notices are treated like parking tickets—after so many are collected the violator is prosecuted. But what does prosecution consist of, given the intimate patterns of social interaction described above? These were not ordinary criminals.

> In the legal division, the agency lawyer emphasized that the principles of criminal law were not a solution, hence the civil

fines. The type of "crime" committed does not merit the "responsible" official being put in jail with "prostitutes and muggers." . . . An interesting footnote to this procedure is that Regulation 1, which does *not* apply to most large industries but to private citizens and land developers, is treated as a misdemeanor where the violator can be put in jail with the "prostitutes and muggers." (P. 33)

Apart from being a useful report on bureaucratic culture, this thirty-seven-page report is the kind of ethnographic information that citizens need prior to an attempt to gain *access* to, or attempt to *use*, a public agency. Such reports would introduce them to the structure and culture of the subgroup in such a way as to allow them to gauge whether the cards are stacked and in what direction they are stacked in terms of real access to, and use of, a public agency.

The study of the California Department of Insurance, and in particular the processing of complaints by the Policy Services Bureau of that same agency, is another attempt to describe the workings of an organization whose acts of omission or commission affect the lives of many (Serber, 1971). Serber concludes (p. 62) that the Department of Complaints does not meet the needs of the people of the State of California because "the vast majority of the people are not aware of its existence." He adds, by means of a quote, a further insight which has been noted by other student studies of governmental agencies (and it is not much different for private agencies that purport to serve the public) and which suggests that such public institutions are not structured for public access:

> It is much worse to deal with someone in the public because you know that you are very limited in what kinds of answers you can give them and the results you can get for them. They expect more and often get impatient. With the industry, it's different: they are usually friendly and polite, at least to our faces; we always know where we stand and how far we can go. It's less stressful because I feel less responsible for the outcome of the conversations. (Insurance Officer III).

The report goes on to note that "there is a qualitative difference in the nature of the interaction between the complainants and the Insurance Officer and the representative of the industry and the Insurance Officer."

> It's not very pleasant to arrive here at a quarter of eight in the morning after battling to cross the Bay Bridge for forty-five minutes and before I can finish a cup of coffee some *hysterical* fat bitch who can hardly talk, she's so stupid and excited, will come in, and they will call me. When I catch sight of her my stomach tightens and my mouth gets dry; sometimes the burning in my pipe starts before I can even get up to the desk, and I'll have to take a sip of water. (Insurance Officer IV)

This same report makes a set of predictions as to what might happen to this Department of Complaints were access by the public easily available; the structure and function of the department would move more closely in line with a major goal of the Department of Insurance "to enforce insurance laws so as to achieve the highest possible degree of protection for the public in general and all policy holders and beneficiaries in particular" (Serber, 1971, p. 64).

The above-stated goal raises a more general question: Who is to decide what is good for the public? Eaton's paper on the Better Business Bureau of Oakland illustrates the dilemma of a value conflict.

> A major limitation in the value of the BBB to the consumer lies in the very fact that it *is* an organization designed to further the interests of legitimate business. The movement assumes that what is good for business is good for the economy and for the consumer. It assumes that the power of conscience and the power of public opinion will triumph over the unbridled profit motive, that an informed public will be able to mold the responsive market to its own desires. These assumptions may be true on some levels, but the picture is not that simple. There are areas of the society in which power is concentrated and areas where it is dispersed or absent altogether. The consumer's complaint has more

weight with the locally competitive retailer than with the faraway corporation which made the product that the retailer sells. The Bureau regulates retail advertising, but the consumer is also exposed to national advertising, especially on television. The retailer is not a free agent: he is limited by the distributor and the supplier. . . .

The Bureau is concerned with truth in advertising, but is it equally concerned about relevance in advertising? There are many things which can be said about a product which are true, but which have very little to do with its significant attributes: durability, safety, efficiency. . . . The consumer is told on the one hand that it is his responsibility to be informed and to exercise his power of choice to bring the market into line with his needs and desires. . . . On the other hand, he is assaulted by national advertising, which stresses the nonpractical attributes of products, and he is confronted with a range of products from different manufacturers which have essentially no differences between them in areas which the consumer may think are significant. He is told to understand the warranty that comes with his new car, but he is not told what he can do if he does not like its terms and finds that all warranties from all companies are just the same. As an individual, he is essentially powerless to bargain in the greater market system that characterizes the modern complex society. (Eaton, 1971, pp. 68–70)

Understanding the differences in the perceptions of producers on the one hand and consumers on the other allows a citizen to evaluate for himself any government statement about the need for government not to encroach on the self-regulatory organizations such as the BBB that are set up by business groups. Eaton's study of the BBB touches but one tiny part of the self-regulatory attempts of business. Since 1966, there has evolved a whole series of "complaint handling mechanisms," from "hot lines" to corporate ombudsmen. A comparative study of such mechanisms would be a much-needed contribution to the literature on the nature of extralegal attempts at voicing complaints and obtaining redress. It would be fascinating to know to what degree "informal law" is dominated by public relations and Madison Avenue techniques in conflict management. The use of advertising in grievance resolution may be related to an upper-class perception of upper-class law and order which says, "Cool it rather than resolve it."

Some years ago, the criminologist Edwin H. Sutherland wrote a book entitled *White-Collar Crime*. A landmark finding documented in that work was the simple fact that white-collar personnel commit crimes, a fact which should have helped combat the belief, at least among social scientists, that the poor had a monopoly on crime. If, as scientists, we are interested in understanding the determinants of crime, then the "discovery" that the rich as well as the poor commit "crimes" (something that is well known to the average citizen and most certainly known by the poor) is very important. The fact that crimes are differentially stigmatized and prosecuted according to class should lead us to disregard oversimplistic theories explaining criminal behavior. Very few sociological works of this type followed Sutherland's study, and indeed there was a long dry period between the muckraking of the turn of the century and Sutherland.

Instead, sociologists such as Lewis Coser (1968) prefer to tell us why some poor do and why some poor do not commit crimes in terms of the theory of related criminal behavior. If we look at the question in relation to a vertical slice, it is a well-known fact that the criminal law has been oriented toward individual crimes, preferably street crime, and collective criminal behavior by an agency or corporation is often dealt with in administrative agencies or in ways which leave very little stigma on those involved (Pound, 1906; Sutherland, 1949). Yet our analyzed data base is slim. Henry Ruth, Director of the National Institute of Law Enforcement and Criminal Justice, noted as late as 1970 that

> the National Institute of Law Enforcement and Criminal Justice has developed an intensive concern that so-called "white-collar crime" receives scant attention from the law

enforcement and research communities. . . . The entire field of white-collar crime represents a national priority for action and research—to define the problem, to examine its many faces, to measure its impact, to look for ways in which its victims can be helped, and to determine how such crime can be prevented, deterred, and effectively prosecuted. (Edelhertz, 1970, p. iii)

With regard to benefit to citizens, it is astounding that in as legalistic a country as the United States, nowhere in the educational system does one get a *working* knowledge of the law as part of a general education. In fact, after years of studying the Zapotec legal system of Oaxaca, Mexico, I would conclude that the single most important difference between the Zapotec legal system of southern Mexico and the American legal system (from the point of view of a middle-class consumer) is that Zapotecs have access to, know how to *use* access to, the legal system. In the United States, most citizens do not have access to the legal system, either because they are ignorant of the workings of the system or because they cannot afford the professional (lawyer) who would have adequate knowledge of the workings of the system. In California, for example—and I imagine this is much more widespread—there are few books for citizens describing the legal system, what it is, and how it works.

This situation is representative of the larger problem of citizen education. Most of what we learn about the law we absorb vicariously from TV westerns and Perry Mason–style shows. Ethnographic works on the subject of law would be filling a scientific and descriptive need, as well as informing the native about a system which at times heavily weights the direction his life takes. For example, one student began a study of the Immigration and Naturalization Service in an effort to find out how immigration and the INS have molded and influenced the communities of third-world immigrants. The basic hypothesis was that the INS is the historical product of negative American attitudes toward non-Northern European immigrants—fear of foreigners, dislike of strange cultures, isolationism, and the like; that while there has been a major liberalization of the laws, the administration of immigration, and indeed recruitment to the agency, continue to be affected by these historical attitudes. Other anthropological studies might involve the use of personal documents—the memoirs of judges, lawyers, and corporate executives are more noticeable for their absence from the bookshelves. The Washington law firms whose lobbying functions have earned them the label of fourth branch of government would be a fascinating place to test some of Elizabeth Bott's hypotheses about networks. What shapes and functions do the networks of such firms have in an organization where, at mid-career, the majority of firm members fan out into positions about Washington, yet still maintain relations with the law firm even after they are no longer on the payroll? What kind of reciprocity is involved here?

OBSTACLES AND OBJECTIONS

But there are those who would not want to entertain any such reorientation of anthropology, and it is important to appreciate the reasons why present-day anthropologists would say "impossible," "improbable," "irrelevant," "off the mark," even "impertinent." The obstacles that are posed are many, but for our purposes here they may be discussed in terms of *access, attitudes, ethics,* and *methodology.*

Departments of anthropology have generally believed that students should do their dissertation field work in a non-Western culture. At some points in time that was a useful policy to implement, if in training anthropologists one valued the importance of culture shock and the detachment which accompanies it. For many students today, the experience of working in a Washington law firm, in a company town, or in an international industrial complex would be more bizarre than anything a student anthropologist could find in a Mexican village, or in New Guinea for that matter. We anthropologists have studied the cultures of the world only to find in the end that ours is one of the most bizarre of all cultures and one, by virtue of its world influence for "bad" or "good," in urgent need of study.

The most usual obstacle is phrased in terms of access. The powerful are out of reach on a number of different planes: they don't want to be studied; it is dangerous to study the powerful; they are busy people; they are not all in one place, and so on. As some of our students found out in their studies of corporate use of the courts:

> The belief that corporations work secretly and surreptitiously in their own interests has been somewhat verified. Their desire for secrecy, their paranoid fear of all but self-fashioned publicity, their refusal to discuss questions on their operation, and the overconscious regard of their lawyers for the confidential nature of the lawyer-client relationship (even when the public's interests are at stake), all serve to eliminate any free flow of information which should be available to the public forum, and are reminiscent of secret societies. The stealth of the corporation is epitomized in those wily chess masters they employ to handle their cases, the corporate lawyers. (Zeff and Bush, 1970)

These difficulties are true of the people that anthropologists have studied in many different places. That problems of access are any different, or at least any more problematic, in studying up in the United States is a proposition which has not been adequately tested. Anthropologists have had problems of access everywhere they have gone; solving such problems of access is part of what constitutes "making rapport." In view of our successes among peoples of the world who have been incredibly hostile, it is rather surprising that anthropologists could be so timid at home (see Riesman, 1954, pp. 440–66). Furthermore, it could be argued that access to bureaucratic organizations (such as governmental agencies) frequented by the wealthy and powerful should be open to social scientists by virtue of laws which protect public access to information affecting the public interest. In addition, there are wealthy anthropologists who would presumably have access "up." Cleveland Amory (1947) and E. Digby Baltzell (1964) have made substantial contributions to understanding the power status of the upper class, although neither one is an anthropologist. No, there must be more plausible reasons why the less powerful are more attractive for study in the United States.

It has been said that anthropologists value studying what they like and liking what they study and, in general, we prefer the underdog. Braroe and Hicks (1967), discussing the mystique of anthropology, make reference again to the traditional alienation from their own culture that characterizes anthropologists, and they explore how such alienation relates to their lack of intense commitment to social reform. This could be phrased more positively: Anthropologists have favored studying non-Western cultures as a way of fulfilling their mission to study the diverse ways of mankind; they have not had an intense commitment to social reform because of their relativistic stance and a belief that such a stance was necessary to a truly "objective, detached, scientific perspective," or because they thought that others, such as sociologists, were involved in social reform. While scientific findings may be ideally viewed as "value-free," certainly the choice of subject for scientific inquiry is most certainly not. Anthropologists of the future will have a greater responsibility for what they choose to study as well as how they study.

The ethical problems that are raised in studying up almost always appear to be confused, particularly in discussing ethics of working in one's own society. One student made the following comment:

> To say that kula-ring participants don't perform in practice what they say they do has very different consequences from saying that a government agency is not living up to its standards. This isn't to say that the government agency shouldn't be studied, or that the fact it isn't living up to its

standards shouldn't be pointed out. The question is: Can the anthropologist do a structural study and then in his role as citizen point out that the agency is screwing the American public?

The same student asked:

> How can we gain access to the same kinds of information as when we "study down" without being dishonest (i.e., a fake secretary or other role)? If we did get information without letting informants know we were social scientists, how could we publish it? It seems that the only "open" way of doing a study would end up being fairly superficial—questionnaires and formal interviews as versus what we learn by participant observation.

The problems raised by this student are ethical problems anthropologists have had to face no matter what culture they are studying. In discussing such ethical questions involved in studying up in our own society, I have the impression that confusion results depending on whether or not one recognizes the implicit double standard—is there one ethic for studying up and another for studying down? Or is it, as this student suggests, that the consequences of describing what may be systemic inadequacies may be greater for government agencies than peasant economic systems or for conflict resolution (or just plain conflict) in a small fishing village, and that therefore our subjects of study should be treated accordingly?

There is an important distinction to be recognized as to "public" and "private," even though informant anonymity may be important to both sectors. For the most part, anthropologists working in the United States can be said to have worked in the "private" sphere: we study families, small groups, those aspects of communities which are more private than public. We should not necessarily apply the same ethics developed for studying the private, and even ethics developed for studying in foreign cultures (where we are guests), to the study of institutions, organizations,

bureaucracies that have a broad public impact. In reinventing anthropology, any discussion of ethics should
consider the public-private dimensions as well as the home-
abroad component. Furthermore, in the present anthropology, work that is considered in the objective social science
mode, when carried out abroad might well be dubbed
"journalistic" by the subjects. Telling it like it is may be
perceived as muckraking by the subjects of study (Oscar
Lewis' work on Mexico was so viewed), *or* by fellow professionals who feel more comfortable if data is presented in
social science jargon which would protect the work from
common consumption.

The concept of participant observation plays a determin-
ing role in *what* anthropologists choose to study. The power
of participant observation as such was only discovered in
the twentieth century. Malinowski and Radcliffe-Brown,
among the first to do field work by the techniques of
participant observation, set a new standard for ethnographic
descriptions. When an anthropologist goes to study the culture of a people, he lives with them; the resultant description is rich in contextual information and is the result of
the many points of view that one is opened to by virtue of
"living with the natives." Hortense Powdermaker has described the components of participant observation as follows:

> The conditions for successful mutual communication include
> 1) physical proximity of the field worker to the people he
> studies, 2) knowledge of their language, and 3) psychological
> involvement. (1966, p. 287)

She goes on to say:

> The ability to be psychologically mobile is important in
> hierarchical situations where it is necessary to move easily
> between different levels in the power structure. Some field
> workers identify so completely with the underdog that they
> are unable to make effective contacts with those on the top
> level of the social (or political) hierarchy. (P. 291)

At the same time that Hortense Powdermaker has described the value of participant observations, she has also alluded to the limitations of such complete acceptance of participant observation as a distinctive feature of all social anthropological field work. When the anthropologist participant observes, he or she resides and generally partakes with the "natives." Such a method has weighed heavily in the decisions as to where anthropologists study: we prefer residential situations, whether the residence is in a primitive village or a modern hospital.

The degree to which our field choices might be determined by whether or not we can observe as participant was made clear to me when two of my students went to Washington to study a law firm that did not want to be studied (even though individual members were willing to cooperate in a limited way). How could they participant-observe if the firm wouldn't let them in the door, and *if they couldn't participant-observe, how could they do anthropology?* These questions have, of course, been raised before in anthropology, and when anthropologists thought it important enough they surmounted the problems raised. Witness the culture-at-a-distance studies that cropped up during World War II, or witness the work of Elizabeth Bott (1957) in her network study of kinship in London, which was based principally on face-to-face interviewing.

The point here is that there is a mystique about participant observation that carries points with it, yet it remains that the anthropologist's image of himself is shattered (Fischer, 1969) if he cannot participant-observe, and for the most part our students are not generally trained in the kinds of techniques that they would need to work on problems in nonresidential settings such as banks, insurance companies, government agencies, electronics industries, and the like. How many anthropologists know how to find out who owns a city? If Sol Tax is right in pointing out that anthropologists are not working on the most relevant problems of the world today—such as population, pollution, and war—

because they cannot participant-observe such problems in a community, then, in reinventing anthropology, we might have to shuffle around the value placed on participant observation that leads us to forget that there are other methods (see Gussow and Tracy, 1971) more useful for some of the problems and situations we might like to investigate. The use of personal documents, memoirs, may substitute for anthropological participation in some areas of culture that take long years of participation to really understand. One student makes the following comments about field methodology:

> The principal research method of the anthropologist, participant observation, is, needless to say, not wholly applicable when one is studying a government agency or elite institution and its interaction with various people. A particular situation can be dealt with, but characteristically the data gleaned would be through observation rather than participation. We can define participation in two ways. One definition would maintain that to say the researcher is a participant means he is able to interact as a native in the situation studied and is therefore able to use himself as an informant. The other definition considers the participant in a status achieved by an outsider, since he is treated as an insider. Ideally, the more intimate the acceptance, the less the participant/observer will influence the situation he is observing and the closer he will be to the status of participant. Considering these two definitions, the term "participant/observer" could not be applicable to the types of situations that the ethnographer would want to study in large-scale institutions, unless he was actually to become a member of the group he is studying. The term "participant/observer" would not truly apply to these researcher's techniques, even in the situations where I was attempting to fulfill the ideal. In studying one's own society, especially if it is complex and highly specialized and heterogeneous, the question is to determine the levels of actual participation and the level barred from participation.

> If the anthropologist is going to make a contribution to the understanding of the institutions which in a complex

way affect the lives of many people, he must take a methodologically eclectic approach. . . . (Serber, 1971, pp. 5–6)

Interviews of various sorts (formal/informal, face-to-face/
telephone) were used by my students. Documents were used
(see the *NACLA Guide*, 1970)—public relations documents
for understanding the preferred self-image of the organization, internal documents on the structure and statistics of
work planned and accomplished by the organization, all
useful in discovering trends and what is thought of as
problematic by the actors. Also important is what Marian
Eaton has labeled "self-analysis"—an awareness on the part
of the student of how he as a social scientist is perceived, run
around, enculturated, and described in the veiled and not-
so-veiled encounters with informants and the members of
organizations and the like whose job it is to deal with outsiders. We may have to give higher priority to traditional
anthropological values such as using our knowledge of others
as a mirror for ourselves and allowing questions to lead us to
methodology (rather than vice versa).

We may have to reorder our conception of urgent anthropology. Surely it should be the needs of mankind for
the study of man that lead the way.

Notes

I am very grateful to Elizabeth Colson, Marian Eaton, Dell Hymes,
and Julio Ruffini for taking the time to read and criticize earlier versions of this paper. Marian Eaton deserves special recognition for helping research and edit these pages. The undergraduate students who
have been pioneering in "studying up" deserve recognition for their
vision, their persevering attitudes, their delight in doing ethnography
of everyday life situations at home, and for trying to do so in better
than the usual way. Physicist Arthur Rosenfeld deserves special thanks
for funding two anthropology students in an early effort to study up in
Washington, D.C., an effort which led to the formulation of ideas for
this paper.

1. See M. N. Srinivas' book *Social Change in Modern India*, Chapter
   5, "Some Thoughts on the Study of One's Own Society," for a discussion of the problems involved in such an endeavor.

References

Adams, Richard Newbold. 1970. *Crucifixion by Power*. Austin: University of Texas Press.

Amory, Cleveland. 1947. *The Proper Bostonians*. New York: E. P. Dutton & Co.

Baltzell, E. Digby. 1964. *The Protestant Establishment: Aristocracy and Caste in America*. New York: Vintage Books.

Benedict, Ruth. 1946. *The Chrysanthemum and the Sword*. Boston: Houghton Mifflin Co.

Bott, Elizabeth. 1957. *Family and Social Network: Roles, Norms and External Relationships in Ordinary Urban Families*. London: Tavistock Publications.

Braroe, Niels Winther, and George L. Hicks. 1967. "Observations on the Mystique of Anthropology." *Sociological Quarterly* 7, No. 2: 173–86.

Colson, Elizabeth. 1971. *The Impact of the Kariba Resettlement upon the Gwembe Tonga*. Manchester: University of Manchester Press.

Coser, Lewis A. 1968. "Violence and the Social Structure." In *Violence in the Streets*, ed. Shalom Endleman. Chicago: Quadrangle Books. Pp. 71–84.

Eaton, Marian. 1971. "An Ethnography of BBB Oakland: One Consumer's View." Unpublished undergraduate thesis, Department of Anthropology, University of California, Berkeley.

Edelhertz, Herbert. 1970. *The Nature, Impact, and Prosecution of White-Collar Crime*. Washington, D.C.: Government Printing Office.

Fellmeth, Robert, ed. 1971. *Power and Land in California, Preliminary Draft*. Center for the Study of Responsive Law, Washington, D.C.

Fischer, Ann. 1969. "The Personality and Subculture of Anthropologists and Their Study of U.S. Negroes." In *Concepts and Assumptions in Contemporary Anthropology*, ed. Stephen A. Tyler. Proceedings of the Southern Anthropological Society No. 3. Athens: University of Georgia Press. Pp. 12–17.

Gellhorn, Walter. 1966. *When Americans Complain*. Cambridge, Mass.: Harvard University Press.

Gladwin, Thomas. 1969. Review of *Culture and Poverty: Critique and Counter-Proposals*, by Charles Valentine. *Current Anthropology*, 10, Nos. 2–3:185.

Gussow, Zachary, and George S. Tracy. 1971. "The Use of Archival Materials in the Analysis and Interpretation of Field Data: A Case Study in the Institutionalization of the Myth of Leprosy as 'Leper.'" *American Anthropologist* 73, No. 3: 695–709.

Hannerz, Ulf. 1969. *Soulside: Inquiries Into Ghetto Culture and Community*. New York: Columbia University Press.

Henry, Jules. 1963. *Culture Against Man.* New York: Random House.

Kluckhohn, Clyde. 1960. *Mirror for Man.* Greenwich, Conn.: Fawcett Publications.

Leacock, Eleanor Burke, ed. 1971. *The Culture of Poverty: A Critique.* New York: Simon & Schuster.

Love, Norma, and Marian Eaton. 1970. "The Bay Area Air Pollution Control District: An Anthropological Perspective." Unpublished undergraduate paper, Department of Anthropology, University of California, Berkeley.

Malinowski, Bronislaw. 1922. *Argonauts of the Western Pacific.* London: Routledge & Kegan Paul.

Mitchell, J. Clyde. 1966. "Theoretical Orientations in African Urban Studies." In *The Social Anthropology of Complex Societies,* ed. Michael Banton. Association of Social Anthropologists Monograph No. 4. London: Tavistock Publications. Pp. 37–68.

Nader, Laura. 1964. "Perspectives Gained from Field Work." In *Horizons of Anthropology,* ed. Sol Tax. Chicago: Aldine Press. Pp. 148–59.

North American Congress on Latin America. 1970. *NACLA Research Methodology Guide.* New York.

Pound, Roscoe. 1906. "The Causes of Popular Dissatisfaction with the Administration of Justice." *Reports of the American Bar Association* 29, Part 1: 395–417.

Powdermaker, Hortense. 1966. *Stranger and Friend: the Way of an Anthropologist.* New York: W. W. Norton & Co.

Resek, Carl. 1960. *Lewis Henry Morgan, American Scholar.* Chicago: University of Chicago Press.

Riesman, David. 1954. *Individualism Reconsidered and Other Essays.* Glencoe, Ill.: Free Press.

Serber, David. 1971. "A Discussion of the Policy Services Bureau of the California Department of Insurance, with Specific Reference to the Interaction with the Insured Public and the Insurance Industry." Unpublished undergraduate thesis, Department of Anthropology, University of California, Berkeley.

Spradley, J. P. 1970. *You Owe Yourself a Drunk: An Ethnography of Urban Nomads.* Boston: Little, Brown & Co.

Srinivas, M. N. 1966. *Social Change in Modern India.* Berkeley: University of California Press.

Sutherland, Edwin H. 1949. *White-Collar Crime.* New York: Dryden Press.

Valentine, Charles. 1969. Book review of his *Culture and Poverty: Critique and Counter-Proposals. Current Anthropology* 10, Nos. 2–3: 181–200.

Weakland, J. H. 1960. " 'The Double Bind' Hypothesis of Schizophrenia and Three-Party Interaction." In *The Etiology of Schizophrenia,* ed. Don D. Jackson. New York: Basic Books.

Wolf, E. 1969. "American Anthropologists and American Society." In *Concepts and Assumptions in Contemporary Anthropology,* ed.

Stephen A. Tyler. Proceedings of the Southern Anthropological Society No. 3. Athens: University of Georgia Press. Pp. 3–11.
ieff, David, and Peggy Bush. 1970. "Corporate Use of the Courts." Unpublished undergraduate paper, Department of Anthropology, University of California, Berkeley.

Counter Culture and Cultural Hegemony: Some Notes on the Youth Rebellion of the 1960s

A. Norman Klein

And as in private life one distinguishes between what a man really thinks and says of himself and what he really is and does, still more in historical struggles must one distinguish the phrases and fancies of parties from their real organism and their real interest, their conception of themselves from their reality.
—Karl Marx, The Eighteenth Brumaire of Louis Bonaparte

I

TO POSE QUESTIONS about the youth rebellion and counter culture of the 1960s, it is necessary to reach outside the conventional boundaries of anthropology. The culture of our industrial complex exhibits different qualities from the tribal and peasant organizations which are the traditional subject matter of cultural anthropology. This difference is more than bigness. Terms like "ruling class," "power elite," and others express a reality in our lives that is nonexistent in tribal societies; they express the fact that very few among us actually make the political and economic decisions that affect us all. This has been the case since the first urban revolutions. It is inherent in the formation of states. In peasant and early capitalist cultures, political power reflects economic interests much more immediately than in our own. In these cultures the state employs its power directly through the coercive mechanism of "political" society—that is, the army, the law courts, and so on. If the peasant—always anxious to hold on to as much of his output as possible—withheld rent or taxes; if the voteless worker of early capitalist society—always pressing to increase his wages—threatened the property or productivity of his employer's plant, they were both coerced back into "their place." A knight, a soldier, a gendarme, a judge, would use the force of military might or custom or law to bring the recalcitrants into line with the interests of the wielders of state power.

In advanced industrial culture, where the majority who do not make the decisions possess the vote, literacy and skills, the older, directly coercive sanctions of previous state forms are obsolete. Such a majority could not remain coerced. On the contrary, as Marcuse points out, the potential tools for exercising power have been transformed into instruments of their own domination.

> Democracy would appear to be the most efficient system of domination. . . . Free election of masters does not abolish the masters or the slaves. . . . The spontaneous reproduction of superimposed needs by the individual does not establish autonomy; it only testifies to the efficiency of the controls. (Marcuse, 1964, pp. 57, 7, 8)

The conception of ideological "hegemony" in the work of the Italian Marxist Antonio Gramsci[1] led me to pose the question of the youth rebellion in terms of the dominant hegemonic culture which was the object of its protest. How, in an advanced industrial complex, does "hegemony" operate to absorb, assimilate, and integrate a variety of forms of protest into its own ideological network? "Hegemony," a Marxist correlate of Lenin's theory of the state, begins with a distinction between "political" and "civil" society. "Political society," already alluded to, is the coercive arm of the state. "Civil society" (defined below) is composed of non-coercive, and even "nonpolitical," elements of our culture. In spite of the fact that the hegemonic interests are those of a very small decision-making group, all groups identify with, or at least acquiesce in, its values, conceptions, and institutions.

A useful introductory definition of hegemony is "an order in which a certain way of life and thought is dominant, in which one conception of reality is diffused throughout society in all its institutional and private manifestations, informing with its spirit all taste, morality, customs, religious and political principles, and all social relations, particularly in their intellectual and moral connotations" (Williams, 1960, p. 587, cited in Cammett, 1967, p. 204). "Hegemony" requires a "hegemonic group," which, according to Gramsci, cannot be defined in simple economic terms.

> The fact of hegemony undoubtedly presupposes that the interests and strivings of the groups over which the hegemony will be exercised are taken account of, that a certain balance of compromises be formed, that, in other words, the leading group makes some sacrifices of an economico-corporative kind; but it is also undoubted that these sacrifices and compromises cannot concern essentials, since if the hegemony is economico-political, it must also be economic, it must have its foundation in the decisive function that the leading group exercises in the decisive sphere of economic activity. (Gramsci, 1957, pp. 154–55)

Gramsci's broad cultural concept is a far cry from the economic determinism usually attributed to Marxists. It encompasses all the forms in our culture which "persuade" us to identify with its dominant, hegemonic interests; which "persuade" us despite our own economic, social, and political interests. Cultural instruments for the exercise of hegemony in the gigantic industrial complex of today's United States include voluntary associations, schools, religious groups; a staggering variety of social, intellectual, and artistic forms; total industries like advertising and public relations, which specialize in the manufacture of taste and values; the media; and even culturally coded private and interpersonal behavior—institutions which Gramsci would include in his "civil" society.

> Our insistence on the depth and efficacy of these controls is open to the objection that we overrate greatly the indoctrinating power of the "media," and that by themselves the people would feel and satisfy the needs which are now imposed upon them. The objection misses the point. The preconditioning does not start with the mass production of radio and television and with the centralization of their control. The people enter this stage as preconditioned receptacles of long standing; the decisive difference is in the flattening out of the contrast (or conflict) between the given and the possible, between the satisfied and the unsatisfied needs. Here, the so-called equalization of class distinction reveals its ideological function. If the worker and his boss enjoy the same television program and visit the same resort places, if the typist is as attractively made up as the daughter of her employer, if the Negro owns a Cadillac, if they all read the same newspaper, then this assimilation indicates not the disappearance of classes, but the extent to which the needs and satisfactions that serve the preservation of the Establishment are shared by the underlying population. (Marcuse, 1964, p. 8)

Ours is a culture in which the coercive arm of political society rarely becomes visible, except when state power is threatened. Cultural hegemony is built into many aspects of the American Myth. It is implicit in the assumptions behind such leveling attitudes as "We are all consumers." The unemployed relief-check recipient is likely to be as avid about the latest luxuries in the American standard of living as he is about the latest astronauts in our conquest of space, while reading his tabloid or watching his television screen. All our cultural codes are saturated with hegemonic messages.

A hegemonic spirit pervades our social science. Anthropology is no exception. The dictates of "structural functionalism" and various psychological approaches—all primarily interested in the mechanics of social equilibrium and harmony—virtually dominated the field until very recently. To focus on competition and conflict between different political-economic vested interests, as expressed in the ideological and social structures of peasant cultures, has indeed become more acceptable than it was a few years ago —even commonplace today. In arguing that the dominant culture has assimilated and subverted the counter-cultural criticism of it, I am far from denying that the underlying interests remain antagonistic and am definitely not arguing that the maintenance of the hegemony was inevitable or desirable. I am arguing that we may be misled by the spectacle of conflict into granting appearance more substance than it actually has, and that such deception can be destructive to real chances of transformation. In keeping with the theme of reinventing anthropology, I should like to discuss some cultural contradictions and conflicts in the present-day United States of America and Western Europe.

It was precisely against the broad cultural front of hegemonic values that the youth of the 1960s finally rebelled. It is hardly an understatement to say that the entire hegemonic culture was the target of the counter culture. I shall argue that:

1) The youthful protest was an integral part of the culture being protested against.
2) Form and content of the protest were assimilated and mobilized by the hegemonic culture in its own defense.
3) The counter-cultural protest of the sixties only partially recognized the absorptive, integrative character of the hegemonic culture it attacked, and, because of this faulty and incomplete understanding, the politics of the counter-culture produced some ironic results:
   a) It rendered itself nonpolitical and
   b) It contributed to the long-run reinforcement of those hegemonic mechanisms in the dominant culture it attacked.

Since so much of what follows flows directly from personal experience, it is inevitable that my feelings come through. I spent many hours talking to, arguing with, and picketing alongside these protesters, and I was, from the beginning, sympathetic to their outcry. I do not claim to be an "impartial" observer or a "value-free" social scientist. On the contrary, I conceive my role as anthropologist in much the same way as Adorno conceived his as "cultural critic"—with all the contradictions and difficulties this implies (Adorno, 1967, pp. 19–34). I am left with a certain ambivalence and sadness in relating what follows. Baudelaire might have been speaking for the protesting youth when he wrote:

> *Je suis la plaie et le couteau!*
> *Je suis le soufflet et la joue!*
> *Je suis les membres et la roue,*
> *Et la victime et le bourreau!*

> (I am the wound and the knife!
> I am the slap and the cheek!
> I am the limbs and the wheel,
> And the victim and the executioner!)

II

A universal feature of the youth revolt that began in the 1960s, whether in Western Europe or the United States, whether at political barricades or in song, whether against United States foreign policy or parents, has been the feeling that some power Up There was and is oppressing them. This feeling has united the explicitly political New Left and Marxist-Leninist sectarians with the only implicitly political hippie flower people in massive demonstrations. It has been against the power and authority of the dominant culture that they all have rebelled. In their career as rebels they have claimed increasing autonomy from their culture of origin, an assertion sloganized as "counter culture," "life-style," "youth culture," and most recently "Consciousness III." In spite of this self-image, I have found it necessary to interpret all these forms of protest as integral aspects of the hegemonic culture they attack. The contradictions that define and characterize the politics and counter culture of the youth rebellion derive from the dominant political and social culture, although in inverted or exaggerated form. This appears when one notices that the differences between the youthful rebellions in Europe and in the United States correspond to differences between the parent cultures.

Common to student protests, whether in Berkeley, Berlin, Paris, or New York, has been their anarchism, but the different political heritages of Western Europe and the United States have produced different anarchisms. On the Continent, Cohn-Bendit, speaking for the students, interprets the rebellion of Parisian students in 1968 as a trigger for what should have been a revolution by workers and peasants. He believes the workers wanted a revolution but were frustrated by the army, police, law courts, and other institutions of state power ("political society") from the right, and even more importantly by the Communist Party from the left. In fact, he says, all traditional political organizations and leaderships neutralize revolutionary impulses by diverting them into antidemocratic, bureaucratic committees and offices which develop their own vested interests. "All revolutionary activity," he writes, "is collective, and hence involves a degree of organization. What we challenge is not the need for this, but the need for a revolutionary leadership, the need for a party" (Cohn-Bendit, 1969, p. 199).

The strongest competitor of this anarchism was the Communist Party, for both movements hoped to win the same constituency of workers and peasants. All European revolutionaries think with the traditional categories of class consciousness and class conflict; Cohn-Bendit is no exception. Unlike the United States, Western European countries, including France, have powerful socialist movements with a mass base. Hence anarchists like Cohn-Bendit have had to expend as much ammunition on Lenin and the leadership of the "Bolshevik" parties as they expended on De Gaulle's establishment; and they have felt the need to find spiritual ancestors among anti-Bolshevik Russian anarchists in the Ukraine and the Red Fleet who were defeated by Trotsky's armies shortly after their seizure of power.

It is difficult to visualize American universities capitulating to masses of students carrying slogans about workers and peasants. Although a small minority belonging to Marxist-Leninist organizations have debated about Lenin, Trotsky, and Stalin, to most Americans this is pretty faraway stuff. An account of Rosa Luxemburg's arguments with Lenin was not the sort of thing that turned on the majority of American student radicals. But participatory democracy did; this was one principle shared by young anarchists on both continents. The revolutionary's credentials were not his library, his intellectual analyses, or his party card. Most important was his engagement in political actions. But students did not occupy university offices and invade city streets because some leaders had passed down the word. As Cohn-Bendit wrote, "we are convinced that the revolutionary cannot and must not be a leader" (1969, p. 251). In the *ad hoc*, informally structured student organizations, everyone had a say and nobody gave orders. Every act was voluntary and collective. Out of the immediacy of issues on strife-torn campuses there flashed a genuinely spontaneous response. The identification with others, the sharing of excitement, enthusiasm, and idealistic purpose, while actively engaged in challenging the system, filled many young people with a sense of democratic participation in political life that they had never experienced before.

Another contrast is between the subtlety of European political distinctions and American political crudity. European students grow up distinguishing among communist, socialist, centrist, conservative, and fascist political lines; Americans are taught to homogenize everything political as either "good"—that is, "democratic," "free," "patriotic" —or "bad"—that is, "communist," "subversive," "un-American." These are affect-triggers, not thought-triggers. A student leader like Cohn-Bendit strikes a familiar chord in his audiences when he cites a Luxemburg to blast a Lenin. He automatically reaches for intellectual weapons among the others in his arsenal. Whatever else might be said for American political culture, it is hardly intellectual. Politicians are supposed to be "men of action," never "eggheads."

In the sixties, American students leaped from crisis to crisis with *ad hoc* solutions and a minimum of analysis. Their political actions were essentially reactive, but they explained that there was "no time" for intellection. This excuse placed the New Left squarely in the American pragmatic tradition, along with the Old Left, from which the young rebels so shrilly differentiated themselves. Vietnam generated a series of intensifying crises. The climax came at the Democratic National Convention in Chicago during the summer of 1968. Spontaneous political engagement seemed imperative to Jerry Rubin's and Abbie Hoffman's "yippies," various factions of a fast-dissolving SDS, and large numbers of respectable young liberals who hoped that the nomination of Senator Eugene McCarthy would bring an end to the war.

After the dust had settled and the conspiracy trial had begun, the most visible and impressive spokesmen arose from among the militant radicals on trial, not the dispersed liberals. Their manner and tactics were novel and compelling. Cohn-Bendit spoke for all when he asserted the need "to rid ourselves, in practice, of the Judeo-Christian ethic, with its call for renunciation and sacrifice. There is only one reason for being a revolutionary—because it is the best way to live" (1969, p. 255). Jerry Rubin, Abbie Hoffman, Tom Hayden, and other Americans went one step further—in Rubin's words, "Do it!"

Participate! The calls for mass participation in every form of protest became louder and more frequent. By the time of Chicago, the liberal, integrationist tactics of passive resistance of the civil rights movement had been swept aside by confrontation and guerrilla theater. Its quiet discipline and organization gave way to loud and aggressive assaults. Discipline and organization had enabled the civil rights movement to sustain defeats without despairing; they had enabled the Old Left, for all its faults, to retain a long-term perspective and ideology without giving way to adventurism. In the face of repeated frustrations, both movements were able to put off immediate political gratification for the sake of future results. The absence of discipline, organization, long-term perspective and programs made defeats intolerable to the New Left. Finally, for many, participation in the massive protests became an end in itself. American students in revolt were redefining politics, collapsing ends into means. In Jerry Rubin's words, "People who say: 'I agree with your goals, but I don't know about your tactics,' smell of foul horseshit. Goals are irrelevant. The tactics, the actions, are critical" (Rubin, 1970, p. 125). "Action is the only reality" in this "existential revolution" (Abbie Hoffman). To "do it" meant that "there's no such thing as a bad tactic. Put down nothing" (Rubin). The objective of political engagement had changed, from such limited aims as integrated public transportation in the Birmingham bus boycott to altogether new states of consciousness and total being. This does not hold true, of course, for all young radicals, among whom were still to be found terrorist Weathermen, pacifist priests, draft refusers, Maoists, and others who in one way or another continued to distinguish between their current actions and their long-range objectives. The mainstream of the counter culture abandoned that distinction, as it abandoned the distinction between past and future in its desire to live in the eternal present. "Revolution," anounced Abbie Hoffman, "is the Highest Trip of Them All." "We create reality wherever we go by living our fantasies" (Rubin). Such a "Politics of Ecstasy" (Timothy Leary) extends to its outer limit Cohn-Bendit's reason for being a revolutionary: "because it is the best way to live."

"Politics" now invaded almost all areas of everyday life. The American youth revolt perceived itself as a revolutionary life-style with a new rhetoric and tactics. In Tom Hayden's words, *"Our crime was that we were beginning to live a new and infectious life-style without official authorization. We were tried* [in the Chicago conspiracy trial] *for being out of control."* This was "a new life-style beyond that of capitalist America" (Hayden, 1970, pp. 20–21; emphasis in original). A new life-style means something bigger than long hair and beads, than psychedelic posters and rock music. The term covers everything from new forms of social relations and political economy, to new thought patterns and affects, to revolutionary self-conceptions by young people in revolt. This implies a new mode of cognition: hence such terms as "counter culture," "youth culture," "new culture," and "life-style."

The culture of protest did not begin as alternative institutions, social forms, or political economies. Instead, it addressed itself first to the hearts and minds of young people. As it spoke to their innermost being, it simultaneously protested, satirized, and parodied the depersonalization and commercialization of life around them, and the Madison Avenue-like manipulation of human beings at home along with their slaughter in Asian paddy fields. It protested the glittering official hypocrisies about sex, marriage, love, democracy, racial equality, and freedom by the same official culture that had dropped The Bomb.

Alongside the new political rhetoric of "revolution for the hell of it," there evolved a "new language" of protest. As in previous religious and political movements, specific verbal usages became insignia of affiliation and identity. It is almost as though millions of young people were carried away by the magic of the word. A new word-magic sprang up to invert the official bureaucratese. Yesterday's whispered obscenity became today's shouted greeting. It seemed that everyone good was "revolutionary," "liberated," and "alienated," all in one, in a united front against armies of "pigs." The novelty of the revolutionary messages seemed to require a new semantics, logic, and power of their own.

> New language becomes a weapon of the movement because it is mysterious, threatening to conventional power. . . . If we were interested in mild improvements to the system, perhaps we would use the prevailing language of the system. But one of the first tasks of those creating a new society is that of creating a new and distinct identity. . . . the old language is depleted. In order to dream, to invoke anger or love, new language becomes necessary. Music and dance are forms of communication partly because they are directly expressive of feelings for which there is yet no language. (Hayden, 1970, pp. 23–24)

The power of language is that it can start people acting. Words can, and have, mobilized millions. Whether it follows that a new language is necessary in order to dream, invoke anger, or love is arguable. Jerry Rubin shows how, in the heat of political action, Hayden's relatively abstract theorizing about the new language and its political rhetoric came alive.

> The yippie political strategy is to ally with Billy Graham. Keep the word "fuck" dirty. At the same time we yippies fight for the right to say "fuck" whenever we want to. It's a contradiction—but in contradictions like this lies the genius of making a revolution. (Rubin, 1970, p. 111)

There is indeed a contradiction between this effort to create a new language, as both weapon and badge of identity, and the young rebels' felt need to transcend all language by means of nonverbal communication. The result is increasing inarticulateness. Witness their heroes: from Marlon Brando to James Dean to *Easy Rider,* we see a progression from mumbles to grunts to long silences taking the place of articulate speech.[2] "Words lie!" seems to have become the slogan of the new wave of young hero types. Look, feel, touch, smell, taste, groove—in fact, do anything but explain.

Language dissembles; the only meaningful experiences cannot be verbalized. Better to dance and make music than to speak. Yet political action requires communication.

Spontaneity has extended past the borders of political protest into the interpersonal tactics of small groups in daily life. A whole new wave of existential psychotherapies, encounter groups, and growth centers has come along to challenge traditional psychotherapeutic theory and practice. Whatever else it contains and whatever questions it poses for psychology, it also has been affected by American anti-intellectual currents. "Intelligence, rationality, and thoughtfulness turn out to be negative values in the encounter culture" (Maliver, 1971, p. 41).

Like encounter groups, radical politics demands "talking from the guts" about the here and now. Brawling with "pigs," ritual collective chanting, the sacraments of self-identity when "telling it like it is"—all are forms of "turning on," significant only for the moment. To abolish past and future is to deprecate intellection in favor of immediate feeling. This attitude derives from chronic American anti-intellectualism and takes it a step further. Its catchword among young scholars is *relevance*. Only yesterday, functionalist anthropology and sociology were criticized from the left for ignoring history; radical young historians are now returning the favor by themselves denying "the pastness of the past" (Susman, 1964, p. 251). As their leading spokesman has written:

> The historian need not be embarrassed if he concerns himself more with the present and the future than with the past. . . . the historian's business with the future is not to predict but to envision. . . . The past is ransacked, not for its own sake, but as a source of alternative models of what the future might become. (Lynd, 1968, p. 107)

Historians of this school use the past to provide models for the future and legitimizations for present tactics, not as a source of understanding of the present. The historian's devaluation of society's past is matched by "existential" psychologists' devaluation of individuals' pasts, evidenced in encounter-group therapy. As one psychologist writes:

> Encounter people . . . care very little about the unconscious and what may have happened in the past. What really matters, they say, is the Here and Now, the existential experience. Talking about the past is a way of "avoiding the honesty of the moment," they contend. (Maliver, 1971, p. 40)

Yesterday is declared irrelevant, because it is considered unnecessary for an understanding of the present. Their common "presentism" justifies both the "relevance" of the past for the historian and its "irrelevance" for the psychologist.

The combination of anti-intellectualism and an ahistorical attitude is typically American. The former is usually associated, in liberal interpretations, with the right, as in the McCarthyism of the 1950s. But it has characterized the left as well; in the 1960s, a new form of radical anti-intellectualism appeared. Its linkup with an antihistorical spirit can be traced to the Beat Generation of the fifties, which foreshadowed a good deal of the pop culture that followed. The attitude toward the past, of the Beats and pop art, has been well summarized:

> For the Beat Generation the past—and even the future—is an enemy, threatening man with a vicious traditionalism (sometimes called conformity) or a series of problems to which there is no solution except individual action. They return to an almost Thoreau-like ritual burning of the past, preferring the immediate sensation, the experience of the moment or the escape into timelessness offered by some oriental philosophies (or their version of them) which are strictly a-historical. Our leading movements in painting, especially abstract expressionism and "pop" art, offer the most immediate kind of experience, more clearly divorced from any sense of history than any other movement in painting since the Renaissance. (Susman, 1964, p. 261)

Such attitudes and values had percolated through mass audiences of young people by the late sixties. What began as the bohemian, Beat expression of the previous decade came to characterize and dominate whole fields of artistic mass culture. Along with Madison Avenue's discovery of "youth" as a commodity, an ahistorical spirit and anti-intellectual attitudes and values focused more and more explicitly on issues of "drugs, sex, and politics" in the lives of American youth. Tens of millions of transistor radios, phonographs, and television sets became carriers of the young search for timeless truths, to oppose an alienating, dehumanizing, and phony culture. What had begun as attempts to come directly to terms with the inner meanings of non-Western religious experience now became the stock in trade of millions of young (and not so young) hippies. A pervasive antirationalism came to the surface. It diffused, along with the drug experience and rock music, through the whole spectrum of mass culture.

This brings us to an essential of the counter culture: "It is nothing new that there should exist antirationalist elements in our midst. What *is* new is that a radical rejection of science and technological values should appear so close to the center of our society, rather than on the negligible margins" (Roszak, 1969, p. 51). Antirationalism is not exactly the same thing as anti-intellectualism. While it is possible, and indeed commonplace today, to be an antirationalist intellectual, anti-intellectual rationalists are rarer. Most intellectuals earn their living by thinking. Rationalism, the doctrine that reason is the highest source of knowledge, went largely unchallenged in the West from about the sixteenth to the nineteenth century.

> About the end of the nineteenth century there appeared in the European countries several new doctrines which challenged the supremacy of reason, as against feeling, in human life; criticized those theories which explained social events in terms of rational motives; and declared their opposition to the trend of the modern societies toward a more rational, technological and industrial way of life. (Bottomore, 1969, p. 128)

The supremacy of reason has been undercut at political rap sessions, yoga and meditation groups, communes, encounter groups, and pop-rock festivals. The flood of existential, psychedelic, and underground arts, together with increasing absorption in versions of Eastern philosophies and religions, intensified the radical bombardment of institutions. Since official culture claimed reason for its own, to blast the authority of reason was to blast the authority of that culture. Spontaneous political and social actions reinforced the priority of affective over cerebral activities, and these affects were fed back into the cathexis of spontaneous participation.

Two related contradictions may be discerned here. The first is the contradiction between a broad cultural definition of politics and a conception of politics reduced to spontaneity. A real "counter culture" must embrace psychological, social, political, and economic culture. Otherwise passing fads may seem to be "epochal transformations."[3] The depth and breadth required for a real counter-culture outlook hardly seem compatible with the "instantaneous, stochastic, abrupt, discontinuous electronic cosmos" (Laing, 1967, p. 12) of the counter culture. Second, there is the contradiction between the spontaneous immediacy of "directly expressed feelings" and the deliberation and learning necessary to formulate the concepts of a counter-cultural revolution; this is a contemporary version of the classic conflict between impulse and forethought.

Counter-culture politics are produced by the middle- and upper-class children of the most affluent economic culture in history. They have come, especially in America, from the permissive social culture of an advanced industrial society, a society that equates happiness with material rewards and status. Never before has any younger generation achieved material gratification so completely and instantly, yet the end product has been alienation instead of happiness. As they had begun to redefine politics, so they now began to redefine the paths to happiness. Such questions could be posed only by those for whom the material preconditions of their culture's ideas of happiness had already been fulfilled.

Young people began an attack, across a broad cultural

front, against the authority of the powers that rejected them. Anti-authoritarianism motivated the demand for participatory democracy. One product of this assault on authoritarianism was the New Left's personalism of political style in the student revolt. It seemed opposed from the beginning to centralized, tightly structured organizations in its informality, the autonomy of local groups, and casual relations between its leaders and members. So far, Cohn-Bendit's anarchist injunctions might have been composed in Ann Arbor or Berkeley. But when these young people insisted on organizational flexibility and personalistic decision-making, they were doing more than rejecting their parents' authority; they were also repudiating the Old Left establishment with its rationalistic formulations ossified to dogma, its organizational rigidity, and its authoritarianism. From left to right, from the administration on top to the family on the bottom, traditional authority came under fire.

Inside this antirationalistic, anti-authoritarian explosion, a new emotional conformism was being born. Not political or social doctrine, not policy or strategy, but the cathexis of active participation—"doing it"—became the universal magnet that drew tens of thousands to monster demonstrations. A young person participating in these spontaneous protests knew he shared with millions of others a feeling of outrage and the ecstasy of engagement. Feelings, not doctrine, gave these people their collective identity. At best, thoughtfulness and patient reasoning were inadequate; at worst, they became the insignia of liberal cowards who would in the end line up with the establishment. What extraordinary emotional pressure on economically secure children of liberal, middle-class America to "get with it," to conform, to belong! This emotional conformism is most obvious in matters of aesthetic taste and style. Let the reader try getting high with a small group of hip friends listening to the latest rock heroes. Then, at the apex of everyone's ecstasy, let him, if he is strong enough, say, "Gee, I don't like it," or, "It doesn't do anything to me." How long would he last in that group? This leaderless but manipulative emotional conformism has been observed in encounter groups.

> Many observers feel that there is in the encounter movement the essence of a profound emotional fascism. Not necessarily a political fascism, but one that elicits emotional conformity, demands the correct behavior and the correct emotion at the designated time, and suppresses criticism. (Maliver, 1971, p. 43)

A psychiatrist, noting the same phenomenon, warns against the tyranny of the group and points out that "the tribe is as oppressive a master as is the machine" (Malcolm, 1971). It is as though, deprived of the experience of parental authority, permissive America's young bestowed that authority on "the group." This contradiction between participatory anti-authoritarian protest and emotional conformism and group authoritarianism[4] reflects the quest of so many young people for real authority. Consider the student who participates in actions against the university authorities only to come back to the commune and resume the search for his guru; the master-disciple relationship is authoritarian by definition. Whatever else it means, in the context of American political and social culture the search for new gurus—from the Mansons to the Maharishis—represents a quest for final truth and authority outside the family and elsewhere than in orthodox values.

Another contradiction in values implicit in the counter culture is the combination of near-cynicism and romanticism. A striking example is in the movie *Easy Rider*. Two guys with no place to go set off on a tragic trip, the (inevitable?) outcome of which is death. More antisaccharine, anti-romantic characters and situations would be hard to find. Yet there is an essential and powerful romantic moment when they meet the pure, silent, back-to-earth flower people on their commune in the Southwest. Here all is warm and vivid daytime, contrasted with the darkened images of an acid trip through nighttime whorehouse, Mardi Gras, and cemetery in New Orleans. Something similar can be said for Bonnie and Clyde, who, after retaliating against their rapacious and brutal culture with its own weapons, finally discover their true selves, their love, and a moment of sublime sexual fulfillment on the eve of their slaughter.

These contradictions in orientation and values reappear in instance after instance of the new youthful mass culture. As in previous nonconformisms, they consist in a reassertion, albeit in more colorful dress, of those very values in the hegemonic culture they assault. Widened affective horizons and deeper introspections accompany a panegyric to impulse. The authority and emotional censorship of the group grows within its anti-authoritarian outcry against official censorship. Romantic reverie about real, silent people gone back to nature coexists with hard-boiled, realistic hero types who have to employ the brutal workings of the system in order to achieve their antiheroism. And so on. That the counter culture is a reactive form of the larger culture is shown in the fact that its "new" values are in every instance an inversion or exaggeration of the orthodox values. But even this is not unprecedented. Writing in the 1930s about the bohemianism of the twenties, Joseph Freeman explained:

> The prosperous middle classes needed a little bohemianism to spend their money in ways not sanctioned by the puritan tradition; the bohemians needed a little puritanism to go with their newly acquired money. Indeed, bohemianism requires a certain amount of social stability. The bohemian wishs to "shock" the bourgeois. For this purpose, the bourgeois must be well entrenched, secure financially, able and willing to be shocked; and the bohemian himself must feel that the road back to the world he is "shocking" is not entirely closed. In the depths of his heart he not only fears but hopes that his eccentricities, which are part of his stock in trade, will earn him a fatted calf as the returning prodigal. It is not capitalism that he hates as a rule, but the respon-

sibilities which any highly developed social system imposes upon its members. (Freeman, 1936, p. 285, as quoted in Aaron 1965, p. 125)

One difference between the bohemianism of the twenties and the youth rebellion of the sixties is sheer size. Whereas in the past bohemians were a small group and therefore on the fringe, now millions seem to have caught some infection from the counter culture's germs of protest. Our culture is much more affluent and can afford many more nonconformists than it could in the twenties, and it seems that now, for something to be heard or seen at all, it has to be gigantic. Millions were spent in the early sixties preparing American audiences for the Beatles' debut. As younger pop-culture audiences were tapped, star performers became younger also. Peer-group egalitarianism, with its participatory democracy, became translated from small-group personalism into the mass-audience mass culture. The young rebellion of the sixties was unprecedented in size and the variety of its forms, but the dominant culture is unprecedented in its absorptive power. For the first time, messages of protest were themselves transformed into commodities by their intended victims. ("Co-opted" is the hip term.) Elements of the new life-style were marketed almost as soon as they appeared. It was the mass media, powered by that same profit motive against which the rebels were rebelling, that made possible the dissemination of their message.

This is a surprise only to those who accept the mythos of the counter culture, that it is an "epochal . . . new culture . . . radically disaffiliated from the mainstream assumptions of our culture" (Roszak, 1969, p. 42).

After the blacks had gone their own way, and after the last gigantic antiwar rallies had dispersed, the political energies of young protesters became more diffused. Life-style and counter culture eclipsed traditional political issues. By calling everything "political," young protesters became less and less relevant to those political issues that had consumed them only a short time before. There are exceptions, from terrorists to draft refusers. But the mainstream of counter-culture political energies flowing out of the student revolt of the sixties seems to be turning inward and Eastward.

The politics of counter culture make most sense when viewed as an integral part of the dominant social-political organism. As to their long-term consequences, I cannot help feeling that they have served as an invaluable school for the future masters of a culture whose rationale is "democracy and freedom." As youthful rebels, they have studied the subtleties of group-imposed conformism and authoritarianism in a milieu of personalistic, democratic, leaderless decision-making. Those who ascend to the top of industry and government will arrive prepared with more subtle manipulative skills than their predecessors. Among all the other things it is becoming, does the counter culture perhaps represent an appropriate self-realization for an alienating culture?

Notes

1. Gramsci, 1957, pp. 154–55 and *Passim*. See also Cammett, 1967, especially pp. 201–12; and Genovese, 1967, pp. 63–107. Unfortunately very little of Gramsci's work is available in English. Cammett's relevant sections and Genovese's review are the best starting points I know for a discussion of ideological hegemony.

2. "Such anti-heroes demand anti-rhetoric, since for them there are no viable, new noble phrases to replace the outworn old ones— only the simplest epithets, and certain short-breathed phrases, not related or subordinated to each other, but loosely linked by the most noncommittal of conjunctions: *and . . . and . . . and. . . .* In a world of non-communication, only a minimal speech, the next best thing to silence, the equivalent of silence, gives a sense of reality." (Fiedler, 1964, p. 131) The author is here referring to "the famous Hemingway style" of the 1920s.

3. Roszak, 1969, p. 44. Roszak's thesis, contrary to my own, is that the counter culture represents a new quality altogether different from its parent culture. For a third view, see Mead, 1970. Mead scorns Roszak's analysis of both contemporary society and counter culture. In the first, she finds a blanket rejection of all forms of

science-based organization of society; in the second, a conception of the young formulated entirely in terms of their presumed mentors (Marcuse, Brown, Goodman, Ginsberg, Watts, Leary, Maslow, and so on). The first analysis she finds irresponsible, in the face of the needs of millions of people in the world, and the second untrue: "Young people today are without any mentors and prophets. They stand alone, without models, struggling with an understanding of the issues of the modern world which they alone understand as birthright members of this new age." Later, she remarks: "The accident that, because they are the oldest of the new generation, they must carry in their extreme youth the burden of the necessary challenge, adds a special poignancy to today's scene."

4. This is one more evidence that the counter culture is squarely in the American tradition, for Alexis de Tocqueville's comments on America's "tyranny of the majority" were published 140 years ago. The forms this tyranny has taken in different generations, and its frightening implications, have been discussed by many historians. See, for example, Louis Hartz: "A sense of community based on a sense of uniformity is a deceptive thing. It looks individualistic, and in part it actually is. It cannot tolerate internal relationships of disparity. . . . the common standard is its very essence, and deviations from that standard inspire it with an irrational fright. The man who is as good as his neighbors is in a tough spot when he confronts all of his neighbors combined." (Hartz, 1955, p. 56) The same point is made by David Potter, 1962, p. 220. See also John P. Roche: "If one begins with the notion that political 'truth' is discovered by counting votes rather than through some process of divination by a self-anointed elite, democratic procedures can result in some eccentric end products. American history is, for example, replete with instances of consensual authoritarianism and a lynching, with only one dissenter, appears as the acme of majoritarianism." (Roche, 1967, p. 140)

References

Aaron, Daniel. 1965. *Writers on the Left.* New York: Avon Books.

Adorno, Theodore W. 1967. *Prisms.* London: Neville Spearman.

Bottomore, T. B. 1969. *Critics of Society: Radical Thought in America.* New York: Vintage Books.

Cammett, John M. 1967. *Antonio Gramsci and the Origins of Italian Communism.* Stanford, Calif.: Stanford University Press.

Cohn-Bendit, G. and D. 1969. *Obsolete Communism, the Left Wing Alternative.* Harmondsworth, Middlesex: Penguin Books.

Fiedler, Leslie A. 1964. *Waiting for the End.* New York: Stein & Day.

Freeman, Joseph. 1936. *An American Testament: A Narrative of Rebels and Romantics.* New York: Farrar & Rinehart.

Genovese, Eugene D. 1967. "On Antonio Gramsci." *Studies on the Left* 7, No. 2: 83–107.

Gramsci, Antonio. 1957. *The Modern Prince.* Trans. Louis Marks. New York: International Publishing Co.

Hartz, Louis. 1955. *The Liberal Tradition in America.* New York: Harcourt, Brace & World, Harvest Books.

Hayden, Tom. 1970. "The Trial." *Ramparts* 9, No. 1 (July). Special issue.

Hoffman, Abbie. 1970. *Revolution for the Hell of It.* New York: Pocket Books.

Laing, R. D. 1967. *The Politics of Experience.* New York: Ballantine Books.

Lynd, Staughton. 1968. *Intellectual Origins of American Radicalism.* New York: Vintage Books.

Malcolm, Andrew I. 1971. Quoted in the *Montreal Star*, February 9, 1971, p. 38.

Maliver, Bruce L. 1971. "Encounter Groupers Up Against the Wall." *New York Times Magazine,* January 31, pp. 4, 41.

Marcuse, Herbert. 1964. *One Dimensional Man.* Boston: Beacon Press.

Mead, Margaret. 1970. "Review of Roszak 1969." *The Critic,* January–February, pp. 77–79.

Potter, David M. 1962. "The Quest for the National Character." In *The Reconstruction of American History,* ed. John Higham. New York: Harper & Row, Torchbooks. Pp. 197–222.

Reich, Charles. 1970. *The Greening of America.* New York: Random House.

Roche, John P. 1967. "Equality in America." In *American Political Thought: From Jefferson to Progressivism,* ed. John P. Roche. New York: Harper & Row, Torchbooks.

Roszak, Theodore. 1969. *The Making of a Counter Culture.* Garden City, N. Y.: Doubleday & Co.

Rubin, Jerry. 1970. *Do It!* New York: Ballantine Books.

Susman, Warren I. 1964. "History and the American Intellectual: Uses of the Usable Past." *American Quarterly* 16, No. 2, Part 2 (Summer): 243–63.

Williams, Gwynn A. 1960. "Gramsci's Concept of Egemonia." *Journal of the History of Ideas* 21, No. 4: 586–99.

Toward an Anthropological Politics of Symbolic Forms
Sol Worth

I

IMAGINE A WORLD where symbolic forms created by one inhabitant are instantaneously *available* to all other inhabitants; a place where "knowing others" means *only* that others know us, and we know them, through the images we all create about ourselves and our world, as we see it, feel it, and choose to make it available to a massive communication network, slavering and hungry for images to fill the capacity of its coaxial cables.

Imagine this place that is so different from the society within which we nourish our middle-class souls, in which symbolic forms are not the property of a "cultured," technological, or economic elite, but rather are ubiquitous and multiplying like a giant cancer (or, conversely, unfolding like a huge and magnificent orchard), and available for instant transmission to the entire world.

Imagine a place where other cultures (in the anthropological sense) and culture (as digested at ladies' teas) are available to all; a place where almost anyone (some will be too young or too infirm physically or mentally ever to be involved) can produce verbal and visual images, where individuals or groups can edit, arrange, and rearrange the visualization of their outer and inner worlds, and a place where these movies, TVs, or tellies (a marvelous word coined from television, and connoting the verb "to tell" so subtly as almost to be overlooked) can be instantaneously available to anyone who chooses to look.

What will the anthropologist as the student of man and his cultures do in this world? Imagine this place; for it is where we are at *now*. Let me review the situation in bald technological terms.

In 1850 information traveled at the speed of man, on foot, on an animal's back, or on a ship at sea. Men knew each other across time by the symbolic mediation of words and the interior images they created. A memory storage of a small portion of the earth created by an even smaller percentage of persons was laboriously collected in libraries. The look of things—a man, a god, a place—was fixed in visual images created by a small group of highly trained and talented men who painted pictures, carved statues, and illustrated books. A man could personally see but few things in the world. *If* he traveled, he could see only the people and places he actually passed through and looked at. Visual knowledge was limited by space and time. All else was known by the words of other men, by their descriptive power, and by the ability of readers and listeners to give body and image to the symbolic event of verbal interaction.

In 1850 information and the knowledge it created still traveled at about the same speed it had attained in 3000 B.C.

In 1900 words and all their magical symbolic fruits were traveling by radio waves at almost the speed of light—from 15 miles an hour to almost 186,000 miles a second in fifty years. Instantaneous communication was possible, and by the time of World War II most men on earth had potentially available to them everything sent out by radio wave. Men sat at home in New York City and twirled a dial, picking up broadcasts from Japan, from India, from Africa, from Germany, and from Russia. And in those places men also twirled dials and listened, knowing for the first time in history that potentially everyone could be listening at the same time to the words of a president proclaiming an infamous act on the part of Japan.

In 1905, the same year that Freud published *Studies in Hysteria* and suggested a new way of making inferences from the symbolic forms created in dreams, Thomas Edison invented the motion-picture camera.

Thus, at the beginning of the twentieth century, at the same time that man was given a new and revolutionary glimpse of inner "reality," the motion-picture camera came into being, hailed as the technology supreme, the machine that would finally allow man to capture the outer world, as it "really" was. For the first time in man's long attempt at symbolizing and representing himself in his environment it became possible to make an image that was, in Peirce's sense, not an icon—a visual resemblance of object reality—but an index. We no longer had to depend on the hand-eye skills of a few highly trained picture-makers who created images that *resembled* objects—more or less.

While the iconic sign of the hand-drawn image was always a resemblance, a similarity to the "real" world, the camera image was accepted as an indexical sign of it, a true mapping, a point-to-point correspondence with the reality before the camera. With indexical signs, we no longer had to doubt the individual notation systems of other cultures. All perspectives were "true," and the puzzles of Chinese perspective or Egyptian profiles and side views were understood as cultural creations reflecting a specific way of creating similarity or resemblance to the "real" world. The indexical sign achieved the status of reality-substitute; it became the base upon which visual imagery rested. We really believe that the camera image records the reality of places, people, and behavior.

By 1905 men had developed the ability to create symbolic forms in modes that had never before been possible. Men could "reproduce" their actual voices, and could send these voices, unaccompanied, all over the globe in such fractions of time as to appear instantaneous. Men could "reproduce"

actual places and people by a technology that created indexical signs without the hand-eye coordination and skill of the
graphic artist. One could produce images and sounds of
anything in the world; one had only to be able to point a
camera and a microphone at the world.

Three-quarters of a century ago we learned to reproduce
sound and to create indexical camera images. By 1930 we
had learned to combine sounds and images to create talking
pictures, and by 1940 we had learned how to make these
images speed unaccompanied around the globe.

II

It is clear that we have learned to produce talking images,
but it is not quite so clear why we use these images as we do,
or how we ought to understand our use of them. We often
tend to forget even the short history of moving pictures and
to assume that the way we use movies now is the way they
were always used, and further, that the way we think of
movies now is the way they will always be. It might be
argued that the fifty-year period between 1930 and 1980
will be considered an aberrant period in the history of the
use of the moving sound image.

Movies developed along a dual path: one direction can be
clearly seen as motivated initially by a naive ethnographic
concern and the other as motivated by a mythmaking, magic,
and storytelling impulse.

It is of central importance to the thrust of this paper to
understand the underlying and continuous influence of the
ethnographic impulse in the development not only of the
technology of film, but of the art as well.

The very first "movies" created in the Edison Laboratories were simple exercises in ethnographic description: a one-
minute film of a sneeze, one minute of a lab assistant playing
his violin, and another minute movie of two lab workers
kissing. The brochure that Thomas Edison printed to de-

scribe his new invention had as its headline "Recordings from Real Life." Lumière in Paris also used the first movie camera invented in Europe to record the ritual behavior of everyday life: workers punching a time clock, workers walking through the factory gates, and Parisians rushing to get on a train at the Gare du Nord. Within several years movies were being "manufactured" on both sides of the Atlantic. These early films shown in the United States in storefronts called nickelodeons continued the ethnographic directions of Edison and Lumière. Films with titles such as "Washing the Baby," "The Train Arrives at the Station," "Cleaning the House," and "Making the Bed" were shocking, delighting, and often frightening to audiences. Early newspaper accounts and interviews with audience members emphasized that these new moving pictures were valued because "they were just like what people really did."

In Germany in 1905 ethnographers going to the field carried with them a motion-picture camera—a new *scientific* instrument with which they could record for further study the behavior and rituals of the "primitive" peoples they observed. As a matter of fact, the very beginnings of the development of the motion-picture camera as we know it today stemmed from what Ray Birdwhistell has termed "kinesics." Edwuard Muybridge, an engineer with the Union Pacific, was asked by Governor Leland Stanford of California to invent a way to settle a bet. Stanford, an owner of racing stables, had wagered a large sum of money on the assertion that a racehorse at a gallop had all four feet off the ground at the same time. Muybridge, who in addition to his engineering skills was interested in the biology of motion, developed a camera that would record the images of a racehorse in motion. It seemed natural, once Muybridge had invented his motion camera, for biologists and anatomists all over the world to consider it not as an artistic instrument but rather as another scientific tool for the recording and reproduction of visual events.

It seems inevitable that the first motion pictures were

"intuitively" about culture, motion, and the ritual of every-day events. The real was available, was captured, and was made into data by motion-picture film on a reel.

The other direction—that moving toward the creation of myth—started with the magic shows of Méliès in Paris in 1902. This movement attempted to provide inexpensive theater. The movie was thought to be an extension of the stage, with more flexibility as to locations portrayed, but still dependent upon actors and playwrights. The period between 1920 and the present seemed to be dominated by the mythmakers and storytellers of the stage. What most people knew about the movies were the story films of Hollywood and the giant studios. The ethnographic impulse, however, continued increasingly to affect film theory and practice. The so-called documentary movement, developed in the Soviet Union as a political tool immediately after the revolution, matured through the documentary film boards of Britain and Canada until, in the late fifties and early sixties, the ethnographic films of Jean Rouch and Edgar Morin of the Musée de l'Homme in Paris became the theoretical inspiration for France's "new wave." Today even "fiction" films are designed with ethnographic theory in mind. The art of the film today in large part is concerned with the depiction of ethnographically valid imagery and symbols. The theorists of film in France, Britain, Poland, Italy, and lately in the United States are supporting their film theories and analyses—rightly or wrongly—with references to Lévi-Strauss, De Saussure, Chomsky, Mead, and a host of other anthropologists and linguists.

The technology that made the "new film" possible—light-weight cameras and portable synchronous sound equipment—was developed originally to support ethnographic research in the field. Rouch and Morin, needing the ability to capture actual behavior with sound in the field, made it possible to do so. It was after seeing their *Chronicle of a Summer* that Truffaut and Godard realized what they could do with the ethnographic method.

III

While all this was happening in movie theaters, the home screen, via electronics and the television tube, was also being developed. After World War II it became possible for millions to sit at home and watch moving pictures of events in any part of the world (and later the universe) *as they occurred.* With the advent of television we thought not of listening to events as with radio, but finally of watching them. The mediation of symbols through which our ontology is in large part created had finally encompassed the image. Symbolic events could now be constructed to match face-to-face observation—or so it seemed.

While everyone can speak, however, not everyone could make movies or television. These forms demanded vast allocations of economic or technological resources beyond the reach of any but a new elite. And, further, movies and television seemed to have built-in limitations. Movies could not be seen at home: they were public events, rivaling theater. Custom decreed it that way, and "home movies" were not fully acceptable until after World War II. Television, however, had even more stringent limitations, set not by custom or economics but by physical law. While radio waves could broadcast multidirectionally and across the entire globe (given a large enough power source), television waves could broadcast only by line of sight—in straight lines, interfered with by tall buildings, mountains, and simple distance on the curvature of the earth. Television was also limited by the amount of the electromagnetic spectrum it consumed in broadcasting. It used up, as it were, much more of the air waves for its signal, and so the granting of licenses to broadcast originally limited the number of communication channels to twelve. And in order to safeguard the integrity of the signal, most localities used only alternating channels, limiting the channel space to six.

It seems "reasonable" under these conditions for societies to control the channels of communication. Control of scarce resources makes sense. With a technological limit of channel space, it seemed appropriate that a new elite—controlling the input devices of television channels—develop. After all, everyone could look without charge. The enlightened new elite fought for its "rights"—the right to show what *they* wanted, the freedom of speech to show what *they* felt important.

Technology in our culture seems almost like the mythic mountain-climber who does what he does because "it's there." Television's limitations were not only technological. This limited broadcast ability also *limited markets.* A toothpaste ad was unavailable to those who lived on the other side of the hill. Consumers could not be created and cultivated out of people who wanted to, but could not, tune in to the commercials.

A small group of entrepreneurs invented a solution. They would build a large antenna on the top of the hill, receiving the TV signal from its input source, and create another channel by *wire,* which would deliver the "message" into the home. People would pay for the wire—the channel—not the message.

This solution of creating another channel of wire to eliminate the inherent limitation of the TV broadcast signal was of such huge import that hardly anyone involved saw what was at stake for the concept of culture. The greatest device for the accomplishment of cultural homogeneity was created to sell toothpaste. For, incredibly enough, wires were not licensed. Anyone—with enough money and political power, that is—could put up an antenna and send received signals by wire. These wires were owned privately and went into only such homes as paid for it or were chosen to have it. The TV broadcaster, that conglomerate elite of fighters for freedom of speech, was at first delighted by wire. Now people would pay to be able to receive his free signal. He was somewhat annoyed at not having a piece of the action—the rental fee for wire—but was basically so happy about the expanded audience market that he allowed the cable TV companies to live. After all, how many mountains are there anyway?

Within five years, however, the cable TV companies had developed their technology to the point where one wire was able to carry up to twenty different signals, and it was clear that a wire could be built that would allow up to several hundred simultaneous signals. Suddenly the cable TV people, the Ford Foundation (an alliance of McGeorge Bundy of the Department of State and Fred Friendly of CBS), Bell Telephone, and even Howard Hughes began to see the magnitude of the future.

This was the situation in 1960. TV broadcasting required incredible economic resources, but TV program origination required even more. Not only money but talent was scarce and hard to find. Imagine the state of the cable TV owner. He had a system that could broadcast (in effect) a hundred programs over the same channel (wire) at almost the same cost as broadcasting one program. No channel-space restriction, no space restriction, and no program-origination cost. With TV satellites, all signals from all over the world could, theoretically, be received by special ground stations and broadcast simultaneously on cable. The set-owner paid only for the wire, and the wire-owner vied to provide the set owner with the greatest number of choices. The problem as it is phrased in the trade is one of "product": "Where the hell are we going to get enough product to fill up the cable?"

IV

We are now past 1970. It is technologically feasible *right now* for a moving image with its accompanying sound to be broadcast from any place in our solar system and to be received in hundreds of millions, or even all, homes attached to the wire—simultaneously. It is further possible for all homes to have their choice of hundreds of messages received simultaneously.

Cable TV, unlike radio and broadcast television, also has output control. When the astronauts broadcast from the moon, *anyone* can watch and listen. With cable any single set or any group of sets can be switched on and off for particular messages. Total control of reception is therefore also possible.

That is the state of channel capacity and control of symbolic forms available to us right now.

What does this mean for the anthropologist concerned with the study of man and his culture, conceived as almost infinitely diverse, hard to find and to understand in its diversity, disappearing with the onslaught of technology and urbanization, and basic to the development of a science of man?

With this background in mind I would like now to describe some of the current problems and plans for the development of what communications technologists are calling the "wired planet." Then I shall try to project some of the very probable developments of the next ten to twenty years. And finally I would like to formulate some of the questions and problems that I see as crucial concerns for the field of anthropology, both in terms of how anthropologists of the future are to be trained and of the anthropological problems that will face the student of culture in the immediate future.

For the first sixty years of the age of the moving image, the production and control of these images were limited to small groups of men who controlled the vast economic resources thought to be necessary for the creation of moving pictures and television. In the first five or ten years after the invention of the motion-picture camera and projector, individual men with no previous training (where could they get it in the beginning?) became the owners of movie cameras and makers of moving pictures. For the next fifty years a myth system was created, implying that only a special group of "artists," "communicators," and later "journalists" could, and should, have access to the making of motion pictures. But the young, brought up since World War II in a world in which the moving image was first a baby-sitter and second their window on the world, began in the late 1950s to demand to have this tool—along with the car—for their own use. All over the Western world, and partic-ularly in the United States, young people began to demand that they be taught the use of the motion-picture camera, not to make "moving snapshots," which their parents made to show to their relatives and friends, but to make "movies" —stories about a world that they could call their own, in ways that were their own.

A few researchers began in the early 1960s to examine what would happen when young middle-class children, ages nine to twelve, black teen-age dropouts, ages ten to fifteen, and college students were taught the technology of the camera and allowed to use film to structure "stories" of their world in their way. John Adair and I taught Navajo Indians in their own community to use the motion-picture camera (Worth and Adair, 1970, 1972). They learned to make movies easily. One of our students, age twenty-three, taught her mother, age fifty-five (who spoke no English and had never seen a movie), to use a 16mm. Bell and Howell triple-lens turret camera in three hours. Everyone who has worked with youngsters in our culture, or with members of other cultures, has reported that no one failed to learn the technology quickly, and that every-one asked seemed, at the very least, interested and most highly motivated. The most "primitive" man can learn to understand a picture or a movie in a very short time. The reports of primitive man's difficulties with movies are an-ecdotal and sparse, but these same reports confirm the speed (hours and, at the most, days) with which any men seem to adapt to symbolic communication through motion pictures. At a fundamental level, universals of visual communication come into play much more readily than those of verbal language. At the same time, we have found that peoples with differing cultures make movies differently. When given instruction only in the technology of the camera and film, they tend to structure their movies according to the rules of their particular language, culture, and myth forms (as in the case of the Navajo) and according to their social roles and cultural attitudes, as in the case of black and white youngsters in our society. In sum, it is not unreasonable to expect that anyone who has mastered enough technology to build his own house or tell his own story in words can learn in a very short time to use a movie camera. It is not unreasonable to expect that the New Guinea native, the American Indian, the Eskimo, the peoples of developing and developed states in Africa and Asia, as well as various segments of our own society, will soon be able to make moving pictures of the world as they see it and to structure these images in *their* own way to show us the stories *they* want to show each other, but which we may also oversee.

Right now, at Mt. Sinai Hospital in New York, the Department of Community Medicine is training doctors and patients (on a limited scale) to make movies about health. The doctors are showing their idea of health, and the patients are showing theirs. This hospital is planning now to install cable TV in several housing projects and health centers, to institute the beginning of a "wired community" in East Harlem, where doctors and community members will have joint access to several channels through which they may "broadcast" whatever they wish. Such projects are being thought of in communities throughout this country and in Europe, for health, for education, and of course for *political control*.

Let us imagine the planet Earth somehow managing to escape the horrors of ecological or atomic disaster for another twenty years. What will its people be like in their capacity to produce and live by visual communication? The large industrialized nations, both East and West, will have a majority of their households wired. Teaching, banking, newspapers, and most shopping will most certainly be done through the "tube" wired to computers and to special videophone outlets connected with the tube. We shall use libraries by video printout or just read off the tube in our study.

Fidel Castro might provide for all of Cuba, or all of the planet, direct TV coverage of the newest methods for harvesting sugar, and of course the United States could (if it chose) broadcast the entire war in Vietnam continuously. The anthropologist in the field could easily broadcast his entire field experience (edited *his* way, of course), supplemented by films or simple continuous broadcast of the stream of behavior as seen by his informants, whom he would have trained to use the camera.

In general, men today need no longer depend on verbal reports of distant places and people. One can see them. One can see the man on the moon by television and see the Dani of New Guinea making war by film. Moreover, while hearing a Greek on radio may have evoked the response, "It's Greek to me," it is harder, if not impossible, to *see* a man laugh, or weep, or die, and feel that he is a stranger. A man going about his day, planting, hunting, or simply sitting alone near a fire, is in a situation that speaking does not make available to us. Movies do.

It would seem to be the case that Malinowski's stricture that the function of the ethnographer was to see the native's culture from the native's own point of view could at last be achieved—literally and not metaphorically.

What would such a world be like, and more importantly, what problems have we to set before our students *now* that will, at the least, not hinder them from coming to an understanding of an age in which man presents himself not in person but through the mediation of *visual* symbolic forms?

Although the problems that I see before us in this area can be divided into three groups—what I shall call the political, ethical, and theoretical areas—it should become clear that none of these categories can in actual practice be separated. It is only for convenience of articulation that I shall start with what seem to be theoretical questions and go on to ethical problems, which are, in the long run, probably all political questions anyway.

By theoretical, in this paper, I mean theories and methods that will have to be developed and articulated in order to understand a world suffering from (or blessed with) the democratization of culture, a world, that is, where all cultures are potentially available to all people via this new visual symbolic mythmaking form.

Epistemological and ontological questions—how we know and what we know—have always been of concern to anthropologists and other students of man. Poetry, myth, stories, and tales have always been created and studied as a singularly important source of the world view mediated by symbolic forms. Language itself has been a central problem in anthropology. But this "language" that we have been mentioning refers only to a verbal output received through an auditory channel—the ear—taking visual form only in the anthropologist's transcription. Our own sense of epistemology and ontology is reflected in the fact that our language carries within it the notion that *the* mediating symbolic system is the word, such that we use "language" (or "grammar") to refer to any organized body of rules or structure in the symbolic domain. Speaking, however, is not limited to the audial mode and grammar alone. It is a multichannel, multimodal communicative system composed of sound, body movements, distances, expressions, inflections, and contexts which grow more complex as our understanding of it becomes clearer. And even verbal language with its accompanying body channels is no longer the sole device by which we become familiar with the world removed from our immediate time and space.

We have passed that stage of anthropological methodology where, as in Boas' time, we had to prepare our students for hundreds of dreary hours of transcribing native ceremonies and speakers by hand. We are now at the point where the anthropologist must know how to teach others to tell him about themselves through movies and television, and further where he must know how to analyze a completely new symbol system by which people will be creating new forms for old myths about themselves. In the past, the field of anthropology could get away with training visual illiterates to study verbal illiterates. It is now no longer possible for the student of culture to ignore the fact that people all over the world have learned, and will continue in great numbers to learn, how to use the visual symbolic mode. Anthropologists must begin to articulate the problems that will face us in trying to understand others when their point of view is known to us primarily through movies distributed by broadcast television and cable. How can we help our students and future colleagues to overcome the inevitable tension between the world they will study and their own cultural backwardness in terms of a mass-distributed visual symbolic mode?

V

An ethnography of communication developed on the basis of verbal language alone cannot cope with man in an age of visual communication. It is necessary to develop theories and methods for describing and analyzing how men show each other who they are and how they are. Theories of vidistics[1] must be developed to supplement linguistic and sociolinguistic theories, in order to describe, analyze, and understand how people who organize their films in different ways than we do are understood or not understood. Just as anthropologists in the field must learn the verbal language of the people they study (or find informants who know the anthropologist's language), so now must they begin to learn the visual "language" of the people they study.

This, however, raises further questions. All anthropologists speak at least one verbal language and report their work in at least one verbal language. The anthropologist is, however, most often "mute" (there is no word in English to refer to those who cannot make movies) in film. He cannot make films, and he certainly has not been trained to analyze them and to infer facts of culture from them.

In a world in which people of other cultures are being taught to make movies, in a world in which our own children are learning to make movies and are being increasingly acculturated and educated through film and television, can the anthropologist afford to remain a "blind mute"? Can a blind mute ever have anything to say to a person who respects visual "speaking"[2] and whose culture demands social interaction through pictures?

I do not mean to imply here a McLuhanesque position that words are out of style. I do not think the advent of mass-distributed visual symbolic forms will replace speaking or reading; on the contrary, I suspect that interest in visual symbolic forms will enhance interest in verbal and written forms. Once one learns to communicate well in one channel, one begins to find needs for further channels. It is significant that the interest and development of films among the young took place spontaneously among those of our youth who were most educated and most literate. What I wish to emphasize is the need to expand our articulatory and analytic powers to cover many modes of symbolic interaction and communication. We have a tendency in academic life to continue examining and thinking about *only* inherited problems, rather than those problems and modes our children, our students, and even we ourselves pay most personal attention to.

What I am suggesting for anthropologists, as a first step, is the development of the capacity to articulate in motion pictures, as an artist if possible, but primarily as a simple "speaker" in this new mode of communication. But anthropologists cannot rest with the "speaker of film" ability alone. The native speaker has no need to articulate his knowledge of how he knows to speak and to understand his language.

The student of language and of culture must know more than how to speak; he must know how he knows to speak and how others speak. He must know how he puts visual events together to convey meaning through film, and how others do it. He must be able to analyze the way people communicate through movies as well as to do so himself. He must, in fact, not only be taught to make movies as children, Navajos, and others all over the world will be taught; he must learn how to teach others and must formulate theories about *what* to teach others.

VI

It is when we begin to think about the problem of teaching film and television to others that we must face a host of ethical problems which anthropology has never had to face before. In teaching people to read, we implicitly teach them *what* to read. When we teach people to speak—and the same is true of most people when they learn to speak—they also learn what to say, what not to say, and to whom and on what occasion to say it. The use of a mode of communication is not easily separable from the specific codes and rules about the content of that mode. Speaking is something that most people do anyway; anthropologists do not have to teach it. Film and television are not something that most people do—at this time. Someone has to teach it. Whoever teaches it will have a large and powerful impact upon the culture of the people using it and viewing it. If anthropology is to study culture, it must begin to understand how the use of new communication forms affects it, how best to introduce a communications technology, and, I suppose, first and foremost how to observe and to study this kind of situation.

Anthropology has always had a kind of doctor-patient relationship with the people it studies. As in the Hippocratic Oath, the first premise has always been, "Do no harm to the people you study."

In the past, it has been the case that one person or at most a handful of people have provided us with the information about many of the cultures of the world. Not only did our knowledge of Highland New Guinea, for example, depend on the observations of a few anthropologists and missionaries, but these same few, it was hoped, could be counted on to protect their informants in every way possible.

Carpenter (1971) reports in *TV Guide* that his own introduction of pictures in 1970 to people in New Guinea created vast changes in a short time. He reports that after the taking of pictures of a circumcision ritual, the people gave up the ritual and substituted pictures for it. He questions his own role in this matter and wonders if he himself had given enough thought to the change he unknowingly created.[3] This change was created, not by teaching people to make and to control their own visual symbolic forms, but merely by showing them pictures he had taken. How much greater might the change have been had he introduced into that culture the ability to make their own movies?

The problem cannot be solved by avoiding it. The anthropologist cannot "save" the people he works with by refusing to introduce motion pictures to them for the simple reason that they will be introduced by others with methods and effects that are in many cases known, but in large part unknown. The effects of commercial television and the aims of economic control and commodity advantage are quite clear. Up to now, political control has been largely a by-product of marketing tendencies and demands. With the advent of cable, and with a greater understanding of the *possibilities* of political control through television, political segments of all societies will begin to see the need for their own programs and procedures. The manipulation of the symbolic environment by elite groups in any society becomes a major focus for the study of culture.

Right now, the major television networks in the United States are giving away complete transmission facilities to developing nations all over the world—giving them away and training technicians to operate them so that these nations will develop a hunger for "product" to fill their air. That hunger is, and will continue to be, filled by American product sold "cheaply" to those who now have transmission facilities. Throughout the world the air is being filled with reruns of "Bonanza" and ads for toothpaste, mouthwash, and vaginal deodorants. Should the anthropologist become the person who teaches the people he studies to present themselves in *their* way, or should he stand back and allow the democratization and subsequent homogenization of culture through "Bonanza" and commercials? If left unchecked, Bantu, Dani, and Vietnamese children as well as our own will be taught to consume culture and learning via thousands of "Sesame Streets," taught not that learning is a creative process in which they participate, but rather that learning is a consumer product like commercials.

If left unchecked, we and perhaps other nations like us will continue to sell the technology which produces visual symbolic forms, while at the same time teaching other peoples *our uses only,* our conceptions, our codes, our mythic and narrative forms. We will, with technology, enforce our notions of what is, what is important, and what is right. The questions that anthropologists have been struggling with (related to whether we as anthropologists should help the oppressed as well as the oppressor), whether we should take sides in questions of culture change or even culture destruction, assume new dimensions when transformed from physical to symbolic forms. While answers are not simple in this area, should we not consider the question whether we who strive to learn about others should take some responsibility for helping others to learn about themselves? Should we not consider whether we have a responsibility, at the very least, to explain to those we study that new technologies of communication *need not* be used only in the ways of the technological societies that introduce them?

Further ethical problems exist. Some of our studies, in which we compared films made by black, white, and Navajo young people, show clear differences in these groups' social organization around film-making, thematic choices of material and subject matter, and attitudes toward the use of film.

For example, from analysis of our current studies it seems that blacks prefer to manipulate *themselves as image,* while whites prefer to manipulate the image of *others* but rarely themselves.

Black teen-agers want to be *in* the film; they want the film to be about themselves, and consider their important role and status in film-making to be the construction of the plot or story and the choice of themselves as actors. They fight over who will be in the film, but rarely over who will make the image, who will operate the camera. They seem to attach little importance or status to who will edit the film, and to consider it a chore to be gotten over with so they themselves can appear on the screen. They will often leave the camera unattended, forgetting that someone has to run it.

By contrast, the white teen-ager almost never appears in his film. "It's not cool," he says. "It's unsophisticated." His film is about others. He competes with his peers in the film group for the role of cameraman, director, or editor. Further, the films made by black groups involve behavior close to home and neighborhood, while the white teen-ager's films are often about the exotic, the distant, the faraway. He rarely shows his own block, his own home, or his own self.

Space does not permit a fuller examination here of the differences noted, but from our studies these differences seem not at all inconsistent with the predominant imperialist ideology of the white Western middle-class world. It is "reasonable" for whites to "capture" the image of others and to manipulate it to tell a story, to make a world based on symbolic events captured from far away and not of themselves. They then find status and pleasure in manipulating these events (often not even of people but of clouds, flowers, and "artistic" images of peeling paint, or crashing seas) to tell about themselves.

Anthropologists, too, are notorious for studying everyone but themselves. The "anthropological film," interestingly enough, has from its very inception always been defined as a film about others, exotic and far away. "Culture," in film, is frequently defined as in the *National Geographic*: strange rituals, exotic dances, and bare breasts. A study of anthropological films reviewed in the *American Anthropologist* shows that not one film reviewed was about us—always about how *they* live. Until the last few years and then only rarely, when used in the classroom, anthropological films were always used to show us about "others."

Our own study of Navajo films shows clearly that what the Navajos show us about themselves in their films is very different from what an anthropologist shows in his. Even in a film about weaving, the Navajo concentrates the bulk of his film on things that are never seen in an anthropologist's film on the same subject (Worth and Adair, 1970).

Can anthropologists in the future learn how to look at other cultures in ways different from the way "our" culture teaches us? Can *we* learn from the way others communicate themselves through film to think of the very term "other cultures" in new ways? Can we teach our students enough about this new mode of cultural communication so that they, perhaps, can develop insights that we do not have?

And what of the ethical problem posed by the very fact of our knowledge of different ways to organize and manipulate visual events on film? Should we teach others *our* way of conceiving the world on film? Should we, as anthropologists, as intellectuals, teach others to study and to reveal themselves when we do not? Should we teach them to go out and make movies of others as we do of them?

And how should we teach other people to protect themselves from the onslaught of a wired planet? Or if "onslaught" is too loaded a term, what is our responsibility to help them to understand a world in which their every act of living can be televised and viewed by a watching world?

In this context, I do not mean only people in other cultures far away. I am thinking of ourselves as well. Several years ago, during a student sit-in and strike at my own university, Pennsylvania, the student and faculty leaders were confronted with television cameras and documentary directors from both the commercial and educational stations. None of them had any idea of either their rights or their responsibilities, or the methods that they could use to control the images of themselves and their ideas that appeared on the air. Although they were aware of the fact that what they were doing could be manipulated and distorted by this process, they felt, and proved to be, helpless. A young faculty member, "sophisticated" and with a knowledge of the situation, was chosen by the striking group to narrate the final "documentary" that would appear on educational television. Although he would never allow anyone to write his books, he was manipulated by the technical crew in such a way that he actually recited their words, in their way. Few of us, in our culture or in others, know how to deal with the images that can be made of us and beamed to all corners of the earth.

It is now, as I have noted earlier, also possible for the anthropologist in the field to broadcast his view of another culture directly from the field. Should he do it? And if so, how? What safeguards can there be, or should there be, on a wired planet? What should he show, or better yet, what should he not show?

One can project this problem further into the future and envision a world in which it would *seem* that the anthropologist need not go to the field at all. The doctor will soon see his patients on video phone and will have to see them face to face only in those rare instances when physical manipulation needs to be performed by him rather than by a machine. The medical student will be able, by next year, to sit in his study cubicle and dial access on the tube to movies of any kind of health event he wants to learn about—from initial interviews for diagnostic purposes, or complete psychotherapy sessions, to examples of every rare disease and every surgical procedure performed. Not only will it be unnecessary to spend much time with patients; it is being planned to teach much of the medicine of the future this way.

Will it perhaps "make sense" to think of ethnographic field work as consisting of sitting in a study watching the movies that people make, or have made, of themselves and of others? Will this mean that the ethnography of the future will be concerned mainly with the view of others we get from the tube? Some anthropologists now feel that trusting the word of one individual who has observed a culture for a short period of time, and reported his singular view of it, is a slipshod way to go about studying culture. Already anthropologists are installing TV cameras in homes and broadcasting the view of the "other" to their offices, where they watch what's going on on the tube and preserve what they feel is important on television tape. For years, many anthropologists have argued that studying how people live by merely looking or listening is too coarse and rough-grained a view. They have argued that only through re-peated and close viewing of a motion-picture film of human behavior can certain aspects of behavior be studied. It seems time now to begin to clarify those aspects of human culture which can best be studied through film.

We need theories and values to help us clarify exactly what justification there is for intruding upon other people's lives in order to study them on film. It is not inconceivable that, in the same way that large segments of American Indian and Asian populations are even now refusing anthro-pologists entrance into their communities, most others will soon refuse to let us study them. Why should not others demand the right to learn the technology of film and tele-vision and to communicate with us as *they* wish, about what *they* wish, when *they* wish?

It might be that we shall be forced to know others only

from the movies they choose to broadcast to us, or that, if they allow us to observe them, they will want a voice about what we show of them. At least until recently, the ethical question often could be blurred when it concerned a written scholarly report. Few read these reports, and the peoples studied did not know our verbal language.[4] With film this argument no longer holds. It will be quite easy for others to view the films we make of them. Should we therefore show only that which another group wants us to show of them? Should we teach them not only to make their own films but to censor ours as well? The problem as I see it is: What reasons do we have *not* to insist that others have the right to control how we show them to the world? Questions such as these stem not so much from the problems of understanding the presentation of self in everyday life as from the presentation of self in symbolic life.

VII

I have mentioned the possibility and the likelihood of a wired planet. I have also introduced the possibility that everyone *can* have access to input channels, but the probability that access will be freely given to all those capable and desirous of access to television is small. Access to channels of communication is too valuable to power elites, who are fast discovering that control of the symbolic environment is as important as control of the physical, biological, and social environments. The political problems that I would like now to touch upon stem directly from the theoretical and ethical questions I have posed. Essentially, they are questions of power and control. Whereas in earlier times power and control were seen as being involved with natural and technological resources and with the control of labor and man's production from that labor, political power now seems to be tied more and more to the control of information.

Any of the arguments of the New Left in the social sciences would lead one inevitably to the realization that anthropologists must make a major effort to study the ways in which societies control the production and distribution of symbolic forms. Anthropologists have always been interested in these areas in terms of culture change and less frequently in terms of cultural stability and the prevention of change. Change, stability, and repression are now intimately affected by the visual forms distributed by the mass media or by individual "tellers of tales" about themselves such as I am proposing here.

Anthropologists have also always been involved with governments; they have always needed, and often sought, permission to go where they wanted to study. Frequently this permission had to be obtained, not from the people they studied, but rather from the imperialist powers that controlled those areas of the planet, or from other groups of elites that controlled areas and societies. The control of information has to a large extent always been in the hands of others and only in minute amounts in the hands of the anthropologist. From permission to go into a territory to funds to pay for field work, the anthropologist has never been totally in control of where he could get information. Frequently, to the dismay of some, and quite properly in the view of others, papers and publications were censored for a variety of reasons.

With the advent of a wired planet, however, the problem of control becomes enormously greater. Children are being taught by television; funds have been and are now available for the production of "anthropological films" for teaching, from first grade to university level. *The only group of professionals involved in the making and use of anthropological films who have no training* AT ALL *in the making, analysis, or use of film are anthropologists.* One can count on the fingers of both hands the anthropologists who are trained to study films, not as a record of some datum of culture, but as a datum of culture in its own right. I have stated elsewhere

(Worth, 1969) that anthropological films seem to mean one thing to anthropologists and quite another to those interested in an ethnography of visual communication. To the anthropologist today film is like the tape recorder or the pencil and notebook—a convenient way of assembling a record of data in the field, a memory aid, a device by which overt *behavior* can be studied microscopically and over and over again, as "real" behavior cannot. Film in this view is quite often thought of—falsely—as an objective record of what's out there.

To the person interested in vidistics or in an ethnography of visual communication, ethnographic or anthropological film cannot be defined by the film itself. A movie is a datum of culture in its own right, and every film *can* be an ethnographic or an anthropological film—if it is looked at anthropologically or ethnographically. The anthropologicalness of a film depends *not on the film but on the mode of analysis of that film*. It is becoming increasingly clear that the films members of other cultures make for *any* purpose can be studied to tell us about that culture. Just as the study of kinship systems, myth, and other rituals and modes of living can be seen as helping to develop an understanding of universals and differences in culture, so must the free exchange of films by broadcast and wire be seen as an integral part of the study of culture.

But just as the anthropologist has been concerned with the problem of culture change in the old ways—how it changed without him and how it changed because of him—he must now become concerned with the fact that culture *will* be changed because of the introduction of film and television on a wired planet.

Politically, many anthropologists have traditionally been categorized as "liberal." Today many, particularly the younger ones, prefer to think of themselves as "radical." What could a radical position be in regard to the democratization of culture through the homogenization of symbolic forms? Should the radical anthropologist cry "Eureka!" at the thought that CBS will introduce film and television to every corner of the planet and that Howard Hughes Enterprises will control most of the input to cable TV in the United States (at the very least)? Should the radical anthropologist take a stance favoring the control by government of input facilities into every home? Should the democratization of culture be thought of as liberating or as potentially regressive and reactionary?

In his report to the Twentieth Congress of the Communist Party of the Soviet Union, Joseph Stalin presented a long section entitled "Nationalities and Language" (attributed to the linguist Margaret Schlauch, who had left the United States for Poland during the McCarthy purges). The "radical" wing of the party supported the position called in that report "the democratization of nationalities." They felt that the nationalities within the Soviet Union should be brought together under one language, one set of customs, and one way of life. Stalin took the "conservative" view. The report stressed the encouragement of individual nationalities, languages, and customs within the framework of socialism.

It seems to me that the anthropologist today faces a somewhat similar problem (without the political power of my previous example, of course). Should he take what might be called the "conservative" view—the view that tends to support the status quo (individual culture in all its diversity)— or should he take the "radical" view that tends to support culture change and technology and what I have called the democratization of culture?

I have stated the problem too broadly, however, for the dichotomy is not quite so clear and is perhaps a false dichotomy altogether. It is a question, not of a battle between the status quo of diversity and the homogeneity of democratization, but rather of an interaction between them. Just as the nature-culture question is falsely seen as a dichotomy rather than a dialectic, so can the previous question be seen as a dialectic between the existing culture of any people and the introduction of a technology enabling all of us to present ourselves to each other.

The problem, it seems to me, can also be seen as a dialectic of power, a struggle for skill and access to production and distribution technologies for the use of symbolic forms. If we are to study culture, we are inevitably involved in the study of the power relationships and control over mechanisms, messages, message-makers, and message-receivers.

But such a dialectic requires an understanding of the politicization of symbolic forms. It requires an ethnography of communication that has developed theories about the politics of the cultural changes that will be brought about by the ability of people to show themselves in their own way. It will require that anthropologists face the fact that they may soon not be allowed to study different cultures on their home grounds, that they must now think about whether they want to teach other people to present themselves and whether they want now to begin training themselves and their students to understand the visual presentations of others that they may be reduced to viewing on the tube in their study.

Anthropologists must, in the coming power struggle over control of men's minds, develop an anthropology that can aid them in attempting to understand, and perhaps even to control by themselves, how men learn about one another through film. They must decide whether the images of their own culture that nurture *them,* on their children's, their students', and their very own television sets, are a proper concern for a new anthropology.

I have tried to present a picture of the planet Earth as it is today and as it is most likely to develop in the next few decades, concentrating on what I consider to be important anthropological problems of which most anthropologists are in large part unaware.[5]

If I were reinventing anthropology in the light of the problems presented here, I would have to invent one that could handle the questions I have barely been able to formulate fully. It would have to be an anthropology that would be equipped theoretically and methodologically to formulate the subtler problems I believe are implied in some of the data and argument I have presented. I would have to invent an anthropology that could deal with culture on a wired planet.

Kluckhohn suggested that anthropology was invented "as the search for oddments by eccentrics." I would like to suggest that we move on to the invention of an anthropological politics of symbolic form.

Notes

1. "Vidistics is concerned, first, with the determination and codification of visual elements as used by the image-maker. Second, it is concerned with the determination of those rules of visual or pictorial symbolic forms by which a viewer infers meaning from cognitive representations and interactions of the elements in sequence and context. Vidistic 'rules' in this sense are thought of as a set describing the interaction of specified elements, operations on these elements, and inferences appropriately made from them in specified contexts." (Worth, 1968)

2. The frustration of not having a word for those who communicate through film, comparable to "speaker," is great. I have resisted coining another jargon word for "speaker through movies," in the hope that the constant frustration of quotation marks and the ambiguity of the word "speaker" will jar on my readers' sensibilities as they do on mine and serve the rhetorical function of constantly reminding us of the fact that we are dealing with something that our verbal language and our culture have not learned to deal with adequately.

3. Stephen L. Schensul (*Newsletter of the American Anthropological Association*, Vol. 12, No. 3, March 1971) feels that "the intent of [Carpenter's] article in elucidating the effects of mass media upon our society by 'experimenting' with a New Guinea group is obviously ridiculous and requires little comment. Further, current ethnographic data from the Sepik River region indicates neither the reported isolation nor the fearful reaction to technological innovations reported by Carpenter. The article contains little that is either conceptually or empirically valid.

"But, the truth of Carpenter's statements aside, I find the nature of his 'experiments' to be highly immoral and unethical and his description of the results at least ethnocentric, if not racist. His methods of developing rapport and the way in which he *thrusts his electronic equipment on these villagers* makes Captain Cook look like a cultural relativist." (My italics)

The "truth" of Schensul's statements aside, his letter points up the highly charged atmosphere in which research dealing with television and people of other cultures is currently being discussed. I repeat that we know very little about what happens when we thrust, or even gently introduce, electronic media or other new symbolic forms to anybody in any context.

4. Sofue (1971) writes: "Kloos has pointed out (*Current Anthropology* 10, p. 511) that 'publishing an item may be harmful to the people concerned, while not publishing is harmful to science.' I would like to see some discussion as to how we are to face this problem. It would be a help to have some concrete examples of cases in which publication was harmful to the informants or others. (*Sun Chief*, by L. W. Simmons, is probably one example.) The problem is very serious in Japan, where all villagers are literate and many have access to ethnographic publications through bookstores in nearby towns."

5. In discussions of this paper with various colleagues, arguments were put forward regarding the probability of occurrence of the events described here. It was felt that other cultures would not, or could not, be made to participate in a wired planet such as I have described. It was argued that the dangers I try to predict are less real or less awful than I make out. The outcome, or the reliability, of these predictions is unfortunately empirical, and must await the future. Should it be the case, however, that we have prepared ourselves to deal with an anthropological politics of symbolic forms and the need is not as great as I have imagined, we will, I am afraid, still be ahead, for the understanding of the effects upon culture of a wired nation (our own) is an urgent matter right now —and one that we are not prepared to cope with at the present.

References

Carpenter, Edmund. 1971. "Television Meets the Stone Age." *TV Guide,* January 16, Pp. 14–16.

Sofue, Takao. 1971. Letter to *Current Anthropology* 12, No. 2: 145.

Worth, Sol. 1968. "Cognitive Aspects of Sequence in Visual Communication." *AV Communication Review* 16, No. 2: 1–25.

———. 1969. "Why the Anthropologist Needs the Film-Maker." Paper presented at the 70th Annual Meeting of the American Anthropological Association, Seattle, Wash.

Worth, Sol, and John Adair. 1970. "Navajo Film-Makers." *American Anthropologist* 72: 9–34.

———. 1972. *Through Navajo Eyes: An Exploration in Film Communication and Anthropology.* Bloomington: Indiana University Press.

V · Responsibilities
of Ethnography

Personal and Extrapersonal Vision in Anthropology
Robert Jay

IN THIS PAPER I consider something about the relation of knowledge to relevance and responsibility in social science research, particularly in social anthropological research. I am not concerned here primarily with the responsibilities involved in choosing a subject for research, in gaining research funds, in intervening in the affairs of those one studies, or in the relevance of the knowledge gained for some kind of social action, though I shall turn to all these at the end. Those things are important, but I want to start farther back, with a more radical and personal rethinking of the problem, namely, how I relate myself to the subjects of my work, what kinds of knowledge I look for, and how the problem becomes part of those relationships. I shall try to show that there are at least two different realms of knowledge to be gained, and that how we relate ourselves to those whose actions are the subjects of our study is intimately connected with these realms, which in anthropology are often confused.

My own position on these matters has gone through a sharp change in the past few years, and I find it increasingly difficult to explain myself in conventional anthropological terms. In order to do so, I shall first consider some difficulties that have disturbed me about the way many anthropologists go about gaining knowledge, the kind they seek, and the way they seek to build theory with it.

In the ordinary way of anthropological research, as I myself practiced it in Java and later in Malaya, we are asked to relate ourselves to our subjects in the field in two ways—as participants in their lives and as detached observers of selected items in those lives. The first relation is sought in order to gain a strategic position for performing the second. It is not, I think, clearly enough realized what are the consequences of this forked, "have-your-cake-and-eat-it-too" relationship on the yields of knowledge often sought by anthropologists.

Ronald Laing (1960, p. 21) says:

> If you are sitting opposite me, I can see you as another person like myself; without you changing or doing anything differently, I can now see you as a complex physical-chemical system, perhaps with its own idiosyncrasies, but chemical nonetheless for that; seen in this way you are no longer a person but an organism. . . .
>
> One's relationship to an organism is different from one's relation to a person. One's description of the other as organism . . . is different from one's description of the other as person . . . similarly, one's theory of the other as organism is remote from any theory of the other as person.[1]

Laing makes his point powerfully by showing at length what expanded understanding of a schizophrenic may result from treating his bizarre behavior and utterances not as symptoms of an organic disorder or mental illness but as modes of personal communication which can be decoded with intimate knowledge of the patient as a person. What results for both the patient and the psychiatrist is a flood of knowledge on the patient's personal case. And such knowledge is not simply of therapeutic value; it is also used to build up general knowledge of personal organization, in terms of what Laing calls a "theory of persons."[2]

Now, I think I am right in asserting that much of anthropological theory, and therefore field work, is aimed at discovering and elucidating processes that show certain similarities to the organic processes Laing speaks of, that is, the processes are generally seen as rooted in extrapersonal bases

—the local psychological or social organization, local ecology, local culture, or some combination. The kinds of knowledge needed, therefore, include what is gained from the subjects by viewing them as different creatures from one's experiencing self, as parts of systems displaying certain organic features.[3]

I feel strongly that such approaches involve a serious moral question as to their dehumanizing effects on our society. In this paper, however, I am concerned rather with the limits and qualifications of the knowledge these approaches yield. Such theory at best admits as useful very little personal knowledge of the individual subjects, and the methods used to observe the subjects, which stress a high degree of personal detachment (as distinct from the methods used to "establish rapport"), indeed provide shallow knowledge of the subjects as whole persons. If one is *primarily* attempting a description of subjects as "organisms," seeking a theory about them as part of "organic" processes, as elements in a system, then one will be primarily perceiving them as such, that is, they will not show through clearly as persons.

The difficulties that have often disturbed me in research arise when anthropologists, using standard methods of observation, attempt theories that require actual knowledge of their subjects as persons. In observing events, social anthropologists are mostly seeking to perceive patterning in the action of their subjects and in the setting of the events. That at least is what I was mostly sensitized to search for as the raw stuff of my observations. It is out of such patterning that the field worker draws up his generalizations, discerns his processes, and matches his data to his theory. When I was studying family relationships in Java, or cooperative labor relations in Malaya, I sought to perceive patterns in the behavior of the members of various families I knew, or in the events of various work parties at which I was present. As I began to see patterns, I increasingly interpreted behavior in their terms—successfully, of course. As time went on, I came more and more to perceive largely through such patterning, to the exclusion of nonpatterned items. I gather most anthropologists in the field proceed in the same manner, making order out of initial chaos and congratulating themselves on mastering the local cultural codes.[4] It has only recently struck me what is overlooked, if seen at all, and what exaggerated importance is thereby given to the content of the patterns.

Let me give an example from the work of two well-known anthropologists, so that the problem will be seen to exist in the very best work. In a recent essay, Eric Wolf (1966) analyzes contrasting bases of personal relationship in a complex society. One basis with which he deals is that of friendship. Drawing heavily from an article by Ruben Reina (1954), he sets up a distinction between what he terms "expressive or emotional friendship" and "instrumental friendship." The first type is one in which partners are drawn into friendship for the emotional rewards they gain from one another. The other kind draws the partners together for the practical uses they can make of one another.

As the paradigm for these types, Wolf cites Reina's study of friendship in a Guatemalan community, using observed patterns which he then used for a total characterization of the nature of personal friendship in the community, or rather for two characterizations—one for the Maya Indians and one for the Ladinos. Wolf takes Reina's characterization of Indian friendships for his first type and of Ladino friendships for his second. He is concerned with the personal basis of friendship (that is, with knowledge of individuals that can be gained only through an intimate relationship with them as persons), for he attributes the form of the "expressive" friendship type to "emotional deficits" inferred as existing in the selves of those entering such friendships. He then asks in what kind of community one would expect to find such personal deficits generated in a considerable number of individuals, and the answer is, in highly solidary communities, where the emotional expression of each individual in his relations with others is severely cramped by "the strains and pressures of role-playing." From there he continues toward a theory of friendship as shaped by the form of the social organization in which it is set.

What Wolf has done, following Reina, is to take certain general patterns of friendship as accurately representing the whole of all actual, particular friendships in a community, or at least as sufficiently representative of them to allow one to derive from those general patterns the *personal conditions* of the particular relationships. From that, he proceeds to hypothesize forms of community which would generate those personal conditions. Now, there may be some intuitive insights hidden here, but the logic of the method is very questionable. In fact, the data, that is, Reina's descriptions plus Wolf's own field of observations, do not contain knowledge in depth of more than a few *particular* friendships, and in writing up his observations, Reina describes and analyzes them in terms of general patterns that contain only very partial expressions of those relationships, expressions selected *just because* they exhibit patterning. Both Reina and Wolf are of course only following a standard operating procedure in anthropology. The result is that behavior within a highly personal relationship is mixed with socially standardized behavior, and both are read in terms of a theory that views people as objects shaped and moved within a field of forces external to their autonomous selves.

In Laing's terms, studying friendship requires modes of observation and analysis appropriate to a theory of persons. Wolf, in fact, initially defines friendship by reference to common experience. Such experience is gained through personal ties of friendship with others, and through empathetic perception of other friendships. Wolf, however, continues his analysis with a categorization of friendship types that I cannot believe derives from his own personal experience, but which instead appears to have derived from the Reina descriptive patterns. He thus takes up into general analysis the observational stance taken by his sources in reporting field experience.

In the field, Reina and his wife, by his report, did what

they could to discourage the Indians they got to know from forming close friendships with them in order to avoid the difficulties, personal and professional, of their demands and jealousies, and succeeded by and large in keeping themselves neutral. They struggled to overcome the pressure for an exclusive relationship that some of their informants put on them by trying to explain their position, but managed mostly only to mystify and alienate those would-be friends. I might very well have been driven to the same means, with probably no better success, but I have come to think that the aloofness so achieved for the sake of efficient field work carries as its price a loss in knowledge which anthropologists generally do not seem willing to admit.

In the field, investigating friendship requires a relationship to your subjects as persons, and that must also include yourself as a person. For if you objectify your interacting self, setting it "over there," apart from your observational self, and relate to that part of you also as an object (an operation often done in the name of "participant-observation"), you will severely limit your power to gain personal knowledge from your subjects. They will not be fooled and will keep their distance accordingly.

The main point I am trying to make in this paper is that the relationships we form with the subjects of our work—for whatever reasons we settle upon those relationships—control the kind of knowledge that the material we gain will yield and also control how we exercise whatever responsibility we may feel to our subjects and to ourselves as persons. I have further been trying to show that there is a certain knowledge relevant for understanding our subjects' lives in the same way we understand one another in our own personal lives, in which we look upon one another as autonomous, mutually responsible selves, and that there is another kind of knowledge relevant to understanding our subjects as shaped and moved by extrapersonal forces allowing at most very limited autonomy or responsibility. The knowledge involved in each kind of understanding is not directly or even readily translatable into that of the other. That disconformity between our direct, personal sight of the universe and the sight that an objective science gives us has been at the root of much intellectual discontent in Western civilization for some time.[5]

What I am trying to say will be made much clearer by examining a recent essay very relevant to my topic by another deservedly admired anthropologist, Clifford Geertz (1968). One of his main points is that communication between the field worker and his subjects is necessarily very partial. The investigator, he says,

> has a passionate wish to become personally valuable to his informants—i.e., a friend—in order to maintain self-respect. The notion that one has been marvelously successful in doing this is the investigator's side of the touching faith coin: he believes in cross-cultural communion (he calls it "rapport") as his subjects believe in tomorrow. It is no wonder that so many anthropologists leave the field seeing tears in the eyes of their informants that, I feel quite sure, are not really there.
>
> I do not wish to be misunderstood here. No more than I feel that significant social progress in the new states is impossible, do I feel that genuine human contact across cultural barriers is impossible. Had I not . . . experienced, now and then, a measure of the second, my work would have been insupportable. . . . [Yet] in a way which is in no sense adventitious, the relationship between an anthropologist and his informants rests on a set of partial fictions half seen through. . . . If the implicit agreement to regard one another, in the face of some very serious indications to the contrary, as members of the same cultural universe breaks down . . . they are shut up once more in their separate, internally coherent uncommunicating worlds.

Dr. Geertz then goes on to give an example of such a breakdown in his own relations with one of his Javanese informants. He had a thirty-year-old man in the town as an informant on traditional myths, legends, and the like, and Geertz was using standard, formal interview techniques for eliciting the material. The man was also an aspiring playwright and regularly borrowed Geertz's typewriter to type up his own material. Geertz felt he was gradually losing the typewriter to the man's demands and decided one day to put on the brakes by politely refusing the loan of it. The man responded by politely refusing his time as an informant for a couple of days. Geertz reports that he then made the fatal error of trying to retract his refusal, thus exposing the pretense of their politeness, and the man responded by breaking off the relationship totally.

Geertz's explanation for the break, consistent with his argument, is that their relationship rested upon a fiction which they both dimly perceived but chose to keep out of mind.

> Borrowing [the typewriter], my informant was, tacitly, assert-ing his demand to be taken seriously as an intellectual, a "writer"—i.e., a peer; lending it, I was, tacitly, granting that demand. . . . We both knew that these agreements could be only partial: we were not really colleagues and not really comrades . . . he was as far from being an inglorious Milton as I was from being a Javanese. . . . When I refused the use of the symbol of our unspoken pact to regard, by a kind of mutual suspension of disbelief, our two cultural worlds as one, his suspicion, always lingering, that I did not take his "work" as seriously as I took my own, broke into conscious-ness . . . and my fear, always there, that he saw me as an inconsequent stranger to whom he was attached by only the most opportunistic of considerations, broke into mine.

Geertz here makes perfectly clear that a theory of culture is irrelevant to explain the event; a theory of persons is wholly adequate. Geertz *did* indeed rather scorn the man's intellectual efforts, and both must have been aware of it. The man *was* highly sensitive to any overt signs of such rejection and responded strongly in the face of one. Geertz *was* fearful and painfully sensitive to the precariousness of his personal position with most of his informants (as I also was in my corner of the field). The reciprocal gestures of rejection escalated, feeding on these fears, to a final breach. Such a situation could, and indeed does, arise in our experience of persons in our own society, and differences in individual experience among us also lessen the margin available for healing such hurts. There is no need at all to draw in notions about difficulties of "cross-cultural communion," separate cultural universes, and the like, to explain such a breakdown. Yet Geertz feels driven to explain the event ultimately by talking in terms of a theory of culture.

It is precisely here that I see the difference between my position in anthropology and that of many, perhaps most, of my colleagues. I want to choose, with full awareness, to relate to my subjects fully as persons, as I would to any other—friend, colleague, student, chance acquaintance. That choice determines the realm of knowledge I shall be able to explore, and it is a realm for which the concept of culture, and for that matter of social structure, ecology, and the like (extrapersonal bases for explaining behavior) are of only peripheral value.

The clear, certain desire to make that choice in my work has come to me, as I said earlier, only within the past few years, as part of radical changes in my personal life and in my teaching. These changes have had the effect, or so it seems clear to me, of bringing to the surface strong yearnings deep within me, long buried, to relate closely and warmly to all others in all parts of my life—as myself and not as one filling a variety of roles. I am one of those who have, in Geertz's words, "a passionate wish to become personally valuable to one's informants," and also a strong wish to know them and become known to them as a person.

When I was doing field work in Java in 1953–1954, and later in my teaching and further field work in Malaya in 1962–1963, I was driven mainly by externally impressed professional values. I related to the villagers in Java primarily in ways to gain from them information not about themselves as persons but as specimens of their total setting, samples of its cultural modulations, ecological modulations, or whatever. Looking at a villager's actions, public or intimate, I scanned them for patterning that connected with other patterns so as to "reveal," or to allow the construction of, system in the village setting, system in the local modes of rice agriculture, in the exercise of social and economic power within the village, and between its members and the wider society, system in their kin relationships, and so on.

This was true of how and what I was choosing to see, because I understood that I was to return with data to define and explicate such systems. Any awareness I had of particular individuals as they related personally to me, to others, and to their own lives, except as it bore on my perception of such patterning, slipped by me, or, if registered because of some intimacy in my relations with them, got set apart into the separate realm of my private life (which was in truth rather starved). In writing up my material, I have often been baffled by my inability to find a place for such powerful recollections of particular persons. They did not fit, or fitted only with distortion, into analyses for professional ends. I gather many anthropologists have similar experience.

The professional urge to fit the qualities of even intimately known "informants" into aspects of their environment is vividly shown by the portraits of such individuals presented in Casagrande (1960), where personal relationships with the anthropologists are, with few exceptions, described not so much to reveal the persons themselves (and certainly not the persons of the anthropologists) as to show them as representatives of their settings—cultural, ecological, and so on. A growing number of books have been appearing recently in which anthropologists have attempted to reveal those personal connections in their field work, such as Hortense Powdermaker (1966), Kenneth Read (1965), David Maybury-Lewis (1965), Carlos Castaneda (1968, 1971), Jean Briggs's superb book (1970), and the vivid, though semifictionalized, account of Laura Bohannan (1954). There is evident, I think, an increasing concern with returning to the roots of how we perceive and know, with a phenomenological view of the problems of field work that I find myself also taking.[6]

I have said that I am concerned in this paper with the interplay of relevance and responsibility. It should be clear by now that I see them as inseparably linked. Relevance has to do with knowledge, and responsibility with action. For me, both begin with the ways in which I relate to the subjects of my work. The choice of relating involves a choice of the knowledge I may gain, and also states something about the mutual responsibility I expect to appear both between myself and those I study and between myself and those I see as the recipients of what knowledge I gain. It states, too, the responsibility I am taking toward myself.

As for responsibility to myself, the major personal meaning my work has for me was clear to me even in Java, revealed through the enormous pleasure I gained from seeing individuals there emerging, through a thick veil of alienness, as particular persons equal in my understanding of them with others I knew as persons elsewhere in my life. But that meaning I set firmly aside as no part of the professional returns expected of my work. Most others I know in my field concur in that judgment: such meaning is "purely a personal matter" or at most "merely of humanistic value" (which is to say, "scientifically of no value"). I have come to see that for me to turn my back, professionally, upon perceptions I gain through such experiencing of individual "subjects" is to lose certain knowledge of them that may be important to them and others, and it is also to fail in responsibility to myself.

What of the responsibilities to my subjects and (for I must deal with them together) to those I see as ultimately benefitting from my research? There are those, quite numerous, social scientists with a clear faith in the ultimate value of science as an instrument toward the solution of particular problems and as a thing valuable for its own sake. They accordingly see their most direct, primary responsibility as being to their fellow scientists. Objective data, devoid of personal involvement, is ordinarily what they require for the discharge of that responsibility, and a highly detached stance toward their own persons as well as those of their subjects is what they feel they must adopt for that end. Knowledge they render from their data through highly selective theory, and they may not see that knowledge as necessarily relevant to any of their subjects' interests. In any case, they certainly do not see their subjects as usefully able to enter into the formulation of the inquiry, the rendering of the data into knowledge, or the application of that knowledge to their own problems. In short, they treat their subjects as objects for study and in some cases as objects for treatment.

My own position on this has been uneven and unclear. Toward the end of my field work in a Malay village in 1963, I was approached by a small delegation of villagers, who said to me, "You are a professor in an American university who has studied our village for a whole year. You must have learned a lot about us in that time that could help us with our problems here. Will you please tell us some of what you know?"

I was taken aback, since I had indeed been thinking of my knowledge as of interest only to my colleagues, and had gathered material toward that end, not material selected out of any sense of what any villagers themselves might want. My attitude toward the villagers had oscillated between seeing them as people with whom I was personally concerned and as representative sources, in their words and action, of knowledge about their society which had no necessary relevance for them. In the first, they counted as persons; in the second, they did not. Here they were asking me to unite the two. I complied, and remember speaking to an assembly of villagers one evening of my observation that in their local cooperative organizations criticisms of the leaders' actions were always aimed at their personal motives rather than at the effectiveness of the actions for the organization. I argued that they would do better to be more impersonal toward one another within their organizations, toward gaining their ends more efficiently. They were polite in their response to my talk, but I had no feeling that my advice made much sense to them.

I have since come to realize how very little meaning my Weberian logic could have had for them, not because they were intellectually unable to grasp it, but because I had never seriously treated any of them as intellectually able to share in any part of my enterprise. Had I done so, I believe I would have learned so much more as to make the knowledge I tried to give them on their organizations seem what I consider it now: a shallow, distorted, even arrogant effort at understanding the problems they faced in organization. In future field work I shall place first a mutual responsibility to my whole self and to those I go to learn from, in agreement with my desire to relate to them as full equals, personal and intellectual. I shall try to use my relationships with them to find out what topics are relevant to each of us, to be investigated through what questions and what modes of questioning, and for what kinds of knowledge. I should wish to make the first report for them, in fact with them; indeed it may be that written reports would seem to us redundant.

Such a linkage of relevance and responsibility will not perhaps appeal to many. I advance it here as illustrative, not as exemplary; one person's effort to break through the compartments into which his life had become divided. We must each start from, and return to, ourselves.

Notes

1. The distinction is that which Martin Buber has brought to our attention in his *I and Thou*, where he deals with it far more broadly than Laing does in *The Divided Self*.
2. The work of Harry Stack Sullivan is an excellent example of such theory-building. Sullivan was a close personal friend of Edward

Sapir, and they deeply influenced each other's thinking. Sapir's article "Culture Genuine and Spurious" (1924) contains an early appeal to anthropologists to give attention to their own personal values in relation to their subjects.

3. In some recent important anthropological theory, notably in the work of Fredrik Barth and Edmund Leach, the local social organization is seen as dominantly shaped by the current sum of the choices the individual members make in dealing with the local power structure or structure of economic resources. The actual autonomy granted the individuals in these theories, and therefore the degree of interest shown in their personal beings, is very scant, however; it is assumed that they choose among a small number of fixed alternatives and that their choices are always determined on the basis of maximizing for themselves the political or economic values that each is striving to gain. Such a Hobbesian point of view, however, does not alter the impersonal nature of the knowledge needed. The personal nature of the choices is not under investigation; it is assumed.

4. I am aware that there are those, "ethnoscientists," who, in order to avoid what they feel to be biases of the observer in the discovery of such patterning, use a very rigorously standardized set of procedures for discovering and ordering them. This method, however, simply eliminates as a problem what I am concerned with here —how the members of a society relate such patterns to their own lives.

5. In a series of lectures delivered in 1934–1935, Kohler attempted a theory of visual perception that cut across the disconformity, but neurovisual research since then has, ironically, moved in just the direction he predicted would increase it.

6. Still, these books are separate from the "official," professional account of the work (except in the case of Castaneda). What is considered known and how it came to be known are still compartmentalized. We are not yet able, or willing, to explain the conditions of our knowledge, as is, say, an experimenter in a laboratory. It is as if field work were two unrelated things—reportable knowledge and personal adventure—and to join the two consciously, let alone publicly, would damage both. [DH]

References

Barth, Fredrik. 1959. "Segmentary Opposition and the Theory of Games: A Study of Pathan Organization." *Journal of the Royal Anthropological Institute* 89, No. 1: 5–22.

[Bohannan, Laura]. 1954. *Return to Laughter*. London: Victor Gollancz. Published under the *nom de plume* Elenore Smith Bowen.

Briggs, Jean. 1970. *Never in Anger: Portrait of an Eskimo Family*. Cambridge, Mass.: Harvard University Press.

Buber, Martin. 1958. *I and Thou*. New York: Charles Scribner's Sons.

Casagrande, Joseph B., ed., 1960. *In the Company of Man: Twenty Portraits by Anthropologists*. New York: Harper & Brothers.

Castaneda, Carlos. 1968. *The Teachings of Don Juan: A Yaqui Way of Knowledge*. Berkeley: University of California Press.

————. 1971. *A Separate Reality: Further Conversations with Don Juan*. New York: Simon & Schuster.

Geertz, Clifford. 1968. "Thinking as a Moral Act: Ethical Dimensions of Anthropological Field Work in the New States." *Antioch Review* 28, No. 2: 139–58.

Kohler, Wolfgang. 1959. *The Place of Value in a World of Facts*. New York: Meridian Books.

Laing, Ronald D. 1960. *The Divided Self*. London: Tavistock Publications.

Leach, Edmund. 1961. *Pul Eliya: A Village in Ceylon*. Cambridge: Cambridge University Press.

Maybury-Lewis, David. 1965. *The Savage and the Innocent*. Cleveland: World Pub. Co.

Powdermaker, Hortense. 1966. *Strangers and Friends: The Way of an Anthropologist*. New York: W. W. Norton & Co.

Read, Kenneth. 1965. *The High Valley*. New York: Charles Scribner's Sons.

Reina, Ruben. 1954. "Two Patterns of Friendship in a Guatemalan Community." *American Anthropologist* 61: 44–50.

Sapir, Edward. 1924. "Culture, Genuine and Spurious." *American Journal of Sociology* 29: 401–29. Reprinted in *Selected Writings of Edward Sapir*, ed. D. G. Mandelbaum. Berkeley: University of California Press.

Wolf, Eric R. 1966. "Kinship, Friendship, and Patron-Client Relations in Complex Societies." In *The Social Anthropology of Complex Societies*, ed. M. Banton. Association of Social Anthropologists Monograph No. 4. London: Tavistock Publications.

Some Questions About Anthropological Linguistics: The Role of Native Knowledge

Kenneth Hale

I

I USE THE TERM "anthropological linguistics" to refer very broadly to any form of research or study dealing with the languages spoken by peoples whose cultures and societies have been the traditional objects of anthropological investigation. Under the term, I include research relating to strictly linguistic matters as well as to matters which pertain to areas in which language is seen as being a part of culture in some sense. My usage is somewhat inaccurate in that many people who view themselves strictly as linguists and as having no connection whatsoever with anthropology are working on a great many of the languages included under the definition loosely formulated above. It is nonetheless true that there exists a tradition of linguistic inquiry which finds a substantial measure of its heritage in the work of scholars who saw themselves, and were seen by others, as general anthropologists. And many of us who now do work which is primarily linguistic, in a technical sense, do feel that we can trace our interests and concerns back to this anthropological tradition. Moreover, for many of us, our professional associations are as much with anthropologists as with linguists. In any event, I do not feel that the remarks I wish to make here are out of place in a book devoted to anthropological concerns.

I would like at this point to characterize my own involvement in anthropological linguistics in order to enable the reader to understand the perspective from which I view the field and the considerations which lead me to have questions about it. I am a student of American Indian and Australian Aboriginal languages, and my professional interests are in the contribution which these languages will make to the development of a general account of linguistic universals. I am thoroughly convinced of the importance of this area of study and am deeply committed to it. My academic training has been primarily in linguistics but also partly in anthropology, and my academic employment has been both in anthropology and in linguistics. I consider myself an anthropological linguist within the tradition alluded to above, and I owe an immense intellectual debt to the people who have worked to build the field.[1]

I have a number of questions, which I consider serious, about the future of this area of linguistics. However, I think it is appropriate to point out that what I shall have to say below is for the most part a personal response to conditions in the field which I see as a student of American Indian and Australian Aboriginal languages. I find it very difficult to speak of my concerns for my area of interest other than in terms of my own personal experience—in some instances, my remarks will fail to generalize beyond this experience. My questions about the field fall roughly under three rubrics: (1) the future of the field as an intellectual endeavor and its contribution to the science of linguistics, (2) professionalism within the field, and (3) the extent to which the field is of service to the people. These concerns are not really separate; they are, in my view, intimately interconnected.

Anthropological linguists typically obtain the data which they study directly from native speakers of the languages involved. Sometimes the research is carried out in the communities where the languages are actually used, and sometimes it is undertaken with the help of speakers who are separated from their home communities. In either case, the linguist depends upon native speakers of the language he studies. It is a prevailing fact about anthropological linguistics, particularly in the areas in which I have worked, that the linguist and the native speaker are not the same individual. There are exceptions, to be sure, but I do not think it incorrect to say that the state of affairs which epitomizes the field is one in which the linguistic investigator is an outsider in the sense that he is not a native speaker of the language he studies nor is he a member of the community in which the language is spoken.

The historical origins of this circumstance are, I feel, abundantly clear and should be faced with honesty. Anthropological linguistics, no less than anthropology itself, is "a child of Western imperialism." Kathleen Gough, in an important paper (Gough, 1968), has given a persuasive account of this view of the development of anthropology as a science. I feel that her account applies without essential change to anthropological linguistics; certainly this is so to the extent that the two fields share a common heritage. Thus, I do not think it is inaccurate to say of anthropological linguistics, as Gough does of anthropology, that it developed as a discipline during "the period in which the Western nations were making their final push to bring practically the whole preindustrial, non-Western world under their political and economic control" (Gough, 1968, pp. 12–13). During this formative period, field work, which has been the essential nutritive component of both disciplines, was carried out, primarily by Westerners, in aboriginal communities which were to a greater or lesser extent subjugated in the course of Western imperialist expansion.

In effect, anthropology and anthropological linguistics became disciplines in which Westerners studied, published, and built teaching and research careers around the cultural and linguistic wealth of non-Western peoples. The extent to which this is true today varies in different parts of the world and in different subfields of anthropology, but in the geographical and disciplinary areas with which I am concerned and of which I have some personal knowledge, it is overwhelmingly true. The study of American Indian languages is dominated by non-Indians; and research in Australian Aboriginal linguistics is, to an even greater extent than is true in the American Indians' case, being carried out by people who are not native speakers of the languages involved.

There is, of course, nothing wrong with studying the language and culture of a community other than one's own; it is essential that the peoples who inhabit this planet come to know one another intimately, and the study of languages and cultures has an obvious central role to play in achieving this goal. Anthropologists and anthropological linguists are often motivated by this consideration, as well as by a deep respect for, and abiding loyalty to, the peoples whose languages and cultures they study. Moreover, the expertise which has developed in connection with the growth of the anthropological disciplines is considerable, and it is potentially of great benefit to humanity. Speaking for my own area of interest, I believe that the detailed study of language teaches the greatest respect for the capabilities of the human mind and, further, that it is of critical importance to this study that as large a number as possible of the world's several thousand rich linguistic traditions make their contributions to it.

In order for any field of inquiry to realize its potential for service to the people, it is a necessary (though not sufficient) condition that it achieve the greatest possible degree of excellence; part of the criterion of excellence for the study of the world's languages is, of course, adequate coverage. For that reason, if for no other, it is extremely important to continue the work which owes so much of its substance to the anthropological linguistic tradition. But I question whether significant advances beyond the present state of knowledge of the world's languages can be made if important sectors of linguistics continue to be dominated by scholars who are not native speakers of the languages they study. To be sure, it would be incorrect to assert that a linguist is absolutely incapable of making important observations about the structure of a language not his own or that such observations as he can make are of limited scientific interest—the evidence against this extreme position is overwhelming. Nonetheless, it has become increasingly clear in recent years, partly as a result of certain advances in the study of the syntax of English and other Indo-European languages, that many important aspects of the structure of a given language are essentially beyond the reach of the scholar who is not a native speaker of it. Even where insights of great importance have been contributed by non-native speakers to the study of English, for example, it is possible to argue that the insights are based on intuitions which, in all essential respects, closely approximate those of a native speaker.

Linguistic information about the structures of American Indian and Australian Aboriginal languages, to use the examples with which I am familiar, is, with a few exceptions, limited to spheres which are more or less readily accessible to the perceptive non-native speaker—that is, to areas which can be studied with minimal appeal to the native speaker's intuitions. Thus, we have a great deal of excellent information on phonology and morphology, but relatively little on syntax. And the extent to which success has been enjoyed has depended a great deal on the efficiency of the partnership between a linguist who was not a native speaker and an informant who was. It could be argued that I am distorting the picture by implying that the paucity of syntactic information is due to the relative lack of involvement of native speakers; one might say that the truth of the matter is that syntax has only recently begun to attract the interest of anthropological linguists and that we can expect great advances with the traditional methods of field work now that we know what to look for, so to speak. I think that this argument is wrong and that it involves a gamble which it is not wise to take. First of all, it is not the case that we know what to look for—this keeps changing, or rather expanding, as the science of linguistics advances. Second, even where we have a clear-cut problem to investigate, the more remote this is from superficial aspects of linguistic structure, the more crucial the native speaker's intuitions become. For some linguistic problems, I really doubt whether the traditional arrangement, in which the linguistic problem is formulated in one mind and the crucial linguistic intuitions reside in another, can work at all—or, where it appears to work, whether it can be said that the native speaker is not, in fact, functioning as a linguist. Again, I can only document this from my own experience, but in the area of syntax dealing with phenomena of pronominal reference and deletion of coreferential elements in complex sentences, to cite an example, I confess my absolute dependence on the searching introspection of a native speaker.

These two circumstances—that is, the proliferation of research problems concomitant with the growth of linguistic science and the dependency relationship between effective research and a native speaker's control of the data—conspire to create a serious problem of logistics. But the problem is greatly reduced if the linguist and the native speaker are the same individual. Since my last contact with native speakers of Walbiri (of Central Australia), for example, activity in the field of linguistics has generated literally scores of questions of relevance to the study of Walbiri syntax and semantics, but I cannot work on any of these questions because I do not have access to a native speaker's competence. What data I have relevant to more recent linguistic concerns is, to a very great extent, accidental. This would not be the case if I were a native speaker of Walbiri. While I feel it is not true that I am unable to say anything at all of interest about the structure of Walbiri, it is true that, with accidental exceptions, my knowledge of Walbiri is limited in a way which makes it impossible for me to bring Walbiri data to bear on new questions which constantly arise in the study of language universals. As matters now stand, if a fellow linguist wishes to know how Walbiri handles a phenomenon with which linguists have not previously concerned themselves, but which may have important implications for universals of language, I am, with accidental exceptions, unable to supply the information needed. I would be surprised if this were not true for most, if not all, linguists who work on languages other than their own. In any event, the degree to which it is not true surely corresponds to the degree to which the linguist's command of the language he studies approximates that of a native speaker.

Assuming that linguists can agree that the problem just outlined is a real one, it seems to me to follow that the future of such fields as American Indian and Australian Aboriginal linguistics will depend critically upon the extent to which they come to be in the hands of scholars who are native speakers of the languages involved. I do not mean to imply that linguists should cease to work on languages other than their own—I tend to agree with those who say that there are certain real advantages to being a detached observer. But a native speaker's control of linguistic data is critical (the advantages here are greater and of a different nature), and it seems to me essential to the future of the field that the state of affairs represented by present-day American Indian and Australian Aboriginal linguistics be reversed. I think that the best and most productive use to which we could put the expertise in anthropological linguistics which has developed, and is continuing to develop in anthropology and linguistics departments, would be in bringing about this reversal.

II

It is my impression in thinking about the history of anthropological linguistics, in North America at least, that the degree of involvement of native speakers in scholarship pertaining to American Indian languages was greater in the nineteenth century and in the early decades of the twentieth than it has been in recent years. This is probably more than an impression, although I cannot claim to have researched the matter thoroughly.[2] There are, of course, outstanding recent examples of linguistic scholarship by American Indians. To cite an instance with which I am particularly impressed personally (because of its value in my own current research), the collaborative efforts of William Morgan and Robert Young, the first of whom is a native speaker of Navajo, have produced a number of extremely important works, among them *The Navaho Language* (1943), which is a classic in American Indian linguistics. This example greatly strengthens the general point about the contribution of a native speaker's knowledge to the study of American Indian languages, as do other works, like Joseph Laurent's on Abnaki (1884), Pablo Tac's on Luiseño (ca. 1834, published by Carlo Tagliavini in 1926), William Jones's on Fox (1911), Ella Deloria's on Dakota (with Franz Boas, 1941), Francis La Flesche's on Osage (1932), and Edward Dozier's on Tewa (1953, and with Harry Hoijer, 1949).[3] By and large, however, the field of American Indian linguistics has developed in a direction which has effectively discouraged precisely the kind of participation which is vital to its growth. The same is true in the case of Australian Aboriginal linguistics.

The reasons for this situation are probably extremely complex, but I feel that a significant contributing factor has been the increased professionalism within the field over the past several decades. By this I mean the tendency to define in increasingly narrow ways the credentials for linguistic scholarship and severely limit the possibilities for finding careers which involve the study of language. There is really only one way in which an individual can prepare himself for a career in linguistics, and that is to obtain an advanced degree from an academic institution. This is not because the study of language, by its very nature in some vaguely understood sense, can be carried out only in the academy, but rather because of the requirement that a particular type of accreditation be obtained. This in itself is not particularly deplorable, but the fact of the matter is that one must obtain an academic degree—at least a master's but preferably a Ph.D.—whose acquisition entails running a course of obstacles which, for the most part, are absolutely irrelevant to the contribution which a gifted person could make both to the study of his language and, through that, to his community. Consider, for example, the gifted person, a native speaker of an American Indian language, who, at the age of thirty or older, and with little or no previous academic training, discovers a deep interest in and talent for the study of his language. Such a person's potential contribution to linguistics is enormous, and I see no principled reason why this person should not be enabled to obtain the strictly relevant training and to receive accreditation which would enable him or her to become involved in a career relating to the study of language. This partly hypothetical case is but one of many that one could think of; I have reason to believe that there are scores of people fitting this or a similar description known to linguists and anthropologists who study in American Indian communities; certainly it has been my experience, and that of a number of my colleagues, to meet such people constantly, in both parts of the world in which I work. But the prevailing tendency in professional linguistics has made it extremely difficult for the field to accommodate the people who could prove to be its richest and most productive resource. One might attempt to counter this argument by pointing out that there are few careers, after all, for people trained specifically for the study of their own languages. But this is the same point. The narrowing of accepted methods of accreditation which has developed as a result of the professionalism I have described has also had the effect of narrowing the range of linguistic career possibilities. Linguistics, not by its nature, but as a matter of fact, is primarily a graduate school subject. For a career involving the study of language, an undergraduate degree in linguistics is, in itself, meaningless, despite the fact that such degrees are granted and despite the fact that recipients of them are in many cases as competent as their graduate-degree counterparts. In the main, linguists are expected to receive advanced degrees and to seek employment in institutions of higher learning.

I seriously question whether this can continue much longer. The subject matter of linguistics is perhaps uniquely amenable to use in education at secondary and primary levels as a means of teaching concepts and methodology of general applicability in scientific inquiry (for example, hypothesis, explanation, empirical evidence, and the construction of supporting argument), and it seems to me entirely reasonable for linguists to explore the possibilities which this suggests for the future position of linguistics and of linguists in general education. But this is a matter of concern to linguistics generally and is somewhat off the track of the present discussion. As regards careers for native-speaking scholars of American Indian languages, for example, the fact is that there are more potential positions in the growing number of American Indian studies and bilingual education programs than there are candidates to fill them. It seems to me that what is to blame for this is the professionalism in the field of American Indian linguistics which has tended to make it the exclusive province of a particular class of people.

Professionalism has also had the effect of isolating the field of linguistics from the people, of making it increasingly difficult for linguists to see how their subject matter is in any way of potential service to the people. This problem has enormous ramifications, some of which are discussed in a recent paper by Newmeyer and Emonds (1971), and has, in some cases, caused students to leave the field after a year or so of graduate work. Linguistics has, to be sure, found application, principally in areas concerned with second-language learning, but also in other areas of education and in fields relating to health. Too often, however, linguistics has responded to the state, rather than to the people, in seeking means of application. Perhaps part of what underlies this is a feeling that the people do not understand enough about linguistics to see its potential value, in education, say. But this is a direct result of the professionalism which has tended to restrict linguistics to institutions of higher learning, the same professionalism which has made linguists themselves unclear about the relevance of their subject matter to society. There are, for example, American Indian communities which are anxious to explore the potential contribution of linguistics to their developing bilingual education programs. They are hampered far less by their own vision of the possibilities than by the unnecessary fact of the isolation of linguistics from them. These communities are addressing themselves to a problem which is extremely concrete, namely, that of ensuring that their own cultural and linguistic wealth play a prominent role in the education of their children. They recognize the importance of their languages to this effort and the importance of devising sound programs for the study of their languages in their schools. Moreover, they realize that there exists a field of inquiry which could be directly relevant to their language programs. An outstanding example of this line of thought in an American Indian community is that represented by the Diné Bi'ólta' Association, based at Chinle, Arizona, which, among other things, conducts summer workshops devoted to the development of materials and the training of teachers for the study of Navajo language and culture in elementary education. This is but one of a growing number of cases in which a community of people has defined a set of concerns which relate in obvious ways to the subject matter included here under the umbrella of anthropological linguistics.

It seems reasonable to suggest that a minimum condition for ensuring that linguistics serve the people is the removal of the barriers of professionalism which tend to separate it from them. In the case of American Indian linguistics, for example, the people who can best decide its relevance to the concerns of American Indian communities are the members of those communities. The distribution of linguistic talent and interest which is to be found in an American Indian community does not necessarily correspond in any way to the distribution of formal education in the Western sense. If this talent is to flourish and be brought to bear in helping determine the particular relevance of the study of language to the communities in which it is located, then ways must be found to enable individuals who fit such descriptions as the hypothetical one given earlier to receive training and accreditation which will enable them to devote their energies to the study of their own languages.[4]

There are a number of things which anthropological linguists could do to work in the directions vaguely suggested above. For example, it would make a great deal of sense to begin to think seriously about ways in which linguistics could be used in primary and secondary education, as a vehicle, say, for the teaching of methods of inquiry. Language is particularly well suited to this, since school-age children and young adults are in complete command of the relevant data; unlike many other sciences, most aspects of linguistics can be carried out without recourse to elaborate equipment, or even a particular physical setting. The use of linguistics in this way would not only have the effect of making linguistics more available to the people, but it would considerably expand the career possibilities for students of language; and it would establish an obvious and essential role for the local language (where that is different from the national one) in education in particular communities.[5]

It would also make sense for those of us who work in anthropological linguistics to think about and to develop means by which talented individuals, regardless of previous academic background, could receive the strictly relevant training and accreditation which would enable them to accept positions in which they could make their potential contribution to education and to linguistics. (This might be accomplished by developing special master's degree programs for, and in collaboration with, gifted individuals who are native speakers of a language whose role in education is being considered by a given community.) Those of us who are involved in teaching students to do linguistic field work might attempt to modify our courses in ways which would be productive in terms of some of the concerns expressed above. For example, instead of designing them with the exclusive purpose of training linguistics or anthropology students to obtain linguistic data from informants, we might design them more along the lines of reciprocal tutorials in which there is an exchange of competences. In the context of such a course, students with some background in linguistics might collaborate on specific linguistic problems with assistants in the course who are not only native speakers of the language(s) being studied, but also individuals interested in learning how linguists make use of primary data in constructing hypotheses about the grammar of a particular language. This idea, of course, extends naturally to field work itself. To an increasing degree, we might seek field situations in which there is an *exchange* of competences between linguists and persons interested in the study of their own languages. And this extends to our grammar-writing as well. Instead of addressing our grammatical writings to a narrow audience of professional linguists, we might write them in such a way as to make them of maximum use to native speakers of the languages involved. In fact, it would make considerable sense to compose them more or less in the form of linguistics textbooks addressed primarily to the community whose language is described. This would in no way lessen their scientific value —in fact, it would increase it by making the writings subject to the criticism of perceptive native speakers; furthermore, such writings would be of obvious use in training native speakers to work on their own languages.

In conclusion, I feel compelled to say that some of the suggestions I have made above must be considered utopian until there are fundamental changes within this society. The required redistribution of wealth, of power, and of opportunity to engage in intellectual endeavor which will enable local communities to develop their cultural resources can be achieved only under a form of socialism which seems an extremely remote possibility in a country whose government at present serves a ruling class dedicated to preventing change toward socialism over most of the world. In this is also to be found the key to a problem which is important to all sciences—namely, the problem of ensuring that knowledge is used for, rather than against, the people.

Notes

This work was supported in part by the National Institutes of Health, Grant No. MH-13390.

1. I have in mind here such people as Franz Boas, Edward Sapir, and Benjamin Whorf, of course, but I owe a special debt to those who have been involved in giving me training in anthropological linguistics: Carl Voegelin and Stanley Newman.
2. The difficulty in documenting this has to do with the fact that much current work by American Indians is not published; some is still in the form of notes. There is, for example, the work in Navajo ethnolinguistics by Kenneth Begishe in collaboration with Oswald Werner (some of which is published, e.g., Werner and Begishe, 1970); there are also Albert Alvarez's two unpublished papers (1969a, b), briefly anticipated in Alvarez and Hale (1970); there is Gordon Francis (1971); and in general, it is probable that the amount of unpublished work, both early and recent, is quite extensive. The work on Papago, largely textual, by Juan Dolores, for example, is still largely unpublished (but cf. Dolores, 1913, 1923). For Australia, there is the work of Ephraim Bani on Mabuiag in collaboration with Terry Klokeid during the summer of 1970, and more recently by correspondence. These notes have been assembled under the title "Papers on the Western Island Language of Torres Strait" (Bani and Klokeid, 1971).
3. Although Francis La Flesche was Omaha rather than Osage, the closeness of the two languages made it inevitable that his native command of Omaha contribute to his work. It is important to keep in mind also the contribution of informants, often unsung, who have contributed an enormous amount to American Indian

linguistic scholarship. An example is Alex Thomas, whose contribution to Sapir's work on Nootka is eloquently described by Sapir in his famous paper "The Psychological Reality of Phonemes" (Mandelbaum, 1949, pp. 46–60).

4. Included among people who should be accommodated in this way are those who, in one way or another, have trained themselves in areas of linguistic scholarship—for example, informants who have learned by observation; and so-called amateurs, who have learned through reading or through practice or both.

5. S. J. Keyser has recently discussed the use of linguistics in the elementary school curriculum in an important paper (Keyser, 1970), and I have attempted to discuss ways in which Navajo linguistics might be used in bilingual education in the Navajo community in Hale (1970).

References

Alvarez, Albert, 1969a. " 'Ó'dham Ñé'okĭ ha-Káidag" [The Sounds of Papago]. Unpublished.

———. 1969b. " 'Ó'odham Ñé'okĭ ha-Cé'idag" [The Expressions of Papago]. Unpublished.

Alvarez, Albert, and Kenneth Hale. 1970. "Toward a Manual of Papago Grammar: Some Phonological Terms." *International Journal of American Linguistics* 36: 83–97.

Bani, Ephraim, and Terry Klokeid. 1971. "Papers on the Western Island Language of Torres Strait." Unpublished.

Boas, Franz, and Ella Deloria. 1941. *Dakota Grammar*. National Academy of Sciences Memoirs, Vol. 23, Part 2. Washington, D.C. Pp. 1–183.

Dolores, Juan. 1913. *Papago Verb Stems*. University of California Publications in American Anthropology and Ethnology, Vol. 10. Berkeley, Calif. Pp. 241–63.

———. 1923. *Papago Nominal·Stems*. University of California Publications in American Anthropology and Ethnology, Vol. 20. Berkeley, Calif. Pp. 17–32.

Dozier, Edward. 1953. "Tewa II: Verb Structure." *International Journal of American Linguistics* 19: 118–27.

Francis, Gordon. 1971. "Mīgëmeöeöôgemg: Ingōtj Amsgöeseöei" [Speaking Micmac: Part 1]. Unpublished.

Gough, Kathleen. 1968. "Anthropology: Child of Imperialism." *Monthly Review* 19, No. 11: 12–27.

Hale, Kenneth. 1969. "American Indians in Linguistics." *Indian Historian* 12, No. 2: 15–18, 28.

———. 1970. *"Navajo Linguistics I, II, III."* Unpublished.

————. 1972. "A New Perspective on American Indian Linguistics and Some Comments Relative to the Pueblos." In *New Perspectives on the Pueblos,* ed. Alfonso Ortiz. Albequerque: University of New Mexico Press. Pp. 87–133.

Hoijer, Harry, and Edward Dozier. 1949. "The Phonemes of Tewa, Santa Clara Dialect." *International Journal of American Linguistics* 15: 139–44.

Jones, William. 1911. "Algonquian (Fox)." In *Handbook of American Indian Languages,* ed. Franz Boas. Bureau of American Ethnology Bulletin No. 40. Washington, D.C. Pp. 753–874.

Keyser, Samuel Jay. 1970. "The Role of Linguistics in the Elementary School Curriculum." *Elementary English* 47: 39–45.

La Flesche, Francis. 1932. *A Dictionary of the Osage Language.* Bureau of American Ethnology Bulletin 109. Washington, D.C.

Laurent, Joseph. 1884. *New Familiar Abnakis and English Dialogues.* Quebec.

Mandelbaum, David, ed. 1949. *Selected Writings of Edward Sapir in Language, Culture, and Personality.* Berkeley: University of California Press.

Newmeyer, Frederick, and Joseph Emonds. 1971. "The Linguist in American Society." Papers from the 7th Regional Meeting of the Chicago Linguistic Society.

Tagliavini, Carlo. 1926. "La Lingua degli indi Luiseños." Biblioteca de l'Archiginnasio, Bologna, Ser. II, No. xxxi: 1–55.

Werner, Oswald, and Kenneth Begishe. 1970. "A Lexemic Typology of Navajo Anatomical Terms I: The Foot." *International Journal of American Linguistics* 36: 247–65.

Young, Robert, and William Morgan. 1943. *The Navaho Language.* Education Division, United States Indian Service, Phoenix, Ariz.

VI · The Root Is Man: Critical Traditions

Anthropology in Question
Stanley Diamond

In a sense, by dint of studying man, we . . . have made ourselves incapable of knowing him.

—*Jean-Jacques Rousseau*

ANTHROPOLOGY, reified as the study of man, is the study of men in crisis by men in crisis. Anthropologists and their objects, the studied, despite opposing positions in the "scientific" equation, have this much in common: they are both, if not equally, objects of contemporary, imperial civilization. The anthropologist who treats the indigene as an object may define himself as relatively free and integrated, a subject, a person, but that is an illusion. In order to objectify the other, one is, at the same time, compelled to objectify the self. On this score, the anthropologist betrays himself as inevitably as he does the native whom he examines. Therefore, when Lévi-Strauss, whom I take to be the most representative and, at the same time, the most elusive of contemporary anthropologists, argues that, as the offspring of colonialism, "anthropology . . . reflects, on the epistemological level, a state of affairs in which one part of mankind treats the other as an object," he tells us only half the truth. The other half is critical, for the anthropologist is himself a victim, and his power of decision is a fiction, embedded as it is in the exploitative foundations of civilization. Edmund Carpenter relates a case in point: the presumed results of an official experiment in communication to which he lent himself in Australian New Guinea.[1] Although questioning the ethic of the undertaking, he argues that the disorganization, indeed the destruction, of the village culture under systematic electronic assault (tape recordings, film, and so on) which his team initiated could be justified only by the knowledge gained of analogous processes in our (the colonizing) society.

Unless the anthropologist confronts his own alienation, which is only a special instance of a general condition, and seeks to understand its roots, and subsequently matures as a relentless critic of his own civilization, the very civilization which objectifies man, he cannot understand or even recognize himself in the other or the other in himself. Thus when Lévi-Strauss finally insists, with an admirable consistency many who share his views fail to achieve, that as an anthropologist he cannot invidiously compare societies, that to assume the legitimacy of one is to legitimate all (Lévi-Strauss, 1961, pp. 384 ff.), he does so as a perfectly abstract relativist, a natural scientist of man. This implies an absolute suspension of what our society dissociatively calls values and all serious reflection or action that might be consequent on such values. Put another way, values become aspects or phases of a cultural paradigm or code: they have no normative implication beyond their position in a syntactical field. This "privileged" situation of the anthropologist is, in fact, the quintessence of alienation. For he must behave *as if* he had no judgment, *as if* his experience were inconsequential, *as if* he denied history, *as if* the contradictions between his origins and his vocation did not exist. Moreover, he will imagine that he has no politics and he will consider that a virtue. One is reminded of Ruth Benedict's argument that if our society created unemployment, it was only logical to assume that the unemployed should be treated with diginity, or, analogously, that under colonial conditions the British did better with proud people, and the Dutch with those who were more accustomed to humiliation. Therefore, a reshuffling of sovereignties was theoretically in order. In this admittedly banal example, which has not yet developed into scientific relativism, symmetry of values, the logical structure of the cultural code, is nonetheless the paramount consideration, the meta-value of the relativistic professional.

He may know better, but he may not admit to knowing better as an anthropologist.

The split between the person and the professional reaches the limits of irony in the study of man. It is, of course, prefigured in military and civilian bureaucracies; in the organization of the state itself, wherein the person assimilates to a single status personality, with a rationalizing "professional" ethic, the ethic of conquest, always at hand. Such a "professional" anthropologist is an alien, although, and perhaps because, he claims the whole of the Western tradition for his ancestry. Claiming everything, he is in danger of being nothing. Indeed, he is estranged three times over: first, in his own society, along with the generality of his fellow citizens; secondly, in the choice of his profession; and finally, in relation to those he studies.

Such an anthropologist must sooner or later define himself, with Lévi-Strauss (1961, p. 397), as an "entropologist" and rest on the prediction of the ultimate thermodynamic leveling of all cultural structures, sinking back without a trace into the flux of matter. If the possibility of self-knowledge is denied by the anthropologist as the goal of his inquiry, as Lévi-Strauss does in response to Ricoeur, then the structures or forms, of which history is merely an aspect, become repetitive ends in themselves and remain entropic. This denial of self-knowledge by Lévi-Strauss, most evident in his confrontation with Ricoeur and others at a symposium organized by *L'Esprit* in 1963 (cited from Lévi-Strauss, 1970), is worth examining because it defines scientism in its ethnological form and at the same time almost succeeds as an abstract and objective, relativistic statement.

OBJECTIFICATION

On two occasions during the round-table discussion Ricoeur asks: "But if I do not understand myself better by understanding [primitive peoples], can I still talk of meaning? If meaning is not a sector of self-understanding, I do not know what it is."

The first time, Levi-Strauss replies: "In my perspective, meaning is never the primary phenomenon: meaning is always reducible. In other words, behind all meaning there is a non-meaning, while the reverse is not the case. As far as I am concerned, significance is always phenomenal."[2]

The second time, Lévi-Strauss replies: "I find it quite legitimate that a philosopher who poses the problem in terms of the person should raise this objection, but I am not obliged to follow suit. What do I understand by meaning? A particular flavor perceived by a consciousness when it tastes a combination of elements of which any one taken alone would not produce a comparable flavor. . . . The ethnologist tries to recover the meaning . . . to reconstitute the meaning . . . by mechanical means; he constructs it, unwraps it, and then after all he is a man, so he tastes it."

Later on, Lévi-Strauss, in response to Jean Lautman's remark "I should like to return to the question of meaning," elaborates: "I am trying to make an analysis of man. . . . This undertaking is to find out how the human mind functions. . . . I have a feeling that the ethnologist does the same thing for collective ensembles that the psychoanalyst does for individuals [with reference to the theory of the mind, not therapeutic praxis]. . . . *I do not believe that the self-analysis undertaken by the mind will improve it; I am completely indifferent as to whether it improves it or no. What interests me is to find out how it works, and that is all.*"

But questions remain. Jean Conilh asks: "I wonder if this problem you have raised is not the following: Each time we attempt an interpretation of savages, is this not always ultimately a way of finding a meaning for them so as to understand ourselves? . . . Is our problem to classify or to find a meaning?"

Lévi-Strauss answers: "To be sure I think that one of the reasons for the attraction ethnology exercises even on non-professionals is that its inquiries have powerful motivations within the heart of our society, interpreting as they do a number of our society's dramas. . . . We ought to recognize that, whether we are ethnologists or merely interested in ethnology, it is for *scientifically impure reasons*. . . . Nevertheless, if ethnology is to deserve recognition some day for its role in the constitution of the human sciences, it will be for other reasons."

The anthropologist implies, in other words, that structuralism, or whatever the name of the contribution ethnology is destined to make to the understanding of mind, is a higher and deeper truth, on the analogy of Freudian psychodynamics, in contrast to psychoanalytic praxis. It is just here that the relativism of Lévi-Strauss breaks down in the espousal of an objective, objectifying, and scientific conceptualism, a conceptualism, moreover, which is, and must be, literally useless; "its importance . . . depends on results whose interest lies on another plane." In this admission, Lévi-Strauss reveals himself as a partisan of the unique theoretical superiority of an immaculately abstract and analytic logical-deductive science of the ultimate forms of reality, which has reached its zenith in Western civilization.[3] Although he refuses to locate himself in any particular philosophic tradition, he has, in fact, become a mediator of final concepts. Alexandre Koyré has precisely situated the origins of that perspective in Plato, that is, in a point of view emerging fully at a certain juncture in the history of our civilization, coincident with the rise of the academy. This meta-value of Lévi-Strauss is, then, academic and ethnocentric.

Despite his intricate concern with the meaning and operation of symbols, Lévi-Strauss stops at the "reality" of structuralist and psychodynamic theory. He fails to consider, for example, that Freud's theory of the mind is one of many possible complementary "explanations" for phenomenal experience; or that it may, perhaps, be taken as a genetic metaphor. It is, therefore, clear that to the paradoxical degree that Lévi-Strauss can be considered a phenomenologist ("significance is always phenomenal") it would have to be in the conceptual vein of Husserl, certainly not in the existential perspective of Merleau-Ponty. Moreover, the only conceivable, but by no means inevitable, proof of psychodynamic theory is in its instrumentation, that is, in psychoanalysis, the latter being the origin of, while remaining dialectically in touch with, the "higher" conceptual effort. More to the point, no scientific concept outlives consistent counterindicative application; and, one should add, the concept divorced from application, as in the instance of Einstein's Unified Field Theory, is an aesthetic curiosity, a deficient category of myth. The history of Western civilization is, after all, littered with dead scientific concepts. It is ironic that Lévi-Strauss understands so well on the one hand the presence of technology in the absence of scientific systems in primitive societies, while insisting on the ultimate superiority of such systems on the other, despite the historicity of the concepts they generate. In any event, it is clear that his concern is to discover no less than the "true" nature of "minding," which, in his idiom, implies an ambition to understand the final character of the human universe. It is equally clear that he believes an inevitable requirement for such understanding is objectification, and that the resultant knowledge is superior to that which all other types of cognition provide us with.

But objectification is a mental operation least of all. Objectification on the scale which concerns us evolves with civilization itself; it is an ensemble of processes—a political process involving the legal subordination and definition of the person within the state; a social process coincident with the elaborate division of labor and the rise and conflict of classes; a psychological process through which the civilized consciousness becomes alienated from labor, nature, society as a whole. Correlatively, objectification finds its intellectual analogue in the analytic-abstract modality of thought which, reflecting further on itself, emerges in one form as "structuralism." We should also bear in mind that Lévi-Strauss is not interested in technology as such, which modern science is to some extent associated with; he is, rather, concerned with a pure principle of understanding, a principle he has succeeded in detaching from both its origins and its social or technical functions. He wishes, it seems, to be a mathematician, whose integers are necessarily devoid of content, of meaning. Jean Conilh intimates this when, during the course of the *L'Esprit* confrontation, he says: "Have you not constituted a philosophy and a philosophy of our time? . . . In that case, I can reject this philosophy and go back to primitive mentality, reading it on another level, the level of symbols, for example, and find a new meaning for it."

But Lévi-Strauss does not interpret objectification as alienation, even though he tells us that "anthropology is the daughter of this era of [colonial] violence." On the contrary, he contends (1966, p. 126) that the "state of affairs in which one part of mankind treats the other as an object" makes it possible *"to assess more objectively the facts pertaining to the human condition."* Therefore, one must conclude that *as an anthropologist* Lévi-Strauss has no important argument to launch against the imperialism that he describes, nor against the condition of his own society; as a matter of fact, as a highly trained member of that society, he is obliged to confess that his understanding of "reality" has been furthered; for him objectification is, above all, a purely mental operation. Ricoeur, who, one imagines, could hardly agree with this implicit assessment, terminates his response to Lévi-Strauss as follows: "As far as you are concerned, there is no 'message': not in the cybernetic but in the kerygmatic sense; you despair of meaning; but you console yourself with the thought that if men have nothing to say, at least they say it so well that their discourse is amenable to structuralism. You retain meaning, but it is the meaning of nonmeaning. The admirable, syntactic arrangement of a discourse which has nothing to say."

The key to Lévi-Strauss's "meaninglessness" is, I believe, in his rejection of self-knowledge, which is in turn the root paradox of modern anthropology. If self-knowledge is irrelevant, so is self-criticism. Indeed, the latter is impossible in the absence of the former. Moreover, both self-knowledge and self-criticism are meaningless in the absence of a normative sense of human nature, which Lévi-Strauss's radical relativism and formalism inevitably contradict. His relativism breaks down, as we have seen, with reference to his own professional task, or perhaps we are obliged to say, more specifically, that his relativism is that of the quintessentially scientific observer and is not a naive cultural relativism. His formalism constricts the human enterprise within an ethnologically derived cultural unconscious, a finite set of universal functions which generate a variety of thinly disguised formal analogues, but there is no real possibility of novelty, volition, substance, synthesis. Lévi-Strauss's complementary oppositions, around which he chooses to organize his ethnographic data, do not permit of synthesis (not to speak of transcendence), and therefore they do not permit of growth, that is, they are not immediately apprehended human ambivalences. It is hard to decide whether so high-pitched a determinism is rooted in a theory of human nature or culture. What is more likely is that we have been presented with a closed hypothesis concerning the nature of culture that is reducible to a dogma concerning the nature of mind. It is equally hard to decide whether Lévi-Strauss is a pure natural scientist or the cold poet of a formalist aesthetic, until one realizes that in his work, more clearly than in that of any thinker of our time, the two visions are shown to be identical. But above all, it is important to recognize the determinism, the negation of history as a human possibility.[4]

Criticism of self or other, of our society or theirs, depends on the definition of human needs, limits, and possibilities arrived at through the constant effort to grasp the meaning of the historical experiences of men. In this anthropological "experiment," which we initiate, it is not they who are the ultimate objects, but ourselves. We study men, that is, we reflect on ourselves studying others, because we must, because man in civilization is the problem. Primitive peoples do not study man; it is not necessary, the subject is given; they say this or that about behavior (who has not been impressed by the wisdom of his informants?); they engage in ritual, they celebrate, but they do not characteristically objectify. We, on the contrary, are engaged in a complex dialectic involving the search for the subject in history as the precondition for a minimal definition of humanity, and, therefore, of self-knowledge as the ground for self-criticism. This dialectic bases itself on certain questions which we bring to history out of the experience of our own need. The task of anthropology is, first of all, to clarify these questions.

THE ENLIGHTENMENT
HERITAGE: ROUSSEAU

Jean Conilh touches upon the problem as follows: "In the eighteenth century we find writers discussing the Good Savage in relation to the questions they were asking about themselves. In the bourgeois colonialist epoch we find a conception of the primitive which presents them as inferior."

Manifestly, these two contrasting views, which are more or less accurately stated, would seem to be merely rationalizations of the interests of the respective pre- and postrevolutionary societies. Certainly, nothing could be clearer than that imperialism was the source of the idea of the inferior savage (cf. Curtin, 1964). But further reflection leads us to a deeper assumption, namely, that in the nineteenth century, the period of bourgeois political and class consolidation within the Euro-American sphere, the very image of man was progressively degraded, and *that* was reflected in the shift in conceptions of the primitive. Put another way, the distrust and suspicion of human nature, the mark of the nineteenth-century bourgeoisie, that basic distrust and repression of themselves, were expressed as anthropological assumptions. The latter, then, were, as always, assumptions about man in general, projected about primitive men, *those others.*

There is a further nuance in the dialectic between the eighteenth-century Good Savage and the nineteenth-century notion of inferiority. Just as, in the nineteenth century, the social organization and techniques of modern industrial capitalism emerge as a world force, so the idea of inevitable progress in the name of science becomes a fixed ideology. The revolutions having succeeded and then, quite obviously, having failed in their social promise, it appears as if all the frustrated passion was mobilized behind the idea of a regnant science. This, in turn, had been foreshadowed in the high expectations, the excitement concerning the future of science so evident in the eighteenth century. But there are very important distinctions. For the eighteenth century, science was to incarnate the spirit of reason (celebrated by the poets), and the vision of the scientific society was utopian, a vision that Saint-Simon and others later tried to realize. Moreover, the celebration of the rational was balanced by a bitter and sophisticated critique of actual social conditions on the one hand, and the sense of the indivisibility of existence, in its aesthetic, sensuous, and rational dimensions, on the other.

In the eighteenth century men can still be rediscovered; mankind is an open system. The great questions concerning the nature of man and culture are being reformulated; it is the axial episode in the modern consciousness. The Good Savage, synonymous with the natural man, was both a historical definition and the ground for the reconstitution (or perfectibility) of man. Rousseau asks: "What experiment would be necessary to achieve knowledge of natural man? What are the means of making these experiments in the midst of society?" He charges: "For the three hundred or four hundred years since the inhabitants of Europe have inundated the other parts of the world, and continuously published new collections of voyages and reports, I am convinced that we know no other men except the Europeans. . . .

Under *the pompous name of the study of man,* everyone
does hardly anything except study the men of his country"
([1750] 1964, p. 114). Rousseau calls for a proper anthropology, the purpose of which is self-knowledge, and the
means, the authentic understanding of others. As a representative of his time, he is interested in a critical and revolutionary discipline. And if one examines the methods and
conclusions of Rousseau, it is possible to understand the
ground of this fruitful and perennial ethnological habit of
concern with the primitive-civilized dichotomy.

Rousseau was concerned with two complementary tasks.
On the one hand, he was engaged in a journey to the center
of the species, in order to understand the "natural" pre-
civilized man as a human possibility. He situated that possibility in prehistory and viewed certain realities in modern
civilization, with which we have become all too familiar, as
a threat to its further realization. On the other hand, he was
engaged in a journey to the center of his own civilized being.
The first task was historical, the second personal, and they
are of course, related. With reference to the former, he
projected a model of primitive society, incorporating limited
data, in quite the way contemporary anthropologists do. He
called, as did Marx later, for a much wider exploration of
the lives of primitive people than had hitherto been possible,
in order to discover "the real foundations of human society."
He was fully aware of the difficulties involved: "It is no
light undertaking to separate what is original from what is
artificial in the nature of man. And to know correctly a state
which no longer exists, which perhaps never existed, which
probably never will exist, and about which it is nevertheless
necessary to have precise notions in order to judge our
present state correctly" (Rousseau, [1750] 1964, p. 93).

What are we to make of this typical Rousseauan paradox?
Rousseau is here, to use our jargon, laying down a rule for
the construction of a model with a normative and comparative intention. At the same time, he consistently refers to
the surprisingly wide range of information available to him,

and he evaluates it in the perspective of the civilized predicament, about which he has incontestable data, and in which he himself is a datum, but not a passive vehicle. He has no illusions about the possibility of a perfectly objective portrait of primitive man, because he clearly recognizes that that portrait must be, on the one hand, the result of his own questions, and on the other, the result of his own introspection. Although Cassirer, among others, is disturbed by the apparent disparity between Rousseau's recourse to data and the projection of a qualitative model, this turns out to be no less than the inevitable method of anthropology.

Rousseau, then, utilizes data, constructs a model, and assumes a logical and historical complementarity between himself, as a prototypical modern man, and the primitive peoples with whom he is concerned. Need it be repeated that he never uses the expression "noble savage"? Along with Morgan and Marx, he sees the deep past as prologue; nor did he ever suggest or imagine the possibility of turning back history. The latter was a charge, as he put it, in the manner of his adversaries, and hardly worth a response. His impulse to understand primitive people is the other side of the impulse to understand the largely unexperienced, but imagined, possibilities of himself as a civilized person. This attempted synthesis, which embraces data, the construction of a model, introspection in the service of self-knowledge, which in turn clarifies further what one is observing, is the first lucid expression, and among the last, of what anthropologists do or should do.

Rousseau, while explaining to us how he arrived at it and what its function is, establishes the primitive-civilized paradigm in modern anthropology, but he did not invent it. Its history is rooted in the history of civilization, but tracing it would be an exercise in an almost infinite regression. One would eventually arrive at that hypothetical point where man in civilization asks the question (in whatever symbolic form): Who am I? And since contrast is the only mode of seeing, he conceives himself against the background of what he assumes himself to have been, in the hope of what he may one day become.

The second aspect of Rousseau's understanding is evident in his *Confessions*. They are among the most enduring revelations of a fully conscious, perhaps the first, modern man. Rousseau strips himself to the bone. And once again he is less interested in the precise sequence or retailing of events than he is in their meaning. He is not a diarist. When his critics accuse him of misrepresentation, they misunderstand the convoluted problems of memory and construction of self, the issue of truth which transcends the presentation of facts. Any confession, like any attempt at ethnology, has in short, to be a fiction, a constitution of reality.

Interestingly enough, anthropologists have frequently attempted these personal and confessional statements, which inevitably deal with the confrontation of self in relation to the people being studied. Among social scientists, such memoirs are, in fact, peculiar to anthropologists. It would seem that anthropologists, no matter how they protest as professionals, maintain their concern with the definition of man.

THE NINETEENTH-CENTURY HERITAGE: MARX

In the nineteenth century, on the other hand, the concept of the primitive no longer implies the search for the "natural" man. In the hardening scientific perspective, primitive characteristics are regarded as remote in time and space; they are at the base of the evolution toward civilization; and civilization has been identified as a unilinear, inevitably progressive movement. Although doubts are evident, for example, in the work of Morgan and Tylor, the secular trend is conceived to be from the inferior to the superior. This investment in the notion of progress in the nineteenth century was the beneficent aspect of a morbid process, which can be epitomized as the conquest of nature—including human nature. Imperialism was a political manifestation of the struggle against nature and man, associated with the notion of the inevitable superiority of Western civilization; the means at hand for conquering primitive and archaic peoples helped rationalize the scientific perspective in which they were viewed as inferior. Coincidentally, the spirit of reason, the scientific utopianism of the eighteenth century, was transformed into functional, or, better, reductive rationality, evident, ideally, in the mechanisms of the market, and embedded in the apparatus of industrial capitalism. The arena for rationalization becomes the whole of human existence; as reason is reduced to rationality, the aesthetic and sensuous aspects of the person are repressed, that is, they are brutalized or sentimentalized. The "performance principle" develops in antagonism to human nature or, rather, constricts the definition of human possibilities.

Even revolutionaries do not escape, they are, after all, shaped by the forces they seek to transcend. Marx, for example, abandoned the scientific utopianism of the eighteenth century, though he acknowledged his indebtedness; he was obliged to take into account, while accounting for, nineteenth-century capitalism both in its domestic and foreign manifestations. Accordingly, the early Marx justified imperialism as being "objectively" progressive; only thus could the frozen structures of archaic civilizations be broken down, and progress become possible. He was to give up this view, which remains the classic rationalization for colonialism, although he never developed any coherent alternative. Similarly, Marx shifted his opinion on the question of Irish liberation. Originally, he was opposed to that movement, because he assumed that the potential solidarity of the British working class and the impoverished Irish could be more important strategically, and more significant historically, than the national question. He changed his mind in later years on the ground that Irish independence would deprive the English establishment of a diversionary tactic and force the English proletariat to express their frustrations against their own ruling class. In each instance—that of imperialism and that of the Irish question—Marx objectified, first with reference to the totality of non-European peoples and then with reference to Irish peasants; and he did so in the language of an abstract, world historical process.

But he displayed no such ambivalence about his own society. Marx anticipated and worked toward a revolution which, he assumed, could occur under the social and material conditions of nineteenth-century capitalism. He did not counsel patience or call upon the workers to await the inception of a more advanced technology. Indeed, as Venable asserts (1945, pp. 151–71), he defined patience as utopian, that is, he did not subordinate what he conceived to be the interests of the European proletariat to any other class or population anywhere in the world. The European proletariat, who had reached the extremity of alienation, were the cutting edge of the world historical process; their actions were the precondition for the freedom of all. Marx, of course, was the seminal theorist of alienation; he understood the human predicament in modern society, and he undoubtedly believed that the social situation which gave rise to it had to be fought through on its own terms, and that any other course would be evasive. His enthusiasm and strangely unreal hopes for the momentary fraternity of the Paris Commune indicate his frustration about the ordinarily alienated character of revolutionary imperatives. Still, in centering on "progressive" Europe, Marx was certainly a man of his time.

Indeed, the most fruitful of the Marxist terms of reference derive from the time. More generally, they relate to "history," that is, in the Marxist lexicon, to civilization. Prehistory, the period of primitive, classless, communal society, and the posthistorical societies, which have presumably freed themselves of alienation, are hardly subject to conventional Marxist analysis. The historical materialist terms of reference, which find their object with the emergence of class and state, with civil society, as Marx identifies the context, and grow more cogent as such societies mature and harden, reflect the conditions of civilization. This is what Rudi Supek, the Yugoslavian sociologist, seems to imply when he writes (1971, p. 39): "Marx's well known statement . . . namely that 'the methods of production of material life condition the process of social, political, and intellectual life in general' is valid only for a firmly structured society with highly developed material production." It follows, therefore, that only in primitive societies can we begin to understand the full potential of the human generic-symbolic capacity.

The extreme division of labor, which dissociates man from himself, the reduction of persons to limited functions situated in classes, and the splitting of the cultural universe into antagonistic economic, social, and ideological sectors are, first of all, real events, and only then do they become analytic categories. Marx emphasized time and again that he was describing, not fantasizing, history. He was not a system-builder, nor can Marxism be turned into a theory of material limitations. If it can be epitomized at all, it is as a theory of social, hence political, constraints on material possibilities. It is, therefore, dialectic in method and must be distinguished from all types of reductive materialism or technological determinism.

To put it another way, Marx recognized the disjunction between available technology and the maximum social use of technology in civilization, as well as the competing economic interests generated by that state of affairs. That is, Marxism is based on the social process of exploitation in terms of class conflict; the question of class consciousness becomes the critical political question. Therefore, Marxists view conventional politics as a screen for economic interests and the economic factor as relatively invariant over the long term. But as Supek points out (1971, p. 39), "Marx, in fact, does not mean that the method of material production conditions the contents but 'the process' of social, political, and intellectual life."

Marxists do not, for example, "reduce" art when they seek to relate the aesthetic process to social and economic constraints; nor do they deny that the artist may "rise above his time." As dialecticians, it would indeed be awkward for them to deny that. The Marxist point is that art is not merely an epiphenomenon on an economic base but a creation which reflects its social limitations, although it can be, like other ideological factors—revolutionary theory and certain aspects of religion—symbolically transcendent. Nonetheless, it is only when men *act* politically, not only through aesthetic and religious symbols, to change the economic basis of their lives in accord with their "truly human" interests that they may begin to make history. It is at this latter juncture that the analytic categories of Marxism, derived from the actual history of civilization, are avowedly negated by its goal—a classless communitarian society. For it is anticipated that in such a society labor will become socially reintegrated, and the primacy of economic interests will diminish, along with the class conflicts they generate; such conflicts will no longer serve as the motivating force in history. Hence in projected communist societies, with the reintegration of labor, the person can be redefined as an indivisible unity of aesthetic, rational, and sensuous components. Analogously, where economic, social, and ideological sectors of culture have been reintegrated, causal analyses, which arise as a result of intolerable disjunctions, such as that between mental and manual labor, become irrelevant. Thus, analytic, objectifying social science will lose its foundation and its function. Even historical materialism was, of course, not conceived as a contribution to academic social science; it was supposed to sharpen its wits in praxis and lose itself in revolutionary success.

In this emphasis on praxis, Marx is very close to Rousseau, who had stated, "Man is not made to meditate, but to act" (Peyre, 1963, p. 105). Rousseau's meditations were, of course, in their relentless, pertinent self-examination, *acts*. For Rousseau, "theory and practice, thought and life, the abstract and the concrete [could not be divorced]" (Peyre, 1963, p. 105). Moreover, in propounding a theory of society most in accord with the possibilities of human nature, the *natural society*, to which, he imagined, all history is tending, Marx extends and completes the tradition of Rousseau. If Rousseau is, in his reach, the paradigmatic thinker of the eighteenth century ("With Rousseau," asserts Goethe, "a new world begins"), Marx plays that role in the nineteenth. He is, so to speak, the Rousseau of the postrevolutionary period of bourgeois class consolidation, but he also conceives himself as living in a revolutionary interim. And he has absorbed most of what is useful in the evolutionary theories of his time. He lives at a time in which Rousseau's (or for that matter, Herder's) worst intimations of the future have been realized.

It is hard to conceive a Marx without a Rousseau; between them, they have constructed an astonishing critique of the origins and fate of the modern consciousness. They are both familiar with the paradoxes of history and they represent a critical tradition which binds their two centuries together. Their differences reveal precisely the discontinuities in their respective periods; indeed, their differences may be said to delineate these periods. Marx, as I have tried to show, is substantially committed to Europe; he faces the juggernaut squarely; and he imagines it transformed through its structural contradictions, understood and acted on politically. Europe is the key to the future, and for most of his life he seemed convinced that progress, despite drawbacks, had occurred in history. Progress is no longer just an eighteenth-century projection; it is for Marx, and for Engels also, a reality. Rousseau, on the other hand, was, from the beginning, alive to the human possibilities that he sensed in the primitive cultures that Europeans had been systematically destroying for the sake of progress and profit. Rousseau believed in the perfectibility of man, but he was profoundly skeptical of the European argument for progress.

The categories of Marxism, then, delineate the realm of alienated history; they are not intended to reveal the details of a liberated, classless society, but only to outline its general character, and, of course, to pronounce on its necessity and desirability. It follows that Marxism provides us with the impulse, but not the means, for understanding the primitive, classless (gentile) cultures of the past. Marx and Engels both borrowed from and converged to Morgan on that score, but their purpose was to chart the *prehistoric evolution of society toward the state.* Primitive cultures were for them the ground of all future historical movement. Moreover, Marx indicated that they *served as the paradigm for the idea of socialism.* "Socialism," said Marx, "would achieve 'that which men had always dreamed about'" (Supek, 1971, p. 32). But primitive cultures are not approached on their own terms, although Engels can be euphoric.[5]

Nonetheless, it would seem that nineteenth-century progressivism inhibited Marx and Engels from a further inquiry into the actual conditions of primitive culture. Marxism did not generate an ethnology, but a critical and revolutionary analysis of civilization, particularly of modern capitalism, based upon the fundamental questions asked of their own time and place.

It is important to realize, however, following Hobsbawm, that there is a precedent in Marx for an anthropology that shares the eighteenth-century vision of the human potential.

It is certain that Marx's own historical interests after the publication of *Capital* (around 1867) were overwhelmingly concerned with [primitive communalism]. . . . [a reason for] Marx's increasing preoccupation with primitive communalism [was] his growing hatred and contempt for capitalist society. . . . it seems probable that he, who had earlier welcomed the impact of Western capitalism as an inhuman but historically progressive force on stagnant precapitalist economies, found himself increasingly appalled by this inhumanity. We know that he has always admired the positive social values embodied, in however backward a form, in the primitive com-

munity, and it is certain that after 1857–8 . . . he increasingly
stressed the viability of the primitive commune, its powers
of resistance to historical disintegration, and even—though
perhaps only in the context of the Narodniki—discussed its
capacity to develop into a higher form of economy without
prior destruction. (Hobsbawm, 1965, pp. 49 ff.)

But this is not to say that the result was a systematic
ethnology. It does, however, imply that the primitive-
civilized paradigm central to the eighteenth century increasingly commanded the attention of Marx, who, in this
sense also, extends and completes the tradition of Rousseau.[6]

A TWENTIETH-CENTURY
OUTCOME: RELATIVISM

The ethnocentric and abstract progressivism of the nineteenth century preadapts anthropology for the uses to which
it is put in the twentieth, the period in which the study of
man becomes rationalized as an academic discipline and
as a way of life for anthropologists. Amateurism evaporates;
the tradition of Rousseau and Marx is not furthered, it is
either misunderstood or abandoned; and the study of man
lends itself to the manipulation of peoples in the very
course of observing them. This is the case not only politically
but intellectually; that is, trivial questions are frequently
asked as part of the price exacted in the search for disciplinary position and academic reward.

At the same time, relativism emerges as the dominant
theme in twentieth-century anthropology and seeks to redress nineteenth-century ethnocentrism with specific reference to the allied notions of progress and the presumed
inferiority of primitive peoples. Therefore, one finds that
evolutionists can be relativists, social anthropologists associated with the British Colonial Office can be relativists, em-
piricists can be relativists, and so on. Relativism is, at its

best, a liberal response to, and a "humane" mediation of, whatever society seems viable in the eye or imagination of the anthropologist. But at its worst, relativism proves popular not only because of its corrective role in the profession of anthropology; it is in accord with the spirit of the time, a perspective congenial in an imperial civilization convinced of its power. Every primitive or archaic culture is conceived as a human possibility that can be "tasted"; it is, after all, harmless. We, at our leisure, convert the experience of other cultures into a kind of sport, just as Veblen's modern hunter mimics and trivializes what was once a way of life. Relativism is the bad faith of the conqueror, who has become secure enough to become a tourist.

Academic relativism knits together anthropologists of diverse "schools." Boas, and those whom he trained, for example, establish (and it is a brilliant achievement) that there are no inferior cultures, races, or languages; and correlatively, that races, languages, and cultures are historically, not functionally, related. They strive to appreciate and understand cultural diversity.

But this twentieth-century abreaction is caught in contradictions from which it cannot escape. Cultural relativism is a purely intellectual attitude; it does not inhibit the anthropologist from participating as a professional in his own milieu; on the contrary, it rationalizes that milieu. Relativism, logically pursued, is self-critical only in the abstract. It does not engage the anthropologist, but rather converts him into a shadowy figure, prone to newsworthy and shallow pronouncements about the cosmic condition of the human race. It does, however, have the effect of mystifying the profession, so that the very term "anthropologist," *student of man,* commands the attention of an increasingly "popular" audience in search of novelty. But the search for self-knowledge, which Montaigne was the first to link to the annihilation of prejudice, is reduced to the experience of culture shock, a phrase used by both anthropologists and the State Department to account for the disorientation that usually follows an encounter with an alien way of life. But culture shock is a condition that one recovers from; it is not experienced as an authentic redefinition of the personality, but as a testing of its tolerance. These experiences have also been compared to psychotherapeutic encounters, and here again the focus of attention is the career of the anthropologist, that hero/heroine of our time, and the goal is the integrity of his professional function, clincially defined. The result to which relativism logically tends, and which it never quite achieves, is to detach the anthropologist from all particular cultures. It does not provide him with a moral center, only a job; he can only strive to become a pure professional.

One is tempted to say that relativism puts the soul of the anthropologist in jeopardy. But in the end, the relativistic stance is usually demystified in practice, and the anthropologist discovers that he is a middle-class Episcopalian Anglo-American, or a second-generation urban American Jew, whose cultural identity reasserts itself along with his humbler prejudices. It is at this recurring point that relativism is abstracted as a professional ideology and divorced from the actual life of the person.

As cultural relativism becomes thoroughly objectified and professionally self-conscious, it passes into scientific relativism and seeks to rid itself of all purposes extraneous to the detached scientific examination of cultural mechanisms. Self-knowledge, engagement, the involvement of the anthropologist in any activity other than his profession, are potential contaminations. The cycle is completed: participation in all cultures finally appears and is scientifically justified as equivalent to participation in none; moreover, *that* is assumed to be the path to an understanding of the human situation. And it is just here that Lévi-Strauss emerges as the anthropologist of his time.[7]

But the avoidance of the implications of the Rousseau-Marx tradition does not work. Reductive materialism, the merely aesthetic appreciation of primitive cultures, the collapsing of the historical sense, the refusal to put one's society in a radically critical perspective, lead only to academism and, in reality, convert the anthropologist into an instrument of that imperial civilization, in dialectical opposition to which his calling arose in the first instance.

A STRATEGY FOR ANTHROPOLOGY

How, then, can anthropology be reconstituted? Intellectually, this is not as formidable a task as it sounds. The problem is one of reformulation, rather than discovery or invention. Nor is it primarily a question of devising new methods or fancy ideas. Anthropologists have always generalized about primitive peoples. The problem is to ask questions of the latter, and of ourselves, in terms of an ethnology in the tradition of Marx and Rousseau. Such an ethnology is possible, but it is obliged to base itself on the converse of the Marxist analytic and critical categories, and is thus axiologically indebted to Marx, since it deals with those cultures that he understood to be antithetical to the State. Only in this way can we provide ourselves with an interpretive, comparative, and historically self-critical description of primitive society. Anthropology has been impoverished to the degree that it did not explicitly center on questions of the following order, which were, of course, anticipated in the eighteenth century:

What is the quality content, form, and function of social life and individual consciousness in a primitive culture in which:

1) there is a predominantly natural division of labor, the person engages in a variety of tasks, and no significant disparity between mental and manual labor exists;
2) neither classes, class conflicts, nor exploitative political structures exist;
3) social contradictions are minimized or resolved; existential contradictions are celebrated and socially experienced;
4) the available technology is maximally utilized for

human needs, that is, where there are no social constraints on material possibilities, and man remains the
subject of, *commands,* the means of production;
5) technology has developed in an empirical, but non-
scientific context, and is embedded in ritual relations;
6) kinship, rather than object-relations, define and link
society and nature;
7) the idea of *social* progress does not exist?

Further, in primitive cultures:
(a) What is the range of definitions of human nature?
(b) What is the character of, and the social occasions for,
violence?
(c) What are the goals and means of education in the absence of formal schooling?

In short, what is concretely meant by the claim that our
sense of primitive communal societies is the archetype for
socialism?

As I have implied, such questions are not new; but by
making them central, we change the ethnological focus. It
is not even a question of further field work, but of reflection
and synthesis. The data is voluminous; the ground for working toward conclusions exists. How many anthropologists
have generalized about primitive peoples (Boas, Kroeber,
Lowie, Radin), and with what surprising consistency, on the
basis of restricted information?

Lowie is typical: "The Eskimo (and most other primitive
peoples) generously share what food and shelter are available"
([1924] 1948, p. 335). How may we dissect that statement? What is meant by "generously"? What are the penal-
ties for not acting that way? How does Lowie know that
most other primitive peoples behave in the same way? What
does the ethnographer mean by primitive? And so on. Such
questions are valid and more or less answerable. But the
answers do not explode the paradigm; they help define it
further. Lowie's statement remains accurate, if imprecise,
and it is not trivial—*in contrast to ourselves, most primitive*

peoples share the necessities of life, and that becomes one of the definitions of the primitive experience. One must note that Lowie's orthodox field work was limited to North American Indians, notable the Crow of the Plains, who had long since been confined, as he himself states, to reservations by the time the anthropologist appeared among them. Obviously no anthropologist has worked in more than two or three primitive societies. In short, anthropologists are in the habit of referring to the primitive modalities of existence in terms of their own immediate experiences, and their colloquial references to "my people" are symptomatic. But "my people" is also a proprietory expression, implying an invention, in which the anthropologist unwittingly includes himself.

This historical construction is not, nor can it be, based upon so-called rigorous examination of the full range of empirical data. The notion that data can somehow exist independently of a paradigm, even if unconscious, is obviously an illusion; such data would be no more than an infinite catalogue of random observations. Goethe put the matter succinctly: "The highest wisdom would be to understand that every fact is already theory." The historical intuition—for the theoretical construction must also be an intuition—is the result of an intellectually inherited paradigm that constantly renews itself in civilized reflection.

The political reconstitution, in contrast to the intellectual reformulation of anthropology, is more complex, because it requires not only reflection and synthesis, but a different kind of work in the world. We are living in a period of unprecedented destruction of languages and cultures, of nations, under the assault of highly centralized bureaucratic states. These states exert, both internally and externally, a steady pressure, reducing culture to a series of technical functions. Put another way, culture, the creation of shared meanings, symbolic interaction, is dissolving into a mere social mechanism guided by signals. This, of course, accounts for the rebellion of youth against functional rationality and their search for some kind of meaning, a rebellion which need not be overt; it also takes the form of cynicism, mock conformity, apathy.

Clearly, the study of man can reconstitute itself only in the struggle against the civilized objectification of men, in our own society and elsewhere. Anthropologists who recognize this may now decide to turn to the arena in which the generality of men, notably peasants and primitives, the conventional "objects" of study, are now re-creating themselves as subjects in the revolutionary dramas of our time. In accordance with their competence, these anthropologists are likely to declare themselves partisans in the movements for (1) national liberation, the nation being the ground for culture, and (2) social reconstruction, which begins with socialism, the name for the ancient and persistent paradigm for the rights and possibilities of man. If field work remains possible for them, it will not be in the pursuit of their careers, but independently, as amateurs, in order to learn, not to "examine," in dynamic and possibly revolutionary circumstances.

But since when has anthropology been comfortable in the academy? And since when have academic concentrations of intellectuals accomplished what they pretend? As the recent Yale University Study Commission on Governance put it: "Considering how overwhelming a proportion of intellectuals are gathered in universities, it has always been puzzling why so few great intellectual achievements spring from them." Moreover "there [is] 'a great deal of truth' in the allegations of radical critics that universities are class institutions with complacent and self-indulgent faculties that forget to ask fundamental questions" (*New York Times,* April 18, 1971, p. 66).

Those anthropologists who choose to reformulate the questions of Rousseau and Marx can at least be sure that the study of man is not an end in itself; it will be negated in the knowledge—and in the actions—of men.

Notes

A short version of this essay has appeared by permission in *Partisan Review* 38, No. 2: 167–201, under the title "Man and Superman."

1. Personal communication, cf. *Newsletter of the American Anthropological Association* 12, No. 3 (March 1971): 15.

2. The ethnologist is actually saying that he is not interested in meaning (significance), which he regards as *merely* (and always) phenomenal. For him, the primary phenomenon is not meaning, but the nonmeaning which lies behind meaning and to which, he believes, meaning is reducible. But the reverse is not true, that is, nonmeaning is never "reducible" to meaning. In short, he is concerned with the primary, or underlying, structures of nonmeaning, which nonetheless govern meaning. Lévi-Strauss, reverses, so to speak, the focus of the phenomenologist; he had, it will be recalled, substantially dismissed phenomenology in *Tristes tropiques* (1961, pp. 61–62).

3. During the *L'Esprit* confrontation Lévi-Strauss seems to disavow the conclusion of *La Pensée sauvage*. There he had made a plea for a synthesis of primitive and civilized modalities of thought, viewing them as complementary to the modern scientific enterprise; their equivalence, therefore, was a live historical issue, not merely an abstract timeless matter. Even so, he seemed to imply that only the modern mind could understand the significance of the synthesis.

4. Contrast this with Rousseau:

> Nature commands every animal, and the beast obeys. Man feels the same impetus, but he realizes that he is free to acquiesce or resist; and it is above all in the consciousness of this freedom that the spirituality of his soul is shown. For physics explains in some way the mechanism of the senses and the formation of ideas; but in the power of willing, or rather of choosing, and in the sentiment of this power are found only purely spiritual acts about which the laws of mechanics explain nothing. ([1750] 1964, p. 114)

5. "What splendid men and women were produced by such a society!"

> . . . all white people who have come into contact with unspoiled Indians [admire] the personal dignity, uprightness, strength of character, and courage of these barbarians.
>
> We have seen examples of this courage quite recently in Africa. The Zulus a few years ago and the Nubians a few months ago—both of them tribes in which gentile institutions have not yet died out—did what no European army can do. Armed only with lances and spears, without firearms, under

a hail of bullets from the breech-loaders of the English infantry—acknowledged the best in the world at fighting in close order—they advanced right up to the bayonets and more than once threw the lines into disorder and even broke them, in spite of the enormous inequality of weapons and in spite of the fact that they have no military service and know nothing of the drill. Their powers of endurance and performance are shown by the complaint of the English that a Kaffir travels farther and faster in twenty-four hours than a horse. His smallest muscle stands out hard and firm like whipcord, says an English painter. That is what men and society were before the division into classes. And when we compare their position with that of the overwhelming majority of civilized men today, an enormous gulf separates the present-day proletarian and small peasant from the free member of the old gentile society.

. . . However impressive the people of this epoch appear to us, they are still attached to the navel string of the primitive community. The power of this primitive community [had to be] broken. But it was broken by influence which from the very start appears as a degradation, a fall from the simple moral greatness of the old gentile society. The lowest interests—base greed, brutal appetites, sordid avarice, selfish robbery of the common wealth—inaugurate the new, civilized class society. It is by the vilest means—theft, violence, fraud, treason—that the old classless gentile society is undermined and overthrown. And the new society itself, during all the two and a half thousand years of its existence, has never been anything else but the development of the small minority at the expense of the great, exploited, and oppressed majority; today it is so more than ever before. (Engels [1891] 1902, pp. 117–19)

6. For an extended analysis of Marx and Engels in relation to the ethnology of their time, see Krader. Krader's study constitutes the introduction to his transcription and edition of Marx's notebooks on ethnology; the part concerning Morgan was extensively used by Engels ([1891] 1902). Besides the authors represented in the notebooks, Marx had earlier been concerned with the work of Taylor, Prescott, and Bancroft (cf. Hobsbawm, 1965, pp. 24 ff). [DH]

7. One can understand why Paul Radin, alone among the anthropologists of his generation, insisted that the only acceptable ethnology is the life history, told by members of an indigenous society themselves. Radin defined this as both the method and the theory of ethnology, which had eventually to be assimilated to history; in this perspective he severely criticized the Boas school, especially Mead and Benedict. Radin's view is necessarily incomplete (he himself continued to ask critical questions throughout

his career), but what is more pertinent is that his view was exactly the reverse of the *objectifying trend;* he spotted it, and tried to combat it early on (Radin, 1933).

References

Benedict, Ruth. N.d. Notes from lectures at Columbia University.

Curtin, Philip D. 1964. *The Image of Africa: British Ideas and Action, 1750–1850.* Madison: University of Wisconsin Press.

Engels, Frederick. [1891] 1902. *The Origin of the Family, Private Property, and the State, in the Light of the Researches of Lewis H. Morgan.* Translated from *Der Ursprung der Familie, des Privateigentums und des Staats* (4th ed.; 1st ed., 1884). Chicago: Charles Kerr. New English translation, New York, International Publishers, 1942; New World Paperbacks, 1963. A new edition with introduction by Eleanor Burke Leacock was published by International Publishers in 1971.

Hobsbawm, E. J. 1965. Introduction to *Pre-capitalist Economic Formations,* by Karl Marx, ed. E. J. Hobsbawm. London: Lawrence & Wishart.

Krader, Lawrence. 1971. "The Works of Marx and Engels in Ethnology Compared." Introduction to *The Ethnological Notebooks of Karl Marx* (studies of Morgan, Phear, Maine, Lubbock), transcriber and ed. Lawrence Krader. Assen: Van Gorcum. In press.

Lévi-Strauss, Claude. 1961. *A World on the Wane.* Translated from *Tristes Tropiques* (1955) by John Russel. New York: Criterion Books.

———. 1966. "Anthropology: Its Achievement and Future." *Current Anthropology* 7: 124–27.

———. et al. 1970. "A Confrontation." *New Left Review* 62: 57–74.

Lowie, Robert H. 1948. *Primitive Religion.* Rev. ed. (1st ed. 1924). New York: Liveright.

Peyre, Henri. 1963. *Literature and Sincerity.* New Haven, Conn.: Yale University Press.

Radin, Paul. 1933. *The Method and Theory of Ethnology: An Essay in Criticism.* New York: McGraw-Hill Book Co. Reprinted New York: Basic Books, 1966.

Rousseau, Jean-Jacques. [1750, 1755] 1964. *The First and Second Discourses,* ed. Roger D. Masters. New York: St. Martin's Press.

Supek, Rudi. 1971. "Sociology and Marxism." *International Journal of Sociology* 1, No. 1.

Venable, Vernon. 1945. *Human Nature: The Marxist View.* New York: Alfred A. Knopf. Reprinted Cleveland and New York: World Publishing Co., Meridian Books, 1966.

Toward a Reflexive and Critical Anthropology
Bob Scholte

THIS ESSAY is motivated by a sense of malaise—a vague sense, admittedly, but one which I think I share with many other anthropologists in this country. I must confess that I do not know either the exact nature of this uneasiness or its sociohistorical genesis. But I do believe that it exists and is not a mere figment of my imagination. Concrete expressions of this malaise are certainly evident both in the anthropological literature (take, for example, the recent "Social Responsibility Symposia" in *Current Anthropology* or the vehement debates surrounding the Ethics Committee's reports in recent AAA *Newsletters*), and at our professional meetings. (In San Diego, 1970, there seemed to be an unusual number of symposia on alternatives in, and to, "traditional" anthropology.)

What is responsible for this professional crisis and moral ferment? Is it the sociopolitical situation in which we find ourselves—both inside and outside academia? Is it the result of thinking in traditional and disciplinary terms when perhaps we should be thinking of urgent and substantive issues? (To many of us the two alternatives no longer seem synonymous or even complementary.) Or is it simply a consequence of "mental entropy" (Remmling, 1967, p. 4) brought about by philosophical uncertainty and moral exhaustion? I really do not know. Even the precise nature of the malaise is difficult to determine. Is it a specific sense of political and moral outrage about the inexcusable plight of so many of our fellow men and women? Or is it a related

sense of institutional dehumanization—both inside and outside anthropology departments? Or is it simply a partial and
momentary symptom of an unsettling crisis in our professional paradigms? Again, I honestly do not know, and these
are not questions I can hope to answer in this paper. They
are, however, the kinds of questions that motivate what I
can try to do: to offer suggestions for the reflexive and
critical study of anthropological traditions and to draw from
such a perspective some programmatic conclusions for
ethnographic praxis.[1]

My working hypothesis is elementary, even obvious: Intellectual paradigms, including anthropological traditions,
are culturally mediated, that is, they are contextually situated and relative. The inference I draw is also elementary
and obvious: If anthropological activity is culturally mediated, it is in turn subject to ethnographic description and
ethnological analysis.[2] If the hypothesis and inference are
correct, we are faced with a deeply problematic situation
whose substantive implications are far from obvious. Ethnographic experience and ethnological analysis presuppose a
condition which transcends scientific investigation as such,
that is, the sociocultural and philosophical nature of anthropological inquiry as itself a part of human praxis transcends
working in procedural problems within anthropology.

Let me state the implications of this situation as categori-
cally as possible—my essay will be devoted largely to their
elucidation. Anthropological activity is never only scientific.
In addition, it is expressive or symptomatic of a presupposed
cultural world of which it is itself an integral part. As anthropologists, we cannot simply take this *Lebenswelt* and its
attendant scientific traditions for granted. We must subject
them to further reflexive understanding, hermeneutic mediation, and philosophical critique. In this sense, epistemological reflection (the assessment of "ethno-logical" assumptions
entailed in the possibility and constitution of any anthropological knowledge whatsoever) must complement, if not
precede, scientific activity proper.[3]

That intellectual paradigms—anthropological traditions

included—are mediated has been amply argued elsewhere
(e.g. Gouldner, 1970; Kuhn, 1962; or Scholte, 1966 and
1970; or, for examples close to current problems, Willis and
Szwed in this volume; Moskos and Bell, 1967; and Leach,
1971, p. 43). What is far less certain are the implications of
this fact. Are any and all aspects of anthropological investigation so mediated? Or can we isolate and hold constant
transcendental principles which will assure a scientific and
progressive anthropology (cf. Rudolph in Berreman *et al.*,
1968, p. 464)? If we have to admit that anthropological activity is partial, "nonobjective," and "culturally determined"
when viewed *in situ* (Bennett, 1946, p. 373), is a truly universal, objective, and transcultural enterprise ever possible
or even desirable?

THE IDEOLOGY OF VALUE-FREE
SOCIAL SCIENCE

Let me paraphrase the "ideal-typical" answers which were
(and still are) quite prevalent in the literature of our
discipline. Critical reflection on diverse anthropological
traditions, it was said, is necessary and liberating insofar as
it is motivated by, bears witness to, and contributes toward
the progressive realization of a value-free and therefore
objective science. Toward this end, we should be concerned
with improving and refining the methodological concepts
and empirical data of our historical predecessors and near
contemporaries. (What is the use of studying them otherwise?) At the same time, we should be humble enough to
critically examine and honestly admit our own limitations
and present failures—that is how science "advances." The
normative import of such self-awareness complements the
emancipatory interest: it first of all assures the historical and
systematic continuity of a self-corrective science, greater
clarity, increased precision, logical coherency, lawful prediction, and so on. Such progressive values will in turn con-

tribute to the pragmatic success and efficient implementation of functional norms generally; they will ensure technical know-how, operational maximization, and workable alternatives in applied domains (science in the service of man). Cultural anthropology, in sum, is emancipatory to the extent that it frees us from prejudices, superstitions, irrationalities, and gives us instead facts, predictions, and rationality. Anthropological activity can be considered normative to the degree that it is objective, informative, and self-corrective, rather than merely ideological, authoritarian, or tautological.[4]

There are many inconsistencies in this point of view—the kinds of frailties which inhere in the very presuppositions and practical consequences of the "answers." Let me briefly illustrate this with a fairly familiar critique.[5] Most importantly, the central idea of a value-free and truly objective social science is logically contradictory and, *de facto*, unattainable. For one, a self-reflexive and self-critical analysis of social scientific paradigms will invariably discover the inescapable presence of one ideological context or another (cf. Mills, 1959, pp. 78 ff.). To this extent, "every theory is (and must be) a discreet obituary or celebration of some social system (or another)" (Gouldner, 1970, p. 47). This means that even the paradigmatic assumptions and procedures of a "value-free" activity entail normative commitments and evaluative results. This may be evident as early as the initial act of "neutral" description: from the point of view of the observed, objective techniques for data-gathering often destroy "the veil of unreality" which is the "emic" basis for the behavior in question (cf. Seely, 1962, p. 58).

If the results of scientific activity are evaluative (especially as far as the people we study are concerned), so are its preconditions. More often than not, the gathering of information and its subsequent appropriation for analytical purposes presuppose such normative values as the "control," "manipulation," and even "exploitation" of both the empirical data and the social world to which they belong (e.g.

Burridge, 1970; Gouldner, 1970, pp. 49 ff.; or Matson, 1964). One can and should go even further: the entire concept of a value-free social science (and the methods proper to such activity) is to a large extent the historical outcome and the cultural consequence of a normative and bourgeois ideology (e.g. Gouldner, 1970). In the current context of academic social science, this ideology is further mediated and concretized in an occupational group which often seeks to merely maintain, justify, and spread its own socio-economic interests and ideological false consciousness under the protective rubric of scientific objectivity and technological efficiency (cf. Gough, 1968; Gouldner, 1962 and 1970; Habermas, 1970; Becker, 1971; or Schroyer, 1970). If this is true (and the evidence seems overwhelming), the logical irony is readily apparent: a so-called value-free perspective in principle embodies and in fact perpetuates a normative ideology.

What is especially disconcerting is the fact that the assumptions and implications of this ideology often run counter to the most cherished and humane values of an emancipatory anthropology—even one which may otherwise be guided by a scientific and utilitarian motive. This is especially evident in the case of applied anthropology. Only recently did we become fully aware of, and deeply disturbed by, the counterrevolutionary setting and reactionary uses of many taken-for-granted assumptions and sociopolitical results of applied anthropology (e.g. Boneil, 1966; Gough, 1968). At first, many anthropologists understandingly deplored the rapidity of culture change, and they justifiably felt that anthropology was and could be involved in practical attempts to humanize these disruptive processes. Perhaps their sympathetic understanding, comparative knowledge, and practical guidance could help to make these inevitable situations more tolerable and less disastrous. But relatively few anthropologists undertook these applied tasks self-critically, that is, they often failed to realize that applied anthropology "functions" according to criteria of operational implementation and with little regard for the ultimate ends envisaged (other than vague and conservative concepts like "stabilization," "integration," and so on). Many belatedly realized that a means-ends logic is merely practical and not necessarily rational, that the technical and functional biases of a "value-free" approach may in reality foster a "bureaucratically ordained partiality" (Habermas, 1965, p. 299), and that, finally, the political misuse or ideological abuse of many of our sincere efforts only bears witness to the vested interests and warped sensibilities of many government funding agents, research foundation strategists, and anthropology's capitalist patrons (cf. Gouldner, 1970, pp. 467 ff.; Radnitzky, 1968, pp. 134 ff.).[6]

If the emancipatory and normative interests of "scientism," especially as practiced in applied domains, are contradictory and illusory, if no position can ever hope to be entirely value-free and transcultural, and if its naive, uncritical application may either simply hide ideological presuppositions or unwittingly generate reactionary political consequences, does not the self-corrective, self-critical, and progressive nature of scientific activity eventually ensure consistency, transparency, and viability? I would argue— following Radnitzky and others[7]—that this would be possible *only* if "scientism" were to embark on a self-reflexive and self-critical course, that is, one which would emancipate it from its own paradigmatic stance. This, of course, is highly unlikely, since the paradigm's own assumptions, procedures, and aims mitigate against a radical and contextual critique. The basic reason for this lack of self-reference lies in the widely held assumption that there is, and should be, a discontinuity between experience and reality, between the investigator and the object investigated. If we accept this assumption (which, ironically, is no longer tenable or practical, even from a strict scientific point of view [cf. Bateson, 1970; Wilden, 1970]), the scientist can afford to remain largely indifferent to his own existential, sociological, historical, and philosophical environment.

Let me elaborate on the nature and implications of this false discontinuity. While "scientism" may express a peripheral interest in the intentional consciousness of scientific investigation, it does so only to use or to purge existential circumstances for the sake of scientific objectivity and replicability. Though it may utilize and contribute to the "ethnomethodologies" available at any given time and may study, manipulate, or implement a culture's norms and values, its professed and ultimate aim lies in transcending the sociocultural settings and particular time periods in which scientific activities are located and developed.[8] Similarly, if progress demands at least some awareness of history, "scientism" nevertheless remains largely indifferent to the *historicity* of scientific praxis as a whole.

If "scientism" also considers itself empirical and problem-oriented, it usually assumes that facts are facts, that objective methods simply select relevant data without further affecting them, and that these "units of analysis" can be processed to yield lawful predictions and functional norms. Its overriding interest in logical clarity and technical precision, realizable within the "manageable" boundaries of "piecemeal" research, further assures only a marginal concern with the ontological grounds and epistemological preconditions which science's own activities nevertheless presuppose or simply take for granted. Finally, when "scientism" is raised to the encompassing status of a philosophical system, its ultimate purpose becomes the rational explanation of a determinable reality in accord with universal principles and objective techniques. Its transcendental aim is to establish and to verify formal laws and eternal verities. Any relativizing or perspectivistic alternatives to scientific dogma are simply considered irrational, impractical, or—worst of all —metaphysical.

I would readily admit that this summary account of "scientism" is simplistic, selective, and prejudicial. I would nonetheless maintain that many social scientists, cultural anthropologists included, have worked, and still work, within the general philosophical context of the aforemen-

tioned paradigm. What is anthropologically (and philosophically) lamentable is not that this position is partial and
relative (which, after all, is true for any paradigm), but that
it basically refuses to critically examine its own sociocultural
circumstances and historicophilosophical limitations as a
paradigm. As long as it fails to do so, I don't believe it can
be really emancipatory and normative. Its concept of emancipation will remain an ethnocentric, self-generating, and
self-fulfilling prophecy; its norms will merely reflect the
utilitarian, technological, and rationalist values of its own
Western environment. If it is so confined, can it ever hope
to realize anthropology's comparative aims: to detail and
to encompass the rich diversity of human circumstance?

My own tentative "solution" to this difficult problem is
somewhat as follows: Neither the possibility nor the desirability of a transcendent, purely scientific anthropology can
or should be taken for granted. We must first subject
anthropological thought itself to ethnographic description
and ethnological understanding and try to determine the
degree to which it is circumscribed or made possible by its
diverse cultural settings. Such anthropological studies should
be radically contextual, immanently dialectical, genuinely
comparative, and emphatically motivated (reflexive anthropology). We must subsequently describe and assess the
effects of the cultural mediation of anthropological inquiry
on the nature of anthropological activity itself and on the
life-styles of those native "others" so investigated. Such
radicalizing studies should have normative and emancipatory interests in mind, that is, they should be evaluative and
liberating (critical anthropology). Finally, we must define
and implement a concrete anthropological praxis which is
in keeping with the distinctive limitations and practical
possibilities of any culturally mediated and intentionally
motivated activity. Such a directive program should be
attentive to both the given and the possible, that is, it
should consist of an actual and a transforming praxis (dialectical anthropology).

In this essay, I cannot possibly defend or detail this

doubtlessly controversial and ambitious program in its entirety. Rather, I shall concentrate on certain aspects of critical anthropology, suggest some of their possible implications for ethnographic activity, and define the place of normative and emancipatory interests in anthropological investigation. I shall assume that the concrete task of a reflexive anthropology has been adequately delineated elsewhere (especially in the related domain of the sociology of knowledge) and that the most difficult problem of all—a specific praxis for dialectical anthropology—can for the present remain unspecified and unresolved.[9]

REFLEXIVE ANTHROPOLOGY: THE ETHNOGRAPHIC SITUATION AS AN EPISTEMOLOGICAL SITUATION

Let me take the relation between ethnography and ethnology as my point of departure.

In response to the question: "How is anthropology done?" we cannot simply reply: "Anthropologists construct scientific and replicable theories on the basis of empirical data." We must also explain how field work and subsequent analysis constitute a unified praxis, the first results of which are mediated by the "in here" as much as by the "out there." The ethnographic situation is defined not only by the native society in question but also by the ethnological tradition "in the head" of the ethnographer. The latter's presuppositions are operative even before entering the field. Once he is actually in the field, the natives' presuppositions also become operative, and the entire situation turns into complex intercultural mediation and a dynamic interpersonal experience. In other words, ethnography entails the personal sensibilities of the field worker, the specific nature of his descriptive methods, *and* the natives' artistry at disguise and the credibility of their information (cf. Berreman, 1962; Den Hollander, 1967; Langness, 1963; Vansina, 1967). Since these factors in turn presuppose a pre-understanding (*Vorverständnis*) on the part of both natives and anthropologists, cultural contexts and personal circumstances precede ethnographic description as such and affect the empirical data gathered.

Epistemological mediation is evident in the existential situation of ethnographic experience itself. As Kurt Wolff has so convincingly and sensitively shown, field work demands a "catch" and a "surrender" to the ethnographic setting. The immediacy of these initial acts is not further reducible. They entail "total involvement, suspension of received notion, pertinence of everything, and risk of being hurt" (Wolff, 1964, p. 237). Nor can "catch" and "surrender" be understood in merely idiosyncratic or psychological terms. Instead, they suggest an important epistemological priority and unique ontological precondition: "Man, in contrast to all other phenomena in the universe, can be done justice to only by surrender and catch—or invention— . . . rather than by the customary varieties of describing, defining, or reducing to instances of generalizations" (Wolff, 1964, p. 241; cf. also Fabian, 1971, pp. 25 ff.). This does not necessarily mean that scientific analyses are irrelevant, but that any ethnographic encounter demands the observer's initial (that is, premethodological) involvement. This "very act of surrendering will [then] determine . . . which elements or aspects are done justice to by the usual procedures of science" (Wolff, 1964, p. 248). In this sense, too, "humanism is the prerequisite for the scientific study of humanity" (Duerr in *Current Anthropology*, 1970, p. 75), not the other way around.

Let me try to elaborate on what I have in mind here. If we adopt an epistemological position, the interactional success of the ethnographic encounter will not only become fundamental, but be undertaken with distinctive aims in mind and have significant consequences for anthropological activity as a whole. As Johannes Fabian remarks: "In anthropological investigation, objectivity lies neither in the logical consistency of a theory, nor in the givenness of the data, but in the foundation (*Begründung*) of human *inter-subjectivity*" (Fabian, 1971, p. 12). Any resultant ethnographic data are never, therefore, mere static particulars that can be reduced to instances of ethnological laws and principles. Rather, they are the result of a dynamic process, a sympathetic identification, and a creative production (cf. Fabian, 1971, pp. 12–17, and Wolff, 1964, pp. 262–63). If so, a descriptively meaningful ethnography presupposes a dialectical and constitutive relation of exchange and communication. Subsequent perception and understanding of ethnographic data are "given [only in this initial] context of communicative interaction" (Fabian, 1971, p. 16). It is not reducible to predictive or psychological processes, any more than hermeneutic *verstehen* can be subsumed under psychological explanation (cf. Radnitzky, 1968, pp. 106 ff.). I would even go so far as to insist that the possibility of communicative interaction is the irreducible epistemological precondition to any anthropological knowledge whatsoever (cf. also Diamond, 1970, p. 4).[10]

It is, of course, a specific language which both mediates the communicative context and allows for its subsequent description. If our perceptions, descriptions, and analyses are influenced by language, and if our language is in turn related to a given cultural setting, then our efforts are potentially subject to various "ethnocentricities of meaning" (Mills, 1963, p. 435; cf. Leach, 1971, p. 43, on American social scientists' interpretations of the nature of Asiatic religions and their relation to modernization). Nor can a scientific language be assumed to be neutral (cf. Pouillon, 1968, pp. 6 ff.). Moreover, any language, scientific discourse included, is process as well as product, and any descriptive activity is constitutive and articulatory, not only representational or instrumental (cf. Fabian, 1971, pp. 17 ff; Radnitzky, 1968, pp. 23 ff.). It follows that all ethnographic descriptions and any ethnological analyses derived from such accounts are, and must be, part hermeneutics, that is, interpretive activities based on contextual information and mediated texts.[11] When we consciously adopt a scientific meta-language, we may irrevocably lose sight of the field's dynamic and interactive reality (cf. Den Hollander, 1967, p. 24; Shands, 1968, p. 72). In the analytical context of ethnological comparison and scientific elaboration, these descriptive "reifications" may be even further embellished. Whether we call it "mouth-talk" (Service, 1969, p. 70), "terminological escapism" (Myrdal, 1969, p. 57), or just "jargon" (Mills, 1959, p. 78), meta-languages can, and often do, turn into dangerous and pedantic abstractions. When they do, they can no longer interpret or emancipate (cf. Apel, 1968, and below). Instead, they either create an objectivistic and "cloudy obscurantism" (Mills, 1959, p. 78), or they reflect a "formal and empty ingenuity," which, as a typical "mannerism of the noncommitted," is in fact partial and ideological (Mills, 1959, pp. 78–79; cf. Gouldner, 1970, pp. 120 ff.).

To bypass these facts is to commit what might be called the "fallacy of objectivism" (Schroyer, 1970, p. 211). To try instead to determine the extent and meaning of the mediation is the distinctive task and hoped-for contribution of a reflexive and critical anthropology.

What seems to me to be urgently required is a genuinely dialectical position, one in which "analytical procedures [and descriptive devices are chosen and] determined by reflection on the nature of the encountered phenomena *and* on the nature of that encounter" (Fabian, 1971, p. 25). This would mean that every procedural step in the constitution of anthropological knowledge is accompanied by radical reflection and epistemological exposition. In other words, if we assume a continuity between experience and reality, that is, if we assume that an anthropological understanding of others is conditioned by our capacity to open ourselves to those others (cf. Huch, 1970, p. 30), we cannot and should not avoid the "hermeneutic circle" (cf. Ricoeur, 1971), but must explicate, as part of our activities, the intentional processes of constitutive reasoning which make both encounter and understanding possible. Indeed, "the question is not . . . how to avoid it, but . . . how to get properly into it" (Radnitzky, 1968, p. 23).

RELATIVITY AND RELEVANCE

A position such as this poses a number of additional problems. Most importantly, to what extent does self-reflexive and critical anthropology preclude the possibility of a cross-culturally valid, scientifically relevant anthropology?

Some might dismiss my entire proposal on the grounds that constant self-reflection and self-critique would ultimately involve us in an unproductive paradox of infinite regress and self-doubt at the expense of matters of political and scientific urgency. Especially among the no-nonsense pragmatists in our profession, such self-conscious efforts at enumerating the contextual frailties of ethnographic and enthnological understanding must seem wasteful. Indeed, does a reflexive and critical "ethnology of anthropological activity" not entail a circular and self-defeating reduction of practical and substantive issues to mere culturally confined assumptions and activities?

Even assuming that reflection and critique can at least serve to illuminate the nature of our own confinements and possibilities, would it really serve to dignify those to whom the anthropologist owes his ultimate allegiance: his fellow human beings? Perhaps self-reflection and self-critique only lend weight to Lienhardt's conclusion that cultural anthropology is less of a social science devoted to the empathetic understanding of "significant others" and more of a circumstantial exercise in exploring the extremities of our own thought and culture (cf. Pouillon, 1968, p. 5). Or is it possible that reflection and critique can become privileged means toward the practical realization of a more inclusive ethnography, a more comprehensive ethnology, and a more emancipated and normative anthropology?

Before trying to show that the latter alternative is indeed possible, let me first indicate some qualifications that will place the hoped-for contribution in perspective. First, to point out that anthropological investigation is existentially, socially, historically, and philosophically mediated is not to debunk one's anthropological colleagues or adversaries in terms of self-centered motives, vested interests, historical naiveté, or warped ideological misrepresentations. The approach assumed here (cf. Scholte, 1970, for details) can be, and has been, put to much use (e.g., Harris, 1968; White, 1966), but this is neither accurate nor necessary in most cases. Context entails derivation, not reduction; criticism implies partiality, not perversion.

Second, let me make it quite clear that reflection and critique can be only a part and never the whole of anthropological activity. I am convinced that it can illuminate and even enhance anthropology's goals and procedures, and I would therefore consider it both intrinsic and necessary to the discipline as a whole; but it cannot and should not replace ethnographic experience nor substitute for ethnological understanding. Whatever the paradigmatic limitations of anthropological activity may be, they still provide us with important ethnographic information and significant ethnological generalizations. As Dell Hymes suggested to me in conversation, perhaps the fact of anthropological knowledge requires an explanation, not merely its contextual relativity. I would readily agree, but would also add the reminder that anthropological activity does not automatically arrive at such knowledge. In fact, it is precisely the self-reflexive and self-critical study of anthropological alternatives (and not merely their internal methodological refinement or "external" empirical verification)[12] which can filter out the particular from the general, the idiosyncratic from the universal, or the relative from the essential (cf. also Krader, 1968). In sum, a reflexive and critical stance is a necessary, though not a sufficient, condition for an encompassing anthropology.

THE ETHNOLOGY OF ETHNOLOGICAL TRADITIONS AS PERSPECTIVISM

With these strictures and limitations in mind, let me turn to the positive role I would ascribe to a self-reflexive and self-critical anthropology—especially as related to the normative and emancipatory functions of anthropological praxis.[13] The initial task is describing and analyzing anthropological traditions or activities as cultural products and processes. Since these anthropological "paradigms" differ from one society to another and from one historical period to another, their contextual study provides additional ethnographic food for ethnological thought (cf. Scholte, 1970). Ideally, these preliminary studies should be dialectical rather than merely analytical, that is, their primary aim should not be to explain or to analyze away a given tradition or praxis, but to understand and to comprehend it.[14] Basing ourselves on such immanent descriptions, we can then hope to determine the paradigmatic assumptions and ethnoscientific limitations of each, and contrast and compare their distinctive approaches and frames of reference. Any subsequent and informed choice between differing or rival positions would be based on such initial descriptions and comparisons. In other words, given two or more alternative positions, "the first step is to ask which of them permits the understanding of the other as a social and human phenomenon, reveals its infrastructure, and clarifies, by means of an immanent critical principle, its consistencies and limitations," (Goldmann, 1969, p. 12; cf. Burke, 1957, pp. 107, 127).[15]

Perspectivism (see Mannheim in Wolff, 1959, p. 571)—with which most anthropologists would probably concur (except when applied to their own paradigms)—does not necessarily preclude ethnographic accuracy or ethnological insight.

It is only by means of this liberating—if at times painful and as yet uncritical—perspectivism that we can hope "to come to the point where the false ideal of a detached, impersonal point of view [can] be replaced by the ideal of an essentially human point of view which is within the limits of human perspective, constantly striving to enlarge itself" (Mannheim, 1936, p. 297).

This leaves a crucial question: "If all anthropological knowledge is relative, how do we meaningfully choose between alternatives? Moreover, in doing so, how do we 'steer clear between the Scylla of historic (and cultural) relativism . . . and the Charybdis of ideologization through utopian historicism (or, as is more frequently the case in cultural anthropology, through either 'primitivism' or 'scientism')?" (Radnitzky, 1968, p. 35.) Both extremes avoid the real issue: to choose intelligently without dogmatic reification. What we need instead is a reflexive position which is contextual, comparative, and perspectivistic *as well as* a critical stance which is evaluative, discontinuous, and radical.

It is certainly true that any criteria for critical judgment will in turn be historically situated (e.g. Derrida, 1967, p. 414; cf. also Derrida, 1970, pp. 247 ff.; Wolff, 1959). Precisely because of this fact, historical consciousness (*Geschichtsbewusstsein*) can fulfill a positive function: to provide contemporaries with a timely, if situated, critical stance. As Pouillon points out, *"prendre conscience d'une tradition c'est trouver dans la passé un héritage mais n'accepter ce dernier que sous bénéfice d'un inventaire dont les critères sont les nôtres"* (1968, p. 9). In other words, reflection and critique must be complementary: "The reflective assimilation of a tradition is something else than the unreflected continuity of tradition" (Ahlers, 1970, p. 116). The reflexive study of anthropological traditions is to this extent diacritical and can provide us with "relevant" criteria of differentiation and "progress": *"Une théorie nouvelle se constitue, non pas*

*à partir d'une théorie antérieure et analogue qui la con-
tiendrait en germe, mais comme réponse à un problème non
résolu, ou, plus souvent, non encore posè."* In this sense, *"les
traditions sont discriminatoires, c'est leur fonction essentielle
et pratique; . . . le recours à une tradition, c'est un moyen de
formuler as différence"* (Pouillon, 1968, pp. 11–12).

Still, the process of comparative differentiation and discrimination does not itself suggest any compelling criteria
for critical judgment. If these are to be found at all, I would
advocate that we seek them in the normative and emancipatory interests of anthropological praxis, that is, in the degree
to which anthropological activity violates or sustains pertinent "life-preserving" values and in the extent to which it
inhibits or realizes human freedom. I am painfully aware of
the fact that this is more easily said than done. I also admit
that I have not as yet arrived at any satisfactory substantive
definitions for these crucially important interests. What I can
try to do is explain the extent to which normative and emancipatory interests are nevertheless integral to anthropological
praxis as a whole.

ANTHROPOLOGY'S EMANCIPATORY
AND NORMATIVE INTERESTS

In defining the emancipatory interest of cultural anthropology as one of knowledge for the sake of freedom (cf. note
13), I have two complementary theses in mind. On the one
hand, anthropological activity should in part be considered
as an explanatory and predictive effort. Its empirical and
analytical function would be to provide causal explanations
for cultural processes, to suggest hypothetical predictions of
sociohistorical events, and to define the infrastructural determinants of human behavior. On the other hand, anthropology should also be considered as a critical and emancipatory
discipline. Its self-reflexive and dialectical aim (based
on its initial awareness of hidden causes or contextual deter-

minants) would be to guide the emancipatory "transcend-ence" (*Aufhebung*) of the historical and cultural deter-minants themselves. In this way, the analytico-empirical and reflexively critical functions would be genuinely comple-mentary. Without a specific knowledge of social contexts and historical causes we would never know the nature of cultural determinants, but without transparency and critical awareness we could never hope to emancipate ourselves from them. Without even a relative emancipation from cul-tural determinants ("historically conditioned autonomy" [Schroyer, 1970, p. 225]), we could never have a conscious knowledge of them in the first place. Nor, finally, would we know what to do with a knowledge of determinants. In sum, the effective possibility of any emancipatory interest whatsoever depends on both a conscious knowledge of infra-structural causality and on the complementary thesis that self-awareness creates at least the possibility of a "modifiable preordained destiny" (Aron quoted in Radnitzky, 1968, p. 125).[16]

The emancipatory interest is not only integral to anthro-pological praxis, the latter also contributes to making that emancipation possible. Cultural anthropology, in seeking to understand the "significant other," first demands an "alienation [from] ordinary self-understanding" (Radnitzky, 1968, p. 72). An ethnographic and ethnological perspective not only distances us from the immediacy of our own cir-cumstances (both literally and figuratively), involvement in and knowledge of other life-styles also invite systematic doubt and self-critical assessment. Whether in the context of a comparison between different cultures or between differ-ing traditions within one society, self-understanding is al-ways mediated by an understanding of others—what Rad-nitzky calls the dialectics of *Selbstverständnis* and *Fremd-verständnis* (1968, p. 43). Finally, the understanding of others not only contributes to our emancipatory interest, but in turn presupposes at least a partial self-emancipation. To quote Radnitzky once again:

If there is . . . any point at all in . . . embarking upon an attempt to establish communication and co-understanding with cultures, religions, etc., not one's own, the following pre-condition must obtain: *one is in a position, despite one's history-boundedness, to philosophize from a platform that is not wholly bound to one's historical [cultural] situation.* If one accepts the bringing about of inter-subjective co-under-standing and content [*Verstandigung*] as the superimposed [i.e., emancipatory and normative] research-guiding interest of the human sciences: i.e., *if one places the human sciences in the service of the historical [and cultural] dialogue which humanity has been conducting with the aim of ever-increasing emancipation, then the problematics of historicism* [i.e., rela-tivity and determinism] is *"aufgehoben"* [transcended]. . . . (Radnitzsky, 1968, p. 39)

We have once again come the full hermeneutic circle: The comparative understanding of others contributes to self-awareness; self-understanding, in turn, allows for self-reflection and (partial) self-emancipation; the emancipatory interest, finally, makes the understanding of others possible. Though this process by no means guarantees nor even implies a total transcendence or a transcultural science, its very circularity, perspectivism, and intentionality make a reflexive, critical, and progressive anthropology more likely and, I would add, more in keeping with anthropological principles themselves.

This brings me to a final question: In what would the normative interest of a self-reflexive and critical anthro-pology lie? This question is an extremely urgent and difficult one to ask. Yet it is also one to which, as I have said, I have no satisfactory reply. I would (intuitively) suggest that if a substantive resolution were forthcoming, it would (espe-cially today) have to be firmly based on the concrete realiza-tion of a dialectical and emancipatory praxis. I do not mean merely in terms of the self-emancipation of anthropological activity, but also in the concomitant context of a radical and political emancipation of concrete humanity. Perhaps this is merely begging the question. After all, to some, the normative interests of cultural anthropology are conservative rather than radical (e.g. Vivas, 1968); to others, they may not be political at all, and for everyone's sake some specific suggestions and compelling arguments would have to be made. At present, I have only opinions, though I would venture to make one final remark: if emancipation and co-understanding are indeed first steps toward the realization of normative interests, cultural anthropology will have a crucially important task to fulfill. Only empathetic and comparative appreciation of human solidarity in cultural difference can possibly bring about "co-understanding and consent about the possibilities and norms of being-in-the-world" (Radnitzky, 1968, p. 12). This mutual consent and co-understanding is, it seems to me, already implicit in most anthropological effort. Perhaps it can be further realized and fully detailed by a self-reflexive, truly critical discipline.

Notes

The present paper is in part derived from two previous essays: one initially prepared for the April 1968 Wenner-Gren Foundation Conference on "The Nature and Function of Anthropological Traditions" (Stanley Diamond and Dell Hymes, cochairmen) and the other written for the September 1970 World Congress of Sociology and presented to the ISA Research Committee on the Sociology of Knowledge (Kurt Wolff, chairman). This latter essay profited enormously from critical suggestions made by Johannes Fabian, Dell Hymes, Lawrence Krader, and Kurt Wolff. Since many of their initial comments are reflected in the present paper as well, I would like to thank them once again for their attentiveness and advice.

1. I am deliberately taking a philosophical stance here. I think this is justifiable if we grant that reflection and critique must precede action and involvement. This is not to deny that theory alone is inadequate and ineffectual. (I am reminded of a villager's advice to Weingrod when it came to discussing a politically sensitive situation: "Don't write about this, or if you do, then write about it *theoretically*: then no one will pay any attention" [Weingrod in Henry, 1966, p. 556].) Though I am convinced that theoretical

reflection can illuminate the concrete nature of anthropological activity, I would readily admit that it cannot, and must not, substitute for such activity.

2. Despite the obviousness of both the hypothesis and the conclusion, there are surprisingly few ethnographic descriptions and ethnological analyses of anthropological traditions as such. (Most studies remain *ab intra* and historical.) Some have indeed called for such a perspective (e.g. Berreman, 1966, p. 350), but few have actually carried out such work. Among those who have, I would single out Hallowell (1965), Krader (1968), Smith (1964), White (1966), Wolf (1969), and especially Bennett (1946).

3. This distinction is as important as it is familiar. Thus, Husserl's monumental critique of scientific objectivism is based on a separation between empirical and eidetic questions (cf. Husserl, [1954] 1970), while comparable efforts have made a similar distinction (e.g. Habermas, 1965; Kockelmans and Kisiel, 1970; Verhaar, 1970). There is, of course, the danger of reifying the eidetic—not so much at the expense of the empirical as such, but at the expense of studying intentional consciousness in its concrete and evaluative relation to the lived reality of the *Lebenswelt* (cf. Holt, 1962; Morakowski, 1969). Despite this danger, I would still agree with Duerr: "One of the main questions should be: What is the *epistemological* character of the relation between reflection upon the categorical framework of empirical theories (traditionally termed the 'conditions of the possibility of knowledge') and the 'morals' which motivate the application of scientific theories to a certain domain?" (Duerr, 1970, p. 72)

4. This is clearly a simplified version, but one that has been more than adequately detailed by others (e.g. Kolakowski, 1968; Matson, 1964). I should add that many anthropologists were not directly exposed to even this summary account of "scientism." I would suspect, however, that this was nonetheless (and perhaps still is) the prevalent, if often implicit, philosophy of Anglo-American social scientists. As a more or less conscious paradigm, it formed an integral part of the over-all value system of anthropology proper. This is not to imply, of course, that alternative paradigms did not exist nor that all Anglo-American anthropologists were uniformly naive in their acceptance of a scientific stance.

5. There are numerous critical assessments of "scientism"—ranging from the sociological (e.g. Mills, 1959) to the philosophical (e.g. Kolakowski, 1968). Since I am giving only a brief and selective summary here, the interested reader might wish to consult some of the relevant literature, especially that of members of the Frankfurt school (cf. Radnitzky, 1968, for an introductory and helpful bibliography).

6. I cannot here detail these rather cryptic conclusions. Recent debates in *Current Anthropology*, the *AAA Newsletter*, and elsewhere will at least attest to the urgency of the problem. Gouldner's

book (1970) provides an exacting and anthropologically relevant account (cf. also Scholte, 1971).

7. The following discussion relies heavily on Radnitzky's summary. Even where I do not quote him directly, I have paraphrased him freely.

8. The aparent contradiction is only partial. The very attempt at transcending historical and social circumstances is itself culture-bound and ideological (cf. Gouldner, 1970, pp. 102 ff.).

9. Let me here rephrase what I already mentioned in the context of note 1. Neither a reflexive nor a critical anthropology is sufficient. We must also confront the practical problem of formulating a concrete anthropological praxis. The fact that I cannot do so here (since it is quite literally a task beyond my present capabilities) should not blind us to the obvious danger of substituting a mere theory of praxis for its actual realization (cf. Therborn, 1970, for a telling critique of the Frankfurt school on these grounds). This essay is merely meant to clear the philosophical grounds for an actual praxis: it is not intended as a substitute for such activity.

10. Though this position is irreducible as a precondition to anthropological activity, it does not necessarily preclude a subsequent reduction or scientific analysis. For example, even a scientific rationalist like Lévi-Strauss agrees that *"le problème ethnographique est un problème de communication"* (Lévi-Strauss, 1950, p. xxxii). Admittedly, he would never subscribe to the consequences I shall myself draw from this conclusion (cf. Lévi-Strauss, 1950, pp. xxviii–xxxi).

11. The specific nature of hermeneutic interpretation, its assumptions, procedure, and aims, is simply too complex and too enormous to summarize or describe here. For a preliminary account, I would recommend Palmer, 1969, and Radnitzky, 1968. For an anthropologically relevant application, I would suggest the work of Paul Ricoeur, e.g. 1969, 1971.

12. We should remember (but often forget) that both methods and facts are epistemologically mediated (e.g. Kuhn, 1962, p. 125; Mills, 1963, p. 459). This means that neither methods nor facts can by themselves substitute for the proper sociophilosophical grounds upon which any concrete activity must ultimately rest. Those no-nonsense pragmatists who deny this fact, and who often mock the "metaphysician" who points it out, are very much like Mannheim's deluded scientist—a man who "glories in his refusal to go beyond the specialized observation dictated by the traditions of his discipline, be they ever so inclusive, and [who makes] a virtue out of a defense mechanism which insures him against questioning his presuppositions" (Mannheim, 1936, p. 101; cf. also Gross, 1968, pp. 22 ff.).

13. By "normative" interest, I mean a concern with what Diamond calls "pertinent life-preserving questions" (Diamond, 1963, p. 4). By "emancipatory" interest, I mean involvement in knowledge

for the sake of freedom. The former presupposes such values as *Lebenspraxis* and *Weltverstandnis* (cf. Radnitzky, 1968, pp. 10 ff.), while the latter assumes that "the truth shall make you free" (cf. Habermas, 1965, pp. 297 ff.). I am asserting not only that these interests exist, but that they should be integral to all social scientific activity (cf. also Schroyer, 1970, pp. 215 ff.). I realize this contention is not universally shared and that many—while perhaps not denying the existence of these interests elsewhere—do not consider them in keeping with the proper definition of the social sciences.

14. Following Piguet, I would suggest that dialectical procedures should be part of any ethnographic and descriptive effort. To quote Piguet:

> *Expliquer une chose, pour la pensée dialectique, c'est alors moins l'expliquer que l'expliciter, c'est à dire dérouler ce qui était enroulé ou explicite ce qui demeurait implicite; c'est amener le phénomène à se dévoiler en manifestant son intelligibilité, en enforçant le phénomène à actualiser l'intelligibilité qu'il possède en lui de manière encore virtuelle, de manière que la raison qui dévoile et la raison de la chose ainsi dévoilée se fondent dans l'unité dialectique de la raison et du réel, dans l'unité retrouvée du logos originel.* (Piguet, 1965, pp. 549–50)

This does not mean, of course, that subsequent analytical procedures do not also have distinct advantages, ones not shared by an exclusively dialectical approach. I would still maintain that a dialectical stance is more in keeping with the "ethnodescriptive" task than a mere analytics. A brief comparison between the two might be helpful here:

> . . . *la force de la pensée analytique réside dans son pouvoir de compréhesion. La pensée analytique est apte à expliquer en moulant les phénomènes à son propre langage; dès lors elle risque de ne pas comprendre ce qui relève de critères distincts d'elle. . . . La pensée dialectique en revanche comprend, en laissant les phénomènes à son propre langage à eux; mais elle explique mal, en refusant tout dualisme méthodologique seul apte à fonder l'explication en raison, à partir de la chose comprise. . . .* (Piguet, 1965, p. 551)

15. Yvan Simonis's *Claude Lévi-Strauss, ou "la passion de l'inceste"* (1968) is a truly brilliant example of a reflexive and critical analysis of an anthropological tradition in the sense that I have in mind here.

16. Karl Marx may have had a similar complementarity in mind when he claimed that on the one hand, man makes his own history, though he may not know the history he makes, while on the other hand, if history's hidden causes were to become transparent, man

might become the conscious master of his own destiny. I think we can safely apply the same argument to anthropological traditions. Though anthropologists create their own paradigms, they often do not know the paradigms they create. But if the contexts and prenotions of these traditions were to become known, anthropologists might become the self-critical masters of their own scientific destinies.

References

Ahlers Rolf. 1970. "Is Technology Intrinsically Repressive?" *Continuum* 8, No. 1: 111–22.

Apel, K.-O. 1968. *Language, Philosophy, and the Geistenwissenschaften.* Dordrecht: Reidel.

Arendt, Hannah. 1958. *The Human Condition.* Chicago: University of Chicago Press.

Aron, Raymond. 1965. *Main Currents in Sociological Thought,* Vol. 2. New York: Basic Books.

Bateson, Gregory. 1970. "Form, Substance, and Difference." 19th Annual Alfred Korzybski Memorial Lecture, January 9, 1970.

Becker, Ernst. 1971. *The Lost Science of Man.* New York: George Braziller.

Bennett, John W. 1946. "The Interpretation of Pueblo Values: A Question of Values." *Southwestern Journal of Anthropology* 2, No. 4: 361–74.

Berreman, Gerald D. 1962. *Behind Many Masks.* Society for Applied Anthropology Monograph No. 4. Ithaca, N.Y.

———. 1966. "Anemic and Emetic Analyses in Social Anthropology." *American Anthropologist* 68, No. 2: 346–354.

———. et al. 1968. "Social Responsibilities Symposium." *Current Anthropology* 9, No. 5: 391–435.

Boneil, Batalla G. 1966. "Conservative Thought in Applied Anthropology: A Critique." *Human Organizations* 25: 89–92.

Burke, Kenneth. 1957. *Philosophy of Literary Form.* New York: Vintage Books.

Burridge, K. O. L. 1970. "Field Work, Explanation, and Experience." Unpublished manuscript.

Copans, Jean. 1967. "Le Métier d'anthropologue (1)." *L'Homme* 7, No. 4: 84–91.

———. 1969. "Le Métier d'anthropologue (2)." *L'Homme* 9, No. 4: 74–91.

Current Anthropology. 1970. "On the Social Responsibilities Symposium." *Current Anthropology* 11, No. 1: 72–79.

Den Hollander, A. N. J. 1967. "Social Description: The Problem of Reliability and Validity." In *Anthropologists in the Field,* eds.

D. G. Jongmans and P. C. W. Gutkind. Assen: Van Gorcum. Pp. 1–34.

Derrida, Jacques. 1967. *L'Écriture et la différence*. Paris: Éditions du Seuil.

———. 1970. "Structure, Sign, and Play in the Discourse of the Human Sciences." In *The Languages of Criticism and the Sciences of Man*, eds. Richard Macksey and Eugenio Donato. Baltimore: Johns Hopkins Press. Pp. 247–72.

Diamond, Stanley. 1963. "The Search for the Primitive.'" In *Man's Place in Medicine and Anthropology*, ed. Iago Goldstein. Institute of Social and Historical Medicine Monograph No. 4. New York: International Universities Press. Pp. 1–60.

———. 1970. "A Revolutionary Discipline." *Critical Anthropology* 1, No.1: 3–13.

Duerr, Hans Peter. 1970. "On the Social Responsibilities Symposium." *Current Anthropology* 11, No. 1: 72–75.

Fabian, Johannes. 1971. "Language, History, and Anthropology." *Journal for the Philosophy of the Social Sciences* 1, No.1: 19–47.

Gadamer, Hans-Georg. 1970. "On the Scope and Function of Hermeneutical Reflection." *Continuum* 8, No. 1: 77–95.

Goldmann, Lucien. 1969. *The Human Sciences and Philosophy*. London: Jonathan Cape.

Gough, Kathleen. 1968. "Anthropology: Child of Imperialism." *Monthly Review* 19, No. 11: 12–27.

Gouldner, Alvin W. 1962. "Anti-Minotaur: The Myth of a Value-Free Sociology." In *Sociology on Trial*, eds. Maurice R. Stein and Arthur J. Vidich. Englewood Cliffs, N.J.: Prentice-Hall. Pp. 35–52.

———. 1970. *The Coming Crisis in Western Sociology*. New York: Basic Books.

Gross, Llewellyn Z. 1968. "Intellectual Journey." *American Behavioral Scientist* 12, No. 1: 10–25.

Habermas, Jurgen. 1965. "Knowledge and Interest." *Inquiry* 9: 285–300.

———. 1970. *Toward a Rational Society*. Boston: Beacon Press.

Hallowell, A. Irving. 1965. "The History of Anthropology as an Anthropological Problem." *Journal of the History of the Behavioral Sciences* 1, No. 1: 24–38.

Harris, Marvin. 1968. *The Rise of Anthropological Theory: A History of Theories of Culture*. New York: Thomas Y. Crowell Co.

Hellesnes, Jon. 1970. "Education and the Concept of Critique." *Continuum* 8, No. 1: 40–51.

Henry, Francis. 1966. "The Role of the Field Worker in an Explosive Situation." *Current Anthropology* 7, No. 5: 552–59.

Holt, Hubert. 1962. *Lebenswelt und Geschichte*. Munich: Verlag Karl Albert Freiburg.

Huch, Kurt Jurgen. 1970. "Interest in Emancipation." *Continuum* 8, No. 1: 27–39.

Husserl, Edmund. [1954] 1970. *The Crisis of European Sciences and Transcendental Phenomenology.* Evanston, Ill.: Northwestern University Press.

Kockelmans, Joseph J., and Theodore J. Kisiel. 1970. *Phenomenology and the Natural Sciences.* Evanston, Ill.: Northwestern University Press.

Kolakowski, Leszek. 1968. *The Alienation of Reason: A History of Positivist Thought.* Garden City, N.Y.: Doubleday & Co., Anchor Books.

Krader, Lawrence. 1968. "The Interrelation of Anthropological Traditions as Dialectic." Paper presented at the Wenner-Gren Foundation conference on "The Nature and Function of Anthropological Traditions," Stanley Diamond and Dell Hymes, cochairmen, New York City, April 1968.

Kuhn, Thomas S. 1962. *The Structure of Scientific Revolutions.* Chicago: University of Chicago Press.

Langness, L. I. 1965. *The Life History in Anthropological Science.* New York: Holt, Rinehart, & Winston.

Leach, E. R. 1971. "The Politics of Karma." Review of books by Spiro, Spencer, and Geertz. *New York Review of Books,* November 18, pp. 43–45.

Lévi-Strauss, Claude. 1950. "Introduction à l'oeuvre de Marcel Mauss." In Marcel Mauss, *Sociologie et anthropologie.* Paris: Presses Universitaires de France. Pp. ix–lii.

———. 1963. "Rousseau: The Father of Anthropology." *UNESCO Courier* 16, No. 3: 10–14.

Mannheim, Karl. 1936. *Ideology and Utopia.* New York: Harcourt, Brace & Co., Harvest Books.

Matson, Floyd W. 1964. *The Broken Image: Man, Science, and Society.* Garden City, N. Y.: Doubleday & Co., Anchor Books.

Merton, Robert K. 1957. *Social Theory and Social Structure.* New York: Free Press.

Mills, C. Wright. 1959. *The Sociological Imagination.* London: Oxford University Press.

———. 1963. *Power, Politics, and People: The Collected Essays of C. Wright Mills.* New York: Ballantine Books.

Morakowski. Stefan. 1969. "Le Marxisme et ses rivages possibles." *L'Homme et la société* 13: 45–168.

Moskos, Charles, and Wendell Bell. 1967. "Emerging Nations and Ideologies of American Social Scientists." *American Sociologist* 2, No. 2: 67–72.

Myrdal, Gunnar. 1969. *Objectivity in Social Research.* New York: Pantheon Books.

Palmer, Richard E. 1969. *Hermeneutics.* Evanston, Ill.: Northwestern University Press.

Piguet, Jean-Claude. 1965. "Les Conflits de l'analyse et de la dialectique." *Annales* 20, No. 3: 547–57.

Pouillon, Jean. 1968. "Tradition: Transmission ou reconstruction?"

Paper presented at the Wenner-Gren Foundation conference on "The Nature and Function of Anthropological Traditions," Stanley Diamond and Dell Hymes, cochairmen, New York City, April 1968.

Radnitzky, Gerard. 1968. *Continental Schools of Meta-Science*. Göteborg: Akademiforlaget.

Remmling, Gunter W. 1967. *Road to Suspicion: A Study of Modern Mentality and the Sociology of Knowledge*. New York: Appleton-Century-Crofts.

Ricoeur, Paul. 1969. *Les Conflits des interprétations: Essais d'hermèneutique*. Paris: Éditions du Seuil.

———. 1971. "The Model Text: Meaningful Action Considered as a Text." *Social Research* 38, No. 3: 528–62.

Scholte, Bob. 1966. "Epistemic Paradigms: Some Problems in Cross-Cultural Research on Social Anthropological Theory and History." *American Anthropologist* 68, No. 5: 1192–1201.

———. 1970. "Toward a Self-reflexive Anthropology." Paper presented at the World Congress of Sociology, Varna, Bulgaria, September 1970.

———. 1971. Review of *The Coming Crisis in Western Sociology*, by Alvin Gouldner. *American Anthropologist* 73, No 2: 308–11.

Schroyer, Trent. 1970. "Toward a Critical Theory for Advanced Industrial Society." In *Recent Sociology No. 2*, ed. Hans Peter Dreitzel. New York: Macmillan Co. Pp. 53–65.

Seely, John R. 1962. "Social Science? Some Probative Problems." In *Sociology on Trial*, eds. Maurice Stein and Arthur Vidich. Englewood Cliffs, No. 1.: Prentice-Hall. Pp. 53–65.

Service, E. R. 1969. "Models for the Methodology of Mouthtalk." *Southwestern Journal of Anthropology* 25, No.1: 68–80.

Shands, Harvey C. 1968. "Outline of a General Theory of Human Communication." *Social Science Information* 7, No. 4: 55–94.

Simonis, Yvan. 1968. *Claude Lévi-Strauss, ou la passion de l'inceste: Introduction au structuralisme*. Paris: Aubier-Montagne.

Smith, Alfred C. 1964. "The Dionysian Innovation." *American Anthropologist* 66, No. 2: 251–65.

Stark, Werner. 1958. *The Sociology of Knowledge: An Essay in Aid of a Deeper Understanding of the History of Ideas*. London: Routledge & Kegan Paul.

Therborn, Goran. 1970. "The Frankfurt School." *New Left Review* 63: 65–96.

Vansina, Jan. 1967. "History in the field." In *Anthropologists in the Field*, eds. D. G. Jongmans and P. C. W. Gutkind. Assen: Van Gorcum. Pp. 102–15.

Verhaar, John. 1970. "Method, Theory, and Phenomenology." In *Method and Theory in Linguistics*, ed. Paul L. Garvin. The Hague and Paris: Mouton. Pp. 42–91.

Vivas, Eliseo. 1968. "Is a Conservative Philosophical Anthropology Possible?" *Social Research* 35, No. 4: 593–615.

White, Leslie A. 1966. *The Social Organization of Ethnological Thought*. Rice University Monographs in Cultural Anthropology, Vol. 52, No. 4. Houston, Texas.

Wilden, Anthony. 1970. "Epistemology and the Biosocial Crisis: The Difference That Makes the Difference." Unpublished manuscript.

Williams, Thomas Rhys. 1967. *Field Methods in the Study of Culture*. New York: Holt, Rinehart & Winston.

Wolf, Eric R. 1969. "American Anthropologists and American Society." In *Concepts and Assumptions in Contemporary Anthropology*, ed. Stephen A. Tyler. Proceedings of the Southern Anthropological Society No. 3. Athens: University of Georgia Press. Pp. 3–11. In this volume pp. oo-ooo.

Wolff, Kurt H. 1959. "The Sociology of Knowledge and Sociological Theory." In *Symposium on Sociological Theory*, ed. Llewellyn Z. Gross. Evanston, Ill.: Row, Peterson & Co., pp. 567–602.

———. 1964. "Surrender and Community Study: The Study of Loma." In *Reflections on Community Studies*, eds. Arthur J. Vidich, Joseph Bensman, and Maurice R. Stein. New York: John Wiley & Sons. Pp. 233–63.

Notes on the Contributors

E. N. ANDERSON, JR., teaches anthropology at the University of California, Riverside, specializing in Chinese society and cultural ecology. He received his B.A. from Harvard University in 1962 and his Ph.D. from the University of California, Berkeley, in 1967. He is the author of *The Floating World of Castle Peak Bay, Essays on South China's Boat People*, and articles in various professional journals, including *American Anthropologist, Anthropos*, and *Pacific Viewpoint*.

GERALD D. BERREMAN, Professor of Anthropology at the University of California, Berkeley, received his B.A. from the University of Oregon in 1952 and his Ph.D. from Cornell University in 1959. He did field research in the Aleutian Islands (1952, 1962) on community organization and social change, and in India (1957–58, 1968–69, 1972), first a community study in the lower Himalayas, followed by a study of urban ethnic identity and interaction. He is the author of *Hindus of the Himalayas: Ethnography and Change, Behind Many Masks: Ethnography and Impression Management in a Himalayan Village*, and papers on the culture and society of India and on ethnic relations and social stratification in India and various other societies. He has also written in several places about the social responsibilities of anthropologists.

MINA DAVIS CAULFIELD teaches anthropology at San Francisco State College and is completing her doctorate work in anthropology at the University of California, Berkeley. Her experiences range from work as a stitcher in various garment factories in Boston and Springfield, Massachusetts, to field research in the West Indies (1970–71). She has written on "Slavery and the Origins of Black Culture" in *Americans from Africa*, edited by Peter Rose.

RICHARD O. CLEMMER has worked among the Hopi Indians of Arizona (1968–70) and more recently among the Western Shoshone Indians of Nevada. His major concerns are resistance to the acculturation effects of non-Indian jurisdiction and ecological issues. He received his B.A.

from the University of California, Santa Barbara, in 1967 and his M.A. from the University of Illinois in 1969, and completed his Ph.D. work in 1972. He was a National Institute of Mental Health Fellow (1970–72), and is presently Visiting Assistant Professor of Anthropology at the State University of New York, Binghamton.

STANLEY DIAMOND is Chairman of the Graduate Anthropology Program, New School for Social Research. His extensive field research includes work in Nigeria, Biafra, the Middle East, and among American Indians. Most recently, he is the author of *Against Civilization* and the forthcoming *African Tragedy: The Meaning of Biafra*. The books he has edited include *Primitive Views of the World*, *The Transformation of East Africa* (with Fred Burke), *Anthropological Perspectives on Education* (with Murray Wax and Fred Gearing), and the forthcoming *Man in Question*. He is a frequent contributor to *Les Temps Modernes*, *The New York Review of Books*, and the *Partisan Review*.

KENNETH HALE is Associate Professor of Linguistics at Massachusetts Institute of Technology, and previously taught anthropology at the University of Illinois and the University of Arizona. He received his B.A. in anthropology from the University of Arizona in 1955, and his M.A. (1956) and Ph.D. (1959) in linguistics from Indiana University. He has done field work in Australia and Mexico.

DELL HYMES left the Department of Anthropology to become Professor of Folklore and Linguistics at the University of Pennsylvania in 1972. He received his B.A. (1950) from Reed College, and his M.A. (1953) and Ph.D. (1955) from Indiana University, and has taught at Harvard University and the University of California, Berkeley. He is the editor of numerous books, including *Pidginization and Creolization of Languages*, *The Use of Computers in Anthropology*, and *Language in Culture and Society*, and of the journal *Language in Society*. He has been a member of the Executive Committee of the Linguistics Society of America, the Executive Board of the American Anthropological Association, and the Board of Directors of the Social Science Research Council, and second vice-president of the American Folklore Society.

ROBERT JAY, Professor of Anthropology at Brown University, received his B.A. (1949), M.A. (1953), and Ph.D. (1957) from Harvard University. His field research includes work in East Java, Perak, Malaysia, and Cape Breton, Nova Scotia. He is the author of *Javanese Villagers: Social Relations in Rural Modjokuto*, and has written for the *Yale Southeast Asia Studies Cultural Report* and various journals, including *Far Eastern Quarterly*. He was the recipient of a National

Institute of Mental Health Special Fellowship and a Research Fellowship from the National Science Foundation.

A. NORMAN KLEIN, Associate Professor of Anthropology at Sir George Williams University, did graduate work at Harvard University and the University of Michigan, and received a Ford Foundation Fellowship. He has written for *Canadian Dimension, Canadian Journal of African Studies,* and *Studies on the Left,* and is currently completing a book on West African history and social anthropology.

LAURA NADER is Professor of Anthropology at the University of California, Berkeley. She received her B.A. from Wells College in 1952 and her Ph.D. from Radcliffe College in 1961. She has done field work among the Zapotec Indians in Oaxaca, Mexico, and among the Shia Moslems in South Lebanon. The producer of the film *To Make the Balance,* she is also the author of *Talea and Juquila* and the editor of *The Ethnography of Law* and *Law in Culture and Society.* She has been a Fellow at the Center for Advanced Study in the Behavioral Sciences at Stanford and a Visiting Professor at Yale Law School.

BOB SCHOLTE is Assistant Professor of Anthropology, Graduate Faculty, New School for Social Research. He received his B.A. from Yale University (1961), his M.A. from Stanford University (1962), and his Ph.D. from the University of California, Berkeley (1969). The editor of several works, including *The Phenomenological and Marxist Critiques of Structural Anthropology,* he has also written frequently for such professional journals as the *American Anthropologist, Critical Anthropology, Social Research,* and *Natural History.* He is Consulting Editor for the New Critics Press and the *International Journal of Sociology,* and Editor-in-Chief of the Northwestern University Studies in Philosophy and Anthropology.

JOHN F. SZWED is Director of the Center for Urban Ethnography at the University of Pennsylvania. He received his Ph.D. in anthropology from Ohio State University, and has done field research in Newfoundland, Trinidad, and the United States. He is the editor of *Black America* and, with Norman E. Whitten, Jr., *Afro-American Anthropology,* and has contributed to various magazines, including *Trans-Action, Journal of American Folklore, Ethnology,* and the *New Republic.*

WILLIAM S. WILLIS, JR., a graduate of Howard University, received his Ph.D. from Columbia University in 1955. His appointment in 1965 to the faculty of Southern Methodist University marked the first integration of that faculty by a black, but he resigned his associate professorship in the spring of 1972 in protest against the treatment he received there. He was a John Hay Whitney Opportunity Fellow, a Fellow of the American Association for the Advancement of Science, and a Fellow of the American Anthropological Association. His articles have appeared in the *Journal of Negro History* and *Ethnohistory,* and his essay "Anthropology and Negroes on the Southern Colonial Frontier" was published in *The Black Experience in America: Selected Essays.*

ERIC R. WOLF is Distinguished Professor of Anthropology at Lehman College of the City University of New York. A Columbia University Ph.D. in anthropology (1951), he has done field work in Puerto Rico, Mexico, and the Italian Alps. He is the author of numerous books, including *Peasant Wars of the Twentieth Century, Peasants,* and *Sons of the Shaking Earth,* and has written for many journals. He was a Guggenheim Fellow and received the National Institutes of Health Career Award.

KURT H. WOLFF is Yellen Professor of Social Relations at Brandeis University. He received his doctorate in philosophy (1935) in Florence after studies at the universities of Frankfurt and Munich. A prolific writer, he edited *Georg Simmel, Emile Durkheim,* and *From Karl Mannheim;* co-edited *The Critical Spirit: Essays in Honor of Herbert Marcuse;* and has written numerous articles for professional journals. From 1966 to 1972, he was Chairman of the Research Committee on the Sociology of Knowledge of the International Sociological Association, and is currently a member of the board of directors of *Sociological Abstracts* and of the advisory board of *Praxis* (Zagreb).

SOL WORTH was a painter, photographer, and filmmaker until 1960, when he came to the study of communications at the University of Pennsylvania. As a Fulbright Professor of Documentary and Education Films in Finland in 1956–57, he founded the Finnish Documentary Film Unit and organized and designed the curriculum for the photography school at the University of Helsinki. While in Finland, he wrote and directed *Teatteri,* a film on the Finnish National Theatre, which won awards at the Cannes and Berlin Film Festivals and was chosen for the Museum of Modern Art's permanent collection of documentary films. He is now Associate Professor of Communications, Director of the Documentary Film Laboratory, and Director of the Media Laboratories Program at the Annenberg School of Communications, University of Pennsylvania. Among his publications are *Through Navajo Eyes: A Study in Film Communication and Anthropology,* "The Development of a Semiotic of Film," "Film as Non-Art," and "Navajo Filmmakers."

Index